The Crisis of Authority
in Catholic Modernity

The Crisis of

Authority

in Catholic

Modernity

EDITED BY

MICHAEL J. LACEY AND

FRANCIS OAKLEY

OXFORD

UNIVERSITY PRESS

Oxford University Press, Inc., publishes works that further
Oxford University's objective of excellence
in research, scholarship, and education.

Oxford   New York
Auckland   Cape Town   Dar es Salaam   Hong Kong   Karachi
Kuala Lumpur   Madrid   Melbourne   Mexico City   Nairobi
New Delhi   Shanghai   Taipei   Toronto

With offices in
Argentina   Austria   Brazil   Chile   Czech Republic   France   Greece
Guatemala   Hungary   Italy   Japan   Poland   Portugal   Singapore
South Korea   Switzerland   Thailand   Turkey   Ukraine   Vietnam

Copyright © 2011 by Oxford University Press, Inc.

Published by Oxford University Press, Inc.
198 Madison Avenue, New York, New York 10016

www.oup.com

Oxford is a registered trademark of Oxford University Press

Library of Congress Cataloging-in-Publication Data

The crisis of authority in Catholic modernity / edited by Michael J. Lacey
and Francis Oakley.
p. cm.
Includes bibliographical references and index.
ISBN 978-0-19-977877-5; 978-0-19-977878-2 (pbk.)
1. Church—Authority. 2. Authority—Religious aspects—Catholic Church.
3. Catholic Church—Doctrines. I. Lacey, Michael James. II. Oakley, Francis.
BX1746.C68 2011
262'.8088282—dc22   2010029620

Printed in the United States of America
on acid-free paper

For John T. Noonan, Jr.: Mentor to many.
Fighter of the good fight.
Keeper of the faith.

Contents

The Crisis of Authority
in Catholic Modernity

Prologue

The Problem of Authority and Its Limits

Michael J. Lacey

This volume was initiated and supported by the Institute for Advanced Catholic Studies at the University of Southern California, Los Angeles, to focus attention on some of the questions and problems that trouble reflective Catholics today about life within their polarized and fretful community of faith. It is oriented mainly to the situation in the United States and in Europe, but the editors feel that the issues dealt with are broad and general enough to be of interest to others as well. They have commissioned and gathered together a set of scholarly essays drawn from a range of disciplines—historical, theological, canonistic, philosophical, social-scientific—and some of those essays explore and assess aspects of the "lived" Catholicism of priesthood and laity.[1]

Although in one way or another most of the essays cut across traditional disciplinary lines and cannot always be readily designated as theoretical rather than practical in nature or, for that matter, vice versa, we have grouped them loosely into three subdivisions. Those in the first part focus on matters historical, on the centrality of the appeal to the witness of the past in the Catholic tradition, and on the degree to which, at one point or another, the understanding and representation of the past has come to be the focus of contention. The essays in the second part can be classified most easily as theological, canonistic, or philosophical. Directly or indirectly, explicitly or implicitly, they all touch upon the neuralgic issue of the role played by ecclesiastical authority in the life of the church. Though perhaps less obviously so, the same remains true of the essays we have grouped together in the third part of the book. These essays, written from a practical rather than a theoretical perspective, engage the "lived" realities of North American Catholicism as they are manifested in the experience of laity and clergy.

The overall purpose of this book is neither to justify nor to repudiate the authority of the church's hierarchy, but to cast some light on the context within which it currently operates, the complexities and ambiguities of the historical tradition of belief and behavior it speaks for, and the kinds of limits it confronts, consciously or otherwise. The hope is not to fix problems, although some of the essays make suggestions that might be useful in that connection and might help to counter the waning sense of common purpose that comes with a climate of prolonged discord. Instead, we wish to contribute to a badly needed intra-Catholic dialogue and debate, without which, we believe, problems will continue to fester and solutions will elude our grasp.

The purpose of this prologue is not to foreground or repeat the arguments that the essays themselves set forth. Rather, by way of background and overview, it is to delineate the context in which the various arguments they advance can be understood most readily. The issue that looms largest in that context is the developing crisis of ecclesiastical authority, particularly the teaching authority of the clerical hierarchy, the magisterium. Consider for a moment the meanings of authority.[2] As the church settles into the twenty-first century, students of Catholicism no less than Catholics themselves are confronted with a paradox regarding the authority of its central institution, the modern papacy: it is stronger than it has ever been, yet frailer than before. Conceived juridically, as something that can be defined and looked up in official sources, the papacy appears to enjoy more institutional power throughout the universal church than it did a century and a half ago before the first Vatican Council (1869–1870), indeed, more than it did at the time of Vatican II (1962–1965).

It is hard to imagine how this formal authority could be more centralized or comprehensive than it is. Some worry, indeed, that the institution may be too powerful for its own good, too strong to fully appreciate the degree of its dependency upon the voluntary cooperation of others and to properly do all that is expected of it by a divided laity. Conceived, on the other hand, in historical or sociological terms, as something that can be studied in action and gauged with scholarly evidence of some kind, it presents a different face. Now it is the frailty of papal authority that comes into view, the apparent limits of the tradition of ultramontane governance that has developed and hardened since the latter part of the nineteenth century. The rather torpid, baffled response to media pressures in connection with the ongoing clerical sex abuse scandals in America and Europe provides but one example.

Those limits and frailties are not formal or constitutional, but they are nonetheless real and ought to enjoy a certain status in the consciousness of all in the leadership for that reason. They are to be found in the minds and hearts of ordinary practicing Catholics, in their estimations of the way the papal office is conducted and the worth of the guidance it passes on in the name of God as to how the Christian life should be lived. The practice is up to them. They cannot be scared into obedience or shamed into piety, and they know it. They can leave if they like and return if they wish. The limits in question are variable—matters of more or less in this context or that. They are influenced not by the teachings of the church alone, but by the believer's response to all the competing forces at work in contemporary culture as these are encountered in what William James called the blooming, buzzing confusions of personal experience.

Practical Limits and the Exemplary Case

To get some practical sense of the limits, one can ask the people of God what they think about things. Here, as Mary Gautier and the other sociologists who wrote chapter 10 of this book demonstrate, the important point is that in encyclicals, the catechism, or statements of bishops, more authority is claimed than accepted, and the gap is apparently widening. Even the extraordinary gifts and energy of a John Paul II failed during his long reign to move the numbers with respect to the underlying trend, and this among people who by and large revered him. Celebrity and vigor and formal authority have not been enough for that. When tensions arise between the official voice of the church, expressed in the teachings of its magisterium, and the voice of the layperson's conscience, the trend is clearly against the voice of authority and in favor of "thinking on one's own," the core value of moral autonomy in liberal modernity, against which the church in its long antiliberal, antimodern phase so stoutly contended.[3]

This quiet insistence upon thinking for oneself is the chief characteristic of Catholic modernity, and it puts stress upon all the inherited conventions of traditional relations between the hierarchy and laity, the ordained and the merely baptized, the teaching church and the learning church. It has to do not with a false sense of the "unencumbered self" or the shallow individualism exploited by consumer culture, though these hazards exist and must be accounted dangerous, but rather with the demand for personal religious experience, understanding, judgment, and integrity. In religious life, subjectivity counts. It does so despite the emphasis in traditional apologetics on the objectivity of doctrines. "If you have a self, take charge of it," says the modern religious spirit, "take responsibility for your own convictions." The spirit does not preclude thinking with others, but it certainly complicates matters.[4]

For good or ill, this shift has gradually become characteristic of life within the church since Vatican II, and those who feel the need, as Cardinal Newman put it long ago, to toast conscience first, and then the pope, are unapologetic. Prior to the council, such people might have drifted away from the faith and been encouraged from above to do so. Today they feel their claims to belonging, reservations and all, are rightful and cannot be trumped simply by appealing to formal authority or citing those passages in scripture that buttress the idea of divinely instituted apostolic succession and its claim to exclusive spiritual powers of discernment.[5] The children of the church have come haphazardly to feel like grown-ups and don't believe they have to abandon the family estate over differences in the family. Catholic life is now more complicated than that, and dealing with the complication is at the heart of the dilemmas confronting ecclesiastical leadership.

Effective authority is not simply power, but legitimate power, and legitimacy cannot be determined satisfactorily by documents and formalities. "Look it up Catholicism" and "think for yourself Catholicism" are in an ongoing state of tension. Legitimacy is a variable quality, too, a matter of more or less, in this situation or that. Today, in civil life no less than in the church, real traction in leadership is hard for authority to find. Leading effectively where people feel obliged to think for themselves is more difficult than it used to be, as the example of John Paul II suggests, and so perhaps is the experience of following. It is no picnic either.

Factions and cliques develop. The noisy, often angry pluralism of one's coreligionists can be a demanding test of faith and stamina for everyone. The temptation to simply drop out is always there, and as a head count of family and friends may quickly confirm (a bit of research will most certainly confirm), many have given in to it and will continue to do so. A quarter to a third of the baptized never go to church, and those who do range from the lukewarm to the ardent, the well informed to the truly ignorant, from right to left on politics and morals, with many points in between. Whatever their degree of commitment and knowledge, their understandings of what the church is and ought to be betray a startling range of variation. On close inspection, one finds many Catholicisms among them.[6]

Rome speaks, but the arguments continue. Perfectly authoritative messages sent out may not be warmly received, or received only selectively, perhaps to be used by one faction in its struggle against others. The best known, best documented, most multifaceted, and fateful case of simple refusal to receive an authoritative message is the nonreception, an awkward but useful term, by the faithful of the reiterated ban on the use of contraceptives by married Catholics contained in *Humanae Vitae* (1968). This is the subject of Leslie Tentler's chapter in this book, and it is a case touched upon by some of the other essayists—Cahill, Kaveny, and Taylor—as well. The episode clearly demonstrates the limits of formal papal authority and the kinds of costs that can come with failure to recognize those limits. Its implications are well worth pondering (the episode ought to be studied in seminary curricula, but that is not likely to happen), and one hopes that the case will prove to be an exception to the rule of normal relations, rather than a symptom of what may be coming to pass more generally. In this respect, there are grounds for worry, however.

Pope Pius VI was advised by some that there were good reasons, practical and theological, to relax the ban, leaving room for the discretion of couples themselves on the regulation of intimacy. And that notion was recommended by the majority of the members of his own commission of inquiry into the subject. Others, however, used the argument of the slippery slope and warned him that relaxing the ban would undermine the authority of his office. What was good enough for the past, they said, should be good enough for the present and the future, the truth doesn't change, and one must not scandalize the faithful by any hint of inconsistency or slow-motion alteration in teaching. It was as if the theory of falling dominoes had a place in moral theology.

Convinced, as his predecessors had been, that contraception was gravely sinful, the pope chose to reiterate the ban. Most in the laity differed and chose to reject it. Soon the practice of going regularly to confession, one of the primary links between priest and people and the traditional setting for provision of personal, spiritual guidance, fell abruptly into decline and has since nearly vanished. One doesn't confess what doesn't seem sinful, and doubt about the unqualified certainty of church teachings on questions of sexual morality easily spreads from one question to another.

It is unlikely that the practice of auricular confession will ever be restored to anything like its former place. A bond has been broken, and an important role for the priesthood, for centuries the practical focus of all that clerical training in moral theology, is being gradually deleted from Catholic life and memory, like fasting and praying the rosary. People have found they can manage without it. It is not clear what the higher clergy has found, but support for the ban on contraception has come into play since 1968 as something of a litmus test in the selection of bishops, and no public criticisms of it are countenanced by Rome.

For more than forty years now, there has been no meeting of minds, hierarchical and lay, on the use of contraception, nor, in consequence, any open discussion of issues of sexual morality more generally, a point strongly registered by Tentler. Ecclesiastical face is involved. There can be no acknowledgment of error or misjudgment on the part of the teaching authority. Instead, an unfortunate misunderstanding on the part of the laity is assumed and sometimes asserted by the leadership. The divide is something that a voluble church has learned it cannot talk about, a costly incapacity that applies to other areas of controversy as well.

Official authority remains unruffled and takes the long view, the *semper idem* view, now speaking of the ban as grounded, not in dubious arguments from natural law that were proffered at the time of *Humanae Vitae*, but in a personalist, mystical theology of the body later propounded by John Paul II that calls for abstaining from contraception in the name of rigorous spiritual and aesthetic discipline for the love of God. But people in the pews find it simply mystifying. From time to time, pro forma reminders are issued by the bishops to the effect that official teaching continues to hold contraception to be a grave evil. The reminders go unheeded. A spirit of reciprocal pretense seems to prevail: "you pretend to teach me, and I'll pretend to learn." How long the living tradition will continue to live in this atmosphere of evasion is uncertain. In the meantime, both sides appear to be content with self-reliance. Charles Taylor remarks that "we should concede to our clergy the right to be wrong." Perhaps eventually they will respond in kind.

Problems of Instructing the Modern Conscience

"I can summon spirits from the vasty deep," Glendower claims in Shakespeare's *Henry IV, Part 1*. "Why, so can I, or so can any man," Hotspur retorts, "But will they come when you do call for them?" Questions of this type should trouble the Vatican, as they have troubled those in other sites of leadership in modern culture. Modern Catholicism has been a tradition of instructed conscience in the strong, top-down sense of the phrase, and instructing conscience is not as easy as it used to be. It was always premised on voluntary cooperation, always dimly understood that the act of faith is worthless unless it is a free act, that God is not pleased by coerced professions of belief, even if subtly coerced, but the voluntary element was more easily overlooked in earlier times of aristocratic clerical dominance than it is now.

As Charles Taylor points out in his chapter on the scope of magisterial authority and how it should be exercised, there are limits in the nature of human exchanges, inherent limits: "authoritative pronouncements on issues where contingent circumstances are crucial to our judgment cannot be taken as definitive, let alone 'infallible.'" The magisterium has not always respected and provided for the inherent limits of its teachings. There has been a habit, Taylor suggests, of oversimplifying its moral prescriptions, of not trusting the laity to deal with the complexities involved. He speaks of the limits of "legalism" and the "false sacralization" that came with favoring a version of Thomist natural law, one rather narrow approach to moral reasoning, over others with equally good claims to respect and use. He also complains of the refusal to leave the enigmatic alone, "a lack of reserve before the enigmatic," the feeling within the Vatican that there must be a moral policy for everything, and the temptation, accordingly, to settle instead for false or misleading certainties.

In the secular world, teachers are legitimate authority figures so long as the pupil is actually learning, making progress. The shared aim of teacher and pupil alike is for the teacher to pass along some degree of mastery and step aside. When the learning stops, respectful relations are likely to continue, perhaps marked by gratitude and even affection, but the quality of the relation is subtly altered. The pupil grows up and moves on. One graduates and comes to share with teachers the status of adulthood and its responsibilities.

In the ecclesial setting, things are different. Here it seems one does not really grow up and move on to independence, but as part of God's plan is expected to remain forever in a state of tutelage. The risk here is what Taylor calls an "infantilization" of the laity, and the faithful are increasingly sensitive about it. It is a distinctively Catholic problem. By tradition, the "teachings" of the clerical hierarchy are to be "obeyed" by the laity as the price of saving their souls.[7] Rooted in earlier times and the social conditions that went with them, this usage reflects the inherited historical mix of the hierarchy's specialized theological competence and the actual jurisdictional power it long shared with civil rulers in the Catholic confessional states of the Old Regime, where the ideal of the unity of throne and altar, religion and politics was dominant, a principle upheld by the hierarchy, though with diminishing conviction, up until Vatican II.

The notions of laws and teachings were confounded. Like the state, the church believed it spoke for the people, even though its authority was not derived from them but directly from God, and like the state, it expected to be obeyed. The tradition dominant in the states of the Old Regime could not withstand the rise of cultural pluralism and the constitutional and legal conventions of the modern state, as Lacey's chapter in this volume makes clear, yet many of the old habits persist, and the notion of obeying teachings (rather than understanding them, reflecting upon them, taking them into account, holding them close to heart, etc.) is one of them.

It is a poor way, a rather ham-fisted way, of getting at the delicacy of the transactions involved: divine inspiration somehow occurs in papal reflection, teaching goes in, and obedience comes out. So in outline providence and continuing revelation operate. Bernard Lonergan has described the model for the workings of belief implicit in this classical perspective on the proceedings of the magisterium: "One must believe and accept whatever the bible or the true church or both believe and accept. But X is in the bible or the true church or both. Therefore one must accept and believe whatever X accepts and believes. Moreover, X believes and accepts a, b, c, d. . . . Therefore, one must believe and accept a, b, c, d. . . ."[8]

It may be true, as far as it goes, but it does not go very far, which of course is the point. The model assumes conditions that have not been met and neglects vital steps and qualifications. It makes things seem unnaturally easy from the standpoint of the magisterium. This illusion can make for a complacent magisterium, one that might drift out of touch with the realities of the lived experience of the laity and provide a rather weak, conventionally pious reading of the signs of the times. The excessive simplicity of the model encourages the notion that on matters of faith and morals, the papacy's traditional, apparently boundless teaching field, belief and behavior around the globe can be centrally programmed to radiate outward from Christ's Vicar in the Vatican, a view that has been called ecclesiastical positivism. It is simply a matter of ensuring that the conditions of formal authority have been met, citing the documents that validate this, recalling appropriate precedents, writing up the lessons one wants to convey in the customary Vatican idiom, and then promulgating them—sending them out and down the line.

For too long, this has been the method of authority. It is founded on the view, not altogether unreasonable or unknown to history, both civil and ecclesiastical, that what counts most vitally is the status of the speaker, rather than the persuasiveness in its own right of what has been spoken. People laugh politely at the unfunny jokes of superiors. The method has worked more or less efficiently over the centuries, but there have been changes, probably irreversible, in the way it works in modernity. Authority, formal or informal, is a constant in society, but what makes for legitimate persuasiveness has changed over time. The status and standing of the speaker remain significant in all civil settings—no one denies that there is neither order nor progress without legitimate authority—but the weight of the reasoning itself, its demonstrable grounds and accessibility, have become more and more significant with the passage of time.

From this angle of approach, at least, and so far as the act of ruling is concerned, the most important historical shift in civil governance in the long course of modernity has been from a focus upon the *right to rule*—kings, like popes, ruled by divine right—to the *duties of rule*, the latter going hand in glove with theories of popular sovereignty, representation, qualifications for voting, rules for settling disagreements, and the long list of things that have come to comprise all the rest of it. Throughout, the aim has been to discipline power, to reduce the element of arbitrary judgment that goes along with its exercise, and to assure that it is not merely self-serving or serving the needs of party or faction under the guise of serving the commonweal.

So far as the contents of ruling are concerned, the shift has been from a genuinely primitive, arbitrary starting point—it was a mark of civil authority that it did not always explain itself, it simply commanded—to a context in which grounds are prepared and referenced, rulings are accompanied by reasons and assurances that relevant matters have been investigated, appropriate bodies of knowledge have been tapped, interested parties have been canvassed, and the likely consequences of the rule are understood and have been prepared for. These are now among the customary duties of rule in civil society, and the need for something more closely comparable to them within the church is becoming increasingly evident.[9]

Norms and Forms

Authority in modern culture cannot be self-justifying, even sacred authority, and the strain is evident whenever the old and the new are placed side by side. In John Beal's discussion of the canon law in chapter 5 of this book, for example, the differences between a self-contained, self-justifying world of rules for a religious community, on the one hand, and the premises of modern common or public statutory law that take into account the conventions of the duties of rule, on the other, are made clear. Strictly speaking, the contents of the canon law are not self-justifying; rather, they are justified by the divine origins of the authority of the pope and bishops, which comes to nearly the same thing, and they are, indeed, self-contained.

Until the rise of the modern state, the canon law and its civil counterparts were broadly compatible, part of the same cultural landscape, not showing much of a gap in basic values and premises. But that is no longer true. As Fr. Beal points out, the purpose of the canon law is to conserve the church and its teachings and to regulate access to God through the sacraments, not to assure justice within the church. Theologically speaking, it assumes that no problem of justice within the church can arise, since the institution is divinely guided and thus incapable of injustice. Why provide remedies for what cannot happen?

It follows that in the modern canon law there is no such thing as learning from individual cases, nothing comparable at any rate to the Anglo-American common law tradition. While she is concerned not with canon law, but with the prospect of retrieving and reframing the practice of Catholic casuistry in the academy, in her chapter Cathleen Kaveny brings to our attention the virtues of the common law tradition as a source of progressive social learning due to its focus on the interplay of contested values and the particularities of changing circumstances, the precise details of the case, its bearing, in other words, on problems of moral casuistry. With nothing really comparable to due process, separation of powers, or reciprocity between hierarchy and laity, the canon law is not set up to spur this type of learning, and yet in the past it was considered, as some commentators have noted, as the handmaiden of the moral theology of the church.

In actual practice, as Fr. Beal observes, canon law collapses into administration at the service of the hierarchy. Its paradigmatic offense, Beal notes, is disobedience. Its dynamic is not teaching and learning, but command and control, and its "social imaginary," a useful term from Charles Taylor's approach to historical analysis, stands in sharp contrast to the burgeoning field of Catholic social teaching, where the promotion and protection of human rights has become the central focus of attention, and where the whole idea of command and control makes no sense.[10]

It has often been pointed out that the Catholic Church is not a democracy, the implication being that it is something much higher and more valuable than that. So in the ideal it is, but what is this feeling of lofty pride in its ecclesial structure all about? Granted that democracy relies upon created human nature, which is known to be subject to sin, and that there is indeed evil in the world. Granted, too, that rationalizing evil may be the most common of sins, the one that makes easy resort to one's conscience morally hazardous. Even so, what is the point of the church's aloofness from the ideals and practices of democratic self-government? For nearly two centuries now, the characteristic achievements and failures of actual democratic governance have been the subject of close study in universities throughout the Western world. Many scholarly methods, historical and social-scientific, have been deployed to that end, and much has been learned.

The resulting professional lore is not for the naive or the starry-eyed. Democratic forms are not trouble free. They have their limits. The lore does not contain a cache of rules for fool-proof politics and government. No one familiar with it would claim that the records of institutional experience in the era of modern democratic life are without blemish. We can readily concede that modern governance, with all its temptations to self-righteousness, hypocrisy, and the feckless populism of left and right, is not guaranteed to obtain justice and the common good; it merely aims to do so.

Is it the case, however, that predemocratic forms of cultural power of the type that called for unity of throne and altar, a call still audible in much of the Islamic world, might do better because of their heavy insulation from popular pressures? As Lacey's chapter shows, in the late nineteenth century, Leo XIII earnestly implored the leaders of the nations of the non-Catholic world, Protestants, secularists, and others who dwelled beyond what he called the arc of salvation, to set aside their historical grievances and misunderstandings of the church and consider converting to the Roman faith. Its yoke was sweet, he said; its burden light. He assured them that with deference to the one true faith and the divinely ordained authority of the pope would come peace, prosperity, and all the blessings of providence. Logically speaking, Leo's solution to global strife was elegant in its simplicity, but does it not betray a certain blindness about the way religious authority is expected to work in the modern consciousness? Does it address the underlying reasons for religious liberty and the need to show respect for the religious traditions of others, a way that is better suggested, perhaps, in the motto of John Henry Newman—"cor ad cor loquitur," heart speaks to heart—whom Leo had appointed cardinal in 1879?

One can distinguish between norms and forms. The shortcomings of life in democracy are measured in critical scholarship not by premodern standards of aristocratic order and discipline, but against the ideals of freedom and self-government that have inspired the democratic ethos and its experiments. The ideals of human rights are morally normative. They took root in the West before they took root in the church, and they remain strong despite the failure to fully achieve them in practice. They provide criteria for judgment about the standing all persons should have in the eyes of authority and the way they ought to be treated. The ideals cannot be compartmentalized into secular and sacred bins. Plainly, it is the steady pressure of these ideals that drives many of the complaints about life in the church today, not the expectation that mere procedures and techniques, popular referenda on moral teachings or direct election of bishops, for example, would make for dependable improvement.

When we are reminded that the church is not a democracy, the reminder, let us hope, is about mere forms. The norms are not being disparaged as passing fancies from the standpoint of eternity. On the contrary, at Vatican II, despite the prominence of forms of speech, dress, and ceremony that derive from long epochs of imperial and aristocratic rule, like the brilliant architecture and steeped-in-time atmosphere of the holy city itself, the norms appropriate to the sacred dignity of the human person were, after much struggle behind the scenes, embraced and proclaimed more directly than ever before. Some insist that they were always there, just neglected on occasion, and that they are rooted in scripture itself. In any case, whatever the "spirit" of Vatican II meant then or means now, it points to the sacred dignity of the human person, created in the divine image, the religious language in which the democratic ideal is presently addressed, and the need to make the sensibility it reflects more at home in the daily life and routines of the sprawling institutions of Catholicism.[11]

History, Tradition, and the Limits of the Ideal

The Catholic tradition, as Fr. Francis Sullivan's chapter in this book indicates, is a complex, compound, multidimensional inheritance. Like a garden, its health and beauty take constant care and pruning. As Sullivan points out in his treatment of the role played by Cardinal Albert Gregory Meyer of Chicago at Vatican II in urging a critical approach to the whole topic, as a dynamic totality of beliefs and practices, the tradition, Meyer insisted, "does not make progress and increase always and in every respect; for when the Church ponders divine things in its pilgrim state, in some respects it can fail, and in fact does fail." The old doctrine that there was no salvation outside the church, for example, about which Fr. Sullivan has written a book, has been pruned to allow new ecumenical and interfaith relations to take root in its life.

A similar care is also now taken in liturgical language that touches on the history and evaluation of Judaism, lest dangerous anti-Judaist misunderstandings arise and fall on fallow ground in the consciousness of those attempting to live the Christian faith. Sullivan quotes comments made on Cardinal Meyer's insight into the necessarily mixed and ambiguous nature of tradition by the young Fr. Joseph Ratzinger, the current pope: "there is a distorting, as well as a legitimate tradition.... Consequently, tradition must not be considered only affirmatively, but also critically." It was unfortunate, Ratzinger said at the time, that the suggestion of the American cardinal had not been taken up and that Vatican II had "more or less ignored the whole question of the criticism of tradition."

No one can say that criticism has been ignored since, and fair or otherwise, criticism is an irritant for those in authority. Critical historical perspectives in particular can be troublesome. They can tempt authority to opposition in the hope that nothing in the recollection of the past will be permitted to interfere with the business of the present. Francis Oakley quotes George Orwell's dictum that he who controls the present controls the past, and he who controls the past controls the future. Oakley's chapter explores a dramatic example of the phenomenon, an instance of truly radical discontinuity in the life of the church, the history of the conciliar movement and conciliar theory. Arising in response to severe crisis within the papacy in the fourteenth and fifteenth centuries, the time of simultaneous multiple popes, each claiming legitimacy, conciliarism is the "council over pope" ecclesiology that was effectively consigned to oblivion with the triumph of ultramontanism at the first Vatican Council, with its twin definitions of papal infallibility and papal jurisdictional primacy throughout the universal church.

Conciliarism sought to limit or balance papal authority. As Oakley shows, conciliar theory attributed to a general ecumenical council acting independently of the pope and in certain critical areas only "a jurisdictional power superior to his." It assumed that the ultimate locus of authority within the church was to be found not in the pope alone, but in the church as a whole, as represented by those who gathered together in a general council. The greatest of these gatherings was the Council of Constance (1414–1418), a kind of representative assembly that was, as one historian cited by Oakley has put it, "as close as the Middle Ages came to the Congress of Vienna (1815) or the United Nations." One of its decrees, *Frequens* (1417), called for making conciliar gatherings regular events in church governance: "the frequent holding of general councils is a preeminent means of cultivating the Lord's patrimony," the fathers declared. "It roots out the briars, thorns and thistles of heresies, errors and schisms, corrects deviations, reforms what is deformed and produces a richly fertile crop for the Lord's vineyard. Neglect of councils, on the other hand, spreads and fosters the aforesaid evils."[12]

Of course, it came to pass that there would be no regular conciliar meetings, and this recommended technique for cultivating the Lord's patrimony has itself been nearly forgotten. After Vatican I, in fact, some observers of life within the church concluded that there would probably be no more general ecumenical councils, since the newly settled powers of the pope rendered moot any need for them for other than celebratory purposes. And indeed, nearly a century would pass, a century marked by revolution, war, and unprecedented bloodshed, played out against the backdrop of the continuing antiliberalism and antimodernism espoused at Rome, before Pope John XXIII, good pope John, startled everyone by calling for Vatican II to deal with the multidimensional pastoral problems that had accumulated in the interval.

Most of the Catholics now living were born after the second Vatican Council (1962–1965) and have no memory of it, perhaps no knowledge of it to speak of. Most scholars of the council's proceedings agree that it was, above all, about the development of doctrine, and that much more needs to be known about how the development of doctrine actually takes place behind closed doors when the policy-relevant thinking and decision making of the Vatican is underway. To oversimplify in the interest of clarity, the question is how does the church make up its mind, and how does it change its mind when it needs to? Is it capable of self-criticism and growth in wisdom? How does it learn from its own institutional experience, including the experience of mediocrity and the failure to always live up to its highest aspirations as the graced embodiment of Christian community?

Is there a conflict of ideas and evaluations involved in the development of doctrine, and if so, how? Observers agree that something like a "battle for the council" involving these matters has taken shape since it closed nearly half a century ago, a battle opposing differing interpretations of the council's achievements and failures and the general bearing of these on all the disagreements that have marked controversies within the church since the mid-1960s. The papacy, of course, has an institutional interest in the issues and how they are perceived and evaluated. How do the popes approach disputes of historical perspectives?

It is rare to find a pope intervening in arcane questions of hermeneutics and actually wrestling to deal with their complexity. A distinguished scholar in his own right and well versed in the problems at stake, Pope Benedict XVI has done so. In his December 22, 2005, reflections on the history of the council, reprinted in the appendix to this volume, the pope notes that "no one can deny that in vast areas of the Church the implementation of the council has been somewhat difficult."

At least part of the difficulty, he suggests, has to do with the frameworks within which its history is interpreted, the ways in which questions of continuity and discontinuity in magisterial teaching are understood and put together. For the reader new to the scene of this battle, the address should make clear the importance of it all—the pope says it "risks ending in a split between the preconciliar Church and the postconciliar Church"—and the scope of the topics involved. As an aid to reflection, Fr. Joseph Komonchak's chapter provides a compact briefing on the council and subsequent arguments about it. For decades himself a distinguished contributor to the ongoing effort to interpret the council, Fr. Komonchak's citations can serve as a starting point for access to the increasingly vast literature of controversy, and his close reading of the pope's address helps to place the papal intervention itself within the broader horizon of the ongoing controversies.

Unity and the Rationale for the Papacy

That controversy over life within the church seems to be forever ongoing, now on the back burner, now on the front, but always present, may be another distinctive feature of Catholic modernity. There is a certain nostalgia felt at times, even by liberal progressives within the church, for the apparent peace and quiet of the pre-Vatican II setup, the church that Pope John XXIII felt had slumbered too long and needed to wake up. Is the peace and quiet of earlier times a real option for us (Charles Taylor thinks not), or is a bit of discord natural and even ineradicable in a church full of people who insist, even if only furtively, on thinking for themselves? If the latter, the question is collectively how to live with the noise of disagreements within the family and even learn from it in the institutional life of Catholicism.

Factions in the laity seem always primed to receive the next Vatican pronouncement as the one that will finally put to rest any spirit of discord on an issue, but such pronouncements never do. *Humanae Vitae*, as we have seen, was intended as such a conversation stopper. So was *Ordinatio Sacerdotalis* (1994), John Paul II's apostolic letter proscribing as beyond the powers of the divinely instituted office of the papacy the ordination of women to the Catholic priesthood. So was his encyclical *Veritatis Splendor* (1993), which prescribed a single method, one particular way of reasoning about moral issues, for all to follow. The list could go on and probably will.

Conservatives insist, to adapt something from Fr. Beal's chapter, that there is no crisis of authority within the church, merely a failure to live according to authority. Any weakness or disease that exists within the ranks of the faithful is caused by "secondary smoke" coming into the pure air of the church from the modern secular culture that surrounds it. For traditionalists of the late Archbishop Marcel LeFebvre's cast of mind, the situation is even worse. The documents of Vatican II for him provided evidence of widespread fatal infection within the leadership itself, and the council's pronouncements with respect to religious liberty, ecumenical relations, and relations with the Jews can claim no legitimacy whatever. They are betrayals of the one true faith.

From the conservative standpoint, any gap between formal and effective authority is illusory. If it measures anything, it measures the scale and spread of apostasy, and its remedy is strict obedience to Rome in thought and deed. Perhaps the gap can be narrowed by cracking down and using some combination of more finely tuned loyalty oaths, doctrinal litmus testing, and careful targeting in exercising the appointment powers of the pope; tightening the reins of training and management from seminaries up through the Vatican bureaus themselves; and making even more tough-minded use than John Paul II and Benedict XVI have done of the world's greatest bully pulpit, the Vatican's.

For others, however, this course of action is dangerously simpleminded and willful. It is a misreading of the signs of the times and a set of recipes for long-term, slow-motion institutional failure. Though developing quietly and off camera, so to speak, there is an underlying crisis of authority, and the laity seems to be learning to deal with it to their own satisfaction by not expecting too much from Rome or from their local ordinaries, who for the most part refuse to acknowledge the existence of any such problem. Here one of Andrew Greeley's observations (see note 5) bears repeating. In terms of formal authority, there is in Catholicism no appeal beyond the pope. His word is the last word. In reality, however, those who practice a selective Catholicism, which includes nearly everyone, justify their choices, their refusal to follow to the letter all the instructions handed down from Rome, by appealing privately from a church that does not understand to a God who does. Their theism is intact, as are their sense of integrity and a spirituality of sorts. These are being used to shield them from what they feel are the shortcomings and shortcuts of ordinary magisterial practice and to fashion a personal appropriation of Catholicism that works well enough for them.

From the standpoint of the meaning of Greeley's selective Catholicism as an emerging new form of Catholic life, which we have been calling Catholic modernity, the gap between clergy and laity does not measure apostasy but rather points to the problems facing merely formal authority and the need to narrow the distance between it and the deeper grades of legitimacy and trust. The gap between the ordained and the merely baptized says something about the size and shape of a failure to think harder about the limits of merely formal authority, to listen more carefully and study the lives of the people subject to it, and to make an effort to learn about what really troubles them and perhaps about how to lead them more effectively in their search for spiritual perfection and friendship with God. For this task, more learning and less authoritative teaching may be called for, fewer certainties and more insights, fallible though they may be.

As things stand, to those who quietly practice selective Catholicism, their leaders appear to live in a clerical echo chamber of sorts, wired at the first Vatican Council to amplify the old method of authority and inhibit the development of newer, suppler ones. The numbers show that for many of them, the leaders of the church seem too remote, too caught up in the formalities of office to be taken seriously, too prone to flattering themselves when they claim that by God's design they speak for everyone on the difficult moral and political issues of life. Most laypeople appear willing to settle for simply keeping the rudiments of the sacramental life conveniently accessible, a hope now jeopardized by the priest shortage. Beyond that, they continue to deal with the rest of the instruction of conscience that comes down from above as best they can.

From this angle, the bark of Peter seems to be adrift, to borrow an image from Peter Steinfel's probing survey of the problems of institutional leadership in the American church (see note 16). The Vatican seems at times oblivious to public sentiment, incapable of anticipating it, as it was for too long in the face of the various national sex abuse scandals, or as it was recently also in the early phases of global reaction to Pope Benedict's announced intention to lift, in the name of unity, the excommunications of a small group of traditionalist bishops, one of whom turned out to be a well-known holocaust denier, and that despite the continuing refusal of those LeFebvrist bishops to publicly accept the teachings of Vatican II.

This episode of Vatican bungling elicited gasps from around the world, from high-ranking civil authorities, Catholic and non-Catholic, as well as from people of faith, Catholic and non-Catholic, and provoked an embarrassed papal apology and clarification. The episode is a passing one, but it speaks to the fundamental problems of inertia and remoteness in sovereign papal governance. It showed that global public expectations of the office of the papacy had not been met. The expectations are implicit and normative, something that even those exercising sacred authority can neglect only at their peril. They are limits. The pope is expected to champion truly universal human values and not get caught up in anything that appears to challenge them, as the traditionalists he seemed to be welcoming back into the fold do in fact challenge them in the name of their preconciliar Catholic orthodoxy.[13]

Any reserves of unconditional trust the hierarchy once enjoyed seem to be slowly eroding in the atmosphere of pluralist modern consciousness and instantaneous communication, and trustworthiness, as Joseph Komonchak has noted, is the functionally equivalent term for legitimate authority.[14] Meanwhile, problems in day-to-day institutional life accumulate and seem to go untended. Sentiment within the Catholic academy, which ought to be regarded as a vital resource for informed leadership, is ignored, though any threat of dissent from magisterial teaching is likely to get attention. Gerard Mannion's chapter conveys some of the frustrations felt by scholars in the world of Catholic higher education over the unresponsiveness of the teaching church to their intellectual struggles for integrity and their need for a free hand, and it reviews some of the rather modest proposals that have been made for improving the clarity and cogency of the workings of the official magisterium to make it more effective.

Sr. Katarina Schuth's report assessing the education of priests and lay ministers in American seminaries today is chock-full of sobering information about one aspect of the lay-clerical gap and its implications. It shows that the vocational crisis is much deeper than falling numbers alone indicate. Candidates for the priesthood are being selected in part for their strong ideological preferences and their hopes for membership in an exclusive cultic priesthood content to proudly stand apart. The educational standards for entry have fallen, academic achievement is unimpressive, a large and growing fraction of entrants are coming from abroad and unfamiliar with American ways, and tomorrow's priests are not likely to have received as background for their work the first-rate classical liberal education many of their predecessors did.

They are being trained, moreover, for a world of easy deference that no longer exists and are unprepared for the encounter they are about to have with parishioners who wish to think for themselves and are leery of any command-and-control attitudes or mannerisms. This is not the stuff of elite intellectual leadership that tomorrow's church will require. Conflict and misunderstanding seem inevitable. Schuth's modest hope is that local priests and bishops will learn to make some serious use of the arts of social analysis, of the sort she is demonstrating, and that bishops will see the need to go beyond ensuring orthodoxy and ensure as well that those in training learn something about the lay-clerical gap and its reasons before they step into it. As it is, they are not being prepared for the many kinds of ethnic and ideological diversity they are sure to run into. It is almost as if they are being programmed to fail.

The papacy exists to symbolize and strengthen the spirit of unity within the universal church. Its basic rationale and principal duty is to provide for that sense of unity, and yet, as popes themselves seem increasingly inclined to admit, despite all their efforts, the unity of times gone by does not exist. By some measures common in other departments of modern life, the office is failing in its duty. At the first Vatican Council, the fathers of the church provided the doctrinal foundation for the radically centralized powers of the ultramontane papacy, convinced that doing so was necessary for the long-term survival and independence of the church as a community of believers. Though not without its critics within the church, who were in the minority, the position was understandable, perhaps even reasonable, at the time.

The papal powers defined at Vatican I were reaffirmed at Vatican II, although a good deal of unease about the ways they had been exercised in the antiliberal, antimodernist interval was registered then as well. The yoke of the papacy may be sweet, but it could stand some loosening. The problem is that it may be strong and ineffective at the same time. The modern situation seems to call for something its centralized institutional strength does not quite reach. It is now bumping up against what appear to be the natural limits of excessively centralized power. It is not alone in so doing. Many other modern institutions have run into the same problem and have sought in various ways to decentralize authority for the purpose of better performance all around. But governments and other kinds of modern corporations are perhaps less constrained than is the church in dealing with their own *semper reformanda* needs.

Has the ultramontane papacy run its course? It is unclear what exactly should be done to close the widening gap between the clergy and the laity and allow for less mechanical, more lifelike relations between center and periphery, top and bottom, the leaders and the led, in an extraordinarily diverse, global community of faith, memory, and hope. The authors of this volume are not of one mind on all the questions involved, and the author of this prologue speaks for no one but himself. Nevertheless, the need for some genuine decentralizing steps seems clear enough to many observers.[15]

A necessary starting point for any improvement in the life of the church is candid discussion and debate within it, a point registered by most of this book's authors. That such a simple thing may be impossible at the moment shows how deep the crisis of authority has become, and observers of church affairs are mindful of the unhappy fate of Cardinal Joseph Bernardin's common ground initiative of 1996, which had this aim. For almost all within his jurisdiction, Cardinal Bernardin was a model for authentic leadership, an example of how to do things right. He showed in his conduct of office what legitimate authority today might look like.

When he proposed to initiate a process of discussion of the problems that divided the faithful, however, he was in a very rare maneuver publicly criticized by four of his fellow cardinals, appointed princes like himself in the American church, led by Cardinal Bernard Law of Boston, who would soon be swept up in public controversy over his handling of the sex abuse crisis at its ground zero location and virtually driven from office by the laity in his charge, an unprecedented event. Bernardin's critics objected on grounds that discussion would only exacerbate things. The overriding need, they felt, was not to talk, but simply to comply with what the sacred authority in which they participated called for. With his untimely death, Bernardin's initiative fizzled out, and he was replaced by one who thought differently about the exercise of leadership and agreed with the critics, Cardinal Francis George.[16]

Feasible or not, the need for earnest talk and the assurance that serious issues will be seriously considered is pressing and will continue to press. Where in fact does deliberation actually go on in the Catholic Church, and why is there so little *public* deliberation on behalf of a far-flung community that now includes more than one billion souls? In its June 27, 2009, issue, *The Tablet* reported an interview (published in *La Repubblica* on June 18) with Cardinal Carlo Maria Martini, the eighty-two-year-old Jesuit and former archbishop of Milan, long admired by Catholic scholars and intellectuals particularly for his candor and independence. Once rumored as "Papabile," Cardinal Martini called for convening, on a regular, periodic basis, general ecumenical councils, claiming it was now necessary to enact what "was decreed by the Council of Constance" in the fifteenth century, a reference to *Frequens*.

Such councils might deal with a restricted number of contentious issues at each of the periodic meetings, every twenty or thirty years, he suggested, perhaps starting with the problems of Catholics who are divorced and remarried and the need for a major overhaul of the Sacrament of Penance. In recent years, Martini has also spoken of the need to rethink celibacy in the priesthood, greater roles for women in the church, and other matters of disputed ecclesiastical practice. While the Cardinal clearly does not expect his proposal to be taken up anytime soon, the mere fact that he makes a gesture pointing to the lost tradition of conciliarism may indicate that the limits of the ultramontane papacy are being felt and that the old conciliar alternative or supplement to it, so worrisome to the papacy in the past, retains some power of precedent and suggestiveness for those who think about church governance.

The aim of those who feel restive about the shortcomings of governance in the church is not to overthrow formal authority, but to find ways for it to work in a more realistic, responsible, effective fashion. Many have noted that Catholicism emerged from Vatican II as, sociologically speaking, a voluntary society, a free-standing church, one that had renounced any wish or hope to be the established religion of the modern states of the world. Ever since then, the struggle has been for a style of governance more responsive to the internal needs of such a church, for evidence of changing norms within established forms that might better live up to the idea of the pilgrim church as a community of graced freedom. Authentic piety all around will not be undermined by criticism of its conventions. The search is for authority without authoritarianism, clergy without clericalism, and acknowledgment from those who hold formal powers that the spirit of unity that must ever be fostered does not entail strict uniformity of thought and behavior. The editors hope that the chapters in this book will be of some interest to those who appreciate the importance of pursuing that search.

As pointed out by Judge John T. Noonan, who has been for so long a mentor to many who seek to learn from the moral history of the church, a long-term member of the board of the Institute for Advanced Catholic Studies, and the person to whom this volume is dedicated, in his letter to the Philippians St. Paul in passing sets out what can be conceived as the start of a useful program. It is my prayer, he says, "that your love abound more and more in knowledge and in insight of every kind, so that you test what is vital" (Phil. 1:9–10). Paul's expectation, Noonan notes, is that "increase in love is increase in knowledge and insight. The increase comes from identification with the other, who is not alien but another self." The love of neighbor is one element in the rule of faith. The other, as Jesus taught, is to "love the Lord your God with your whole heart, your whole soul, your whole mind, and your whole strength" (Matt. 22–37). The twin commandments make up the rule of faith, and authentic development, Noonan concludes, "proceeds directed by this rule. The love of God generates, reinforces, and seals the love of neighbor. What is required is found in the community's experience as it tests what is vital. On the surface, contradictions appear. At the deeper level, the course is clear." This insight into the rule of faith is worth remembering when we ponder the difficulties of authority in the church.[17]

NOTES

1. Joseph Komonchak's chapter is a revised version of an article published under the same title in *Christianesimo nella Storia* 28 (2007): 323–37. William D'Antonio, James Davidson, Dean Hoge, and Mary Gautier's chapter is excerpted from their *American Catholics Today: New Realities of Their Faith and Their Church* (Lanham, MD: Rowman and Littlefield, 2007). They are published with permission.

2. A useful ventilation of the issues in a Catholic context is provided in a volume resulting from the second Cardinal Bernardin Conference of the Catholic Common Ground Initiative, *Church Authority in American Culture* (New York: Crossroad, 1999), with an introduction by Philip J. Murnion. The rich conference discussions published here from transcripts are comprised of responses—questions and answers—to four essays provided by Cardinal Avery Dulles, "*Humanae Vitae* and *Ordinatio Sacerdotalis*: Problems of Reception"; Joseph Komonchak, "Authority and Its Exercise"; James Coriden, "Church Authority in American Culture: Case and Observations"; and Philip Selznick, "Authority in America."

3. The study of voting behavior is another indicator of the limits of official authority. Professional analysis of Catholic voting makes it clear that there is no longer any such thing as a Catholic vote that mirrors the teachings of the hierarchy. In America, at any rate, the faithful seem to reflect in microcosm all the lines of cleavage that mark partisan divisions in the culture as a whole. See Kristin Heyer, Mark Rozell, and Michael A. Genovese, eds., *Catholics and Politics: The Dynamic Tension between Faith and Power* (Washington, DC: Georgetown University Press, 2008). In a discussion of the book in the *CARA Report* (Spring 2009), it was pointed out that when Catholics are asked about the sources of their political views, "only 37 percent said they seriously consider Church statements on social, political, and moral issues, while 59 percent believed their own conscience is more important than Church teachings." On thinking for oneself, it should be noted that anti-Catholicism, now receding, was one of the deepest cultural biases in America's history, the last "acceptable prejudice" entertained by many intellectuals. The notion was that Catholics were not permitted by their faith to think for themselves, but rather were required as religious duty to follow the lead of the Vatican on all things. On the depth and scope of this bias and the prominence of the intellectual elites who believed it, see John T. McGreevey, "Thinking on One's Own: Catholicism in the American Intellectual Imagination, 1928–1960," *Journal of American History* 84, no. 1 (1997): 97–131. McGreevey's *Catholicism and American Freedom: A History* (New York: W. W. Norton, 2003) explores in depth the tensions between Catholic belief and American ideals of individual liberty. For a discussion of the sociological evidence indicating that many Americans continue to doubt the

intellectual independence of Catholics for the same reason (subservience to Rome), see Andrew Greeley, "Can Catholics Think for Themselves?" *Commonweal*, September 9, 2005, 12–13.

4. Charles Taylor, a Catholic thinker, is the leading philosophical expositor and historian of the shifting historical horizons of the personal element in religious experience. His work has been as influential as it has because of his feeling for the origins of modernity in religious aspirations and ideals. He concentrates on the changing context of the personal element in spiritual life and all the demands for authenticity it has entailed throughout the course of modern history. These concerns drive his major works: *Sources of the Self: The Making of the Modern Identity* (Cambridge: Cambridge University Press, 1989) and *A Secular Age* (Cambridge, MA: Belknap Press of Harvard University Press, 2007). The "unencumbered self" is shorthand from Michael Sandel for the notion in liberal political theory and apologetics that the only moral obligations that matter are those that are freely chosen by the individual, and that government and law should be strictly neutral with respect to competing conceptions of the good. Leading communitarian thinkers, such as Sandel, Taylor, Philip Selznick, and Hans Joas, attack these ideas regarding the nature of liberty, the self, and the state as badly misreading the liberal tradition and tending to undermine its valid achievements. See Sandel's *Public Philosophy: Essays in Morality and Politics* (Cambridge, MA: Harvard University Press, 2005), Philip Selznick's *The Communitarian Persuasion* (Washington, DC: Woodrow Wilson Center Press, 2002) and *A Humanist Science: Values and Ideals in Social Inquiry* (Stanford, CA: Stanford University Press, 2008), and Hans Joas's *Do We Need Religion? On the Experience of Self-Transcendence* (Boulder, CO: Paradigm, 2008).

5. Andrew Greeley, whose data-rich interpretations on what is happening within the church have been persuasive and consistent over the decades, stresses the point that those who differ from church teaching on questions of morality, especially sexual morality, do not feel that they are any less Catholic for doing so: "Catholics were rejecting the old rules, but not rejecting the Church or God. Rather they were shifting their appeal from a Church that did not understand to a God that did." The shift is momentous and gathering momentum. The dissidents are not surly or loud, but generally well behaved and devout. See Greeley's *The Catholic Revolution: New Wine, Old Wineskins, and the Second Vatican Council* (Berkeley: University of California Press, 2004). Quotation appears on p. 78. Greeley notes on the following page that "the devout dissidents are rejecting any claim by the leadership to have a monopoly on God. The dynamics that make selective Catholicism possible seem to be impervious to the influence of the magisterium." Greeley's "selective Catholicism" is a descriptive phrase that points to patterns of data. The phrase "cafeteria Catholicism" is a pejorative phrase used by conservative Catholics, who presumably do not make choices themselves and have no issues with magisterial teachings, to denounce their coreligionists.

6. A kind of mapping of the factions, right and left, together with accounts of their movements and ideas, is provided in two related studies: Mary Jo Weaver and Scott Appleby, eds., *Being Right: Conservative Catholics in America* (Bloomington: Indiana University Press, 1995), and Mary Jo Weaver, *What's Left? Liberal American Catholics* (Bloomington: Indiana University Press, 1999).

7. In the "Formula for the Profession of Faith," the successor to the antimodernist oath that all clergy were required to sign up until the time of Vatican II, now required by the revised code of canon law to be taken by all persons, clerical or lay, who have any official responsibilities in the church, the concluding paragraph states: "I adhere with religious submission of will and intellect to the doctrines either the Roman Pontiff or the College of bishops propose, when they exercise their authoritative teaching office, even though they do not intend to proclaim those doctrines by definitive act." This means that noninfallible teachings, which by definition are possibly fallible teachings, are to be obeyed, accorded "religious submission of will and intellect," whatever the difficulties one may have in personally appropriating them. The class of noninfallible, authoritative teachings is a very large one. It includes all the points of the church's social teaching and almost all of its moral teachings, on contraception, abortion, premarital sex, divorce and remarriage, homosexuality, euthanasia, stem-cell research, advance medical directives, and many other questions. While laypeople other than those with official duties are not required to sign the formula, the expectation of the hierarchy is that the norms apply to all.

8. Bernard Lonergan, *Method in Theology* (Minneapolis: Seabury, 1972), p. 270. For Lonergan's perspective on a properly Catholic understanding of moral autonomy, see my "Moral Autonomy in the Church: Bernard Lonergan and the Natural Law," in *Tradition and Pluralism: Essays in Honor of William M. Shea*, Studies of Religion and the Social Order, ed. Kenneth L. Parker, Peter A. Huff, and Michael J. G. Pahls, 81–113 (New York: University Press of America, 2009).

9. These remarks about rights, duties, and the changing grounds for civil rule are derived and adapted from Gianfranco Poggi's seminal article, "The Modern State and the Idea of Progress," in *Progress and Its Discontents*, ed. Gabriel Almond, Marvin Chodorow, and Roy Harvey Pierce, 337–360 (Berkeley: University of California Press, 1982). Poggi stresses the rights/duties shift. He is concerned with relations between knowledge and authority, the exercise of power, on the one hand, and the rise of modern natural scientific, social-scientific, historical, and juridical knowledge, on the other. He did not have questions of ecclesiastical authority in mind when he wrote the article, but for those who are concerned with church authority, the comparisons are hard to miss.

10. One of the reasons that many Catholic scholars and intellectuals feel more at home with Catholic social teaching than they do with other areas of church teaching is precisely because the vocabulary of command and control has no place in it. Its characteristic language, instead, is that of an evolving Christian humanism that appeals to the universal values inherent in the sacred dignity of all human beings, rather than the juridical authority of the pope. See, for example, the Pontifical Council for Justice and Peace volume, *Compendium of the Social Doctrine of the Church* (Washington, DC: United States Conference of Catholic Bishops, 2005). As Lisa Sowell Cahill's chapter on moral theology since Vatican II in the present book shows, the gravitational pull of the norms of "social ethics" and Catholic social thought have become increasingly influential in Catholic academic circles in coloring other areas of moral inquiry. The entire field of moral theology, she demonstrates, has become more biblical in its inspiration and sources, more sensitive to change and historicity, and has become the

province of lay theologians as well as clergy, a fateful development that plays a role in Cathleen Kaveny's chapter as well. That official social teaching has a kind of vital influence on Catholic academic thought that official moral teaching does not manifest to the same degree suggests that authority is working better in the one area than in the other. Those in authority might ask themselves why and make a study of it.

11. In Pope Benedict's remarks on frameworks for interpreting Vatican II, reprinted in the appendix, the reader will notice that at the crucial point in his argument, the pope invokes a distinction between norms and forms, guiding principles and variable circumstances: "we must learn to understand more practically than before the Church's decisions on contingent matters—for example, certain practical forms of liberalism or a free interpretation of the Bible—should necessarily be contingent themselves, precisely because they refer to a specific reality that is changeable in itself. It was necessary to recognize that in these decisions it is only the principles that express the permanent aspect, since they remain as an undercurrent, motivating decisions from within." If this sensibility were reflected in other areas of papal teaching—in moral teaching, for example—it would make living with papal authority less stressful, perhaps, and the whole business of the authoritative instruction of conscience more fruitful than it seems to have been when no distinction between ideals and contingent circumstances is acknowledged.

12. Giuseppe Alberigo and Norman P. Tanner, eds., *Decrees of the Ecumenical Councils*, Vol. 1 (Washington, DC: Georgetown University Press, 1990), 438–439.

13. Jose Casanova, in his chapter "Globalizing Catholicism and the Return to a 'Universal' Church," in *Transnational Religion and Fading States*, ed. Susanne Rudolph and James Piscatori (Boulder, CO: Westview, 1997), argues that the Catholicism emerging from Vatican II was different from its earlier forms in three regards: (1) evident consciousness of a broadened, diverse, universal audience and wider publication of papal encyclicals dealing not only with matters of internal Catholic practice but also with issues of the secular age affecting all humanity; (2) an increasingly active and vocal role for the papacy in dealing with international conflicts and world peace issues; and (3) a new kind of public visibility for the person of the pope as what Casanova calls "the first citizen of a global, civil society" and the "high priest of a new, civil religion of humanity." Where once Catholicism was associated with antidemocratic, antimodern values and arguments, in his (relatively) new role as the leading public champion for the sacred dignity of the human person, made in the divine image, the pope advocates a form of theist, global, universal humanism. There has been, in other words, a "sacralization" of human rights, which puts the church on a new footing so far as democratic values are concerned. Frictions within the church and the drama of its future development involve, Casanova notes, conflict between the old and new papal roles. The role of high priest for a new, universal, theist humanism is "often in tension with his other role as infallible head and supreme guardian of the particular doctrines, laws, rituals and traditions of the Una, Sancta, Catholica, and Apostolica Roman Church." If the Catholic Church wants to live up to its new universalistic claims, Casanova concludes, "it will have to learn to live with social and cultural pluralism both outside and especially inside the Church."

14. See Joseph A. Komonchak, "Authority and Conversion or: the Limits of Authority," *Christianesimo nella Storia* 21 (2000): 207–229. Fr. Komonchak observes that Catholic theological reflection on church authority has traditionally emphasized its *objectivity*, its positive status over and against the individual believer, given its divine origin and the belief that the hierarchy participates in the authority of Christ. In this article, Komonchak explores some of the limits of the old view, drawing upon sociology and history. He notes that, functionally speaking, authority can be translated into trustworthiness and develops its relation to the idea that "graced freedom" is constitutive of the church and of all relations within it. Under conditions of graced freedom, all authority is "co-constituted" by the trust of those who acknowledge it. The church is operating as a free church in a free culture that generates conditions of free choice unknown to much of Christian history. Komonchak's perspective on the actual operations of authority under these conditions points to the necessity of genuine conversion in both the subjects and bearers of authority. It follows that effective authority, as distinct from merely formal authority, must deal with the subjectivity and intersubjectivity of Christian conversion on an open, ongoing basis. Inherited attitudes and practices of command and control are understandable from the historical standpoint but can hit wide of the mark when it comes to the need for ongoing, lifelong conversion under contemporary conditions.

15. On the ways in which some decentralization might be achieved and the kinds of practical questions that are necessarily involved, see Thomas J. Reese, S.J., "Reforming the Vatican: What the Church Can Learn from Other Institutions," *Commonweal*, April 25, 2008, 15–17. See also Archbishop John R. Quinn's *Reform of the Papacy: The Costly Call to Christian Unity* (New York: Herder and Herder, 1999).

16. For information on the common ground initiative, see Cardinal Joseph Bernardin and Archbishop Oscar H. Lipscomb, *Catholic Common Ground Initiative: Foundational Documents*, with an introduction by Philip J. Murnion (New York: Cross-roads, 1997). The story of the initiative and its fate is recounted in the first chapter of Peter Steinfels, *A People Adrift: The Crisis of the Roman Catholic Church in America* (New York: Simon and Schuster, 2003).

17. John T. Noonan Jr., *A Church That Can and Cannot Change: The Development of Catholic Moral Teaching* (Notre Dame, IN: University of Notre Dame Press, 2005), 220–222, passim.

SECTION I

Historical Background

Contested Pasts

I

History and the Return of the Repressed in Catholic Modernity

The Dilemma Posed by Constance

Francis Oakley

From Yogi Berra (or, possibly, the Berra Apocrypha), I draw the inimitable dictum that "the past isn't what it used to be." And it is already clear that the past as apprehended from the contemporary Catholic scene—worldwide no less than European or American—isn't what it once was. Not, at least, what it used to be in the years before the proceedings of the Second Vatican Council made change in belief and practice an immediately palpable feature of modern ecclesial life and, in effect, along with the papal crown and *sedia gestatoria*, retired to museum status the hallowed motto semper idem, "always the same."

It was not, of course, that change or development in such matters had somehow failed to occur before or, more to the point, that Catholic theologians had not for long centuries concerned themselves with elaborating theories capable of encompassing the nature of that process of change. Across the centuries, after all, the church had repeatedly defined doctrines to be held *de fide*, and medieval scholastic thinkers—Bonaventure, Aquinas, and Scotus among them—as well as the seventeenth-century Spanish theologians of the "second scholasticism," had been at pains to make clear that, in so doing, it was not attempting to supplement a revelation that was, in fact, immutable. Instead, it was simply "displaying more clearly the inner content of the revelation, explicating [if you wish] what was implicit."[1] In so arguing, the later scholastics were led to capitalize on the fact that words like *explicit* and *implicit* had been drawn from the vocabulary deployed in the logic of the day and to take the syllogism, accordingly, as their model for what we would call doctrinal development. Thus, or so they argued, "the deduction from two premises is *implicated* in those premises," and "the conclusion of the syllogism is an *explication* of a truth which before was implied by, but perhaps concealed in, the premises."[2] Similarly, with doctrinal definitions. Rather than involving any departure from the original revelation, they were simply necessary inferences from what had been revealed, timely clarifications, or declarations of what was implicit in the revelation.

Around that basic intuition, the seventeenth-century Spanish scholastics erected a formidable body of argumentation. But none of it seemed to have made its way into the broader stream of John Henry Newman's thinking or to have informed the highly influential if hotly disputed theory he elaborated in his *Essay on the Development of Christian Doctrine* (1845; revised in 1878). When he wrote that work, he appears to have known nothing about the older scholastic views on doctrinal development. Even if he had, his own distrust of syllogistic reasoning would probably have constituted an obstacle to his appropriating the central intuition that informed them.[3] Instead, his own approach was far more naturalistic.[4] Acknowledging the formative influence exerted over his thinking by Butler's *Analogy of Religion* and alluding in passing to the notions of development lodged in the thinking of Joseph de Maistre and J. A. Möhler, Newman argued that, so far as "the history of a philosophy or belief" goes, far from being like a stream that is "clearest near the spring," it is "on the contrary, . . . more equable, and purer, and stronger, when its bed has become deep, and broad, and full."[5]

But whatever their nature, neither scholastic notions of doctrinal development as logical inference nor Newman's later and more capacious approach appears to have cut much ice with those in positions of ecclesiastical authority or done much to calm the misgivings of contemporary critics, whether Catholic or Protestant. Certainly, being himself largely ignorant of the scholastic argument and in his scholarly orientation more the historian by temperament, the great Bishop Bossuet was not deflected in the late seventeenth century from trumpeting forth his own confidence in the static, immutable nature of the Christian faith, subject, it may be, to a process of *clarification* of what had been implicit from the start but not to any *variation*, which was always and everywhere a sure sign of error.[6] Nor, in mid-nineteenth century, did the American Catholic Orestes Brownson hesitate, radicalizing Bossuet's traditionalism, to dismiss Newman's *Essay* as "utterly repugnant to her [the church's] claims to be the authoritative and infallible Church of God." For it was the view of the church itself that "there has been no progress, no increase, no variation in faith; that what she believes and teaches now is precisely what she always and everywhere believed and taught from the first. . . . [So that] if you [Newman] believe the Church you cannot assert development in your sense of the term: if you do not believe her, you are no Catholic."[7]

While later Catholic commentators did not usually push their criticisms of Newman to that extreme, the misgivings they felt about his theory of doctrinal development seem, if anything, to have deepened across the century ensuing.[8] Part of the reason for that may well have been the fact that the neoscholastic revival of the late nineteenth century, along with its papally mandated place in Catholic clerical formation right down to the era of Vatican II, tended, when it came to matters of faith, to encourage intimations of immutability and to confer enhanced credibility on a frame of mind that was to a marked degree ahistorical. So, too, in somewhat cruder fashion, did Pius X's condemnation of Modernism in the decree *Pascendi* (1907), as also the very explicit antiModernist oath subsequently imposed on all clerics from 1910 to 1967. Among other things, after all, that oath required them to affirm "the absolute and unchangeable truth presented by the Apostles from the beginning," to reject "the heretical invention of the evolution of dogmas, to the effect that these would change their meaning from that previously held by the Church," and to deny that "it would be lawful for the historian to uphold views which are in contradiction with the faith of the believer."[9]

The prevalent fear, and it was especially evident in those of markedly antiModernist sensibilities, was that the pursuit in theology of historically oriented approaches inevitably carried with it some sort of a threat to orthodoxy. But that notwithstanding, the carapace of neoscholastic essentialism that shielded so much of early-twentieth-century Catholic intellectual life from the historian's preoccupation with contingency, novelty, and change proved powerless in the end to prevent the seepage of historical preoccupations into the thinking of so many of the theologians whose views came to the fore in the debates of Vatican II. I think especially of Henri de Lubac, Yves Congar, and Hans Küng. In Bernard Lonergan's terms, those debates and affiliated discussions were to reflect the shift made by so many of those involved from "a classical world-view" to a species of "historical mindedness." And it was that shift, presumably, that John Courtney Murray had in mind when he concluded that "development of doctrine" was "*the* issue underlying all issues at Vatican II."[10]

"Development," however, as Newman had himself conceded, is a complex notion susceptible of more than one meaning. And while, in the debates about the interpretation of Vatican II's achievement that have rumbled on into the present, the unquestionable reality of development and change has had necessarily to be conceded, sharp disagreement has nonetheless persisted, but with the focus of that disagreement shifting now to the precise *nature* of the change involved.[11] In that respect, a particularly acute anxiety has come to attend upon any suggestion that John XXIII's aggiornamento may have come at the council to mean not simply some sort of updating reform, but rather rupture, revolution, the insertion into the course of church history of a species of marked discontinuity. And so far as the interpretation of Vatican II goes, the sharp distinction Benedict XVI made in 2005 between a confusing "hermeneutic of discontinuity or rupture" and a fruitful "hermeneutic of reform" itself witnesses powerfully to the prevalence of that sort of anxiety.[12]

That this should be the case is readily comprehensible. Of the seven "notes . . . to discriminate healthy developments of an idea from its state of corruption and decay" that Newman was at pains to identify in his *Essay on Development*, the second, after all, was "Continuity of Principle."[13] It is not at all clear that his theory is capable of encompassing (or domesticating) the type of sharp and sudden discontinuity with previous teaching that some would claim to have occurred at Vatican II, and still less, the type of rupture that others would now insist had been evident long before that in the way in which Catholic belief and practice had mutated across the centuries. John Noonan, for example, has recently traced the convoluted process whereby a pattern of behavior once denounced as contrary to nature has modulated across time into the routinely acceptable, whereas another such pattern, once taken for granted as unexceptionable, has come to be viewed as totally unacceptable, perhaps even "intrinsically evil."[14] Noonan takes as his prime examples witnessing to radical change contemporary Catholic teaching on usury, slavery, and religious freedom. It is true that on such matters Catholics have succeeded in accommodating to seismic shifts in official church teaching with a surprising degree of equanimity. But if that is indeed the case, it may largely be due to the empire that the present continues to exert over the past in so much of Catholic institutional thinking. And it certainly reflects the measure of genial institutional forgetfulness that seems to attend inevitably upon that state of affairs.[15] Under certain circumstances, moreover, casual forgetfulness has betrayed a disagreeable tendency to mutate into a proactive politics of oblivion reflective of the Orwellian conclusion that if he who controls the past controls the future, then he who controls the present would be well advised to control the past.[16] And that tendency has come powerfully into play at moments when the waves of change have come to break upon the very bastions of ecclesiastical authority.

It is, then, upon one particular instance of radically discontinuous change touching upon the ultimate locus of authority in the church, as well as upon the persistent ecclesiastical attempt to brush that threatening instance to one side or to consign it to oblivion, that I wish in this essay to dwell. I do so, let it be confessed, with a certain measure of diffidence. In both historical and theological terms, the issues involved are themselves unusually intricate ones. Across time, moreover, they have come to be occluded by a complex combination of ideological repression, historiographic self-censorship, and, eventually, widespread institutional forgetfulness. Since the triumph of ultramontane sentiment in the nineteenth century, indeed, they have come to seem hopelessly recondite, of interest perhaps to the blinkered denizens of research libraries, manuscript collections, and rare book rooms, but of questionable relevance to the pressing challenges confronting the Catholic Church today. It is my claim, however, that that is far from being the case. And in what follows, it will be my purpose to try to put that claim beyond the reach of reasonable doubt.

The instance of radical doctrinal discontinuity in question is the great gulf that yawns between the position the general councils of Constance (1414–1418) and Basel (1431–1449) affirmed concerning the ultimate locus of authority in the universal church and that staked out in 1870 by Vatican I in its twin definitions of papal jurisdictional primacy and papal infallibility, both definitions unambiguously reaffirmed by Vatican II in its great constitution, *Lumen gentium* (1964). It is the gulf between an essentially conciliarist ecclesiology that attributes to the general council, acting independently of the pope and in certain critical areas, a jurisdictional power superior to his and one that locates the supreme ecclesiastical authority either in the supreme pontiff acting alone (thus Vatican I) or in addition (at least since Vatican II) in the college of bishops united with its papal head. And even in the latter case, Vatican II made it clear that, as head of the episcopal college, the pope "alone can perform certain acts which are in no way within the competence of the bishops"; can proceed, taking "into consideration the good of the Church" and "according to his own discretion" in "setting up, encouraging and approving collegial activity"; and, "as supreme pastor of the church, exercise his power at all times *as he thinks best*" (*suam potestatem omni tempore ad placitum exercere potest*).[17]

Neither Constance nor Basel is exactly a household name today, but, however conflicted, neither was a fly-by-night affair. In size alone, Constance was one of the most imposing of all medieval representative assemblies, whether civil or ecclesiastical. Far better attended than most of the earlier medieval general councils had been or, for that matter, than the Council of Trent itself was to be in its first two sessions at least, it attracted into its magnetic field not only the papal but also the imperial chancery and became for a while the international crossroads at which much of Europe's diplomatic business was conducted. In effect, as one historian has put it, it was "as close as the Middle Ages came to the Congress of Vienna [1815] or to the United Nations."[18] Nor was it size alone that set the council apart. It was the greatest and certainly the most memorable of the general councils held by the medieval Latin Church, and one distinguished by its success in putting an end to the worst crisis ever to have overtaken that church. The crisis in question was the protracted scandal of the Great Schism of the West, which, after the confused and disputed election of 1378, had seen, first, two lines of rival claimants, Roman and Avignonese, vying destructively for the papal office. And then, still worse, after the failed attempt of the Council of Pisa in 1409 to end the schism by deposing both rival claimants and electing Pope Alexander V, it had seen the addition of a third, or Pisan, line of claimants, of whom John XXIII was the second. And it was John who convoked the Council of Constance.

He did so, however, under imperial pressure, and when, later, he began to fear that he might be coerced into resigning his high office, he sought to encompass the council's ruin by fleeing Constance and leaving it effectually headless. It was under those circumstances of crisis that the council fathers, encouraged by the emperor-elect Sigismund and rallied by the great French theologian Jean Gerson, determined to proceed even in the pope's absence. In April 1415, then, they formally promulgated the celebrated superiority decree *Haec sancta synodus*, a historic expression of the moderate version of what has come to be called conciliarism or conciliar theory. The decree declared that the Council of Constance was a legitimate general council representing the catholic church militant, that it derived its authority immediately from Christ, and that all Christians—the pope included—were bound on pain of punishment to obey it and all future general councils in matters pertaining to the faith, the ending of schism, and the reform of the church in head and members.[19] The following month, they acted on the provisions of that decree by trying and deposing John XXIII, who had been taken prisoner and returned to Constance. Shortly thereafter, even though he had in fact been deposed already at Pisa, they negotiated the resignation of the Roman claimant, Gregory XII. And after failing to secure a similarly negotiated settlement with the Avignonese claimant, Benedict XIII, they proceeded in 1417 to try him in absentia and declare him deposed. That done, and having first in the decree *Frequens* attempted to give constitutional teeth to *Haec sancta* by mandating for the future the regular and automatic assembly of general councils, they proceeded in November 1417 to elect as pope Martin V, originally one of the cardinals of the Roman obedience but one who, like many another churchman, had switched his allegiance to the Pisan pontiffs.

Surrounded still by a tiny coterie of adamant supporters, the Avignonese pontiff, Benedict XIII, persisted right down to his death in 1423 in his claim to be the true pope. But that notwithstanding, it has been customary to regard the Great Schism as having come to an end in 1417 with the election of Martin V.

There is nothing, I believe, tendentious about the brief account just given. Nothing, that is, to preclude its acceptance by most informed commentators, whatever their disposition on matters ecclesiological. And it is clear enough, so far as it goes. Unfortunately, and for purposes of interpreting the whole conciliar episode, it does not go far enough. In this case, and to an unusual degree, the devil lies, alas, in the details. And in relation to those details, the questions that call for resolution are multiple. Disputed election and papal depositions notwithstanding, is it warranted to claim that we today are some-how in a better position than were contemporaries when it comes to determin-ing to which of the competing lines of claimants—Roman, Avignonese, Pisan—legitimacy properly attached? If so, on what grounds? And to which line? If the Roman and not the Pisan, then, given the prevailing canonistic norm that to claim legitimacy a council had to be convoked by a (legitimate) pope and its decrees confirmed in the same way, can Constance really lay any claim to having been a legitimate general council before its convocation by Gregory XII immediately prior to his resignation? If not, then *Haec sancta*, not being the enactment of a legitimate general council, can possess no validity. Unless, of course, Martin V retroactively confirmed all the conciliar enact-ments of the Constance assembly. But if *Haec sancta* was not the decree of a legitimate general council, by what alchemy could Martin V, whose own papal title depended upon its legitimacy, transmute it into such? As Jean Gerson pointed out to him in 1418 (and Cardinal Cesarini, the papal legate presiding at the Council of Basel, pointed out later on to Eugenius IV), if *Haec sancta* somehow lacked validity, then so, too, did the actions that Constance had grounded on it, not excluding the trial and deposition of the rival claimants and the subsequent election of Martin V.[20] And if Martin's title is invalid, what then is to be said (at least in terms of the traditional understanding of papal succession) about the validity of the titles of all subsequent popes down to the present?[21]

And so on. A veritable cat's-cradle of overlapping and intersecting ques-tions are involved, and, over the years, a bewildering array of responses, often mutually incompatible, have been given to them. But that notwithstanding, in the wake of Vatican I, the lineaments of a constitutive narrative, high papalist in its orientation and governing the whole conciliar episode, may be said to have emerged. In its broad outlines, that narrative succeeded in inserting itself into the older standard histories and textbooks, and not only those of Catholic provenance.

In terms of this traditional narrative and so far as the big picture is involved, the whole conciliar episode is portrayed as emerging, reassuringly enough, once the ideological dust is allowed to settle, as nothing more than a stutter, hiccup, or interruption in the long history of the Latin Catholic Church. That it was an unfortunate, dangerous, and revolutionary episode is not to be gainsaid. But if it was radical in its origins, so also, we are assured, was it rapid in its demise. If it got underway with the disputed papal election of 1378, by 1440, and even before Pope Eugenius IV's great struggle with his conciliarist opponents at the Council of Basel was over, it was already unambiguously heading toward its demise. That year, as the French historian Paul Ourliac claimed rather grandly (and not much more than a quarter of a century ago), was a great ideological and ecclesiological hinge or turning point, after which theologians, canonists, and humanists alike turned eagerly to what he called the "constructive" task of engineering "the triumph of the papal monarchy."[22] The victory of Pope Eugenius IV over the Council of Basel marked the end of the conciliar movement. And if conciliar *theory* survived a little longer, it was to enjoy not much more than a shadowy half-life, or, put differently, it was destined ultimately to become little more than a minor perturbation on the outermost orbit of the ecclesiological consciousness.

That's the big, sweeping picture conveyed by the traditional constitutive narrative. Within its overall framework, attention is focused especially on the facts of the matter concerning the disputed papal election of 1378 and the unfolding of events at the Council of Constance, as well as on matters ideological, on the origins, nature, and destiny of the conciliar theory itself. Thus, so far as the disputed election of 1378 goes, the view taken is that whatever the claims made for the legitimacy of Clement VII (1378–1394) and his successors in the Avignonese line of claimants to the papal throne, they have to be seen as politically conditioned and diplomatically driven. The legitimate pope was Urban VI (1378–1389), the one first elected, and the legitimate papal line was the Roman line of his successors down to Gregory XII, who resigned his high office in 1415 during the Council of Constance. As a result, no validity attached to his deposition (along with his Avignonese rival, Benedict XIII) at the Council of Pisa in 1409. Nor did any validity attach to the elections, first of Alexander V and then of John XXIII, who together composed the third, or Pisan, line of claimants. Hence the Council of Constance, not having been convoked by a legitimate pope, cannot be regarded as a legitimate general council prior to its convocation by Gregory XII, just before his resignation on July 4, 1415. For the council fathers, in the course of negotiating for his resignation, had accorded him that privilege. That means that the decree *Haec sancta*, which had been enacted on April 6 of that year, was not the decree of a legitimate general council, and the invocation of its authority by the conciliarist opponents of Eugenius IV at the Council of Basel, no less than its subsequent invocation by members of the anti-infallibilist Minority at Vatican I,[23] was an unambiguous sign of the doctrinal deviancy and theological bankruptcy characteristic of both groups.

That said, in its view of the conciliar theory itself, the ideological under-pinnings, after all, of the Constance decree, *Haec sancta*, the traditional narra-tive took as its own the damaging case first made by the Dominican theologian, Juan de Torquemada, papal ideologist and propagandist for Eugenius IV at the Council of Basel. According to that case, the doctrinal genealogy was suspect and the verdict clear. The conciliar theory was nothing other than a revolution-ary and heterodox position drawn from the polemical antipapal writings of the two leading imperialist propagandists of the early fourteenth century, Marsiglio of Padua and William of Ockham. Such noxious ideas had come to the fore only because the turbulent conditions of the schism had opened a veritable Pandora's box that not even Eugenius IV had been able fully to close. That task fell instead to Pope Pius II, who, in 1460 in the celebrated bull *Execrabilis*, prohibited the practice of appealing from the judgment of the pope to that of a future general council, and to the Fifth Lateran Council, which, in 1516, added to that prohibition "a condemnation of the [conciliar] theory itself."[24] Even then, tattered remnants of the conciliarist ecclesiology were to be found in the seventeenth, eighteenth, and early nineteenth centuries, caught up in those provincial (i.e., French, German, Austrian) ideologies that we know as Gallicanism, Richerism, Febronianism, and Josephinism. But those "isms" were, in fact, essentially *statist* ideologies, used to provide cover and justifica-tion for the illegitimate extension of French and Austrian state control over the church. And one of the great achievements of Vatican I was to have succeeded at last in erecting a firm doctrinal bulwark against such detestable ideological maneuvers.

All of that said, I would note that not even the firmness of Vatican I succeeded in eliminating all the awkward trailing ends still attaching to this high papalist narrative. Even among those who embraced it, a residual uneasi-ness clearly persisted, and marginal mopping-up operations were still being conducted well into the twentieth century. Thus, early in the century, even so learned a work as the *Dictionnaire de théologie catholique* took the extraordinary step of simply excising the Councils of Pisa, Constance, and Basel from its list of general councils. That list, therefore, simply jumped from the Council of Vienne in 1311–1312 to the Council of Florence in 1439–1445. A remarkably bold exercise in the politics of oblivion! In a similar but Anglophone exercise conducted around the same time, the editors of the *Catholic Encyclopedia*, a pretty scholarly piece of work, by simply opting to include no article on the subject, made it clear that conciliar theory was to be viewed as a dead issue, an ecclesiological fossil, something lodged deep in the lower Carboniferous of the dogmatic geology.[25] Moreover, the need seems to have been felt to continue cleanup operations right down into the mid-century. In the nineteenth century, it had become customary in *Roman* theological circles, at least, to label the Avignonese line of papal claimants during the Great Schism simply as "antipopes," but Alexander V and John XXIII, the claimants stemming from the Council of Pisa's failed effort in 1409 to end the schism, had been handled in a more gingerly fashion and left in limbo.[26] In 1947, however, Angelo Mercati, prefect of the Vatican archives, published a new semiofficial listing of popes in the *Annuario Pontificio* in which the Pisan claimants, too, were now, for the first time, demoted to the status of antipopes. He gave no historical explanation for that move but grounded it, presumably, on the unspecified "theological-canonistic criteria" to which he refers elsewhere in his listing.[27] That notwithstanding, historians in general do not seem to have felt disposed to question his judgment, and his listing has become the standard one to be found in such general works as the *Oxford Dictionary of the Popes* (1986) and the *New Encyclopedia Britannica* (1991).[28] Indeed, it is even, ironically enough, reflected in the tourist-oriented signage to be seen (of all places) in the Palace of the Popes at Avignon.

Even after that move, however, some residual uneasiness seems still to have survived, at least among Vatican officials. And it was to manifest itself in 1958, when Angelo Roncalli, newly elected as pope, announced that he was taking the name of John. At the time, he himself noted that the name John had been borne by twenty-two papal predecessors, adding, however, the qualifying phrase *extra legitimitatis discussiones* (i.e., apart from disputes about legitimacy)—by that significant qualification making it clear that he himself was passing no judgment on the legitimacy of the Pisan line or the first John XXIII (who is described, after all, on his tomb in the baptistery of the duomo in Florence simply as "John XXIII ... *quondam papa*"). But papal authorship notwithstanding, this way of handling the historical record in relation to what appears still to have been viewed as a sensitive issue did not accord with the approach favored by the officials of the papal curia. And they clearly felt themselves charged with the duty of keeping the papal voice on frequency—or "on message," as presidential handlers would say today. From the later official version of the speech published in the *Acta Apostolicae Sedis*, then, the offending qualifying phrase can be seen to have been quietly deleted. Soon the claim was being made that the pope had indeed taken the opportunity to deny the legitimacy of the Pisan line.[29]

The degree of insecurity evident in such recent moves reflects, I suspect, the degree to which the traditional high-papalist narrative had itself constituted a somewhat anxious attempt to cast a species of lifeline across the veritable abyss of disagreement and confusion evident in the judgments Catholic scholars have made over the years about the conciliar episode in general and the respective status of the various lines of papal claimants in particular. The type of confusion involved can readily be illustrated from the disarray characteristic of the pertinent articles printed in the standard twentieth-century Catholic encyclopedias and handbooks. And it is reflective of the differential degree to which their authors permitted modern theological and canonistic considerations to intrude anachronistically upon the interpretation of the historical data.[30] Thus, in some cases, the Council of Pisa is either passed over in silence or rejected outright; in others, the question of its ecumenicity is portrayed as having yet to be decided.[31] In most cases, the Avignonese claimants are treated consistently as antipopes, but in some, the matter of their legitimacy is left in limbo.[32] Similarly, the Pisan pontiffs are listed as legitimate popes or dismissed as antipopes sometimes even in articles appearing in the same encyclopedia.[33] The most striking instance of disarray is in the *New Catholic Encyclopedia* (first ed., 1967), where Mollat insists that "the question of the legitimacy of [John XXIII's] ... claim to the Papal See is still unanswered" but does so, ironically, in an article titled (editorially?) "John XXIII, Antipope."[34]

It should be noted, however, that in all of this the point of view reflected in encyclopedias and handbooks does evince a certain evolution across time. And it is an evolution that puts it increasingly at odds with "curialist" opinion and the high-papalist orientation of the traditional narrative. This shift is clearly evident in the fine articles contributed in 1964 to the fourth volume of the Jedin-Dolan *Handbook of Church History* by K. A. Fink, at that time the leading historical expert on the Council of Constance.[35] It is evident also in the pertinent articles contributed to the most recent (third) edition of the *Lexikon für Theologie und Kirche*. That work was published between 1995 and 2001 and maintains, both in its general listing of the popes and in its entries for the individual Roman, Avignonese, and Pisan pontiffs, a studied impartiality, simply identifying all of them by their respective "obediences."[36] And it is evident again in the fact that in Alberigo and Tanner's *Decrees of the General Councils*, though the proceedings of Pisa still go unmentioned, the entire legislative output of Constance from its onset in 1414 to its dissolution in 1418 is printed.[37]

Here I would note that ever since the vast documentary labors of Heinrich Finke in the early decades of the twentieth century, which succeeded in putting research into the work of the Council of Constance "on a new footing,"[38] the flow of historical scholarship on the Great Schism, on Constance itself, and on the conciliar theory has been simply enormous. In its overall dimensions, it has also been out of all proportion with the much less impressive amount of explicitly theological attention devoted to the ecclesiological issues involved. (In 1993, a listing of work published over the past hundred years on Constance alone ran to more than 1,500 items.)[39] And it has affected, in complex ways, our understanding of almost the whole conciliar episode, from the circumstances surrounding the outbreak of the schism to the Councils of Pisa, Constance, and Basel themselves, and to the origins, nature, and subsequent destiny of the conciliar theory. It has, in effect, transformed the whole picture and intensified the need for theologians to step out finally from the long shadow cast by Vatican I and embark on a fresh appraisal of the ecclesiological issues raised by the whole episode. The limitations of space here preclude a full descriptive analysis of the nature of this transformation in all its dimensions.[40] I will limit myself, accordingly, to focusing on just three issues, all of them, however, issues of fundamental importance.

First is the outbreak of the Great Schism itself. Here, renewed investigation of the disputed election and the contextual factors surrounding it has converged on the conclusion that, despite other motives traditionally imputed to them, the cardinals unquestionably had some perfectly legitimate grounds for questioning the validity of the original election of Urban VI (including well-justified doubts about his mental stability), and their failure to pursue that questioning in the days immediately following the election appears to have been the outcome, on their part, of coercion and of fear in the face of what had emerged as a "pathological personality" who later proved himself willing, if need be, to torture dissident cardinals, despite their dignity and advanced years. Their subsequent repudiation of the election, once they got away from Rome and were beyond the reach of papal anger, and their election of Clement VII, the first of what was to become the Avignonese line of papal claimants, left people at the time—prominent among them those intimately involved in the whole sorry chain of events—in a state of "invincible ignorance" about which of the two claimants was the true pope. Nor, despite the common reflexive dismissal of the claim of the Avignonese line to legitimacy, are historians today in any better position. The *historical* evidence, certainly, does not permit one simply to insist on the exclusive legitimacy of Urban's title to the papacy (and, therefore, the legitimacy of his successors in the Roman line). If that claim is now enshrined in the current official listing of popes, it should be recognized that it has been advanced quite explicitly on theological or canonistic rather than historical grounds. For long centuries, indeed, it was not part of the standard case put forward even by papal apologists like Torquemada, who tended most frequently to argue that it was only in 1417, after the representatives of all three obediences came together, that the assembly at Constance mutated into a legitimate general council.[41] Instead, though canvassed earlier on from time to time, it was only in the early nineteenth century, with the dramatic rise to prominence of ultramontane sentiment, that claims for the exclusive legitimacy of Gregory XII and the Roman line really came to the fore.[42]

Second, that being the case, the claim that the Council of Constance became a legitimately assembled council only after the Roman claimant, Gregory XII, as part of the deal involved in his resignation in July 1415, was permitted by the council to convoke it also falls by the wayside. So, too, does the affiliated papalist claim that, in permitting Gregory XII so to convoke it, the members of the Council of Constance were themselves tacitly conceding the fact that he was the legitimate pope. Their overriding objective instead was unity, and in pursuit of that end, they were willing to be quite pragmatic. Certainly, they were even less disposed to fuss about a formality that very few of them took seriously than they had been the previous year when they had treated the ambassadors of both Gregory XII and his Avignonese rival, Benedict XIII, as official papal delegates rather than merely as private Christians. For that matter, later on, they were also not inclined to fuss, when, in an attempt to persuade Benedict XIII to resign so that they could finish the business at hand, they extended to him the same privilege of convocation as they had extended to his Roman rival.[43] And that happened despite the fact that they themselves had endorsed the sentence of Pisa deposing *both* the Roman and Avignonese claimants and had recognized John XXIII himself as sole legitimate pope.[44]

That means, of course, that there is no reason not to regard Constance as a legitimate general council right from the time of its assembly in 1414 and, *Haec sancta*, accordingly, as a binding conciliar decree. That would appear to be the conclusion Alberigo and Tanner drew in 1990 when they included it in their edition of the *Decrees of the Ecumenical Councils*. It should be noted, however, that there still remains room for disagreement about the precise nature of the decree, whether it is to be regarded as some sort of formal statement of dogma or, rather, as "a permanently binding statement of positive constitutional law," albeit one possessed of an important doctrinal penumbra, rich in "theological consequences" touching "upon the very nature of the Church."[45]

The third issue is conciliar theory itself. Here the claim that it was heterodox in its origins and rapid in its demise has not held up under closer scrutiny. As a skilled propagandist doing his best to vindicate the cause of Eugenius IV against his conciliarist opponents at Basel, Torquemada can perhaps be forgiven for attempting to attach to that theory a helpfully suspect and heterodox genealogy. But the historical facts, it turns out, lend no credence to that shrewd move. And here the truly pathbreaking work was that of Brian Tierney of Cornell University in his splendid *Foundations of the Conciliar Theory*, published more than fifty years ago and as powerful and persuasive now as it was when he wrote it.[46] The case he made so successfully was that the conciliar theory, far from being a heterodox reaction *against* canonistic teaching or an alien importation of secular constitutional notions onto ecclesial soil, had instead deep (and impeccably orthodox) roots in the ecclesiological tradition of the pre-Marsiglian era. And if it unquestionably drew a great deal of inspiration from the essentially synodal or conciliar mode of governance that had characterized the ancient church (and for long centuries after the Council of Nicaea in 325), it derived much of the structural precision crucial to its practical implementation from elements in the canon law itself and from the vast ocean of commentary on that law produced in the twelfth, thirteenth, and fourteenth centuries, notably from canonistic corporation theory and the earlier standard canonistic teaching on the case of papal heresy. Hence, conciliar theory is not to be brushed to one side as "something accidental and external, thrust upon the Church from the outside," but recognized for what it was, namely, "a logical culmination of ideas that were [deeply] embedded in the law and doctrines of the Church itself."[47]

A similarly transformative, if not quite so dramatic or widely known, historiographical shift has been engineered by other scholars pursuing research on the career of conciliar theory during the centuries subsequent to the ending of the Council of Basel in 1449. And here the general message, the politics of oblivion to the contrary, is that it did indeed have such a career, and a very significant one at that. The impact and importance of Pius II's bull *Execrabilis* turn out to have been much exaggerated. And as the great French Bishop Bossuet pointed out in the seventeenth century, it was only with considerable strain that the few oblique phrases embedded in the Fifth Lateran Council's decree, *Pastor aeternus*, could be construed as anything so formal as an explicit condemnation of the conciliar theory itself.[48]

Despite, then, the defeat of the conciliarist party at Basel, the tradition of conciliarist constitutionalism not only survived but also lived on until well into the nineteenth century.[49] In the aftermath of Basel, it remained deeply entrenched in the religious orders and in universities right across northern Europe from Paris to Kraków, was strong enough in the early sixteenth century to eventuate in the assembly of an antipapal council at Pisa, was vital enough to find prominent exponents at the papal court itself, was intimidating enough to the beleaguered popes of the Reformation era to dissuade them for decades from convoking the general council to address the Protestant challenge that contemporaries were urgently calling for, and, when such a council had finally assembled at Trent, enjoyed enough support among the council fathers to preclude the possibility of promulgating a papally sponsored decree on the nature of the church that would finally resolve in favor of the papacy the issue of the relationship of council to pope. Because of acute and mounting tensions on that very issue, indeed, the papal legates heaved something akin to a sigh of relief when the council came to an end.[50] From the early-fifteenth to the late-nineteenth centuries, the preeminent theology faculty at Paris defended that tradition of conciliarist constitutionalism as integral to the Catholic faith itself. In 1682, it became part of the Gallican orthodoxy at large when it was incorporated into the four Gallican articles issued by a national assembly of the French clergy. In the eighteenth century, it enjoyed a great flowering among churchmen in the German and Austrian territories on both sides of the Alps, especially after the 1763 publication of an enormously influential work by Johann Nikolaus von Hontheim, auxiliary bishop of Trier, who wrote under the pseudonym of Febronius.[51]

Thirty years ago, I myself assumed Febronianism, like Gallicanism before it, to be *political* in inspiration, a statist ideology used to put a good face on the extension of state control over the French, German, and Austrian churches. But having since pursued the tradition of conciliarist constitutionalism first into the sixteenth and seventeenth centuries and more recently into the eighteenth and nineteenth, I no longer believe that to be anything like the whole story. *Theological* Gallicanism may have lent itself to the advancement of royal claims, but it did not do so consistently or continuously. The same was true of Febronian ideas. At the theological heart of both, and of conciliarist constitutionalism in general, lay something else: an earnest and principled attempt to find some space within the regal church structures characteristic of the ancien régime for the pursuit of an ecclesiological middle way, one that shrugged off both statist and high-papalist domination, one that remained faithful to the more communitarian ethos of the ancient church and the corporatist formulation it had received in the Middle Ages.

The stretch of history involved is at once both lengthy and intricate,[52] and I must limit myself here to illustrating the vitality of the conciliarist tradition even in the nineteenth century and on the very eve of Vatican I. Thus in 1869, in a two-volume work, *Du concile général*, written as a preparatory memorandum for that council, Henri Maret, last dean of the Sorbonne theology faculty and titular bishop of Sura, evoked once more, and with great faithfulness and precision, the constitutionalist ecclesiological vision of the great fifteenth-century conciliarists. He discussed the Constance decree *Haec sancta* at length, viewing it as a binding "constitutional law" that was faithful to the witness of scripture, tradition, and conciliar history alike. Having as its object, he said, the regulation of the exercise of ecclesiastical power, it had been recognized by successive popes and taught over the preceding four centuries by his learned predecessors in the Parisian faculty of theology. That being so, he viewed the decree as precluding the sort of "pure, absolute and indivisible monarchy" that Cardinal Bellarmine in particular and the Roman theological school in general had attributed to the papal office. Instead, being tempered by the divinely ordained governing role of the bishops, it was, rather, a "monarchy essentially aristocratic and deliberative," what has sometimes been called a mixed government, one framed upon much the same lines, he said, as "constitutional and representative monarchy" in the world of secular governmental regimes. He said the bishops possessed by divine right a share in the church's sovereign power. That power they were to wield in general councils regularly assembled, as *Frequens* had stipulated, working to reform the abuses that centuries of overcentralization had spawned and forming a permanent part of the church's constitutional machinery. And as *Haec sancta* had specified, in certain extraordinary cases—schism, matters pertaining to the faith, reform in head and members—the bishops assembled in council, acting alone or in opposition to the pope (a true pope and not simply some pope of doubtful legitimacy), could, by a determinative and not merely declaratory judgment, stand in judgment over him, punish him, and, if need be, proceed to depose him.[53]

That was 1869, and by the time Maret wrote, views such as his had enjoyed a continuous history in the church for more than half a millennium. They were, in effect, an integral part of the church's tradition. Indeed, they had become so widespread by the start of the nineteenth century that Henry Hallam, the English historian, had written of them in 1814 as "the Whig principles of the Catholic Church" and had described the Constance decree *Haec Sancta* as one of "the great pillars of that moderate theory with respect to papal authority which . . . is embraced by almost all laymen and the major part of ecclesiastics on this [i.e., the northern] side of the Alps."[54] In light of what we now know about the continuing vitality of the conciliarist tradition and from the historical point of view certainly, there is really nothing startling about such an observation. What *is* startling, instead, is the astonishing fact that by the end of the century, what Hallam had seen as a live and commonplace ecclesiological option for the Catholics of his day had been transformed into an effectively proscribed and largely forgotten heterodoxy, a matter of interest only to the archaeologists of defunct ideologies.

In the past, historians spilled much scholarly ink in an effort to explain how the seeds of such an ecclesiology could have come to germinate in the stonily monarchical soil of the medieval Latin church. But the past, of course, isn't what it used to be. Given what we now know about the depth of its roots in the ecclesiological consciousness of Latin Christendom and the strength with which it endured across long centuries down into the modern era, the real question about conciliarism for the historian is a very different one, namely, how and why that essentially constitutionalist ecclesiology came to perish in the latter half of the nineteenth century, yielding the field to the victorious champions of an imperial papacy and, in so doing, leaving so very little trace on our modern ecclesial consciousness.

That is the real, the puzzling question for historians at least.[55] For theologians and canonists, however, the pertinent question is a very different one. Should they choose to take it up, it is a question that will call them to come to terms with an instance of radically discontinuous doctrinal change in a highly sensitive area pertaining to the reach of papal jurisdictional power and the ultimate locus of authority in the universal church.

Alone among theologians writing during the run-up to Vatican II, Hans Küng chose to take up this nettlesome question. As the Belgian church historian Dom Paul de Vooght commented at the time—and with justice—no contemporary Catholic theologian had before accepted the "incontestable historical data" now available concerning the conciliarist episode and had forthrightly admitted the validity of the Constance decree concerning the jurisdictional superiority in certain critical cases of council to pope.[56] And certainly, insisting that "the binding character of the decrees of Constance is not to be evaded," Küng concluded (in much the same way as had the philosopher Leibniz centuries earlier)[57] that "the Church might have been able to avoid many misfortunes after the Council of Constance had ... [its] ... fundamental position ... papal primacy and a definite 'conciliar control' been upheld."[58]

Having looked back and reflected on the work of the great twentieth-century Catholic theologians, Hans Küng among them, Fergus Kerr has recently suggested that no one can now doubt that "sooner or later the Roman Catholic Church will have to come to terms with what was true in the tradition of conciliarism."[59] With that sentiment I heartily concur, though with the rueful caveat that going about that task will involve, unless I am mistaken, the need to face questions far more intractable in nature than anything confronting the historians.

It is true that commentators who have been moved by, or found themselves sympathetic with, the newer, revisionist historical understanding of the conciliar episode have tended to locate the whole discussion in the context of the push for some sort of quasi democratization of ecclesiastical structures, the yearning to make church governance more genuinely participatory, or, at the least, the manifest need to give the doctrine of episcopal collegiality more viable and explicit constitutional expression. Thus, for example, Brian Tierney, affirming the validity of *Haec sancta* but tending to minimize the radicalism of its provisions, viewed it in the 1960s as no more than a clumsy and imprecise reflection of the "ancient and never forgotten doctrine of 'collegiality'" that was eventually to come to the fore at Vatican II.[60] And thus, again, Cardinal König of Vienna suggested in 1964, when Vatican II was still in progress, that it was up to the council to effect some sort of synthesis of (or comparison between) the positions hammered out by Constance and Vatican I.[61] And it would certainly be easy enough, accordingly, to argue that if the validity of *Haec sancta* were taken seriously, then it would have to be admitted that the Catholic ecclesiological tradition was richer and more pluralistic than it had been customary, heretofore, to concede; that, on the one hand, it would admit of limitations on papal authority far more extensive than those conceded in the standard modern manuals to have survived the definitions of Vatican I and the provisions of the 1917 and 1983 Codes of Canon Law; and that, on the other, the degree of papal control over the convocation, composition, agenda, activity, and modes of procedure of the general council (and, by analogy, of the synod of bishops) would be far less than those stipulated from the Fifth Lateran Council (1512–1517) onward and enshrined in the provisions of contemporary canon law.

And so on. This is not an unappealing line of march, and the arguments to be advanced in its favor are not lightly to be dismissed. Unfortunately, however, they appear to be predicated on the assumption that it is somehow both possible and legitimate to sidestep the provisions of Vatican I's *Pastor aeternus*, with its twin solemn definitions of the papal primacy of jurisdiction and papal infallibility. And it is hard to imagine that being an assumption that Catholic theologians would readily concede. Should they move, as Kerr suggests, to undertake the task of coming "to terms with what was true in the tradition of conciliarism," it appears that they will have to come to some decision about the relationship between the rival ecclesiologies of Constance and Vatican I and squarely confront what appears to be nothing other than an outright contradiction between the provisions of *Haec sancta* and the definitions embedded in *Pastor aeternus*. And that decision will have to be more satisfactory in nature than that proposed with elegant circularity by Cardinal Bellarmine in the early seventeenth century when, locked in combat with the Venetian theologian Paolo Sarpi, who had set the teaching of Constance and Basel against that of the Fifth Lateran Council, he argued that to suggest that legitimate councils could actually contradict one another smacked of nothing less than "the reasoning of heretics," for "legitimate councils do not contradict one another, and that [council] alone is legitimate which has asserted the authority of the pope to be superior to all the councils."[62]

Forty and more years ago, Helmut Riedlinger laid down the ground rules for such a confrontation in a sobering series of hermeneutical reflections on the matter that, while he himself proffered no definitive conclusion, left little doubt about the formidable nature of the interpretative challenge confronting anyone who believed *Haec sancta* to possess some sort of doctrinal validity and wished, accordingly, to harmonize it with Vatican I's *Pastor aeternus*. From a reading of his careful essay, one comes away feeling, indeed, as if one has been skillfully guided through an exercise in advanced hermeneutical handwringing.[63] Riedlinger was particularly insistent on the need to penetrate beneath the obvious sense of the conciliar definitions, to be aware of the time-conditioned nature of such formulations, to be familiar with the concrete historical circumstances of Constance and Vatican I, and to reach out to comprehend the intentions of those who, operating within the limiting context of those circumstances, formulated those definitions. Such moves, of course, are indeed called for and entirely proper. Unfortunately, thirty and more years ago, it was my own experience that, even after studying the decrees in their respective historical contexts, in the light of the conciliar debates that helped produce them, in the light of the changes they underwent in their several drafts as a result of those debates, and in view of the commentaries written about them immediately after their promulgation, I could perceive a certain narrowing in the gap or radical discontinuity between the thinking of the two councils, but I could see no way to bridge it. I concluded, as a result, that we were confronted with an instance in which two legitimate ecumenical councils of the Latin church were in contradiction on a doctrinal issue concerning the very locus of ultimate authority in the church. Moving beyond the role of historian and embarking (somewhat impetuously) on a exercise in do-it-yourself theology, I was led, then, to grasp the nettle and argue in radical fashion for the historically conditioned, reformable, and essentially provisional nature of all doctrinal formulations, ecclesiologies, and church structures—all ecclesiologies, that is, conciliarist no less than ultramontane.[64]

Others pursuing different tacks or discerning more room for interpretative maneuver than I did may end up, rightly or wrongly, in a less uncomfortable place. Indeed, among those who have grappled with these intractable issues, some have succeeded in doing precisely that. By way of conclusion, then, though I view the first of them as unsustainable on historical grounds and the second as problematic on theological grounds, let me adduce two approaches adopted by twentieth-century Catholic historians and theologians who, while still working under the long shadow cast by the Vatican I definitions, sympathized, nonetheless, with the more highly nuanced (and less polemically determined) historical understanding of the conciliar epoch that was taking (or had taken) shape in their own day. None of them was tempted to brush *Haec sancta* to one side in traditional fashion as the ephemeral product of an illegitimate general council, and all treated it, therefore, as the understandable and historically significant response of concerned churchmen to a supremely difficult crisis situation. But they did not all seek to come to terms with it in the same way.

The first approach, taken by Johannes Hollnsteiner early in the century and Hubert Jedin and Walter Brandmüller in mid-century, treated the decree not as an enactment of continuing validity for the future but as an emergency measure. They saw it, in effect, as possessed of a certain validity, but a validity limited in scope and time to the extraordinary crisis conditions then prevailing when (they said) three claimants of no more than doubtful legitimacy contended for the papal office.[65] But this approach, while failing to respond sufficiently (as Jedin later conceded)[66] to the very wording of *Haec sancta* itself, founders also on the fact that the greater part of Christendom had clearly accepted as valid the depositions of the Roman and Avignonese claimants by the Council of Pisa. The fathers assembled at Constance, even at the moment when they deposed John XXIII, held firmly to the view that he was the true pope.[67]

The second approach accepted the fact that *Haec sancta* was no mere emergency measure but a conciliar enactment of enduring validity. But it took some of the sting out of that acceptance by subordinating its provisions to the teaching of Vatican I. In effect, it understood *Haec sancta* in terms of the room left by that later teaching and by the 1917 Code of Canon Law for the existence of limitations on the exercise of papal authority. And those limitations, it need hardly be stressed, are not very impressive. Here I have particularly in mind the position that Hans Küng himself adopted in his *Structures of the Church* (1962) and continued, it seems, to affirm in *The Church* (1967).[68] Nowhere did he state the theoretical grounds for adopting such a position. But one can hardly accept as a principle of doctrinal elucidation or development the subordination of the doctrinal determinations of an earlier general council to the diametrically opposed doctrinal definition of a later one. Or one can hardly do so, at least, without envisaging with equanimity the possibility, for example, of the abrogation of Vatican I's *Pastor aeternus* by a future general council committed to an ecclesiology akin to that of Constance. And if one is willing to envisage that, how far would it be, after all, from an outright concession of the essentially provisional and time-bound nature of doctrinal formulations at large?

The past, therefore, is certainly not what it used to be. After long years of ideological repression or ecclesiological self-censorship in the wake of Vatican I, Constance and what it taught and did has been reinjected once more into the Catholic ecclesial consciousness in such a way as to suggest that traditional theories of essentially continuous doctrinal development will have to be rethought—and rethought in such a way as to render them capable of accounting for radically discontinuous change in doctrinal matters central to the church's very self-understanding. Whether that will prove to be possible remains to be seen. The understandable reluctance of their nervous predecessors notwithstanding,[69] what is not in doubt is the urgent need for contemporary Catholic theologians to accept the fact that doctrinal rupture or radically discontinuous change has in the past been an unquestionable reality in the life of the church and, that conceded, to undertake the bracing challenge of coming to terms with that intractable fact. One does not have to share Lord Acton's providentialist confidence that it is possible to detect the validating finger of God in the stupefying scramble of historical events to concur in the rectitude of his affiliated insistence that "no ecclesiastical exigency can alter a fact."[70]

NOTES

This chapter includes in revised form some material drawn from Francis Oakley, "The Conciliar Heritage and the Politics of Oblivion," in *The Church, The Councils, and Reform: The Legacy of the Fifteenth Century*, ed. Gerald Christianson, Thomas M.Izbicki, and Christopher M. Bellito (Catholic University of America Press, 2008), 82–97, and is reprinted here with permission of the original publisher.

1. Owen Chadwick, *From Bossuet to Newman*, 2nd ed. (Cambridge: Cambridge University Press, 1987), 22–23. In what immediately follows, I depend on Chadwick's careful analysis.

2. Ibid., 25.

3. Ibid., 48.

4. On which, see Frank M. Turner, *John Henry Newman: The Challenge to Evangelical Religion* (New Haven, CT: Yale University Press, 2002), 583–584.

5. John Henry Newman, *An Essay on the Development of Christian Doctrine*, revised 1878 ed. (New York: Image Books, 1960), 63.

6. Chadwick, *From Bossuet to Newman*, 1, 17, 19–20, 198–199.

7. Ibid., 171; cf. Turner, *John Henry Newman*, 580–581, 591.

8. Turner, *John Henry Newman*, 561, cites William J. Philbin (writing in 1945) to the effect that "the reserve with which the *Essay on Development* was originally received seems to have *increased* rather than diminished with the passing of a century."

9. An English text of the oath is conveniently printed in the Appendix to Fergus Kerr, *Twentieth-Century Catholic Theologians: From Neoscholasticism to Nuptial Mysticism* (Oxford: Blackwell, 2007), 223–225.

10. Bernard Lonergan, "The Transition from a Classicist World View to Historical-Mindedness," in Lonergan, *A Second Collection* (Philadelphia: Westminster, 1975), 1–10. I cite John Courtney Murray's statement from John W. O'Malley, S.J., *Tradition and Transition: Historical Perspectives on Vatican II* (Wilmington, DE: Michael Glazier, 1989), 14.

11. See the helpful discussion by Joseph A. Komonchack, "Interpreting the Council: Catholic Attitudes Towards Vatican II," in *Being Right: Conservative Catholics in America*, ed. Mary Jo Weaver and F. Scott Appleby (Bloomington: Indiana University Press, 1995), 17–36, and O'Malley, *Tradition and Transition*, esp. 44–125.

12. "Address of His Holiness Benedict XVI to the Roman Curia," Thursday, December 22, 2005, 5–8. The text is available at http://vatican.va/holy_father/benedict_xvi/speeches/2005/december/documents/hf_ben_xvi_spe_20051222_roman-curia_en.html. An excerpt is printed below in the Appendix.

13. Newman, *Essay on the Development of Christian Doctrine*, 177–189.

14. John T. Noonan Jr., *A Church That Can and Cannot Change: The Development of Catholic Moral Teaching* (Notre Dame, IN: University of Notre Dame Press, 2005).

15. In this respect, a considerable pertinence attaches to the observation of Mary Douglas, *How Institutions Think* (Syracuse, NY: Syracuse University Press, 1986), 80, to the effect that "the mirror is a poor metaphor of the public memory.... When we look closely at the construction of past time, we find the process has very little to do with the past at all and everything to do with the present. Institutions create shadowed places in which nothing can be seen and no questions asked. They make other areas show finely discriminating detail, which is closely scrutinized and ordered."

16. George Orwell, *1984* (London: Secker and Warburg, 1949).

17. *Lumen gentium*, cap. 3, §§21–23, in *Decrees of the Ecumenical Councils*, 2 vols., ed. Giuseppe Alberigo and Norman P. Tanner, 2:865–867 (London and Washington, DC: Sheed and Ward and Georgetown University Press, 1990). Cf. ibid., 899–900, the *Nota explicativa praevia*.

18. C. M. D. Crowder, *Unity, Heresy and Reform* (New York: St. Martin's Press, 1977), 24.

19. Alberigo and Tanner, *Decrees of the Ecumenical Councils*, 1:409. The central section of the decree goes as follows (italics mine):

> In the name of the holy and undivided Trinity, Father and Son and holy Spirit. Amen. This holy synod of Constance, which is a general council, for the eradication of the present schism and for bringing unity and reform to God's church in head and members, legitimately assembled in the holy Spirit to the praise of almighty God, ordains, defines, decrees, discerns and declares as follows, in order that this union and reform of God's church may be obtained the more easily, securely, fruitfully and freely.
>
> First it declares that, legitimately assembled in the holy Spirit, constituting a general council and representing the catholic church militant, it has power immediately from Christ; and that *everyone of whatever state or dignity, even papal*, is bound to obey it in those matters which pertain to the

faith, the eradication of the said schism and the general reform of the said church of God in head and members.

Next, it declares that *anyone of whatever condition, state or dignity, even papal,* who contumaciously refuses to obey the past or future mandates, statutes, ordinances or precepts of this sacred council *or of any other legitimately assembled general council,* regarding the aforesaid things or matters pertaining to them, shall be subjected to well-deserved penance, unless he repents, and shall be duly punished, even by having recourse, if necessary, to other supports of the law.

20. Francis Oakley, *The Conciliarist Tradition: Constitutionalism in the Catholic Church 1300–1870* (Oxford: Oxford University Press, 2003), 43, 97.

21. For which point, see Hans Küng, *Strukturen der Kirche* (Freiburg, Germany: Herder 1962); trans. by Salvatore Attanasio as *Structures of the Church* (New York: Thomas Nelson and Sons, 1964), 270: "The (traditionally understood) legitimacy of Martin V and all other subsequent popes up to the present day depends on the legitimacy of the Council of Constance and its procedure in the question of the popes."

22. Paul Ourliac and Henri Gilles, "La Problématique de l'époque: Les Sources," in *Histoire de droit et des institutions de l'église en Occident,* 18 vols., ed. Gabriel Le Bras (Paris: Sirey, 1965–84), 13:1, 51; cf. Ourliac in *L'Église au temps du Grand Schisme et de la crise conciliare: 1379–1449,* 2 vols., ed. E. Delaruelle, E.-R. Labande, and P. Ourliac (Paris: Bloud and Gay, 1962–1964), 1:285.

23. People like Henri Maret, dean of the Sorbonne Faculty of Theology and titular Bishop of Sura, or the irrepressible August Vérot, bishop of St. Augustine in Florida. See Oakley, *The Conciliarist Tradition,* 207–216.

24. Thus Hubert Jedin, *A History of the Council of Trent,* 2 vols., trans. Ernest Graf (London: Thomas Nelson and Sons, 1952–1961), 1:133.

25. *Dictionnaire de théologie catholique,* 15 vols. (Paris: Letourzey and Ané, 1903–1950), s.v. "Conciles"; *The Catholic Encyclopedia,* 14 vols. (New York: Robert Appleton, 1907–1914). In its article on "Gallicanism" (6:355), it drove the point home by stating that "stricken to death, as a free opinion, by the Council of the Vatican, [theological] Gallicanism could survive only as a heresy; the Old Catholics have endeavoured to keep it alive under this form. Judged by the paucity of adherents whom they have recruited daily becoming fewer—in Germany and Switzerland, it seems very evident that the historical evolution of these ideas has reached its completion."

26. E.g., Rodrigo Borgia, by adopting in 1492 the papal title of Alexander VI, would seem to have recognized Alexander V as a legitimate predecessor in the papal office.

27. *Annuario Pontificio* (Città del Vaticano: Tipografia Poliglotta Vaticana, 1947), and Angelo Mercati, "The New List of Popes," *Mediaeval Studies* 9 (1947): 71–80; see 76, n. 19, for his reference to the unspecified "theological-canonical" criteria. For telling commentary, see K. A. Fink, "Zur Beurteilung des grossen abendländischen Schismas," *Zeitschrift für Kirchengeschichte* 73 (1962): 335–343 (at 335–337).

28. J. N. D. Kelly, *Oxford Dictionary of the Popes* (Oxford: Oxford University Press, 1986); *The New Encyclopedia Britannica,* Micropedia 9:123, s.v. "Popes and Antipopes." Similarly, R. P. McBrien, ed., *Lives of the Popes* (San Francisco: Harper San Francisco,

1997), and Eamon Duffy, *Saints and Sinners* (New Haven, CT: Yale University Press, 1997), App. A, 293–299.

29. And not without effect. In his recent book, *Twentieth-Century Catholic Theologians*, p. 154, n. 19., Fergus Kerr (unconsciously?) echoes the curial position when he says that "Cardinal Baldassare Cossa . . . was long listed as an antipope and definitively brushed out when Cardinal Angelo Roncalli took the name and style of John XXIII in 1958." It was the then reigning expert on the Council of Constance, Karl August Fink, who in 1962 drew attention to this whole curious exercise in the politics of oblivion; see his "Zur Beurteilung des grossen abendländischen Schismas," 335–336.

30. For a more extended discussion of this striking phenomenon, see Francis Oakley, *Council over Pope? Towards a Provisional Ecclesiology* (New York: Herder and Herder, 1969), 121–128; Oakley, *The Conciliarist Tradition*, 253–255.

31. *Catholic Encyclopedia*, s.v. "Pisa"; *Lexikon für Theologie und Kirche*, 2nd. ed., 10 vols. (Freiburg, Germany: Herder, 1957–1965), s.v. "Papstliste"; *The New Catholic Encyclopedia*, 17 vols. (New York: McGraw-Hill, 1967–1979), s.v. "Councils, General (History of)."

32. *Lexikon für Theologie und Kirche*, 2nd ed., s.v. "Papstliste"; *New Catholic Encyclopedia*.

33. See *Catholic Encyclopedia*, s.v. "Pope," "Alexander V, Pope," and "John XXIII, antipope of the Pisan Party." Similarly, in the *Lexikon für Theologie und Kirche*, 2nd ed., while in one place it is said that no certain decision can be made on the legitimacy of the Avignonese popes and while it is indicated that a strong case can be made for the legitimacy of the Pisan popes, in another place Clement VII, Benedict XIII, and Alexander V are all described as "antipopes," and in yet another place John XXIII is described as "Konzilspapst" (s.v. "Papstliste," "Alexander V," "Benedict XIII," "Clemens VII," "Johannes XXIII"). In the *New Catholic Encyclopedia*, s.v. "Pisa, Council of," Leonard Boyle states flatly that "since the Council of Pisa was not convoked by papal authority, it is not recognized by the Church as ecumenical," and goes on to venture the comment that what it did ended by making imperative "the solution adopted at the Council of Constance in 1415, when the three contending popes *were persuaded to retire*" (italics mine). Euphemism with a vengeance!

34. *New Catholic Encyclopedia*, s.v. "John XXIII, Antipope."

35. Hans-Georg Beck et al., *From the High Middle Ages to the Eve of the Reformation*, vol. 4 of *Handbook of Church History*, 7 vols., ed. Hubert Jedin and John Dolan, trans. Anselm Biggs (Freiburg, Germany, and Montreal, Canada: Herder and Palm, 1965–1982), chapters 46, 49 and 50, pp. 401–425, 448–487. Cf. Fink, "Zür Beurteilung des grossen abendländischen Schismas."

36. *Lexikon für Theologie und Kirche*, 3rd ed., 11 vols. (Freiburg, Germany: Herder, 1993–2001).

37. Alberigo and Tanner, eds., *Decrees of the Ecumenical Councils*, 1:402–451. Cf. Norman Tanner, *The Councils of the Church: A Short History* (New York: Crossroad, 1999), which treats Constance as "a general council of the western church" and (p. 70) affirms the authenticity of *Haec sancta* and *Frequens*.

38. Thus Hans Schneider, *Das Konziliarismus als Problem der neueren Katholischen Theologie* (Berlin: de Gruyter, 1976), 227, who notes also (in 94) that Finke supervised

no fewer than forty dissertations on the era of the Great Schism and on the fifteenth-century councils.

39. See A. Frencken, "Die Erforschung der Konstanzer Konzils (1414–1418) in den letzten 100 Jahren," *Annuarium Historiae Conciliorum* 25 (1993): 1–509.

40. For a book-length analysis, see Oakley, *The Conciliarist Tradition*.

41. Thomas Izbicki, "Papalist Reaction to the Council of Constance: Juan de Torquemada to the Present," *Church History* 55, no. 1 (1986): 7–20.

42. Ibid.

43. Oakley, *The Conciliarist Tradition*, 86–87.

44. Ibid., 37–42, 84–87.

45. I draw these words from Thomas E. Morrissey, "After Six Hundred Years: The Great Schism, Conciliarism, and Constance," *Theological Studies* 40 (1979): 495–509 (at 501), and Morrissey, "The Decree 'Haec Sancta' and Cardinal Zabarella: His Role in Its Formulation and Interpretation," *Annuarium Historiae Conciliorum* 10 (1978): 145–176 (at 173); I. H. Pichler, *Die Verbindlichkeit der Konstanzer Dekrete* (Vienna: Herder, 1967), 50–51. Cf. Paul De Vooght, "Les controverses sur les pouvoirs du concile et l'autorité du pape au Concile de Constance," *Revue théologique de Louvain* 1 (1970): 45–75 (at 46): "il est indéniable que le décret est doctrinal par son objet." The trouble is that unless one is willing, with commentators like Hubert Jedin and August Franzen, to turn to the definitions of Vatican I as a timeless (and, therefore, retroactively applicable) touchstone on such matters, it turns out to be surprisingly difficult to be certain about what it would have taken in the early years of the fifteenth century to frame a conciliar pronouncement in such a way as to make it constitute a formal dogmatic definition. See the discussion in Oakley, *The Conciliarist Tradition*, 87–99.

46. On which, see Francis Oakley, "'Verius est licet difficilius': Tierney's *Foundations of the Conciliar Theory* after Forty Years," in Oakley, *Politics and Eternity: Studies in the History of Medieval and Early-Modern Political Thought* (Leiden, Netherlands: Brill, 1999), 73–95.

47. Brian Tierney, *Foundations of the Conciliar Theory: The Contribution of the Medieval Canonists from Gratian to the Great Schism* (Cambridge: Cambridge University Press, 1955), 13.

48. For *Pastor aeternus*, see Oakley, "Conciliarism at the Fifth Lateran Council?" *Church History* 41 (1972): 452–463.

49. For this compelling story of survival, I venture to refer again to Oakley, *The Conciliarist Tradition* and the literature referred to therein.

50. Though they were at pains to convey to the pope their own worried sense that peace in the church would continue to prove elusive and recurring divisions inevitable so long as the neuralgic questions concerning the nature and reach of papal power and its relation to conciliar authority were left undecided. See Hubert Jedin, *Geschichte des Konzils von Trient*, 4 vols. (Freiburg, Germany: Herder, 1948–1978), 2:57.

51. Justinus Febronius, *De Statu Ecclesiae et legitima potestate Romani Pontificis. Liber singularis, et reuniendos dissidente in religione christianos compositae* (Frankfurt, 1765).

52. For a reasonably full sense of it, see, again, Oakley, *The Conciliarist Tradition*, III–249.

53. Henri Maret, *Du concile général et de la paix religieuse*, 2 vols. (Paris: Henri Plon, 1969), 1:117–119, 129–130, 342, 417–419, 332–338, 379–468, 530–543. For recent studies of Maret's ecclesiology, see Claude Bressolette, *Le pouvoir dans la société et dans l'Église: L'ecclésiologie politique du Monseigneur Maret* (Paris: Éditions du Cerf, 1984); A. Riccardi, *Neogallicanismo e cattolicesimo borghese: Henri Maret e il Concilio Vaticano I* (Bologna, Italy: Il Mulino, 1976).

54. Henry Hallam, *View of the State of Europe in the Middle Ages*, 3 vols. (London, 1901: first published in 1818), 3:243–245.

55. In any attempt to answer it, the enormously destructive impact of the French Revolution and its ideologically polarizing aftermath on the churches of the European ancien régime in general and the French national church in particular must necessarily bulk large. See Oakley, *The Conciliarist Tradition*, 195–207.

56. Paul de Vooght, "Le conciliarisme aux conciles de Constance et de Bâle (Compléments et précisions)," *Irénikon* 36 (1963): 61–75 (at 74–75). During these years and after considerable research, de Vooght himself had come to embrace the revisionist view of the whole conciliar episode and, with it, the validity of *Haec* sancta. He was to sum up his findings in *Les Pouvoirs du concile et l'autorité du pape au concile de Constance* (Paris: Éditions du Cerf, 1965). In this work, having argued that *Haec sancta* met all the conditions necessary to make it a legitimate decree and one which "in its authentic sense" binds in faith, he concluded (p. 198) that "there is no longer today any motive for maintaining the [traditional] ostracism of a dogmatic decree which clarifies and confirms a point of doctrine always admitted in the Church and always taught in the schools." For my own interventions in the debate, see Oakley, *Council over Pope?* and "The 'New Conciliarism' and Its Implications: A Problem in History and Hermeneutics," *Journal of Ecumenical Studies* 8, no. 4 (1971): 815–839. The former (pp. 105–131), along with Paul de Vooght, "Les controverses sur les pouvoirs du concile et l'autorité du pape," *Revue théologique de Louvain* 1 (1970): 45–75, conveys a sense of the nature and range of the pertinent controversial literature that enjoyed a brief flowering in the 1960s.

57. See his "Observations on the Abbé de St. Pierre's 'Project for Perpetual Peace' (1715)," in G. W. Leibniz, *Political Writings*, 2nd ed., ed. and trans. Patrick Riley (Cambridge: Cambridge University Press, 1988), 180: "I believe that if there had been Popes with a great reputation for wisdom and virtue, who had wanted to follow the measures taken at Constance, they could have remedied the abuses, prevented the rupture [occasioned by the Protestant Reformation], and sustained or even advanced Christian society."

58. Küng, *Structures of the Church*, chapter 7, and esp. 268–319 in that edition. The words quoted appear at 284–285.

59. Kerr, *Twentieth-Century Catholic Theologians*, 207; cf. 154–158.

60. Brian Tierney, "Roots of Western Constitutionalism in the Church's Own Tradition," in *We, the People of God*, ed. J. A. Coriden (Huntington, IN: Canon Law Society of America, 1968), 123–37 (at 124–26), and Tierney, "Hermeneutics and History:

The Problem of *Haec* sancta," in *Essays in Medieval History for Presentation to Bertie Wilkinson*, ed. T. A. Sandquist and M. R. Powicke, 354–370 (Toronto, Canada: University of Toronto Press, 1969), 363–367.

61. Franz König, "Die konzilsidee von Konstanz bis Vaticanum II," in *Konzil der Einheit: 550 Jahrfeier des Konzils zu Konstanz*, 15–30 (Karlsruhe, Germany: Badenia Verlag, 1964), 28–30.

62. *Risposta de Card. Bellarmino al Trattato de i sette Theologi di Venetia sopra l'interdetto della Santità di Nostre Signore Papa Paolo Quinto* (Roma, 1606), 27–28, concluding with the words: "Et cosi non sono tra se contrarii, li Concilii legitimi, et quello solo è legittimo che affermo l'autorità del Papa essere superiore à tutti li Concilii."

63. Helmut Riedlinger, "Hermeneutische Überlegungen zu den Konstanzer Dekreten," in *Das Konzil von Konstanz: Beiträge zu seiner Geschichte und Theologie*, ed. A. Frantzen and W. Müller (Freiburg, Germany: Herder, 1964), 214–238.

64. See Oakley, *Council over Pope?* 151–185; and "The 'New Conciliarism' and Its Implications," esp. 827–840. Responses to my conclusion ranged from the sympathetic to the apoplectic. For the former, see, e.g., Felix Malmberg's review in *Bijdragen* 31, no. 1 (1970): 98–99, and his article "Naar ein Wezenlijk-provisorische Ecclesiologie," *Bijdragen* 31, no. 1 (1970): 33–52. For the latter, see Albert C. Outler's review in the *Journal of Ecumenical Studies* 7 (1970): 804–806. For my own somewhat puzzled response to this oddly disheveled review, see my "Papacy under Fire: A Rejoinder," *Journal of Ecumenical Studies* 8 (1971): 382–384. There is an accurate and balanced (if not altogether uncritical) appraisal in Schneider, *Der Konziliarismus als Problem der neueren Katholischen Theologie*, 264–273.

65. Johannes Hollnsteiner, "Das Konstanzer Konzil in der Geschichte der christlichen Kirche," *Mitteilungen des östereichischen Instituts für Geschichtsforschung* 11 (1929): 395–420; Hubert Jedin, *Bischöfliches Konzil oder Kirchenparlament: Ein Beitrag zur ekklesiologie der Konzilien von Konstanz und Basel*, 2nd ed. (Basel and Stuttgart: Helbing and Lichtenhahn, 1965); Walter Brandmüller, "Besitzt des Konstanzer Dekret *Haec sancta* dogmatische Verbindlichkeit?" *Römische Quartalschrift* 62 (1967): 1–17; Brandmüller, *Das Konzil von Konstanz 1414–1418*, 2 vols. (Paderborn, Germany: F. Schöningh, 1991–1999), 1:232–259, esp. 252–256, where Brandmüller tries, in a strained and highly unconvincing fashion, to interpret the language of *Haec sancta* in such a way as to make it say what it clearly does not say (see Oakley, *The Conciliarist Tradition*, 92–93). This instance of exegetical desperation attests powerfully to the degree of doctrinal anxiety that *Haec sancta* is capable of arousing.

66. Jedin, *Bischöfliches Konzil*, 39.

67. For all of this, see Oakley, *The Conciliarist Tradition*, 91–99.

68. Küng, *Structures of the Church*, 224–341, esp. 282–288 and 310ff. Cf. Küng, *Die Kirche* (Freiburg, Germany: Herder, 1967), trans. Ray and Rosaleen Ockenden as *The Church* (New York: Sheed and Ward, 1967). See my criticism of his stance in *Council over Pope?* 134–141, under the rubric of "deductive timidity!"

69. And on matters pertaining to the nature and dimensions of the papal prerogative, the lineage of nervous predecessors extends well back into the Middle Ages.

Thus, in the early fifteenth century, after ruminating provocatively in one of his academic writings about the source of some aspects of the papal power of coercive jurisdiction, the Parisian theologian Jean Courtecuisse (Johannes Breviscoxe) wryly noted, tongue firmly in scholastic cheek: "But *this I do not assert.* For it is perilous to speak of this matter—more perilous, perhaps, than to speak of the Trinity or the Incarnation of Jesus Christ, our Savior." See Breviscoxe, *Tractatus de fide et ecclesia, Romano Pontifice et concilio generali,* in Jean Gerson, *Opera omnia,* ed. Louis Ellies Dupin, 5 vols. (Antwerp, 1706), 1:882 (italics mine).

70. Acton's full statement is: "God's handwriting exists in history independently of the Church, and no ecclesiastical exigency can alter a fact." See Lord Acton, *The History of Freedom and Other Essays,* ed. J. N. Figgis and R. V. Laurence (London: Macmillan, 1907), 473.

2

Leo's Church and Our Own

Michael J. Lacey

For much of his priestly career, Pope Benedict XVI, who as a young cleric attended the second Vatican Council as an expert theological adviser, has wrestled with its contested legacy and sought to work out a balanced view of what it had done and left undone. He once remarked that "the Council understood itself as a great examination of conscience by the Catholic Church; it wanted ultimately to be an act of penance, of conversion." He spoke of the "almost painful willingness to take seriously the whole arsenal of complaints against the Church," which led "not only to uncertainty about the Church's own identity, which is always being questioned, but especially to a deep rift in her relationship to her own history, which seemed to be everywhere sullied." Although "it was both necessary and good," he said, even self-examination has its limits. Speaking of the polarizing confusion of its aftermath, he pointed out "it was the Council that first urged man on and then disappointed him, just as the public examination of conscience at first enlightened and then alienated him." The time had come to move on, to "reawaken our joy in the reality of an unbroken community of faith in Jesus Christ."[1]

In his own sorting out the meanings of the second Vatican Council, the pope has observed that when taken together, three of the documents it produced (*Gaudium et Spes, Dignatatis Humanae,* and *Nostra Aetate*) add up to "a kind of counter-syllabus," a reversal of the attitudes reflected in the *Syllabus of Errors* (1864) that continued up through and beyond the antimodernist condemnations of the early twentieth century under St. Pius X. These attitudes and arguments were directed against "the determining forces of the 19th century: against the scientific and political world view of liberalism," and they plainly went too far. There was a certain "one-sidedness of the position adopted by the Church" in that era, a failing the countersyllabus had now addressed. As a composite set of affirmations, it represented "an attempt at an official reconciliation with the new era inaugurated in 1789," a reevaluation, in other words, of the liberal tradition and modernity that moves beyond the one-sidedness of the past.[2] The countersyllabus, it might be said, marks what John Courtney Murray would have called "the growing end" of the church's tradition.

This chapter will recall what the one-sidedness of the church in its antil- iberal, antimodern phase was like from the papal point of view, in the hope that the contrast with today's situation will sharpen our appreciation for what was accomplished at Vatican II. It will look into what was called "the mind of the Church" in the late nineteenth century, following the centralizing changes in governance and authority wrought by the first Vatican Council (1869–1870). I will sketch the conservative communitarian intellectual tradition of the modern papacy as laid out by Gioacchino Vincenzo Pecci, Pope Leo XIII (1878–1903), whose encyclical letters offer the best official, single-source articulation of it. The heart of it was his case against liberalism and popular sovereignty, as expressed in the gradual rise of the modern, democratic nation-state. Leo was sharply focused on this master trend, which he regarded as apostasy in motion, a falling away from the ideal unity of religion and politics, throne and altar.

That ideal had been realized historically, he believed, and had been ex- pressed in the medieval doctrine of the two swords, spiritual and temporal, with the spiritual primary. After the Reformation, it lingered in the close cooperation of the civil and ecclesiastical orders in the long era of the confes- sional states—both Catholic and Protestant—that lasted into the twentieth century. Premised on the unity of religion and politics, one aspect of which in the Catholic world was a customary sharing of authority with regard to the appointment of bishops, a practice which Leo denounced as "regalism," the confessional state was eroding, however, in the wake of the French Revolution and the turmoil that followed it. It was being displaced by new ideals of religious liberty and what Leo referred to as "the fatal theory of the need of separation of Church and State." His papacy was devoted to the effort to arrest its momentum in the Catholic states and, if possible, to reverse it, rescuing what he could of the "two swords" way of life, in which various forms of public support—fiscal, administrative, and legal—together with a certain deference to the church on moral questions, were taken for granted. For this reason, he was bitterly op- posed, as his immediate predecessors had been, to the fledgling liberal Catholic movement of his time. An enthusiasm of only a small minority of intellectuals in the church, the movement had begun in France but soon spread elsewhere in the Catholic world. With its motto of a "free church in a free state," it contradicted Leo's view but foreshadowed the ideal that the church would finally embrace at Vatican II.

With its famous definitions of papal jurisdictional primacy and infallibility, the first Vatican Council marked the triumph of the slow-growing ultramontane movement within the church, and it fell to Leo to make ultramontanism actually work in terms of church program and policy. He had been a participant at the council and was an expert on its background and proceedings. A cardinal since 1853, he had joined with others in the compilation of the *Syllabus of Errors* and was aware that the council's *Dogmatic Constitution on the Catholic Faith* incorporated into itself in open-ended fashion the accumulated list of antiliberal anathemas previously propounded, thus giving a highly particularized, ideological quality to Catholic doctrine on society and politics. "Since it is not enough to avoid the contamination of heresy unless those errors are carefully shunned which approach it in greater or lesser degree," the council fathers had written, "we warn all of their duty to observe the constitutions and decrees in which such wrong opinions, though not expressly mentioned in this document, have been banned and forbidden by the holy see."[3]

"Let him be anathema" were the last published words of the council, directed at anyone who would not approve the sweeping centralization of authority expressed in the new definitions. To a far greater degree than his predecessors (or his immediate successor, St. Pius X, it should be noted), Leo understood the limits of this ancient form of holy cursing as a way of public teaching. Although his own writings bristle with resentment over the crisis situation in which his church was struggling against the growing opposition of its "educated enemies," Leo did not issue any anathemas of his own. He tried rather to state positively the reasons for the condemnations of the past and to surface their deeper logic, an effort that made him the first true teaching pope in the modern sense of the phrase. So far as his ideas were concerned, he was not, strictly speaking, an innovator. Innovation, in fact, was a term of abuse in the culture of leadership he inherited, since the identity of the church he led was conceived as uniquely time proof and beyond change. On the other hand, he has been called with reason a "public intellectual" and the author of "masterpieces of political theology" that add up to "the Leonine synthesis" of the church's tradition. His best letters are devoted to articulating basic principles and linking them together in the effort to refute, rather than simply denounce, liberal values and their premises. In this they reflect a novel attitude and tone in papal writings. He thought of them himself as a unified body of work, something more than a miscellany of occasional pieces, and commended them to readers who wished to learn what the church had to say about "the ideal of an upright life."[4]

Leo is most often remembered today for two of his encyclicals, *Aeterni Patris* (1879) and *Rerum Novarum* (1891). The latter marks the beginning of modern Catholic social thought, a now flourishing tradition of social analysis and commentary, a kind of Catholic midrash. The former marked the beginning of an unprecedented attempt to centralize and direct the course of intellectual life within the church under the heading of the neo-Thomist revival, an effort that stalled out by the 1950s and has yielded by all accounts mixed results at best. Leo's thought is much broader than these encyclicals alone suggest, however. The main themes in his writing are the principles of the "upright life," meaning those of the Christian polity; the "true and genuine idea of domestic life," meaning sacramental marriage and the need to protect it against the inroads of the emerging practice of civil marriage and divorce threatening the foundations of social order; and the relations between religious thought and political practice, meaning his case against modern philosophy and the need for neo-Thomism as a counter to it. Others include the principled indifference of the church to the mere forms of government, including democracy, so long as the common good is pursued as its aim; the importance of mass Catholic education to the future of the faith; and the urgent need for intensive clerical education and an elite, highly skilled priesthood, capable of mastering and teaching the art of arts, "the government of souls."

Another Leonine theme is the darkness of modernity, his view of modern history as a story of apostasy, both personal and institutional, a dynamic spiral of decline beginning in the sixteenth century with the assertion of Protestant rights of private judgment and the emergence of civil society, a sector independent of both church and state, tending to secularism, false notions of liberty and progress, "doing as one likes," rootless subjectivism, and the waxing powers of the Godless state. Finally, there is the theme of Jesus as institution builder, architect of the church as a "perfect society," possessing all the inherent powers necessary for self-government and capable of functioning, if need be, as a spiritual "army in battle array." God himself assigned to the church the duty "not only to interpose resistance, if at any time the State rule should run counter to religion, but further, to make a strong endeavor that the power of the Gospel may pervade the law and institutions of the nations."[5]

Perhaps at this point, a brief road map of the chapter would be helpful. In what follows, we will explore Leo's project by examining what he considered to be the ultimate challenge facing his church: the dynamic momentum of erroneous opinions about human rights and the duty to God and his church expressed in the liberalism of the nineteenth century. We will inquire briefly into the carriers of liberal ideas in his view of things, what they held, and what he proposed to do about it, emphasizing his hopes for a centralized Catholic intellectual life and a mobilized transnational counterculture under Roman direction. We will outline his own ideas on liberty, his view of the papal office and its mission to establish unity within the church, his conviction that to be workable unity required of believers the strictest conformity with his pronouncements, and his hope for the reunion of Christendom. We will point to his nightmare vision of the way things might go if his own program of mobilization and resistance failed, his fear that with the rise of the new, democratic state and the triumph of the idea of separation, the church might end up as just another voluntary association, a kind of ecclesiastical self-improvement club that people were free to join and to leave as they liked.

Finally, the last third of the chapter comments on the differences between Leo's church and the post–Vatican II church. Three points will be stressed: (1) the transformational character of the acceptance of human rights as an aspect of the image of God in which human beings are created, and the new, more challenging kind of commitment to universal values that came with it; (2) the deep importance of ecumenical and interfaith relations as both the test and the expression of the new universalism; and finally, (3) the appearance of a more open, pluralistic (though hotly contested) intellectual atmosphere within the church that stems from its troubled conscience regarding the proclamation of yesterday's heresies, Americanism and modernism, and the harm done by attempting to overcentralize and police the life of the mind of the people of God.

A World of Erroneous Opinions

It was one Leo's deepest convictions that the crisis of the church was above all an intellectual crisis: "the cause of the evils which oppose us, as well as those which menace, lies in the fact that erroneous opinions on all subjects, human and divine, have gradually percolated from philosophical schools through all ranks of society, and have come to be accepted by a large number of minds."[6] This called for changing the way people think, providing a more satisfactory model for how it should be done. One of the most important of Leo's initiatives was *Aeterni Patris*, his 1879 encyclical on the restoration of Christian philosophy. The encyclical held up the tradition of scholastic philosophy and theology, particularly the thought of St. Thomas Aquinas, greatest of the scholastics, as the foundation for the adversarial counterculture Leo intended to organize. Henceforth in the Catholic world, neo-Thomism became the chosen way to demonstrate the reasonableness of Catholic Christianity and its implications for law, morals, and politics.

The pope warned against the rationalism and materialism of his time. He expressed a strong aversion to Kantian thought and the idealism that arose out of it, by then deeply rooted not only in Germany and France but also in England and America. He cautioned Catholic thinkers to beware "this fallacious and dangerous philosophy" of "foreign importation and Protestant origin" that led to doctrinal skepticism.[7] Despite the fact that Thomas himself had had no inkling of modern science, the modern state, modern pluralism, or modern reasoning on liberty, Thomism had sterling Catholic credentials and buttressed church doctrine. Leo had been engaged in the Jesuit-led neo-Thomist revival of the nineteenth century for decades prior to his election as supreme pontiff in 1878. That movement, begun in Italy, was at the heart of all his thinking about seminary education and educational reform more generally. Well read in the texts himself, Leo could "think Thomist" and was at home with scholastic exposition. All his encyclicals on political principles and Christian duties are cast in the neo-Thomist idiom.

There were reasons, however, why the neo-Thomist movement was an attempted revival rather than a flourishing school of thought. Since the seventeenth century, scholasticism as a school of thought had slipped into decline and come to seem averse in principle to modern scientific thinking. The *Syllabus of Errors* (1864) condemned the opinion that "the method and principles by which the old scholastic doctors cultivated theology are no longer suitable to the demands of our times and to the progress of the sciences," suggesting that there were indeed critics of the tradition even within the household of faith. In any case, Leo made it clear in his encyclical that "the Angelic Doctor" had never been without influence in church thinking. He cited papal tributes to Aquinas over the centuries and claimed that ecumenical councils had held him "in singular honor." The bishops at Trent "made it part of the order of conclave to lay upon the altar, together with the sacred Scripture and the decrees of the Supreme Pontiffs, the *Summa* of Thomas Aquinas, whence to seek counsel, reason and inspiration." At the recent Vatican Council, he noted, "one might almost say that Thomas took part and presided over the deliberations and decrees of the Fathers," and, indeed, there is a strong scholastic provenance to its documents, in which Thomist natural theology, his proofs for the existence of God, figure prominently. Those who would not accede to the five proofs were anathematized.[8]

St. Thomas appealed to Leo for a number of reasons. His thinking summarized and yet transcended Christian philosophical development up to his own time. Thus, if we set aside the ups and downs of the reception of Thomism since his death in 1274, a pattern Leo felt he was correcting, it seemed to offer the prospect of an open-ended continuity in Christian spiritual and intellectual development. It had roots in the marriage of Athens and Jerusalem and thus brought with it the prestige and continuing influence of classical Greek philosophy, as well as its own Christian ethos, promising to open up a broad new front in the battle of the ancients and the moderns. Both Thomas and Aristotle, for example, vindicated metaphysics as a discipline that opened the pathway to theism, helping to "fortify the road to true faith, and to prepare the souls of its disciples for the fit reception of revelation," as Leo put it. It was not that Greek philosophy made the gospel truth more powerful, he explained, "but inasmuch as it weakens the contrary arguments of the sophists and repels the veiled attacks against the truth, it has been fitly called the hedge and fence of the vine."

There was also the hostility of many Protestant thinkers regarding natural theology in the Thomist style, a tradition culminating in Karl Barth in the twentieth century. For Leo, this aversion, too, well known in his time, was another plus. Among the leaders of heretical sects, he observed, "there were some who openly declared that, if the teaching of Thomas Aquinas were only taken away, they could easily battle with all Catholic teachers, gain the victory, and abolish the Church. A vain hope, indeed, but no vain testimony." Above all, there was the example of Thomas's success in using his philosophic method for the patient, clinical refutation of error: "single handed, he victoriously combated the errors of former times, and supplied invincible arms to put those to rout which might in after-times spring up."

Here was the prospect, in other words, of a new kind of Thomism with teeth, a body of principles that could help to inspire and direct the fighting faith that Leo sought for the Catholic revival. Thus he mandated *ressourcement* of the Thomist philosophical and theological tradition. He put neo-Thomism at the center of Catholic intellectual life because it went beyond "take it or leave it" fideism and fit so well the antimodern apologetic Leo was articulating. While the liberals were preaching naturalism and the moral autonomy of the individual, both notions alien to the medieval worldview, neo-Thomism preached something quite different—an integralism that stressed the presence of God in all things and the duty to God inherent in all aspects of human living. For the countermobilization of the church, "the teachings of Thomas on the true meaning of liberty, which at this time is running into license, on the divine origin of all authority, on laws and their force, on the paternal and just rule of princes, on obedience to higher powers, on mutual charity toward one another—on all of these and kindred subjects—have very great and invincible force to overturn those principles of the new order which are well known to be dangerous to the peaceful order of things and to public safety."

To his credit, Leo seems to have glimpsed some of the problems confronting any mandated philosophy, chiefly the corruptions that come with learning by rote and the differences in power and resourcefulness that distinguish masters from ordinary disciples. He was urging restoration of "the golden wisdom" of St. Thomas, Leo insisted, not his every thought. "The wisdom of St. Thomas, We say: for if anything is taken up with too great subtlety by the Scholastic doctors, or too carelessly stated—if there be anything that ill agrees with the discoveries of a later age, or, in a word, is improbable in whatever way—it does not enter Our mind to propose that for imitation to Our age." Nevertheless, the need for a common framework of ideas binding faith and reason was pressing, and papal action called for it. Scholastic learning had been available for those who wished to cultivate it for centuries, and yet it had not prospered. Most of the core religious orders were devoted to the study of Aquinas to some degree of mastery, but beyond this rather specialized sector of church life, there was no genuine common knowledge of his thought in the episcopacy or the ranks of ordinary working clergy.

Leo wanted to change all this. In the future, neo-Thomism was to be thoroughly institutionalized and mandatory in all educational agencies throughout the Catholic world. He held out the prospect of "a far more peaceful and secure existence if a more wholesome doctrine were taught in the universities and high schools—one in conformity with the teaching of the Church, such as is contained in the works of Thomas Aquinas." Bishops were instructed to "let carefully selected teachers endeavor to implant the doctrine of St. Thomas in the minds of students, and set forth clearly his solidity and excellence over others." Seminary education was to set aside a special place for the teachings of the Angelic Doctor. "Let the universities already founded or to be founded by you," he said to the bishops, "illustrate and defend this doctrine, and use it for the refutation of prevailing errors." Eventually, Catholicism and neo-Thomism became so closely identified that it was hard to see any daylight between them or to recall a time when there were multiple and diverse Catholic approaches to philosophy and theology.

Who were the liberals, the "educated enemies" in Leo's consciousness, the advocates for the principles of the new order that needed to be overturned? What he had in mind was a loose network of voluntary groups devoted mainly to humanitarian causes, political reform, secular philanthropy, and self-improvement that seemed to work together in the common cause of social amelioration. Frequently he referred to these associations as "sects" because of the quasi-religious aura that liberal causes and values had for their members. By far the most important and dangerous of the sects, he believed, were the Freemasons of Continental Europe, a choice that will seem odd to twenty-first-century readers. Freemasonry was "the sect of darkness" that claimed to spread the light. It was a secret society—meaning its membership, rites, and proceedings were hidden from public inspection—of freethinkers made up of political and intellectual elites, and the church had been alarmed about their membership and views since the first half of the eighteenth century. Freemasons were indeed adversaries of church doctrines and advocates for the teachings finally brought together and condemned in the *Syllabus of Errors*. Every important government minister in France's Third Republic was a Freemason. They were also prominent in the Risorgimento (Garibaldi and Mazzini were Masons, for example) and in the government of liberal Italy, which from the start of political nationhood was at loggerheads with the Vatican.

Leo spoke of the Freemasons "generically," as he put it, to make the point that they were part of a class of groups with a shared liberal outlook. "There are several organized bodies which, though different in name, in ceremonial, in form and origin, are nevertheless so bound together by a community of purpose and by the similarity of their main opinions," he wrote, "as to make in fact one thing with the sect of Freemasons." They made up a composite, negative reference group. Altogether he wrote four encyclicals on Freemasonry that focus on "the plan of the sects" and the need for the church to curb it. His own program of church mobilization—"that is what you will do, beloved children, opposing press to press, school to school, organization to organization, congress to congress, action to action"—was designed as a mirror image opposite to their promotional activities and advocacy.

While space does not permit detailed exposition of the point, these letters lay out the particular liberal ideas and arguments that Leo found most objectionable. In them, he addressed what he called the "doctrines" of the sects on politics, religion, morals, and education, which added up collectively to what he called "the code of revolution." Their arguments were all "naturalist," meaning they did not depend on supernatural warrants or sanctions but claimed to be normative and universal nonetheless. Thus in morals they advocated "independent" or "civil" or "free" perspectives on the sources of ethical obligation. On domestic life, they held that "marriage belongs to the genus of commercial contracts, which can be rightly revoked by the will of those who made them, and that civil rulers of the State have power over the matrimonial bond," meaning that what had long been an area of church monopoly was in peril. They advocated public education free of any required religious education. And on politics, of course, they insisted "that all men have the same right, and are in every respect of equal and like condition; that each one is naturally free; that no one has a right to command another; that it is an act of violence to require men to obey any authority other than that which is obtained from themselves."[9]

Leo on Liberty

There are two kinds of liberty in Leo's thought: liberty of the church and those he referred to as "the so called *modern liberties*," so called because what was valid in them was ancient and sanctioned by the church, while the remainder was tainted by the false opinions of the modern age. These were "cankered" liberties. Liberty of the church, on the other hand, was the central concern of all Leo's teaching and diplomacy. It was about the institutional freedoms of the church. Promoting and protecting it was the fundamental issue in ultramontanist policy, both diplomatic and internal. It meant freedom *from* the entanglements of the shared powers of the earlier regalist tradition and the regulation of some elements of church life by civil authority in the confessional state. It meant institutional autonomy, freedom *for* self-governance on the part of the church as a transnational community of believers. It was derived from the doctrine of the church as a perfect society, meaning "a society chartered as of right divine, perfect in its nature and in its title, to possess in itself, through the will and loving kindness of its Founder, all needful provision for its maintenance and action."[10] The stress is on the idea of divine right, with its warrants in scripture. For Leo, it stood in contrast to any merely human, voluntary association of civil society, such as the sects, for example, or the Baptists, Muslims, Methodists, vegetarians, or antivivisectionists. "The Church is a society as distinct from civil society as their reason for existence and ends are different; it follows that she is an indispensible society, for all mankind, since all are called to Christian life, and so they who refuse to enter it, or leave it are separated forever from life eternal; and it is a society eminently independent, and above all others, because of the excellence of the heavenly and immortal blessings towards which it tends."[11]

The liberty of the church, therefore, meant the liberty of the Bishop of Rome to exercise his primacy of jurisdiction and govern the universal church. It was Leo's divine right to rule. It included "the power of handing down Christian doctrine, of giving the Sacraments, of exercising divine worship, of regulating and ruling all ecclesiastical discipline, with which gifts and offices God willed that his Church should be invested and strengthened, and by an admirable providence willed too that She alone should possess. To Her alone has he given in charge all He has revealed to men and established as sole interpreter, judge and mistress, most wise and infallible, of the truth, whose precepts states as well as individuals must accept." The pope was exasperated by any attempt to hedge or trim this liberty, complaining "it is unjustly that the civil powers take offense at the freedom of the Church, since the principle of civil and religious power is one and the same, namely, God."[12]

The rising new states in the Catholic world did take offense, however, as his frequent criticisms of their policies indicate. Thus there were conflicts over civil marriage and divorce, the contents and control of state-provided education, the regulation of church property, the supervision of clerical personnel, the suppression of religious orders, and the worrisome scope of the new civil rights that were coming into being, threatening to hive off believers and loosen bonds of loyalty within the church. Civil rights, as the term suggests, were derived from the status of citizenship, an importantly different thing from the status of the laity conceived by the hierarchy as the subjects of ecclesiastical rule. Civil rights were actionable; states were expected to uphold and defend them through the rule of law. There were no actionable rights within the church, other than the hierarchy's divine right to rule, the core value around which, with the passage of time, the canon law itself had grown up.

Most of the moral prohibitions of the church, those against murder and theft, for example, were of course policed by the state. Crimes and sins are different concepts, however, and the difference seemed rightly to the Vatican to be expanding in the nineteenth century. With respect to some of its moral regulations—its censorship of publications or restrictions on free speech or its prohibition of divorce, for example—the church could no longer rely on the cooperation of the state. And so far as Leo's argument about the origin of authority is concerned, statesmen might concede with a shrug that ultimately, of course, it was from God; proximately, however, it was from the people, and the constitutional doctrine of popular sovereignty was rejected by the church as incompatible with its own divine institution, its conviction that while forms of government and social organization could vary with time and circumstance, its own form of ecclesiastical government and spiritual organization could not do so.

In Leo's historical perspective, the troubles of his times began with the rebellion of the Protestant "innovators" of the sixteenth century and their sacralizing of the idea of freedom of conscience. "Since that epoch, not only has the multitude striven after a liberty greater than is just, but it has seen fit to fashion the origin and construction of the civil society of men in accordance with its own will."[13] From this wellspring "burst forth all those later tenets of unbridled license which, in the terrible upheavals of the last century, were wildly conceived and boldly proclaimed as the foundation of that new conception of law which was not merely previously unknown, but was at variance on many points with not only the Christian, but even the natural law."[14] He was referring mainly to the French Revolution and to what eventually would come to be called in jurisprudence legal positivism and the sociological conception of sovereignty, both of which placed political will at the center of lawmaking, and did so in the service of various classes of rights.

There are two claims emphasized in Leo's critique of modern liberties: the argument that human thinking is inherently normative, meaning the sense of good and evil is inherent or built into human nature, and the argument that truth trumps rights, meaning there is no moral right to choose or do wrong. He summarized as follows: "man, by a necessity of his nature, is wholly subject to the most faithful and ever enduring power of God; and that, as a consequence, any liberty, except that which consists in submission to God and in subjection to His will, is unintelligible. To deny the existence of this authority in God, or to refuse to submit to it, means to act, not as a free man, but as one who treasonably abuses his liberty; and in such a disposition of mind the chief and deadly vice of liberalism chiefly consists." All the modern liberties justified by the "independent morality" of the sects were open to abuse and excess and thus to sin. "The form of the sin is manifold; for in more ways and degrees than one can the will depart from the obedience which is due to God or to those who share in the divine power."[15]

By "the necessity of his nature," Leo meant to invoke the idea of the natural law, the "higher law" as it was called in Protestant traditions, said to be "engraved in the mind of every man" disposing him to do good and avoid evil, the first precept of the natural law. For Leo, following St. Thomas, it was "the same thing as the *eternal* law, implanted in rational creatures, and inclining them *to their right action and end*, and can be nothing else but the eternal reason of God, the Creator and Ruler of all the world." It followed that "the eternal law of God is the sole standard and rule of human liberty." Therefore, "the true liberty of human society does not consist in every man doing what he pleases," but rather in this, "that through the injunctions of the civil law all may more easily conform to the prescriptions of the eternal law."[16] The civil law, in other words, was a polished up version of the natural law. His point was that liberty and law are not opposites, but reciprocals. In a more contemporary idiom, he was asserting that human consciousness was normative, a fact of life experienced in the pulls and counterpulls of conscience in acts of moral deliberation. In terms of policy goals, he wanted the church to be consulted and deferred to by those involved in polishing up the natural law for specific purposes. He wanted its privileged position in the spiritual and moral leadership of the past restored, secured, sustained, and, indeed, expanded.

It was axiomatic that "on the use that is made of liberty the highest good and the greatest evil alike depend," the starting point for communitarian thinking in any age. In Leo's perspective, the besetting sin of liberalism was its selfish indifference to the consequences of immoral acts. It was willing to risk general moral decline to secure individual liberties. Liberals focused too much on rights, not enough on duties, he claimed. Under the guise of toleration, they allowed "boundless license." They were willing to "exceed all limits, and end at last by making no apparent distinction between truth and error, honesty and dishonesty." Thus they pressed against the grain of objective moral truth, which constrained all choices. "Even the infinitely perfect God," Leo observed, cannot "choose evil; neither can the angels and saints, who enjoy the beatific vision." Frequently he cited St. Augustine and St. Thomas to the effect that "the possibility of sinning is not freedom, but slavery." "The death of the soul is worse than freedom of error," as Augustine was wont to say. Properly understood, therefore, a right is "a moral power" that "it is absurd to suppose that nature has accorded indifferently to truth and falsehood." In a nutshell, as Catholic moralists sometimes put it, error has no rights.[17]

The application of this line of reasoning to questions of freedom of speech, freedom of the press, and academic freedom are obvious: all are to be regulated by those in possession of the truth and charged with upholding it. Leo wanted the Catholic states to supervise and regulate these rights, employing the same standards the church would use. He summarized the position of the church by concluding that "it is quite unlawful to demand, to defend, or to grant unconditional freedom of thought, of speech, or writing, or of worship, as if these were so many rights given by nature to man." If that were true, "it would be lawful to refuse obedience to God, and there would be no restraint on human liberty." "Freedom in these things may be tolerated," he observed, "wherever there is just cause, but only with such moderation as will prevent its degenerating into license and excess." Wherever such liberties are in use, the guiding principle he offered was simply that "men should employ them in doing good, and should estimate them as the Church does."[18]

Of all the rights that the church was contesting, the one that most concerned Leo was liberty of worship, "based on the principle that every man is free to profess as he may choose any religion or none." The idea was associated with what on many occasions he called "the fatal theory of the need of separation between Church and State." The concept had been rejected by Rome from the beginning. It was condemned in *Mirari Vos* and *The Syllabus of Errors*. For Leo, it meant "the power is given to pervert or abandon with impunity the most sacred of duties, and to exchange the unchangeable good for evil." The need for unity of religion and politics, for what Gregory XVI had called "mutual concord between temporal authority and the priesthood," was the unquestioned premise of church thinking on this issue. It was held to be self-evident. Reason itself forbids "the State to be godless, to treat the various religions (as they call them) alike, and to bestow upon them promiscuously equal rights and privileges." It followed that "that religion must be professed which alone is true, and which can be recognized without difficulty, especially in Catholic States, because the marks of truth are, as it were, engraved upon it."

In states where Catholics were in the minority, separation was to be tolerated on grounds that it served not only the immediate needs of the church but also the greater good of social peace. Even in these situations, however, as Leo made clear to the American bishops in *Longinqua Oceani* (1889), the ideal of the Catholic confessional state in which the church enjoyed "favor of the laws and the patronage of the public authority" was to be upheld as a matter of principle. This particular principle was, of course, seized upon by religious outsiders and adversaries of the Vatican as gross hypocrisy. By the time of Vatican II, most of the church fathers quietly agreed.

Advocates for religious liberty sometimes referred to it as freedom of conscience. Leo distinguished the two, opposing the former but supporting the latter. The church, he argued, had always defended freedom of conscience, rightly understood. He could not quite bring himself to say that the idea of coerced faith was itself displeasing to God, but he did gesture in that direction. The church's doctrine on the nature of the soul, he pointed out—immaterial and immortal—stressed the logical necessity of free will as a precondition for moral achievement and spiritual development: "at no time, and in no place, has she held truce with *fatalism*," meaning theologies that undermined the importance of human effort, from the Manichaeans to the Jansenists and Calvinists of the Reformation and beyond. On the other hand, liberty of conscience was not to be invoked *against* the church, which would be an offense against God and those who shared in his divine authority, but rather against the state. It meant for Leo "that every man in the State may follow the will of God and, from a consciousness of duty and free from every obstacle, obey His commands." It was the liberty of the Apostles, which "the martyrs in vast numbers consecrated by their blood." It had "nothing in common with a seditious and rebellious mind."[19] It came down to the right of individual Catholics to perform their moral duties as these were determined and specified by the ecclesiastical hierarchy.

Leo on Unity

The need for unity was the basic rationale for the sovereign powers of the papacy. Correct belief and righteous behavior were signs of the action of God in society and history, and the church had been in the vanguard of bringing them to fruition in human life. That was its mission. "In truth," Leo remarked, "thought is the principle of action, and hence there cannot exist agreement of will, or similarity of action, if people all speak differently from one another." The fathers at the Vatican Council were convinced that with their definitions of papal jurisdictional primacy and infallibility, they had finally laid to rest any possible subsequent threats of schism and heresy in the religious life of the West. A favorite text of Leo's was from Paul's first letter to the Corinthians: "Now I beseech you, brethren, by the name of our Lord Jesus Christ, that you all speak the same thing, and that there be no schisms among you: but that you be perfectly in the same mind, and in the same judgment." Repeatedly, he argued that the church was not merely a voluntary organization, "an association of Christians brought together by chance," but a divinely established institution with spiritual powers enabling her "to govern the minds of men in defending the 'kingdom of God, and His justice,' a task she is wholly bent upon accomplishing."[20]

God had provided the "means" and "method" to achieve this aim by granting to the hierarchy its threefold powers of sanctifying, governing, and teaching. The foundation of all three was in Christ's promise "that he would send the Spirit of Truth to His Disciples to remain with them forever." The power of performing and administering the divine mysteries, together with the authority of ruling and governing, "was not bestowed by God on all Christians indiscriminately, but on certain chosen persons," namely, the pope and bishops in union with him. Together, they made up the magisterium or teaching power of the church. The root here is the Latin *magister*, pointing to those who had mastered the lore and learning of the tradition. Leo spoke of the magisterium as living, authoritative, and permanent. Founded by Christ, "its teachings should be received as if they were His own." It was to be trusted without question. It was incapable of fundamental error. "If it could in any way be false, an evident contradiction follows; for then God Himself would be the author of error in man." It followed that "it was no more allowable to repudiate one iota of the Apostles' teaching than to reject any point of the doctrine of Christ Himself."[21]

Leo's reading of his own authority stressed the total sovereignty of the papal office and its apparently limitless jurisdiction. It started with his divinely privileged relation to the scriptures: "For the things contained in the divine oracles have reference to God in part, and in part to man, and to whatever is necessary for the attainment of his eternal salvation." Both of these, "what we are bound to believe and what we are obliged to do," are laid down "by the Church using her divine right, and in the Church by the Supreme Pontiff. Wherefore it belongs to the Pope to judge authoritatively what things the sacred oracles contain, as well as what doctrines are in harmony, and what in disagreement, with them; and also, for the same reason, to show forth what things are to be accepted as right, and what things to be rejected as worthless; what it is necessary to do and what to avoid doing, in order to attain eternal salvation."[22]

Obedience is the first test of authority, and Leo observed that "Christian usage attaches such value to the perfection of obedience that it has been, and will ever be, accounted the distinguishing mark by which we are able to recognize Catholics."[23] Conformity with the mind of the pope was not childlike dependency or mental slavery, as liberal critics charged, but willed subordination, a mark of respect, spiritual discipline and depth. It was conceived as an element in the spiritual discipline through which humanity as a whole would be elevated from natural to supernatural life, rising above the merely temporal level of things and securing salvation. No more than his successors did Leo want to quibble over the degrees of authority carried in his own words as they were put forth in various contexts or encourage the parsing of papal documents with an eye to qualifying them.

He understood the kind of unity willed by Christ to be straightforward, absolute, and exclusive. There was to be no picking and choosing, no resort to distinctions separating core dogmas from more peripheral doctrines. "It is evident that he who clings to the doctrines of the Church as to an infallible rule yields his assent to everything the Church teaches," he wrote, "but otherwise, if with reference to what the Church teaches he holds what he likes but does not hold what he does not like, he adheres not to the teaching of the Church as an infallible rule, but to his own will."[24] Such is the very nature of the faith as Leo understood it "that nothing can be more absurd than to accept some things and reject others." True Catholics were assumed to be "all in," and that was that. As a practical matter, then, Leo can be taken to mean that the salvation of souls depends not simply on faith or works alone, to invoke the poles of Reformation controversy (he would insist that both were required in some measure), but on obedience—fidelity to the inspirations and evaluations given in the first instance through the Holy Spirit by the promise of Christ not to all the faithful, but only to those sacramentally ordained persons who together made up the magisterium and provided its voice.

He spoke of the traditional sanctions for disobedience and dissent: "eternal reward for those who believe and eternal punishment for those who do not." The church, Leo noted, "regarded as rebels and expelled from the ranks of her children all who held beliefs on any point of doctrine different from her own." He spoke of excommunication as a "divinely instituted means for the preservation of unity." Should bishops fall into disagreement with the pope, they would be "a lawless and disorderly crowd." Dissenting or apostate priests revealed "want of discipline and a certain evilness of life." Those who opposed the magisterium risked "perdition" and eternal damnation, and there was no salvation to be found elsewhere. "The Church alone offers to the human race that religion—that state of absolute perfection—which He wished, as it were, to be *incorporated* in it. And it alone supplies those means of salvation which accord with the ordinary counsels of Providence."[25]

Reunionism

For Leo, therefore, the roots of modernity were in religion, a very modern insight, but unfortunately the religion was false. It was heretically Protestant in provenance, involved false notions of conscience and subjective rights, and eventuated in the downward spiral of modern history that resulted in the moral corruptions of the secular city and a politics of pandering to the mob. So what was to be done? Toward the end of his long pontificate, Leo remarked that all his work had been devoted to two chief ends: "the restoration, both in rulers and peoples, of the principles of the Christian life in civil and domestic society" and promotion of "the reunion of those who have fallen away from the Catholic Church either by heresy or by schism, since it is most undoubtedly the will of Christ that all should be united in one flock under one Shepherd."[26] He was distressed and perhaps a bit baffled by the sheer size and vitality of those political communities that lived "outside the arc of salvation," as he called it, where Catholics were either absent or in the minority.[27] To many observers, including Catholic observers in France and Italy, it appeared that the Protestant world, led by Germany, Great Britain, and the United States, was in the forefront of advancing modern, scientific civilization and could hardly be influenced or deterred by Leo's program of revival. In the same vein, it occurred to them that the cost of continued deference to the church in matters of public policy might be to live in a condition of social and economic backwardness, a concern Leo tried to meet by arguing that once the church had been the friend of progress in the arts and sciences and might be yet again.

What did he mean by his effort to promote the reunion of those who had fallen away? Did he imagine that religious differences, centuries deep and battlefield tested, might somehow be reconciled and Christendom restored? On several occasions, he reached out to the Protestant world, and even to nonbelievers, those whom "the foul breath of irreligion" had not ruined altogether. He also reached out to the Orthodox traditions of the East. When he spoke of reunion, however, he did not have in mind acknowledging the legitimacy of those who differed from the Roman way. The European communion closest to Roman Catholicism in its ecclesiastical form and liturgy was the Anglican Church, and Leo's papal bull *Apostolicae Curae* of 1896 pronounced Anglican ordinations to the priesthood "utterly null and void," thus making it clear that there would be no compromising historically rooted differences on faith or governance elsewhere in the Protestant world. His plan, rather, was to publicly lay out the reasons the Roman way was the one true way, why there was no salvation outside it, and then to await such responses as God might inspire. He would make it clear to all why the unity commanded by Christ meant unity of faith and church governance together, that these could not be sundered, and that all outside the arc of salvation who were prepared to acknowledge as much were welcome to return to Rome. In time, he believed, those who did so would come to feel the truth of "the divine saying: 'My yoke is sweet and my burden light.'"[28]

In his apostolic exhortation of June 24, 1894, *Praeclara Gratulationis Publicae* on the reunion of Christendom, he appealed to all the sheep not in the fold, Orthodox and Protestant, "beseeching them with fatherly love to put an end to their dissentions and return again to unity," so that they, too, could feel "the gladness that filled all Catholic hearts." He expressed the wish to reach out beyond them to the ends of the earth and address "men of every race and clime," including the most "unfortunate of all nations who have never received the light of the Gospel...and live in the depths of error." Regarding the political and ecclesiastical leaders of the Protestant world, he said: "let them forget the various events of time gone by, let them raise their thoughts far above all that is human, and seeking only truth and salvation, reflect within their hearts upon the Church as it was constituted by Christ." He invited them "to compare that Church with their own communions," confident that "they will easily acknowledge" that "they have drifted away on many and important points, into the novelty of various errors," so that "there now scarcely remains to them any article of belief that is really certain and supported by authority."

This drifting away, the pope explained, "was an inevitable consequence when they granted to all the right to private interpretation. Hence, too, the acceptance of individual conscience as the sole guide and rule of conduct to the exclusion of any other; hence those conflicting opinions and numerous sects that fall away so often into the doctrines of Naturalism and Rationalism." Again, he called the attention of the world to the dangers posed by the society of Freemasons, alerting everyone to their plans "to root out from the minds of men all respect for authority, whether human or divine." Again, he pressed his case for the cooperation of church and state, civil authority and the priesthood. God "intended them to remain distinct, indeed, but by no means disconnected and at war with each other." On the contrary, he proclaimed, "both the will of God and the common weal of human society imperatively require that the civil power should be in accord with the ecclesiastical in its rule and administration."

The benefits that would come to humanity from the reunion of Christendom would be enormous, Leo insisted. "There would be a marked increase of union among the nations, a thing most desirable to ward off the horrors of war." But beyond increasing the prospects for perpetual peace, there was the probability that the church might once again resume its role of spiritual leadership in the progress of human civilization, as in the centuries before the Reformation. "For as she has been given by God as a teacher and guide to the human race, she can contribute assistance which is peculiarly adapted to direct even the most radical transformations of time to the common good, to solve the most complicated questions, and to promote uprightness and justice, which are the most solid foundations of the commonwealth." These aspirations to promote the common good, uprightness, and justice, of course, would be expressed in an ongoing, open-ended fashion in the subsequent development of Catholic social thought, a tradition of papal commentary on social and political issues begun by Leo with his *Rerum Novarum*.

And so the Catholics of the world stood ready to receive all who wished to come, including those who had been lost to heresy and schism. Leo's reunionism meant that in the House of the Lord, the lights would be left on and the doors left open. He knew how quixotic his call would seem, given that the other traditions were indeed traditions in the strong sense of the term and their adherents evidently satisfied with their lot. "It may be that there are those who consider that We are far too sanguine and look for things that are rather to be wished than to be expected," he remarked. He was not daunted by this, however. Great things had been achieved in times past "by the folly of the Cross and its preaching, to the astonishment and confusion of the wisdom of the world." Christ had promised that "There will be one Fold and one Shepherd," and if the promise was not to be taken literally, how was it to be taken? In closing, he appealed to all civil authorities: "We beg of princes and rulers of States, appealing to their statesmanship and earnest solicitude for the people, to weigh Our counsels in the balance of truth and second them with their authority and favor."[29]

Leo's Nightmare and the Second Vatican Council

Breaking away from the pervasive influence of the church in all departments of social and political life was necessary for modern secular culture to take root and spread. If that culture is worthwhile and in some meaningful sense an advance upon those out of which it grew, as *Gaudium et Spes* (1965) suggests it is, then the one-sidedness of the Leonine view of liberty and history had to be overcome. Where institutional religion is strong enough to overshadow government, subjective rights in today's sense will fall upon stony ground, as a glance at the news of global political and religious struggles will indicate. Where anything like the ideal of the confessional state prevails, then government serves mainly as an agency of the believing community and its leadership. Outsiders may be in peril. According to political scientist James Q. Wilson, today's struggle against terrorism exists because the nation-states of the Western world have learned how to reconcile religion and personal liberty, while most nations in the Islamic world, with weak governments awash in a sea of faith and clerical influence predominant, have not yet managed it. Why do so many who cherish Islamic Shariah law feel averse to subjective rights in the Western style? "People who believe that there is one set of moral rules superior to all others," Wilson observes, "laid down by God and sometimes enforced by fear of eternal punishment, will understandably expect their nation to observe and impose these rules; to do otherwise would be to repudiate deeply held convictions, offend a divine being, and corrupt society. This is the view of many Muslims; it was also the view of Pope Leo XIII—who said in 1888 that men find freedom in obedience to the authority of God."[30]

This, of course, was the gist of Leo's view of freedom and authority, and as we have seen, he would have stressed the duty to obey not only God but also those who shared in the divine power. It remains the view of the church, but in a far more nuanced and qualified fashion than Leo could have given it. The manners of the magisterium are slowly changing under the pressures of modern pluralism. While its "yoke is sweet and its burden light," the church that Leo sought to promote and defend was a compulsory institution. He believed the church would endure "though the nations fell away," but he did not believe that it could *flourish* without "the favor of the laws and the patronage of the public authority," a condition that brought to his mind martyrdom and the persecutions of the pagan era. His nightmare was that liberal secularism, to which he devoted so much attention, would eventually bring an end to political Christendom, and he was correct. The church of God, he feared, would be elbowed out of its place at the center of Western culture and treated "like any voluntary association of citizens," shorn of its ancient jurisdiction and privileges, forced to make its way in the world on the basis of its intrinsic appeal in preaching the gospel or not at all. The advocates for separation would "despoil her of the nature and rights of a perfect society, and maintain that it does not belong to her to legislate, to judge, or to punish, but only to exhort, to advise, and to rule her subjects in accordance with their own consent and will." Her "whole efficiency" was at stake.[31] If the separationists prevailed, the church might simply vanish.

For Roman Catholicism, a church that cannot compel righteous belief and behavior, but only exhort and advise and rule the faithful in accordance with their own consent and will, is a new kind of church, one that takes some getting used to. Doing so is a stressful process that is still underway.[32] The stress is evident in the "confusion" and "discord" that the Vatican says perplex today's faithful and reflect the troubled reception of the second Vatican Council. Herein lies the first major difference between Leo's church and our own. The council issued no anathemas and did not defend the anathemas of the past. There were many documents produced that Leo could have read with understanding, if not wholehearted approval. Two of them, however, would surely have brought him up short: *Dignitatis Humanae* (1965), the *Declaration on Religious Liberty,* and *Gaudium et Spes* (1965), the *Pastoral Constitution on the Church in the Modern World.* Two others would have given him great difficulty: *Unititatis Redintegratio* (1964), the *Decree on Ecumenism*; and *Nostra Aetate* (1965), the *Declaration on the Relation of the Church to Non Christian Religions.* For analytical purposes, these are equivalent to those the present pope has called the countersyllabus, which came out of the council's work, inaugurating its reconciliation with the liberal tradition and modernity.

The prelates at the council decided after prolonged and heated argument that theirs was now a free church, sociologically speaking. Just as they had declared independence from regalism and the sharing of powers over the national churches in the Catholic world at Vatican I, so they declared voluntary disestablishment at Vatican II, a move that marked the end of the confessional state as a Catholic ideal. It would have gladdened the hearts of the liberal Catholics who were chastised in the nineteenth century. Leo's steadfast opposition to "the fatal theory" of separation was abandoned, together with most of the hedging on rights. The move, which had been anticipated in the papacy of John XXIII, officially made Catholicism safe for democracy, rather than one of its most persistent and suspicious critics. In its aftermath, the papacy would take on a new role in global culture as an advocate for human rights and democracy. The conservative communitarianism of Leo's church is accordingly in the midst of transformation into some version of liberal communitarianism as the result of its new appreciation for the nature and importance of human rights.

Dignitatis Humanae (1965) held that the "right of the human person to religious freedom must be given such a recognition in the constitutional order of society as will make it a civil right." It claimed that all should "enjoy both psychological freedom and immunity from external coercion." Human rights were founded not in subjectivism or indifferentism or naturalism, as Leo believed, but in the very nature of the human person: "For this reason the right to this immunity continues to exist even in those who do not live up to their obligation of seeking the truth and adhering to it,"[33] a group that presumably includes practicing Catholics. It had become clear to the fathers in the course of the twentieth century, with its ruinous wars and catastrophic persecutions, that while error may have no rights, *persons in error* do have them, an insight that has implications for the ways the magisterium goes about its work. Internal coercion has its limits. As noted in *Gaudium et Spes* (1965), the errant person "never loses the dignity of being a person even when he is flawed by false or inadequate religious notions. God alone is the judge and searcher of hearts; for that reason He forbids us to make judgments about the internal guilt of anyone."[34] The Leonine church was not so diffident.

For Leo, the doctrine of the perfect society was conceived as a God-given franchise. The franchise was exclusive, as was the liberty of the church derived from it.[35] *Dignitatis Humanae*, however, insists that freedom of the church applies in principle to all religious communities: "A harmony exists therefore between freedom of the Church and that religious freedom which must be recognized as the right of all men and all communities and must be sanctioned by constitutional law." As a universal right rather than a matter of local custom and preference, it carries an obligation to advocacy. It means that freedom of religion of the kind now espoused by the church should be upheld in the Islamic world, in parts of which apostasy is viewed as a crime punishable by death; in secular China, where birth rates are regulated by the state, which also claims the right to approve (as did others in the days of regalism) the appointment of bishops for its small minority of Catholic citizens; and in all other parts of the globe where human rights doctrines are suspect as self-interested Western fictions and are not, in fact, sanctioned by constitutional law or practice.

Thus there is a new, more demanding type of universalism to be considered and protected in the conduct of church diplomacy, ecumenical and interfaith relations. This new universalism requires the Vatican to lift its sights and look beyond the limits of its traditional focus on the liberty of the church, which encouraged a kind of tunnel vision with unfortunate results in the concordats with Germany and Italy in the era of the Second World War, and to address itself respectfully to all humanity in its countless divisions rather than to Catholic humanity alone.

There is a sense, it should be noted, in which commitment to liberty of conscience remains suspect within the leadership of the church, though it is not likely to linger for long. There is an ambiguity in *Dignitatis Humanae* that marks its origin in compromise. The text asserts that the right "has to do with freedom from coercion in civil society," meaning that "it leaves intact the traditional Catholic teaching on the moral duty of individuals and societies towards the true religion and the one Church of Christ."[36] If taken at face value, it means that the fathers believed it was possible to have their cake and eat it, too, that psychological coercion within the church was acceptable. Leo might have written the qualifier. He cast the traditional teaching referred to almost exclusively in terms of submission and obedience, "the distinguishing mark by which we are able to recognize Catholics." His idea, too, of liberty of conscience, "rightly understood," was a right against the state, said to be exemplified in and consecrated by the blood of martyrs. Given its assurance of divine help, he reasoned, the church was a different kind of reality altogether. Here, seriously mistaken judgments, moral failures, and oversights were unlikely to occur and could not displace its supernatural character and aspirations in any case. There were no rights of conscience against the church. Nevertheless, to gloss the new doctrinal language on liberty of conscience and freedom from psychological coercion as intended to apply to every person and institution on earth save one, however, would simply highlight the issues at stake. Had the fathers really intended that meaning, they might have struggled a bit harder to spell it out. This ambiguity aside, therefore, *Dignitatis* stands as milestone in the development of Catholic doctrine.

A second important difference from the Leonine church is evident in the council's opening to ecumenical and interfaith relations and with it the continued softening of the traditional belief that there is no salvation outside the church. If that doctrine suggested service to a jealous God, trimming it suggests an appropriate emerging sense of theological and historical humility. For Leo, it was fundamental that "those who refuse to enter the perfect society or leave it are separated forever from life eternal."[37] In the *Decree on Ecumenism* (1964), on the other hand, heretics and schismatics have become "separated brethren." They "have a right to be called Christians and with good reason" to be "accepted as brothers by the children of the Catholic Church."[38] While all the elements necessary for salvation are said to "subsist" in their "fullness" in the Catholic Church, "which in the Creed we profess to be one, holy, catholic and apostolic," it is nevertheless true, according to *Lumen Gentium*, that "many elements of sanctification and of truth are found outside its visible confines."[39] In other words, there is no sacred monopoly on holiness and truth, a teaching that Leo would have regarded as undermining the basic mission of the church. As Karl Rahner made the point, there has been a growing recognition that "many whom God has, the Church does not have; and many whom the Church has, God does not have."[40]

The transforming response to the new universalism is evident here as well. The late Avery Cardinal Dulles concluded a recent review of the development of church teaching on the question of who can be saved with these observations: "Catholics can be saved if they believe the Word of God as taught by the Church and if they obey the commandments. Other Christians can be saved if they submit their lives to Christ and join the community where they think he wills to be found. Jews can be saved if they look forward in hope to the Messiah and try to ascertain whether God's promise has been fulfilled. Adherents of other religions can be saved if, with the help of grace, they sincerely seek God and strive to do his will. Even atheists can be saved if they worship God under some other name and place their lives at the service of truth and justice. God's saving grace, channeled through Christ the one Mediator, leaves no one unassisted."[41] Theologically speaking, while Dulles holds that all grace is mediated through the one, triune God, he does not insist, as Leo felt he had to do, that it is mediated exclusively through the one true church. The postconciliar church reads history and culture differently from the way the Leonine church read them.

Yesterday's Heresies and a Troubled Conscience

A third difference between Leo's church and our own has to do with the changing atmosphere of intellectual life within it. Whether the change comes from exhaustion in opposing it or from some deeper well of principle, there is a new openness in the intellectual life of Catholicism that makes it a qualitatively different institution. Two heresies have been condemned by Rome since the first Vatican Council: "Americanism" by Leo in *Testem Benevolentiae Nostrae* (1899), his encyclical letter to James Cardinal Gibbons, and "modernism," described as the "synthesis of all heresies" by his successor, Saint Pius X, in *Pascendi Dominici Gregis* (1907). Both were aimed at deviant thinking, liberalism, and modernism, to use the unsatisfactory bucket terms, and both failed to adequately focus in depth on the issues involved and went too far.

It may come as a surprise to twenty-first-century readers, accustomed to Rome's current embrace of human rights and the principle of separation of church and state, that there ever was such a thing as an Americanist heresy. As Leo used the term, Americanism was a set of opinions that differed from the antiliberal tenor of his encyclicals *Immortale Dei* and *Libertas*. Among other things, he had in mind some of the opinions of Isaac Hecker. As reflected in the thought of Hecker, an American convert to Catholicism and founder of the Paulist Fathers as a missionary society in New York in 1858, the open, pluralist, American way of life necessarily inspired the search for a stronger, more vivid personal element in Catholic spirituality, a preference for the active over the passive virtues, an ethics of self-realization as opposed to one of suffering and self-denial, and an impulse to reach out and foster improved ecumenical relations, leaving separatism and its standoffish psychology behind.

The core of Americanism, however, was its confidence in individual liberty and rights, which Hecker and his disciples understood to be theologically validated by the notion of the indwelling of the spirit, the unmediated openness to the presence of the Holy Spirit in all human beings. In Leo's portrait of them, Americanists maintained that since the church had in fact flourished in the United States under a regime of separation of church and state and a widespread commitment to individual liberties, it might in the future flourish everywhere else by adopting the American way and providing a greater measure of individual liberty within the church. In their positive view of religious liberty, Leo noted, Catholic enthusiasts for the American way "hold such liberty should be allowed in the Church, that her supervision and watchfulness being in some sense lessened, allowance be granted the faithful, each one to follow out more freely the leading of his own mind and the trend of his own proper activity." This desire and tendency, Leo believed, was a misapprehension of the divinely instituted relationship between the magisterium and the individual believer, and a challenge to Leo's understanding of what Christian unity was and required. It was accordingly condemned.[42]

While the inclination to liberal and modernist ideas was strongly condemned, the condemnations did not hold up well as they made their way through time. They troubled the conscience of the church, as eventually the second Vatican Council would show. In both cases, Americanism and modernism, the remedy for deviant thought had been neo-Thomism, and its fate is another indicator of the difference between Leo's church and our own. Leo was convinced that centralizing Catholic intellectual life under the rubric of neo-Thomism was both possible and desirable. His ideal church was also a philosophical school, one with antiliberal, antimodern leanings. He hoped a new Thomism would provide depth, unity, and discipline for a common intellectual culture within the hierarchy and the priesthood, and among the educated laity as well. He thought it might be a bridge connecting them, enabling them to address effectively the non-Catholic world also, refuting their errors. By the time of Vatican II, however, it was widely conceded by Catholic observers that neo-Thomism was a lost cause, a failed experiment.[43]

Here the Leonine legacy is mixed and ambiguous. The movement stimulated extraordinary energy and effort throughout the Catholic world, so much so that there is nothing quite like it in history, unless one looks, perhaps, to the rapid global diffusion of Marxist thought over roughly the same period. Leo's movement contributed powerfully to keeping alive the heritage not only of Christian philosophy but also of classical metaphysics and ethics. Impressive neo-Thomist writing was and continues to be produced. For all this, however, no one would argue that it adds up to a vital movement in modern thought.

Without its ecclesiastical provenance, it would barely exist at all, as in the period before *Aeterni Patris*. A common opinion among Catholic scholars holds that there is truth in Thomas, but no monopoly of truth, and the ecclesiastical push to establish a monopoly did significant harm by crowding out other sources of light and inspiration that might have contributed to the life of the church.

In *Fides et Ratio*, which is rumored to have been drafted in part by Cardinal Ratzinger, the current pope, John Paul II expresses his admiration for *Aeterni Patris* and the revival of learning it inaugurated. He makes it clear, however, that there are many philosophies compatible with the church's commitment to the convergence of faith and reason, the aspect of Thomism that has always been at the heart of its appeal. "The Church," he notes, "has no philosophy of her own, nor does she canonize any one particular philosophy in preference to others," a remark that would have taken Leo aback. The hierarchy has a duty to criticize ideas that undermine the faith, John Paul II insists, but "it is neither the task or the competence of the magisterium to intervene in order to make good the lacunas of deficient philosophical discourse."[44] In the council's *Optatam Totius* (1965), the decree on the training of priests, Thomism retains a place above the salt. "With Saint Thomas as teacher," the fathers remark, students are encouraged to learn "all aspects of the mysteries of salvation, and to perceive their interconnection." On the other hand, where Leo saw Thomism as the antidote to modern philosophies and warned against the possibly contaminating study of other traditions, today's priests are encouraged to "take account of modern philosophical studies, especially those which have greater influence in their own country" so as to be prepared "to enter into dialogue with their contemporaries."[45] Had these modest qualifications been inserted into *Aeterni Patris*, the story of Catholic intellectual life over the past century might have been much richer and more dynamic than has been the case. Surely there would have been less to apologize for.

Whatever the accomplishments of the neo-Thomist movement, its legacy also includes a shameful episode in the record of the one-sided church: the unleashing upon Catholic thinkers, primarily clergy but laypersons as well, of that neo-Thomism with teeth that was implicit in the movement from the start. Leo's successor, Pope St. Pius X, did the unleashing. His *Pascendi Dominici Gregis* (1907), issued four years after Leo's death, was intended as a companion piece for *Aeterni Patris* (1878). St. Pius made it clear just how far the Vatican was prepared to go in the coercion of belief and the policing of opinion. He condemned modernism as "the synthesis of all heresies" and installed in every diocese throughout the Catholic world, and in every religious order as well, an organized program of heresy hunting that lasted for decades, stifling the intellectual life of the church. The encyclical was targeted on the enemy within, which included "many who belong to the Catholic laity" and many "from the ranks of the priesthood itself" who lacked "the firm protection of philosophy and theology." They were considered a threat because they claimed to be within the fold as loyal Catholics: "they lead a life of the greatest activity, of assiduous and ardent application to every branch of learning." They possess "as a rule, a reputation for the strictest morality." And yet "they disdain all authority and brook no restraint; and relying upon a false conscience, they attempt to ascribe to a love of truth that which in reality is the result of pride and obstinacy."[46]

In the sainted pope's depiction of him as a general type, the modernist played many roles: "he is a philosopher, a believer, a theologian, an historian, a critic, an apologist, a reformer." Each of these self-understandings was tinged with presumption, he believed, and the very questions that troubled the modernists were regarded as being trumped up and blameworthy. Their intellectual concerns with natural theology, the evolution of doctrines, the nature of religious sentiment and inspiration, the character of religious experience, and the meaning of ideas of vital immanence—all were taken up in the encyclical and found wanting because they skirted the commonsense apprehension of the teachings of the magisterium and thereby threatened to undermine its effectiveness.

As St. Pius X saw matters, the intellectual framework for Catholic thinkers had been authoritatively settled by Leo, and there was no point in criticizing it or attempting to devise new ones. The basic offense of the modernists, he claimed, was that they had neglected or "twisted" the words of Leo's directives regarding study of the Angelic Doctor so as to permit their own programs of research and writing. He spoke in this vein of the moral and intellectual causes of modernism. The primary moral cause was "a perversion of the mind." The more remote moral causes "seem to us to be reduced to two: curiosity and pride." The chief intellectual cause was "contempt for scholasticism." Certain it is, St. Pius argued, "that the passion for novelty is always united in them with hatred of scholasticism, and there is no surer sign that a man is on the way to Modernism than when he begins to show his dislike for this system."[47] The remedies the pope demanded began with a reassertion of Leo's directive: "We will and ordain that scholastic philosophy be made the basis of the sacred sciences." He declared that "all the ordinances of Our Predecessor on this subject continue fully in force, and as far as may be necessary, We do decree anew, and confirm, and ordain that they be by all strictly observed."[48]

Personnel policy in all seminaries, universities, and religious institutes was now geared to rooting out the disease. "Anybody who in any way is found to be imbued with Modernism is to be excluded without compunction" from any church office, "and those who already hold them are to be withdrawn." "You cannot be too watchful or too constant," Pius told the bishops, and warned them to be on the watch for anyone "criticizing scholasticism, the Holy Father," or "ecclesiastical authority in any of its depositories." They were to be alert "to those who show a love of novelty in history, archeology, biblical exegesis, and finally those who neglect the sacred sciences or appear to prefer to them the profane." There was a call for tighter censorship and renewed episcopal vigilance over publications: "it is not enough to hinder the reading and sale of bad books—it is also necessary to prevent them from being printed."

The pope recommended that "a special Censor for newspapers and periodicals written by Catholics" be appointed, and that congresses of priests not be permitted "except on rare occasions," lest they encourage the emergence of a possibly adversarial form of group consciousness. St. Pius X decreed that "in every diocese a 'Council of Vigilance' be instituted without delay," to monitor the local situation, and that at three-year intervals every bishop "furnish the Holy See with a diligent and sworn report on all the prescriptions" contained in *Pascendi*.[49] In a *motu proprio* on September 1, 1910, he issued the *Oath against Modernism*, which all Catholic clergy, preachers, confessors, and seminary professors were required to sign until it was abrogated in 1967, eventually to be replaced by the *Oath of Fidelity*, which laypeople in the employ of the church, in addition to clergy, are required to take at present.

If silence can be taken for assent, the antimodernist campaign was at first a great success. There was little public protest, and only a few priests left the church on principle. As various studies have shown, the highfliers who were excommunicated or came under suspicion at the time, Alfred Loisy, Maurice Blondel, George Tyrell, or Friedrich von Hügel, for example, were doing valuable work and deserved far better from their church and the saint directing it on God's behalf. They are still read with profit, while it takes a special gift to get through the privileged neo-Thomist writings of the day. After *Pascendi*, a repressive culture of clerical surveillance and backbiting set in, and many of the best minds in the church soon ran afoul of it. As late as the 1950s, some were silenced by authority for a time—Henri DeLubac, John Courtney Murray, Marie-Dominique Chenu, or Yves Congar, to mention a few who would be influential later on at Vatican II—and those who escaped discipline were nevertheless troubled and inhibited in their work by the peculiar risks involved in fighting under the lash. For Catholic thinkers, the cost of salvation, it seemed, might be the forfeit of intellectual integrity.[50]

The reputation of Catholic scholarship suffered. In the United States in the 1950s, the so-called "Catholic intellectualism" debate got underway, a many-faceted concern with why Catholic scholarly and intellectual life seemed so anemic and secondhand in comparison with the broader American scene, that foreshadowed the secular professional "upgrading" of Catholic university faculties that was to come. Most of the fathers at the council had their professional formation in this system of episcopal vigilance and reporting that St. Pius X put in place. Many in the majority supportive of the council's innovations had grown weary of it, perhaps even embarrassed. They had seen enough to have criticisms of the "Roman" or "curial" or "manualist" tradition, as it was variously called, while the conservative minority who opposed them were strongly supportive of its antiliberal, antimodern elements and the machinery to enforce them. So far as the basic pattern of Catholic intellectual history is concerned, there can be no doubt, as Bishop (now Cardinal) Walter Kasper put it in 1987, "that the outstanding event in the Catholic theology of our century is the surmounting of neo-scholasticism."[51]

In the longer run, therefore, the antimodernist campaign was a failure, as was the antiliberal campaign before it. What they had in common was the neo-Thomist remedy, which has fallen by the wayside, and a view of the magisterium as rightly engaged in the ambitious regulation of intellectual life, which is now apparently being reconsidered in view of its evident limits. While the policing of theological writing continues, especially the writings of ordained theologians on Catholic faculties who can be easily reached by the magisterial authorities, the situation has changed. Only the most extreme right-wing traditionalists call for a restoration of the culture of heresy hunting and repression, a policy virtually guaranteed to fail.[52] Any such effort would be strongly opposed by conservatives, liberals, radicals, feminists, and other contending groups within the church, thus providing, ironically, a measure of unity that has so far eluded the powers of the papacy to bring about. In their opposition, this otherwise unlikely united front would appeal to Vatican II—and specifically to the spirit and affirmations of the countersyllabus, as it was called by Cardinal Ratzinger.

Unity Again

A final comment on the difference between Leo's church and our own seems called for in light of the foregoing. Pope Leo spoke of unity, not solidarity, its more nuanced offspring, as we do today. He rightly cherished unity, which he understood to be essential for religious life and at the heart of the meaning of the liturgy of the Eucharist around which the church has evolved over the millennia. He and his advisers gave little thought, however, to the nature of unity itself and its limits. On reflection, unity is a fragile and even mysterious aspect of community life in its higher reaches and, for that reason, a central problem in philosophy and theology. Leo can hardly be said to have taken the full measure of the issues at stake. The temptation to coerce conformity in the interest of the common good is a natural impulse familiar to all parents. It is familiar also to the leadership of all formal organizations, divinely instituted or not, not to mention political parties and associations of lesser grandeur. Perhaps we should observe as well that conformity itself is not a phenomenon to be derided, provided it is rightly understood. We do believe in the communion of saints, for example, and when we have it, we can enjoy the state of being agreed,—assuming, of course, that the bonds of community are righteous.

Just what makes the bonds righteous, however, is the nub of the problem. The beginning, at least, of the solution is bound up with the need for free acts of assent and immunity from psychological coercion, criteria that do not promise efficiency, but rather mark the contemporary challenge of making a liberal communitarian religious worldview actually work in human affairs. From the experience of families to the experience of nations, it is evident that the spirit of unity is a variable quality, not a constant, a question of how much and of what kind, rather than either/or, whether or not. For Leo, it was either/or. There was nothing between unity and heresy or schism, and it was "all or nothing" as well.

Charles Taylor has pointed out that the ancient Greek word *katholou* connotes wholeness and inclusion, rather than uniformity. His essay on Catholicism and modernity explores the tensions between this unity-across-difference, on the one hand, and unity-in-identity, on the other. Since Vatican II, the church has been engaged in the search for unity-across-difference, a demanding modern, religious quest, far more difficult for both leaders and led than the countercultural Leonine mobilization was. Though there have been episodes of internal conflict and occasions for disappointment along the way, with charges of restorationism on the one hand and capitulation and infidelity to this or that doctrine or practice on the other, the postconciliar popes have been devoted to the search and shown no serious inclination to call it off. Created human nature being what it is, conflicts and disappointments are likely to continue, but this is what we might expect from a free church in what we hope will become through peaceful engagement a global community of free states. "Human diversity," Taylor notes, "is part of the way in which we are made in the image of God," and perhaps the Trinitarian apprehension of God has something to teach about the nature of community itself. After all, Catholic Christians do not pray each week to live in the uniformity of the Holy Spirit, but in its unity.[53]

NOTES

1. Joseph Cardinal Ratzinger, *Principles of Catholic Theology: Building Stones for a Fundamental Theology* (San Francisco, Ignatius, 1987), 371–374, passim.

2. Ibid. pp.381–82.

3. Norman P. Tanner, ed., *Decrees of the Ecumenical Councils*, Vol. 2, *Trent to Vatican II* (London: Sheed and Ward, 1990), 811.

4. For a single-volume edition of eighty-five of his letters, see Claudia Carlin, ed., *The Papal Encyclicals, 1878–1903* (Wilmington, NC, McGrath, 1981). The Carlin collection does not include two important Leonine letters, either through oversight or the application of some specialized criteria as to what properly constitutes the genre of encyclical letters. They are *Preclara Gratulationis Pubicae* (1894), his apostolic exhortation on the reunion of Christendom, and *Testem Benevolentiae* (1897), his condemnation of Americanism. Both are available online. Unless otherwise noted, all quotations attributed to Leo are from the Carlin volume, indicated simply by the name of the encyclical and the page on which the quotation is to be found. His remark about his letters as instruction on the upright life is from *Longinqua Oceani* (1895) on Catholicism in the United States. The phrase "Leonine synthesis" is taken from Russell Hittinger, as is the notion of Leo as a public intellectual and the author of masterpieces of political theology. See his "Introduction to Modern Catholicism," in *The Teachings of Modern Christianity on Law, Politics, and Human Nature*, Vol. 1, ed. John Witte Jr. and Frank S. Alexander, 3–38 (New York: Columbia University Press, 2006), and in the same volume, his chapter "Pope Leo XIII," 39–74. The reader should note that my focus here is narrowly on what Leo said, his articulations, and only on selected points. For reasons of space, there is no attempt to put his words in detailed context, which full justice would require. Suffice it to say that he had reasons for his worries. He lived in the midst of one of the most stressful crisis periods in the history of the modern church, a fact symbolized perhaps by the church's loss of its "temporalities," the Papal States, some 16,000 square miles of the Italian peninsula, to the new unified government of liberal Italy. Leo had been born in the Papal States and educated to be one of its clerical administrators. He was the first pope since the Middle Ages to try to function without "the temporalities," as they were called. For him, the root meaning of secularization—the alienation of church property—was a matter of lived experience, and it was not clear to him whether the church could long survive without the independence it provided. For a start on Leo in the deeper context of his time, see Owen Chadwick, *A History of the Popes: 1830–1914* (Oxford: Clarendon, 1998); Hubert Jedin, ed., *History of the Church*, abridged ed., *The Church in the Industrial Age* (New York: Crossroad, 1993); Eamon Duffy, "Ultramontanism with a Human Face," in *Saints and Sinners: A History of the Popes*, 235–244 (New Haven, CT: Yale University Press, 1997); and Hittenger, "Pope Leo XIII."

5. *Sapientiae Christianae*, 218.

6. *Depuis le jour*, 458. This is also a leading theme in *Aeterni Patris*.

7. Ibid.

8. *Aeterni Patris*. All of Leo's remarks in connection with the restoration of Thomism are taken from 17–26, passim.

9. Quotations are from *Humanum Genus* (1884). The other letters on Freemasonry are *Dell'alto Dell'Apostolico Seggio* (1890), *Inimica Vis* (1892), and *Custodi Di Quella Fede* (1892).

10. *Immortale Dei*, 109.

11. *Officio sanctissimo*, 154.

12. Ibid.

13. *Diuturnum*, 52.

14. *Immortale Dei*, 112.

15. *Libertas*, 179.

16. Ibid., 171.

17. Ibid., 176.

18. Ibid., 180.

19. Ibid., 178.

20. *Sapientiae Christianae*, 216–217, passim. In *Dogmatic Constitution on the Church* (Tanner, *Decrees of the Ecumenical Councils*, 2:816), the council fathers state that the gifts of truth and never-failing faith were divinely conferred "on Peter and his successors in this see so that they might discharge their exalted office for the salvation of all, and so that the whole flock of Christ might be kept away by them from the poisonous food of error and be nourished with the sustenance of heavenly doctrine. Thus the tendency to schism is removed and the whole church is preserved in unity, and, resting on this foundation, can stand against the gates of hell."

21. *Satis Cognitum*, 394–95, passim.

22. *Sapientiae Christianae*, 217.

23. *Immortale Dei*, 111.

24. *Sapientiae Christianae*, 216.

25. *Satis Cognitum*, 392–401, passim.

26. *Divinum illud munus*, 410.

27. *Quod Anniversarius*, 157.

28. *Satis Cognitum*, 387.

29. This encyclical, *Praeclara Gratulationis Publicae*, is available online at www.papalencyclicals.net/Leo13/l13praec.htm. All quoted matter is taken from 1–6.

30. James Q. Wilson, "The Reform Islam Needs," *City Journal*, Autumn 2002.

31. *Libertas*, 179–180.

32. Consider John Paul II's attraction to Leo, for example. Like Leo before him, John Paul II chafed at the idea that magisterial statements might be taken by faithful readers as something less than the deliverances of scripture. In *Veritatis Splendor* (1994), the first of his encyclicals on moral theology, he observes (4.2) with evident disapproval that today "certain of the Church's moral teachings are found simply unacceptable; and the Magisterium itself is considered capable of intervening in matters of morality only in order to 'exhort consciences' and to 'propose values,' in the light of which each individual will independently make his or her decisions and life choices." Leo's writings on true liberty as conformity with the law of God and the teachings of his church, together with his criticisms of what he called "the spirit of misunderstood liberty," were a source of influence on John Paul II's writings about false notions of moral autonomy that issue in "the culture of death." Like Leo, he thinks of martyrs as exemplifying liberty of conscience, and both stress the idea that truth is trumps when it comes to the exercise of individual rights. While Wojtyla avoids the argument that error has no rights,

he comes very close to it in *Veritatis Splendor* in his treatment of the workings of exceptionless moral norms that brook neither argument nor analysis. Though they differed on ecumenical and interfaith questions, John Paul II also reflected much of Leo's negative view of modern history and his vision of the church as an adversarial counterculture under the direction of Rome. So insistent was John Paul II on the need to prohibit through law abortion and euthanasia that he came very close to Leo's view that a Catholic confessional state in which church teachings enjoyed the favor of the laws might not be such a bad idea after all.

33. Austin Flannery, ed., *Vatican Council II: The Conciliar and Post Conciliar Documents* (Northport, NY: Costello, 1975), 800–801.

34. Ibid., *Gaudium et Spes*, 929. The phrase "voluntary disestablishment" is taken from Jose Casanova's "Global Catholicism and the Politics of Civil Society," *Sociological Inquiry* 66, no. 3 (1996): 356–373, which discusses the transformation of the politics of Catholicism worldwide in the wake of Vatican II. Casanova emphasizes the importance of the point that the national churches no longer aspire to be compulsory institutions and that the papacy has assumed the vacant role of spokesman for humanity, champion of the sacred dignity of all human persons, for world peace, and a better division of labor and power in the world political system.

35. For a critique of the foundation myth of the church in terms of what he calls its "franchise theology," see Catholic theologian James P. Mackey's systematic theology, *Christianity and Creation: The Essence of the Christian Faith and Its Future among Religions* (New York: Continuum, 2006), from which I have benefited. As shorthand for the foundation myth, Mackey coins the phrase "franchise theology" to refer to the "superstructure model of grace above and beyond nature, and of revelation above and beyond history," together with the claim of the hierarchy that Jesus "entrusted to them the privilege and responsibility to make grace and truth known to all nations and all ages, down to the last limit of place and time" (20). The ecumenical and interfaith implication of franchise theology that Mackey draws from the relevant Vatican II documents is that other religions and Christian churches are officially understood to be instances of the *"preparatio evangelica,"* which means they "really ought to disappear as such by merging into the one true Church" that enjoys the fullness of grace and truth.

36. *Dignitatis Humanae*, 800. Though the final vote on it was 2,308 to 70, the final text of *Dignitatis Humanae* was the result of heated controversy and prolonged struggle. According to John O'Malley, *What Happened at Vatican II* (Cambridge, MA: Belknap Press of Harvard University Press, 2008), 216, the main issues were the heritage of antiliberalism and the continuing strength of the position that error had no rights. Cardinal Fernando Quiroga y Palacios argued that the text simply ignored traditional teaching: it moved the church into "novelty" from which "unbridled license would follow." The concept of liberty it proposed "is not only extolled with great praise but seems to be proposed as a solemn definition. Thus you could say that Liberalism, so often condemned by the Church, is now solemnly approved by Vatican Council II." Cardinal Ottaviani, a leader of the opposition, head of the Holy Office and a member of the Preparatory Commission, was the author of a widely disseminated textbook on

canon law that asserted that freedom of conscience was an expression introduced to legitimate religious indifferentism, as had Leo, Pius IX, and Gregory XIV. In a speech at the council in opposition to the proposed text of *Dignatatis*, he said, "I do not understand why a person who errs is worthy of honor. I understand that the person is worthy of consideration, of tolerance, of cordiality, of charity. But I do not understand why worthy of honor." In his chapter on *Dignitatis Humanae* in *Vatican II: Renewal within Tradition*, ed. Matthew L. Lamb and Matthew Levering (New York: Oxford University Press, 2008), Russell Hittinger offers a minimalist reading of the text, arguing that it "adopted a carefully calculated silence on the establishment of religion, at least insofar as it was understood according to the older model" (364). The main issue, he suggests, is still the liberty of the church (as distinct from the liberty of the individual), and the best that can be said for the text is that "the Church's claim for its own liberty must be complemented with a claim for the liberty of others" (375).

37. Carlin, *Officio Sanctissimo*, 154. For historical analysis of the doctrine, see Francis A. Sullivan, *Salvation outside the Church?* (Mahwah, NJ: Paulist, 1992).

38. Flannery, *Decree on Ecumenism*, 455.

39. Ibid. *Lumen Gentium*, p. 357

40. Quoted in Richard P. McBrien, *The Church: The Evolution of Catholicism* (New York: Harper Collins, 2008), 51. McBrien provides a well-documented synthetic overview of the development of Catholic ecclesiology, with emphasis on the period since the mid-nineteenth century.

41. Avery Cardinal Dulles, "Who Can Be Saved?" *First Things*, February 2008, 22.

42. For the context of the condemnation of Americanism, see Gerald P. Fogarty, *The Vatican and the Americanist Crisis: Denis J. O'Connell, American Agent in Rome, 1885–1903* (Rome: Gregorian University Press, 1974) and *The Vatican and the American Hierarchy from 1870 to 1965* (Wilmington, DE: Michael Glazier, 1985), especially chapter 5, "Americanism Condemned: The End of Intellectual Life." For insight into the life and thought of the person who unwittingly sparked it, see David J. O'Brien, *Isaac Hecker: An American Catholic* (Mahwah, NJ: Paulist, 1992). For the argument that the Americanism condemned by Leo becomes the framework in the postconciliar period for "public Catholicism" in the United States, a framework shared by left and right within the American church, see R. Scott Appleby, "The Triumph of Americanism: Common Ground for U.S. Catholics in the Twentieth Century," in *Being Right: Conservative Catholics in America*, ed. Mary Jo Weaver and R. Scott Appleby, 37–62 (Bloomington: Indiana University Press, 1995). Finally, note that two issues of *U.S.Catholic Historian* (summer 1993 and winter 1999) have been devoted to discussion by leading scholars of the implications and aftermath of the controversy.

43. For the story of the rise and then the faltering and fragmentation of the movement, see Gerald McCool, *The Neo-Thomists* (Milwaukee, WI: Marquette University Press, 1994), and Fergus Kerr, *After Aquinas: Versions of Thomism* (Oxford, Blackwell, 2002). See also Philip Gleason, *Keeping the Faith: American Catholicism Past and Present* (Notre Dame, IN: University of Notre Dame Press, 1987), 136–177, and William M. Halsey, *The Survival of American Innocence: Catholicism in an Era of Disillusionment* (Notre Dame, IN: University of Notre Dame Press, 1980).

44. John Paul II, *Fides et Ratio* (Washington, DC: USCCB, 1998), paragraph 49. The impulse "to make good the lacunas of philosophical discourse" is difficult for the papal magisterium to resist, however, particularly if the pope is a scholar-intellectual in his own right. John Paul II's *Veritatis Splendor* (1993) addresses the moral philosophy of natural law and insists that only a single reading of that tradition—one stressing the notion of moral absolutes as "exceptionless" norms that prescind conscientious deliberation and choice, meaning there is no point in trying to think through the consequences of the actions they call for—is acceptable for Catholic thinkers.

45. Flannery, *Optatum Totius*, 718–719.

46. *Pascendi Dominici Gregis*, 2–3, passim.

47. Ibid., 40–41, passim.

48. Ibid., 44.

49. Ibid., 48–56, passim.

50. The tradition of denouncing scholarship inclined to modernist opinions was continued at mid-century by Pius XII in his encyclical *Humani Generis* (1950), which condemned a number of "false opinions threatening to undermine the foundations of Catholic doctrine," among them certain approaches to human evolution. For understanding the antimodernist project, starting points are Lester R. Kurtz, *The Politics of Heresy: The Modernist Crisis in Roman Catholicism* (Berkeley: University of California Press, 1986), and Gabriel Daly, *Transcendence and Immanence: A Study in Catholic Modernism and Integralism* (Oxford: Clarendon, 1980). See also Darrell Jodock, ed., *Catholicism Contending with Modernity: Roman Catholic Modernism and Anti-Modernism in Historical Context* (Cambridge: Cambridge University Press, 2000), and David Schultenhover, *A View from Rome on the Eve of the Modernist Crisis* (New York: Fordham University Press, 1993). See also Marvin R. O'Connell, *Critics on Trial: An Introduction to the Catholic Modernist Crisis* (Washington, DC: Catholic University Press, 1994). For the American response, see Scott Appleby, "Church and Age Unite!" in *The Modernist Impulse in American Catholicism* (Notre Dame, IN: University of Notre Dame Press, 1992). Finally, for insight into the intellectual alienation of the priesthood under the antimodernist regime, see Michael V. Gannon, "Before and after Modernism: The Intellectual Isolation of the American Priest," in *The Catholic Priest in the United States: Historical Investigations*, ed. John Tracy Ellis, 293–383 (Collegeville, MN: St. John's University Press, 1971).

51. Quoted in Felix Kerr, *Twentieth Century Catholic Theologians: From Neoscholasticism to Nuptial Mysticism* (Oxford: Blackwell, 2007), vii. Kerr's groundbreaking study brings home the truth and importance of Kasper's remark. He deals with the problems of "reason under oath" in the preconciliar period and provides analyses of the work of ten theologians: Marie Dominique Chenu, Edward Schillebeecks, Henri de Lubac, Yves Congar, Karl Rahner, Bernard Lonergan, Hans Urs von Balthasar, Hans Küng, Karol Wojtyla, and Joseph Ratzinger. He notes that by 1914 the Vatican had boiled down the vast corpus of St. Thomas's writings to twenty-four Thomist theses that were issued to guide all clerical students in their philosophical preparation for examinations. The theses are available online at www.scottmsullivan.com/24Theses.htm.

52. See, for example, Christopher A. Ferrara and Thomas E. Woods, *The Great Façade: Vatican II and the Regime of Novelty in the Roman Catholic Church* (Forest Lake,

MN: Remnant Press, 2002), which argues "that the only way out of the crisis is *the full restoration of Roman Catholic ecclesiastical tradition, classical theology, classical preaching, and Scholastic philosophy*" (italics theirs), 381.

53. James L. Heft, ed., *A Catholic Modernity? Charles Taylor's Marianist Award Lecture* (New York: Oxford University Press, 1999), 13–37, passim.

3

Benedict XVI and the Interpretation of Vatican II

Joseph A. Komonchak

Fifty years ago, on January 25, 1959, Pope John XXIII announced that he intended to convoke an ecumenical council. In various talks and official documents over the next two and a half years, he set out three large goals for the council: spiritual renewal, updating (aggiorna-mento), and promotion of Christian unity. His request for proposals for the conciliar agenda elicited from bishops, heads of clerical religious orders, pontifical faculties, and universities no fewer than two thousand documents which suggested, it seemed, that the council treat *de omni re scibili et quibusdam aliis.* The most detailed study of these *vota* saw three groups represented in the responses: one that pretty well neglected the pope's aims and wished the council simply to confirm the flinty face that the Catholic Church had set against the principles of liberal modernity, a group that favored the pope's desire for renewal and reform both within the church and in its relations with others, and a group, largely clerics from the Third World, that does not readily fall into the other groups and shows attention to the challenges represented by their circumstances.[1] Two years of preparation for the council were in good part marked by a struggle to define what it should say and do. The greatest openness to pastoral renewal was reflected in the texts prepared by the preparatory commission on the liturgy and by the Secretariat for Promoting Christian Unity; the texts prepared by the preparatory doctrinal commission sought the council's endorsement of the orientations and emphases of the papal magisterium over the previous century and a half.[2]

This struggle defined the drama of the first session of the council in the fall of 1962. After lengthy and lively debate, an overwhelming majority of the bishops endorsed a draft text that set out principles and proposals for substantial liturgical reform. After a shorter but even more passionate discussion, a smaller but still significant majority declared that they did not wish to issue the kind of doctrinal texts prepared for them (exemplified in the draft "On the Sources of Revelation"). The two votes ratified the vision of the council that Pope John had set out in his opening speech, which outlined an exercise of the conciliar magisterium that would be positive, would refrain from condemnations, and, while zealous in preserving the faith, would devote itself to finding a way of expressing it that would be accessible and intelligible to contemporaries. By the end of the first session, it was clear that a new preparation of the council would be necessary and that leadership of the council had passed to a group of prelates and theologians who had largely been marginal to the preparation. The feeling was widespread that something dramatic had happened. People indulged in grand descriptions of what was underway: it was "the end of the Counter-Reformation, of Tridentine Catholicism"; it was "the end of the Middle Ages"; it was "the end of the Constantinian Era"! Pope John's prayer for the council had asked that it be a "new Pentecost" for the church, and some people said that this was how it felt.

The work of producing the sixteen documents that embody the teachings of Vatican II was carried out in the next three sessions of the council (1963–1965). Some topics engaged the bishops more fully than others and revealed diverse positions passionately defended, as, for example, with regard to papal primacy and episcopal collegiality, the place and role of the Blessed Virgin Mary, the interpretation of the Bible, religious freedom, contraception, and nuclear weapons. An easy, lazy division of lines of force between "progressives" and "conservatives" obscures the complexities of the discussions as the council proceeded. In the end, the conciliar process of conversation, confrontation, conciliation, and compromise resulted in four constitutions, nine decrees, and three declarations, all of which were passed by majorities of more than 85 percent.

By the end of the council, the reform of the liturgy had already begun to be implemented, and this was only the most visible of the many changes that in many parts of the world were so to alter everyday Catholic life that one observer was moved to write: "It was as if the North Star had not only dimmed, but moved!" Some of these changes were officially permitted or even required; some went far beyond what the council had called for; some, indeed, would have given many bishops second thoughts if they had been foreseen. Many Catholics enthusiastically embraced the changes, and some of them wished to see even more: within a very few years of the close of the council, its texts were being called outdated, and calls were heard for a Vatican III. Many Catholics deplored the changes and the loss of the tight Catholic identity the church had displayed in the century before Vatican II met. Some blamed the postconciliar confusion on the hijacking of the council by liberal theologians and journalists, while others, of whom Archbishop Marcel Lefebvre was the most famous, did not hesitate to blame it on the council itself. Still others claim to find dozens of heresies in the conciliar texts and argue that the popes who have endorsed the council have fallen into heresy themselves and that the See of Peter is therefore vacant (Sedevacantists), and a few of them, to supply for this lack, have elected their own replacement.

By far the majority of Catholics in the world today were not yet born when the council ended. (Parents of the last undergraduate class I taught on Vatican II are among them.) For them the council, so far from being a remembered experience, has to be reconstructed pretty much from scratch. What a teacher has to do in a classroom, historians are attempting to do by the methods of their discipline. A five-volume *History of Vatican II* has attempted to reconstruct the experience of the council from the day it was announced by Pope John XXIII until the day it was brought to a solemn end by Pope Paul VI.[3] A host of books and articles are exploring the redactional histories of the various conciliar texts, while studies of their reception into the life of the church extend the timeline to include the impact of the council.[4] More recently, a considerable literature on the general interpretation of the council has appeared, in some of which it is not rare to hear echoed some of the same disputes that followed Pope John's announcement and marked many moments in the council's evolution.[5]

In certain circles, the issue is put as one between "discontinuity" and "continuity," that is, whether in interpreting the council the emphasis should fall on elements of novelty and even of reversal, both in the conciliar event itself or in the texts that resulted from it, or whether it should fall instead on the elements that show the rootedness of the texts in the ancient tradition of the church. The history of the council edited by Giuseppe Alberigo has been singled out as representing a "hermeneutics of discontinuity or rupture," and the historiographical concept of an "event" has been taken to call into question the identity of the church before and after the council. A few Italian prelates welcomed a volume highly critical of Alberigo's *History* as a "counter-weight" that would end an alleged "hegemony" enjoyed by the hermeneutics of discontinuity.[6] When Pope Benedict XVI himself addressed the question of conciliar hermeneutics in a speech to the Roman Curia on December 22, 2005 (an excerpted version is presented for the reader as an appendix in this book), his remarks were taken by some as confirming this position, and a volume of studies on the conciliar documents has recently been published that claims to be following the pope's line of interpretation in opposition to claims that the council represented rupture and discontinuity. Since the pope's position has often been considerably oversimplified by some commentators, it is worthwhile to give it a close reading.

The Pope's Christmas Address to the Roman Curia

The much-anticipated remarks of the new pope appeared as a part of his year-end address to the Roman Curia on December 22, 2005.[7] Interest in his views was all the greater because he had himself participated in the council as the chief theological *peritus* for Joseph Cardinal Frings and as an active member of the progressive wing of theologians. In addition, he had on several occasions already published on the council and its aftermath, most famously and controversially in a book of interviews with Vittorio Messori.[8]

Pope Benedict began his speech to the Curia with a set of questions that recall those for which John Paul II convoked the extraordinary session of the Synod of Bishops in 1985: "What has been the result of the Council? Has it been well received? In the reception of the Council, what has been good and what has been inadequate or mistaken? What still remains to be done?" The pope does not attempt to answer them in this address except insofar as this is implicit in the remark that "in vast areas of the Church the reception of the Council has been somewhat difficult." Both the difficulties and the vast areas they affected are left unspecified, but one suspects that he has in mind the Western world, that is, Western Europe and the Americas.

The difficulties in the implementation of the council, he says, derive from the fact that "two opposing hermeneutics confronted and contested one another. One caused confusion, the other, silently but more and more visibly, has borne and is bearing fruit." The former hermeneutics will be called "the hermeneutics of discontinuity or rupture," the latter "the hermeneutics of reform."

At first sight, the pope's choice of names for these rival interpretative orientations may strike one as odd. In contrast to one that stresses discontinuity, one might have expected a "hermeneutics of continuity or of fidelity." Similarly, in contrast to a "hermeneutics of reform," one might have expected the other view to be called "a hermeneutics of revolution." Instead, we have "discontinuity" and "reform" set in contrast to one another. One suspects that the pope had a reason for not using the easy contrasts and for entitling his preferred method as one of "reform." In fact, as we shall see, the larger part of his discussion of the hermeneutics of reform is devoted to showing how it required some measure of discontinuity.

It is also somewhat odd that the pope speaks of only two competing interpretations of the council when, in fact, there are more than two of them, and this holds whether one is interpreting the council theologically or explaining it historically or sociologically.[9] Since I do not think that the pope is unaware of the complexities of this literature, I take it that he has simplified matters for the sake of his rhetorical argument and in view of what I believe to be the primary intention of his remarks. But first, a close analysis of the talk.

The Hermeneutics of Discontinuity

Pope Benedict is so brief in considering the "hermeneutics of discontinuity and rupture" that one must conclude that it was not the main point of his talk.[10] Two aspects of it are pointed out. First, it "risks ending with a break between the pre-conciliar Church and the post-conciliar Church." This danger is simply noted without comment, which is somewhat surprising, given that Cardinal Ratzinger in other writings had taken pains to criticize the idea that there are "ruptures" in the life of the church. Instead, in this talk to the Roman Curia, the pope goes on immediately to mention a second feature of this mistaken hermeneutics, namely, the view that, because they were the result of compromise, the final documents of Vatican II cannot be said to yield the real "spirit of the Council," which is to be found instead in "the impulses toward the new that underlie the texts." A passion for the new would thus be true fidelity to "the spirit of Vatican II."

In criticism of this view, the pope rightly points out how vague this alleged "spirit of the Council" is, and what a large variety of proposals might be, and have been, included under it. He then offers a comparison that illustrates more clearly the sort of view he is opposing. He says that this view conceives of an ecumenical council as a sort of constitutional convention or constituent assembly, at which one constitution might be done away with and another written. No such mandate is ever given to bishops, Pope Benedict comments, even when gathered in council; their only role is to serve as stewards of the constitution Christ gave to his church. The gift they minister is one that has to be kept alive so that it can bear fruit; the Gospel parables make it clear "how in a Council dynamism and fidelity must be the same thing."

It is difficult to know to whom this idea of the council as a constituent assembly may refer. The Italian juridical scholar Paolo Pombeni did discuss the relationship between "event" and "decisions" in parliaments and constituent assemblies, but his essay ended without his drawing links to Vatican II, a task for which he admits he is not competent.[11] Perhaps Pope Benedict had in mind the view of the German theologian Peter Hünermann, who has proposed that the texts of Vatican II be understood as "constitutional" in character,[12] although he certainly did not suggest that a council has any authority to undo Christ's will for the church. Hünermann's view is only one of many recent efforts to set out possibilities for a hermeneutics of the council, and it does not seem to have attracted much support.

It is, of course, not an uncommon procedure for Roman documents to take a view that is considered dangerous and to push it a little (or even a lot) further, and then to repudiate the exaggerated position. Perhaps Benedict XVI by this comparison wished to warn that "the hermeneutics of discontinuity," taken to extremes, is a hermeneutics that sees the council as revolutionary, at least in its "spirit."

The Hermeneutics of Reform

To ground the interpretative key he favors, Benedict XVI turns to two papal speeches at the council, the one with which Pope John XXIII opened the council on October 11, 1962, and the other the one with which Pope Paul VI closed it on December 8, 1965. (It was perhaps the intention of the pope to show a fundamental kinship between the two popes of Vatican II, against the idea that Paul VI had somehow betrayed John XXIII's vision.) The pope cites first the famous passage in which John XXIII insisted that the council could not be concerned only with preserving the faith, as if it were an antiquity, but also had to explore how that faith was to be "studied and presented in a way that corresponds to the needs of our time." This requires the famous distinction between "the substance of the ancient doctrine of the deposit of faith" and "the way in which it is presented." In his brief reflection on this passage, Pope Benedict stresses what new things this required: new thinking about Christian truth, a new and vital relationship with it, a new formulation of it. A fruitful interpretation of the council thus would combine fidelity and dynamism.

It is striking that only these two brief paragraphs are devoted to the council's effort at a restatement of central Christian doctrine in a way that would make it more intelligible and attractive to contemporaries. This is somewhat surprising from a former professor of theology, particularly since he was himself the author of several important and illuminating commentaries on conciliar texts and themes. In an earlier essay, he had even maintained that one might distinguish interpretations of the council on the basis of which texts were considered primary: the doctrinal texts (*Sacrosanctum Concilium; Lumen gentium; Dei verbum*) or the texts on the church's relationship with the world (*Dignitatis humanae; Nostra aetate; Gaudium et spes*).[13] Once again, there must have been a reason that Benedict did not choose to illustrate his hermeneutics of reform by reference to the primarily doctrinal texts but instead turned for the larger part of his exposition to texts in which the council engaged the modern world.

Pope Benedict does not cite a specific text in Paul VI's concluding speech, but the page reference given in his text is to a section in which that pope had spoken of the alienation of church and society in the nineteenth and twentieth centuries.[14] This estrangement Benedict uses to indicate the urgency of the question of the relation between the church and the contemporary world or, as he seems to prefer to refer to it, the modern age. The council's attempt to end this estrangement is a reason that "a hermeneutic of discontinuity can seem convincing."

The pope offers a rapid historical survey of the difficulties the church had experienced over the previous four centuries, beginning with the trial of Galileo (described with some understatement as a "very problematic begin-ning"), moving on to Kant's reductive religion and to the "radical phase" of the French Revolution, which left no room for the church and faith, and ending with the "radical liberalism" of the nineteenth century and with natural sciences that claimed they had no need of the "God-hypothesis." Under Pope Pius IX, the church had responded with such "harsh and radical condemna-tions of such a spirit of the modern age" that it appeared "that there were no longer any grounds for a positive and fruitful understanding," given also the equally drastic refusals of those who considered themselves "representatives of the modern era." This impasse, and the implied criticism of Pius IX, provides the background against which Benedict sets out the novelty of Vatican II.

It was prepared, he says, by certain developments. In a statement that would have pleased John Courtney Murray, the pope points to the recognition that the American political experiment offers "a model of the modern state different from that theorized by the radical tendencies that had emerged in the second phase of the French Revolution." Meanwhile, the natural sciences were learning more modesty about their range and limits. Developments were also taking place in the church. Between the two world wars and especially after the second, "Catholic statesmen had shown that a modern lay state can exist that, nonetheless, is not neutral with respect to values but lives by reaching back to the great ethical sources opened by Christianity." Finally, Catholic social teach-ing was developing and offering a "third way" between radical liberalism and Marxist theory.

As a result of all this, as the council opened, three circles of questions, defining a single general problem, awaited responses, requiring new ways of defining the church's attitude to them: (1) the relation between faith and the modern sciences, including also modern history, presented by the pope as if it were as reductive as the natural sciences had been; (2) the relation between the church and the modern state, the latter described as one "that was making room for citizens of various religions and ideologies, acting impartially towards these religions and simply assuming responsibility for orderly and tolerant co-existence among citizens and for their freedom to exercise their own religion" (Murray would also have welcomed this limited role for the state); and (3) the relation between Christian faith and the world religions, especially Judaism. The adjective *new* occurs four times in this section, and the pope flatly states "that in all these areas, which all together form a single problem, some kind of discontinuity might emerge and that in fact it did emerge."

In the pope's remarks about the developments that led to this situation, one can hear echoes of the position he had set out thirty years earlier when he said that *Gaudium et spes, Dignitatis humanae,* and *Nostra aetate* represent "a revision of the *Syllabus* of Pius IX, a kind of counter-syllabus." Then he had spoken of twentieth-century developments, beginning with Pius XI, as correcting *via facti* the one-sidedness of the positions held by earlier popes. What was lacking, however, was a "new basic statement of the relationship that should exist between the Church and the world that had come into existence after 1789." Prerevolutionary attitudes "continued to exist in countries with strong Catholic majorities. Hardly anyone today will deny that the Spanish and Italian Concordats strove to preserve too much of a view of the world that no longer corresponded to the facts." He even spoke of church-state relationships that were "obsolete." Seen against this background, he had written, *Gaudium et spes* can be interpreted as "an attempt at an official reconciliation with the new era inaugurated in 1789."[15]

The discontinuity that such a reconciliation entailed, however, should not be allowed to obscure "the continuity of principles." There follows an important statement, almost a definition, that many interpreters have overlooked: "It is precisely in this combination of continuity and discontinuity at different levels that the very nature of true reform consists." Properly understanding and evaluating the discontinuity that this effort entailed, then, requires one to make certain distinctions. The first is that "between concrete historical situations and their demands," on the one hand, and "principles," on the other. This was, of course, the distinction in the matter of church and state that was urged by people like Jacques Maritain and Murray and was rejected by their Roman and American critics, for whom the Catholic confessional state was an ideal theologically, even dogmatically, required. For Pope Benedict, however, it is a valid and important distinction.

We have here the explanation of why Pope Benedict does not simply call his view the "hermeneutics of continuity": true reform itself requires a degree of discontinuity at some level. An affirmation of discontinuity in relation to Vatican II, then, is common to the two hermeneutics that the pope has counterposed. The clash between the pope's rival hermeneutics, then, does not revolve around the issue of continuity versus discontinuity.

The pope goes on to explain and illustrate his distinction. Church decisions with regard to certain forms of liberalism or to liberal interpretations of the Bible had themselves to be contingent because they referred to concrete and changeable realities. Here he is referring to condemnations of religious freedom in the last two centuries and to decrees of the Pontifical Biblical Commission at the beginning of the last century. In the remarks with which he had presented his Congregation's "Instruction on the Ecclesial Vocation of the Theologian" (Donum veritatis, 1990), Cardinal Ratzinger had already pointed to such official texts as examples of magisterial decisions that "cannot be the last word on a subject as such"; "provisional dispositions," they are valid at their core but may need "further rectification" with respect to "individual details influenced by the circumstances at the time." He then maintained that "as a warning-cry against hasty and superficial adaptations, they remain fully justified; . . . but the details of the determinations of their contents were later superseded once they had carried out their pastoral duty at a particular moment."[16]

In his 2005 remarks to the Roman Curia, Benedict XVI makes a perhaps more valid distinction when he says that only the principles express the lasting element; "the concrete forms" instead are dependent on the historical situation and are therefore changeable. "Thus the basic decisions can remain valid while the forms of their application to new contexts can change." The pope then offers an illustration: "if religious freedom is associated with agnosticism and relativism, it is only natural that it be rejected by those who believe us capable of knowing the truth about God." Quite different is a view of religious freedom that links it to the need of social co-existence and derives it from the fact that "the truth can never be imposed from without but must be appropriated by a person only through a process of being convinced." Religious freedom in the first sense, therefore, the church can only condemn; religious freedom in the second sense, the church can embrace.

That this is a good illustration of the distinction between principles and concrete applications is not entirely clear. The difference here is not a matter of circumstances, but of two different notions of religious freedom. The same principles could quite logically lead to a rejection of the first and an acceptance of the second. That this distinction also explains the whole history of the magisterium's teaching with regard to religious freedom from Gregory XVI (who called it "madness") to John Paul II (who regarded it as the most basic human right) is also debatable. For the 150 years before Vatican II, there were Catholics who advocated religious freedom in the modern state but did not do

so on agnostic or relativistic grounds, which did not prevent many of them
from becoming the object of ecclesiastical suspicion and censure. It was
the Roman failure to consider that there was some possible middle ground
between indifferentism and establishment that causes sadness when one reviews this whole history. What were in fact variable applications of principle,
as, for example, the ideal of the confessional state, were taken as necessary
logical consequences of unchangeable doctrine. Where principle left off and
contingent application began was the whole point at issue.

With *Dignitatis humanae*, the pope goes on, the council recognized and made
its own "an essential principle of the modern State," but at the same time, he says,
the council also returned in a new way to " the deeper patrimony of the Church";
with this statement, the church could find itself in full harmony with the teaching
of Jesus and the examples of the martyrs. The latter are said to have clearly rejected
the state religion and died for freedom of conscience and for the freedom to
profess their own faith—"a profession that can be imposed by no state, but
instead can only be appropriated by the grace of God, in freedom of conscience."
A missionary church today, he says, has to commit itself to freedom of faith. The
pope here has leapt back over the centuries of Christendom to the example of the
church of the martyrs, who illustrate the "deeper patrimony of the Church." This
is, of course, an implicit criticism of the intervening centuries.

As Pope Benedict neared the end of his remarks, he returned to the
question of continuity and discontinuity:

> The Second Vatican Council, with its new definition of the relation
> between the faith of the Church and certain essential elements of
> modern thought, has revised and even corrected some historical
> decisions, but in spite of this apparent discontinuity it has maintained
> and deepened its inner nature and its true identity. The Church is,
> as much before as after the Council, the same Church, one, holy,
> catholic and apostolic on a journey across time.

After all he has said so far, it is surprising to find the pope referring to the
discontinuity as simply "apparent." He had already said that elements of
discontinuity had appeared in the conciliar texts on the church's relation to
the modern age and that on the question of religious freedom, the council had
permitted the church to rejoin the example of Christ and the testimony of the
martyrs. His point seems to be that this real discontinuity did not threaten the
true nature and identity of the church but permitted the church to recover
elements that had been compromised.

It might also be worth exploring what could be meant by "church" in the
paragraph just cited: what is it or, better, *who* is it that remains the same in the

midst of such new relationships? After all, it is not just the world that has changed over the last few centuries, and the whole point that the pope has been making is that the church has had to come up with new definitions of the relation between its faith and the modern world. If it now understands itself differently in relation to that world and acts in accordance with the new understanding and the new relationships, then it is in that respect and to that degree not "the same Church." A church that was ready to condemn Jacques Maritain for his idea of a "new Christendom" and a church that proclaims a right to religious freedom based upon human dignity is not in all respects the same church.[17]

In the final paragraphs, the pope summarizes what the council did as "a basic 'Yes' to the modern era" and as "the step taken by the Council toward the modern era." He is at pains to point out that this was not and could not be an indiscriminate yes and that there are important respects in which the church must remain "a sign of contradiction." Repeating something he has said often in other places, he says that the council did away with "mistaken or superfluous contradictions in order to present to this world of ours the demands of the Gospel in all their greatness and purity."

The pope went on to compare this latest way of dealing with the perennial problem of the relation between faith and reason to events in earlier ages. Biblically, there was St. Peter's exhortation to Christians to be ready to give a reason for the hope that is in them, the task that was undertaken in the great patristic encounter with Greek culture. The second great example is that of the thirteenth century, with the encounter between Christian thought and Aristotelianism, mediated by Jewish and Arab philosophers. Because tradition was so imbued with Platonism, there was now the danger of thinking that there was an "irreconcilable contradiction" between faith and reason. It took the genius of Aquinas to promote "a positive relationship with the form of reason dominant at the time." Sadly, the pope cannot refer in the centuries after Aquinas to any positive engagement with forms of contemporary reason of the quality or success of the patristic and the Thomist endeavors. That is a long time—700 years! After once more evoking the negative case of Galileo and after a vague reference to the many phases of "the difficult dispute between modern reason and Christian faith," he says that "with Vatican II the hour arrived in which a broad rethinking was required." In the conciliar documents may be found the broad outline, the general direction, in which this dialogue between faith and reason must be undertaken.

To Whom Was the Pope Speaking?

Some commentators on the pope's speech have seen it as an implied criticism of the *History of Vatican II*, published under the general editorship of Giuseppe

Alberigo. There are reasons to think that this work is not the chief target and certainly not the only one. Neither the editors nor the authors of individual chapters in the five volumes entertain the exaggerated hermeneutics of discontinuity that the pope criticizes. None of them denies the church's continuity in the faith. They do point to rupture or discontinuity in two areas. First, the council represented a departure from the tight system of thought and discipline that in the decades before the council had cast suspicion on most of the movements of *ressourcement* and aggiornamento, of renewal and reform, that made the council possible. Second, these authors found discontinuity precisely where the pope has placed it: in the council's effort at a more successful engagement with the modern world than had been achieved by the antimodern attitudes and strategies adopted by the papacy since the French Revolution. This was *"la svolta epochale"* that Giuseppe Alberigo proposed as the historic significance of the Second Vatican Council, and so far from being repudiated, it seems to me that it was affirmed and confirmed by Pope Benedict XVI.

That the mythical "Bologna school" was not in the pope's mind is also suggested by his choice of the question of religious freedom to illustrate the "reform," the "dynamism in fidelity," and the "novelty in continuity" that he wishes to counterpose to the hermeneutics of "discontinuity." The impassioned and at times even bitter debate about religious freedom and the complex history of the redaction of *Dignitatis humanae* were covered in the volumes of the *History of Vatican II*, but that treatment has not been given any particular attention by the louder critics of that work. Why, then, did the pope choose this topic?

I suggest that his chief aim was to try to persuade traditionalists whose rejection of the council depends in no small part on their belief that its teachings on church and state and on religious freedom represent a revolutionary discontinuity in official church doctrine. It had long been notorious among the Lefebvrists and among other traditionalist groups that in 1982 then Cardinal Ratzinger had stated that *Gaudium et spes, Dignitatis humanae*, and *Nostra aetate* represented "a revision of the *Syllabus*, a kind of counter-syllabus, . . . an attempt at an official reconciliation with the new age inaugurated in 1789." They provided the long-needed "new basic statement of the relationship that should exist between the Church and the world that had come into existence after 1789." Leaving behind one-sided and obsolete stances, the council taught that the church must relinquish many of the things that have hitherto spelled security for it and that it has taken for granted. " She must demolish long-standing bastions and trust solely to the shield of faith."[18]

Archbishop Marcel Lefebvre dismissed these comments as "liberal banalities" that show only scorn for "the support that the Catholic state and the institutions that flow from it constitute for the faith."[19] In 2002, Lefebvre's successor as head of the Society of Pius X, Bernard Fellay, invoked these paragraphs of Ratzinger as illustrating the points of serious disagreement that remain between Rome and Ecône. While his group believed in "the homogeneous development of doctrine," it could not, short of doing away with the principle of noncontradiction, accept the council's teaching on religious freedom.[20] This remains one of the points on which the Lefebvrites believe that Vatican II needs not only a correct hermeneutic but also revision and correction.

Pope Benedict seems to have used his speech to the Curia to invite these traditionalists to see in the council's teaching on religious freedom, not a revolutionary shift in the church's teaching, but a development that applies enduring principles to new circumstances. That it will be successful one may doubt: the issue remains where it was when Catholic thinkers like John Courtney Murray were arguing their case; what they considered as changeable concrete applications—in particular, the Catholic state—their critics took to be dogmatically required. Lefebvre himself said that the union of church and state is "a principle of Catholic doctrine as immutable as is the doctrine itself."[21]

Continuity and Discontinuity at Vatican II

In the end, the sharp disjunction between rival hermeneutical orientations with which the pope began his remarks on the council was blunted in the course of his argument. The "reform" that Benedict sees as the heart of the council's achievement is itself a matter of "novelty in continuity," of "fidelity and dynamism"; indeed, in what is something like a definition, the pope says that "true reform" consists precisely in a "combination of continuity and discontinuity at different levels." It oversimplifies his position to see it as counterposing continuity and discontinuity, as is often done.

It is no less an oversimplification to reduce the question of interpreting Vatican II to the same choice between continuity and discontinuity. Is there anyone who sees only continuity in the council, or anyone who sees only discontinuity? Pope Benedict's description of "true reform" invites an effort to discern where elements of continuity and elements of discontinuity may be found.[22] Anyone undertaking that task may find it helpful to keep in mind two sets of distinctions.

In the debates about the council, one finds that things are often complicated and confused because people often mean different things by the term "Vatican II." Some take it to mean the sixteen documents that were produced

in the course of the four years during which the bishops met in council and
that represent the indispensable reference point for anyone wishing to know
what "Vatican II" taught.

The phrase is also used to refer to what happened between two dates,
January 25, 1959, when Pope John XXIII announced that he intended to
convoke an ecumenical council, and December 8, 1965, when Pope Paul VI
brought it to a solemn close. Between these two dates, the council was planned
and prepared and then unfolded in the four autumnal sessions that produced
the sixteen final texts. This might be called the "experience" (or "experiences")
of Vatican II and refers, first, to what the popes, bishops, experts, observers,
and others in Rome said and did within that time frame. This was, however, the
experience not only of preparing texts but also of the total human and ecclesial
phenomenon of an ecumenical council in course.[23] In addition, what was
happening in Rome was being observed and considered by people who were
not actively involved in the conciliar process but were closely watching it, whether
from nearby or from afar, and knew themselves involved in it. Their experience,
too, was part of what was meant and often still is meant by "Vatican II."

As that description of what counts as Vatican II goes beyond the protago-
nists of the council and includes the reactions of people observing it, so also
other meanings of the phrase expand it beyond the conciliar time frame to
include what happened after the council and even because of the council in
either of the two senses already distinguished. As a set of documents that offer
an agenda of renewal and reform, the council had many and great officially
authorized effects, most visibly perhaps in the reform of every single one of the
sacraments but in very many other areas as well, in fact in every one of the
areas the conciliar texts addressed. But just as the council was not a publishing
house producing documents but a lived experience, so also what happened
after and even because of the council cannot be restricted to what was officially
authorized but has to include many other changes and even transformations in
ordinary Catholic life, some of which were in harmony with the authorized
changes and some of which were not. Some people writing about "Vatican II"
mean, then, not only the texts and not only the incidents that constituted the
experience of the council but also its aftermath, however they may judge or
evaluate the latter.

Still broader and vaguer in sense is the phrase "the spirit of Vatican II." This
is sometimes used to refer to the spirit of renewal and reform that the calling of
the council evoked and that the texts of Vatican II were meant to embody and
articulate. But it is also used, and rather often, to refer to the spirit that is thought
to have been at work in the conciliar process and to have provided its distinctive
character, which, if it was indeed embodied and articulated in the final texts,

cannot be reduced to what they say. Sometimes it even seems to mean what "Vatican II" would have said and done if no conservatives had been present in Rome during those years and the spirit of renewal and reform had not been forced into channels too narrow for its full flood into the life of the church.

The question of continuity and discontinuity will look different as one thinks of Vatican II in one or another of these senses. It will also be asked and answered in different ways, depending on the standpoint from which it is being asked. Three such standpoints may be distinguished: doctrinal, theological, and sociological or historical. Doctrinally, there is clear continuity: Vatican II did not discard any dogma of the church, and it did not promulgate any new dogma. On the other hand, part of its novelty was that the council recovered important doctrines that had been relatively neglected in the previous centuries, including the collegiality of bishops, the priesthood of all the baptized, the theology of the local church, and the importance of scripture. Reasserting such things meant placing other doctrines in broader and richer contexts than before. Finally, the council departed from the normal language of ecumenical councils such as Trent and Vatican I and followed Pope John's injunction that it offer a positive vision of the faith in a more accessible rhetoric, particularly, as he also urged, by abstaining from the sort of anathemas that had punctuated previous ecumenical councils.

Theologically, the council was the fruit of movements of theological renewal in the twentieth century: in biblical, patristic, and medieval studies; in liturgical theology; in ecumenical conversation; in new, more positive encounters with modern philosophy; in rethinking the church-world relation; and in reflecting on the role of laypeople in the church. Most, if not all, of these movements had fallen under some degree of official suspicion or disapproval in the decades prior to the council, an attitude reflected in the official texts prepared for Vatican II. There was real drama in the first session of the council (1962), when those texts were severely criticized for falling short of the theological and pastoral renewal that had been underway for decades. The leadership of the council was transferred to prelates who were open to such renewal, and theologians who had been under a cloud for years were brought in as official experts. In all this, there was considerable discontinuity.

From the standpoints of sociology and of history, one looks at the council against a broader backdrop, and one cannot limit oneself to the intentions of the popes and bishops or to the final texts. One is now studying the impact of the council as experienced, as observed, and as implemented. It is hard, from these standpoints, not to stress the discontinuity, the experience of an *event*, of a break with routine. This is the common language used by participants and by observers at the time—the young Joseph Ratzinger's reflections after each session, published in English as *Theological Highlights of Vatican II*, are a good example.[24] It is from this perspective that James Hitchcock calls Vatican II "the most important event within the Church in the past four hundred years," and the French historian-sociologist Emile Poulat points out that the Catholic Church changed more in the ten years after Vatican II than it did in the previous hundred years.[25] Similar positions are held by people along the whole length of the ideological spectrum. Whether they regard what happened as good or as bad, they all agree that "something happened."

It would be helpful if such distinctions of standpoint were kept in mind. They could help to identify precisely where differences in the interpretation of Vatican II really lie and to assess whether they are really in conflict with one another. Pope Benedict's own performance in his 2005 speech to the Roman Curia is itself an example of a serious effort at discernment and would greatly elevate the level of discussion if it were given the close attention it deserves.

NOTES

1. See Étienne Fouilloux, "The Antepreparatory Phase: The Slow Emergence from Inertia (January, 1959–October, 1962)," in *History of Vatican II*, vol. 1, ed. Giuseppe Alberigo and Joseph A. Komonchak, 109–132 (Maryknoll, NY: Orbis, 1995).

2. See Joseph A. Komonchak, "The Struggle for the Council during the Preparation of Vatican II (1960–1962)," in *History of Vatican II*, vol. 1, 167–356.

3. *History of Vatican II*, 5 vols., ed. Giuseppe Alberigo; English version ed. Joseph A. Komonchak (Maryknoll, NY: Orbis, 1995–2006). A fine single-volume history, with attention to the contemporary debate about interpretations of the council, is John W. O'Malley, *What Happened at Vatican II* (Cambridge, MA: Harvard University Press, 2008).

4. Regular chronicles of publications on Vatican II have been produced by G. Routhier: "Recherches et publications récentes autour de Vatican II," *Laval théologique et philosophique* 53 (1997): 435–454; 55 (1999): 115–149; 56 (2000): 543–583; 58 (2002): 177–203; 59 (2003): 583–606; 60 (2004): 561–577; 61 (2005): 613–653. Massimo Faggioli has two bibliographical essays in *Cristianesimo nella Storia* 24 (2005): 335–360; 26 (2005): 743–769.

5. *Chi ha paura del Vaicano II?* ed. Alberto Melloni and Giuseppe Ruggieri (Rome: Carrocci, 2009);Gilles Routhier, *Vatican II: Herméneutique et réception* (Québec: Fides, 2006); Ormond Rush, *Still Interpreting Vatican II: Some Hermeneutical Principles* (New York: Paulist, 2004); *Vatican II: Did Anything Happen?* (New York: Continuum, 2008); *Vatican II sous le regard des historiens*, ed. Christoph Theobald (Paris: Médiasèvres, 2006).

6. Agostino Marchetto, *Il Concilio Ecumenico Vaticano II: Contrappunto per la sua storia* (Libreria Editrice Vaticana, 2005).

7. The full text may be found in Latin in *Acta Apostolicae Sedis* 98 (2006): 40–55, and in six languages at the Vatican Web site.

8. See *The Ratzinger Report* (San Francisco: Ignatius, 1985); for earlier essays, "Catholicism after the Council," *Furrow* 18 (1967): 3–23; "Zehn Jahre nach Konzilsbeginn: Wo stehen wir?" in *Dogma und Verkündigung*, 433–441 (München: Wewel, 1977); *Principles of Catholic Theology: Building Stones for a Fundamental Theology* (San Francisco: Ignatius, 1987), 367–393.

9. A threefold typology is offered by Étienne Fouilloux, "Histoire et événement: Vatican II," *Cristianesimo nella Storia* 13 (1992): 515–538, and by myself in "Interpreting the Second Vatican Council," *Landas* 1 (1987): 81–90, and in "Interpreting the Council: Catholic Attitudes toward Vatican II," in *Being Right: Conservative Catholics in America*, ed. Mary Jo Weaver and R. Scott Appleby, 17–36 (Bloomington: Indiana University Press, 1995).

10. By word count, only 15 percent of the pope's remarks about the council are devoted to describing and discrediting a hermeneutics of discontinuity; all the rest of it is dedicated to explaining a hermeneutics of reform for which discontinuity is a major element!

11. Paolo Pombeni, "La dialettica evento-decisioni nella ricostruzione delle grandi assemblee: I parlamenti et le assemblee constituenti," in *L'evento e le decisioni: Studi sulle dinamiche del concilio Vaticano II*, ed. M. T. Fattori and A. Melloni, 17–49 (Bologna, Italy: Il Mulino, 1997).

12. For a brief statement of his thesis, along with full bibliographical indications, see Peter Hünermann, "Der 'Text': Eine *Ergänzung* zur Hermeneutik des II. Vatikanische Konzils," *Cristianesimo nella Storia* 28 (2007): 339–358.

13. See Joseph Ratzinger, *Principles of Catholic Theology*, 378–379.

14. Paul VI spoke of the church's having been for the last centuries "absent and distant from secular culture"; see Sacrosanctum Concilium Oecumenicum Vaticanum II, *Constitutiones, Decreta, Declaratones* (Typis Polyglottis Vaticanis, 1974), 1067.

15. Joseph Ratzinger, *Principles of Catholic Theology*, 381–382.

16. Joseph Ratzinger, "Theology Is Not Private Idea of Theologian," *L'Osservatore Romano* (English ed.), July 2, 1990, 5.

17. Ratzinger himself had made this point some years ago: "Christianity has never existed in a purely world-less state. Because it exists in men, whose behavior is 'the world,' it never appears concretely except in a relationship to the world. This interweaving with the world may mean that in an apparent clash between faith and world, it is not Christianity itself that is being defended against the world, but only a particular form of its relationship to the world that is being defended against another form. For example, what may seem to be a conflict between faith and world may really be a conflict between the thirteenth century and the twentieth, because the thirteenth century's polarizing of Christian existence is being identified with the faith itself." See "Der Christ und die Welt von heute," in *Dogma und Verkündigung*, 187.

18. Joseph Ratzinger, *Principles of Catholic Theology*, 391.

19. Marcel Lefebvre, *Ils l'ont découronné: Du libéralisme à l'apostasie; la tragédie conciliaire* (Escurolles, France: Ed. Fideliter, 1987), 239.

20. See Bernard Fellay, "Letter to Friends and Benefactors," June 7, 2002, which can be found at www.sspx.org/superior_generals_ltrs/supgen_62.htm.

21. Lefebvre, *Ils l'ont découronné*, 238.

22. A failure to treat with equal seriousness and emphasis the elements of continuity and discontinuity unfortunately marks the majority of the essays in *Vatican II: Renewal within Tradition*, ed. Matthew L. Lamb and Matthew Levering (New York: Oxford University Press, 2008). While the editors offer the volume as exemplifying the kind of hermeneutic Pope Benedict urges, most of the essays do not try to imitate the example he gave in his famous speech.

23. It was to recapture that experience of the council that the five-volume *History of Vatican II* was conceived and carried out.

24. Joseph Ratzinger, *Theological Highlights of Vatican II* (New York, Paulist, 1966).

25. James Hitchcock, *Catholicism and Modernity: Confrontation or Capitulation?* (New York: Seabury, 1979), 75; Emile Poulat, *Une Eglise ébranlée: Changement, conflit et continuité de Pie XII à Jean Paul II* (Paris: Casterman, 1980), 41.

SECTION II

Theological, Canonistic, and Philosophical Issues

Stubborn Challenges, Emerging Directions

4

Catholic Tradition and Traditions

Francis A. Sullivan, S.J.

I shall begin by citing an intervention that Cardinal Meyer, the archbishop of Chicago, made at the Second Vatican Council. This was by no means the only time he addressed the council; in fact, Robert Trisco, who wrote the article about him in the Catholic Encyclopedia, says: "By the end of the third session Meyer had addressed the Council more often than any other American bishop and had emerged as the unrivaled intellectual leader of the hierarchy of the U.S."[1] Unfortunately, the third session was the last he attended, as he died during the interval before the fourth one.

Albert Gregory Meyer did his studies for the priesthood in Rome and was ordained there in 1926. He did not attend the Gregorian University, because the students at the North American College went to the Propaganda College for their classes until 1930. However, after ordination, he studied with the Jesuits at the Pontifical Biblical Institute, where he obtained the Licentiate in Sacred Scripture. He subsequently taught courses in Scripture at St. Francis Seminary in Milwaukee, and he continued to deepen his knowledge of the Bible throughout his life. So it is no surprise that at Vatican II he was named to the commission that drafted the Constitution on Divine Revelation, and he addressed the council more than once concerning that text. The intervention to which I refer had to do with tradition, which was treated in chapter 2. Here is what he said about it:

What I have to say in this brief intervention has to do specially with chapter 2, paragraph 8 of our schema. The whole of chapter 2 pleases me very much, and in particular the way in which paragraph 8 shows that tradition is living, is dynamic, is total, that is, it consists not only of doctrinal propositions, but also of the worship and practice of the whole Church. . . . However, this paragraph, if I have understood it correctly, . . . presents the life and worship of the Church only in its positive aspect. As I understand it, tradition, in this paragraph, extends beyond the limits of infallible magisterium. If this interpretation is correct, then this tradition is subject to the limits and failings of the pilgrim Church, which is a Church of sinners, that knows divine things "indistinctly, as in a mirror." The history of the Church offers multiple proofs of such failings, for example, the fact that the theological doctrine of the Resurrection of Christ was for a long time obscured, that moral doctrine involved an exaggerated casuistry, that piety was non-liturgical, that Sacred Scripture was neglected, and other like things. Consequently, this paragraph needs to be completed by adding words about these failings that are always possible in this life, and by proposing remedies for them. I therefore suggest to the Fathers the following formula: . . . "However, this living tradition does not make progress and increase always and in every respect. For, when the Church ponders divine things in its pilgrim state, in some respects it can fail, and in fact does fail. For this reason it carries Sacred Scripture in itself as a perpetual norm, so that it can unceasingly correct and perfect itself by conforming its life to this norm."[2]

My attention was called to this intervention of Cardinal Meyer by none other than the present Holy Father, in the commentary on chapter 2 of *Dei Verbum* that he wrote back in the late 1960s, when he was Professor Joseph Ratzinger at the University of Tübingen. There he said:

Article 8 . . . is an attempt to meet a widely expressed need for a clear and positive account of what is meant by tradition. The first section points out the total nature of tradition: primarily it means simply the many-layered yet one presence of the mystery of Christ throughout all the ages: it means the totality of the presence of Christ in this world. . . . Teaching, life and worship are named as the three ways in which tradition is handed on. It has a place not only in the explicitly traditional statements of Church doctrine, but in the unstated—and often unstatable—elements of the whole service of the Christian worship of God and the life of the Church. This is the basis of the final comprehensive formulation of tradition as the "perpetuation," the constant continuation and making present of everything that the Church is, of everything that it believes. Tradition is identified, and thus defined, with the being and faith of the Church. The danger that lurks in this statement... had been pointed out by Cardinal Meyer in an important speech on 30 September, 1964: not everything that exists in the Church must for that reason be also a legitimate tradition; in other words, not every tradition that arises in the Church is a true celebration and keeping present of the mystery of Christ. There is a distorting, as well as a legitimate, tradition.... Consequently, tradition must not be considered only affirmatively, but also critically; we have Scripture as a criterion for this indispensable criticism of tradition, and tradition must therefore always be related back to it and measured by it.... It is to be regretted that the suggestion of the American Cardinal was not, in fact, taken up.... On this point Vatican II has unfortunately not made any progress, but has more or less ignored the whole question of the criticism of tradition. There is, in fact, no explicit mention of the possibility of distorting tradition... which means that a most important side of the problem of tradition, as shown by the history of the Church—has been overlooked.[3]

In his commentary on the way the question of tradition was handled by Vatican II, Ratzinger made a positive reference to the way this same question had been treated by the Faith and Order Commission of the World Council of Churches in a conference that took place in Montréal in July 1963, between the first and second sessions of Vatican II. It is illuminating to see how the report of that conference anticipated the question raised by Meyer and Ratzinger about the need to distinguish between authentic and inauthentic traditions. The report began by distinguishing between different meanings of the word *tradition*. It said: "We speak of the *Tradition* (with a capital T), *tradition* (with a small t) and *traditions*. By *the Tradition* is meant the Gospel itself, transmitted from generation to generation in and by the Church, Christ himself present in the life of the Church. By *tradition* is meant the traditionary process. The term *traditions* is used in two senses, to indicate both the diversity of forms of expression and also what we call confessional traditions, for instance the Lutheran tradition or the Reformed tradition."[4]

The report gave a fuller explanation of what it meant by *the Tradition* in a passage that Ratzinger quoted with approval in his commentary on *Dei Verbum*. There the Faith and Order Conference had said: "Thus we can say that we exist as Christians by the Tradition of the Gospel (the *paradosis* of the *kerygma*) testified in Scripture, transmitted in and by the Church through the power of the Holy Spirit. Tradition taken in this sense is actualized in the preaching of the Word, in the administration of the Sacraments and worship, in Christian teaching and theology, and in mission and witness to Christ by the lives of the members of the Church."[5]

The report went on to speak of traditions and of their evaluation. It said:

> But this Tradition which is the work of the Holy Spirit is embodied in traditions (in the two senses of the word, both as referring to diversity in forms of expression, and in the sense of separate communions). The traditions in Christian history are distinct from, and yet connected with, the Tradition. They are the expressions and manifestations in diverse historical forms of the one truth and reality which is Christ. This evaluation of the traditions poses serious problems. For some, questions such as these are raised. Is it possible to determine more precisely what the content of the one Tradition is, and by what means? Do all traditions which claim to be Christian contain the Tradition? How can we distinguish between traditions embodying the true Tradition and merely human traditions? Where do we find the genuine Tradition, and where impoverished tradition or even distortion of Tradition? Tradition can be a faithful transmission of the Gospel, but also a distortion of it. In this ambiguity the seriousness of the problem of tradition is indicated. These questions imply a search for a criterion. This has been a main concern for the Church since the beginning.[6]

There is a remarkable agreement between the point that Cardinal Meyer raised in his intervention at the Second Vatican Council, the commentary that Joseph Ratzinger wrote on chapter 2 of *Dei Verbum,* and the report of the Faith and Order Commission of the World Council of Churches. All three agree on the necessity of distinguishing between *Tradition,* as the whole mystery of Christ as it has been handed on in the teaching, life, and worship of the church, and *traditions,* which are the particular beliefs and practices in which that mystery has been embodied in the ongoing life of the church. Obviously, such beliefs and practices must have a venerable history and be widely shared to justify speaking of them as "traditions." But the problem is, whether the venerable history and wide diffusion of a particular tradition necessarily means that this is an authentic rather than a distorting tradition; in other words, whether it is a genuine embodiment of divine *Tradition* or a merely human tradition.

Karl Rahner raised precisely this question in a commentary he wrote on the "Declaration on the Question of the Admission of Women to the Ministerial Priesthood," which was published by the Congregation for the Doctrine of the Faith in 1976. In this document, which has the Latin title *Inter insigniores,* the Congregation explained why the Catholic Church does not consider itself authorized to admit women to priestly ordination. It summed up those reasons by saying: "This practice of the Church therefore has a normative character: in the fact of conferring priestly ordination only on men, it is a question of an unbroken tradition throughout the history of the Church, universal in the East and in the West, and alert to repress abuses immediately. This norm, based on Christ's example, has been and is still observed because it is considered to conform to God's plan for his Church."[7]

Since he was dealing with a nondefinitive statement issued by the Congregation for the Doctrine of the Faith (CDF), Rahner judged himself free to raise questions about the cogency of the argument it offered for the exclusion of women from the priesthood. I invoke his discussion of this question because the CDF based its argument on the fact that this was "an unbroken tradition," and Rahner's critique involved the question whether this was a merely human tradition and not a divine tradition: that is, an element of the gospel as handed on in the teaching, life, and worship of the church. A far more authoritative statement on the question of the ordination of women was to be made by Pope John Paul II ten years after Rahner had gone to his reward, and it is not my intention to discuss that question in its present state. I am interested in Rahner's insistence on the necessity of distinguishing between divine and human traditions. For instance, he said:

> If the Declaration appeals to an uninterrupted tradition, this appeal is not necessarily and justifiably an appeal to an absolutely and definitively binding tradition, an appeal to a tradition which simply presents and transmits a "divine" revelation in the strict sense, since there is obviously a purely human tradition in the Church which offers no guarantee of truth even if it has long been undisputed and taken for granted. With this Declaration, which has an authentic but not defining character, the fundamental question is whether this appeal is to a "divine" or a merely human tradition.[8]
> It does not seem to be proved that the actual behavior of Jesus and the Apostles implies a norm of divine revelation in the strict sense of the term. This practice [of ordaining only men to the priesthood] even it if existed for a long time and without being questioned, can certainly be understood as a "human" tradition like other traditions in the Church which were once unquestioned, had existed for a long time and nevertheless became obsolete as a result of sociological and cultural change.[9]

The conclusion I draw at this point is that the critical observation that Cardinal Meyer made about tradition in his intervention at Vatican II is one that two of the most respected Catholic theologians of our time, Joseph Ratzinger and Karl Rahner, as well as the Faith and Order Commission of the World Council of Churches, have recognized as raising a crucial question: how can one be sure that particular traditions are authentic embodiments of the Tradition? To put the question in Rahner's terms, how can one be sure that a tradition that was unquestioned and existed for a long time will not become obsolete? Rahner evidently takes for granted that this has actually happened, but in this context, he does not give any examples of particular traditions that have been recognized as inconsistent with the Tradition and have been set aside.

But there certainly are examples of Catholic traditions that have become obsolete in the course of time. Judge John T. Noonan described several such traditions in the Erasmus Lectures he gave at Notre Dame that have been published in his book, *A Church That Can and Cannot Change.*[10] Noonan's thesis is that while the Catholic Church cannot change in holding to the deposit of faith, its moral doctrine has changed with regard to slavery, usury, religious liberty, and the dissolubility of nonsacramental marriages. I shall focus on two of these: slavery and religious liberty. For many centuries, the Catholic Church held slavery to be a morally acceptable social institution, and it practiced and authorized the coercive suppression of unorthodox beliefs, even by the execution of obstinate heretics. I agree with John Noonan that we have good reason to present these as examples of long-standing traditions that can no longer be described as expressions of the belief and practice of the Catholic Church.

In my discussion of these two examples of change in the church's moral doctrine, I shall take into account the contrary position that Avery Cardinal Dulles has defended in the lengthy review of Noonan's book that he published in *First Things.*[11] The title "Development or Reversal?" that Dulles gave to his review sums up his thesis, which is that in regard to those traditions, one can speak of development but not of the reversal of church doctrine.

Noonan treats slavery as the prime case of change in moral doctrine. He observes that no condemnation of this institution as immoral is found in scripture or in the writings of the great medieval theologians or in those of such an authority on moral questions as St. Alphonsus Liguori. In the colonial period, several popes did condemn the unjust enslavement of innocent people, and in 1839, Pope Gregory XVI condemned the slave trade as "that inhuman commerce by which Negroes, as if they were not human beings but mere brute animals, having been reduced to slavery in ways that are contrary to the laws of justice and humanity, are bought, sold, and subjected to the hardest and most exhausting labors."[12] It strikes me that the pope's description of the indignities to which slaves are subjected could well be understood as a papal condemnation of slavery as an institution, but two of the most respected Catholic bishops in the United States at that time, John England, Bishop of Charleston, and Francis Patrick Kenrick, Coadjutor Bishop of Philadelphia, insisted that while the pope had clearly condemned the slave trade, he had not condemned slavery as it was then practiced in the United States. In fact, in the treatise on moral theology Kenrick published in 1860, when he was archbishop of Baltimore, he began his chapter on slavery by saying: "Since by the law of nature all men are equal, no one is by nature the master of another; however, by the law of nations not only the power of government, but also the power of ownership is allowed to men over other men: and this is ratified by the Old Testament."[13] He raised and answered a question that might have troubled the conscience of Catholic slave owners in view of the papal condemnation of the slave trade: "May the masters continue to hold their slaves, seeing that it was by injustice that their forebears were brought here from Africa?" His answer was "Yes, because the defect of their title to ownership should be held as remedied by the very long lapse of time, since otherwise the condition of society would remain forever uncertain, with the gravest danger of tumults. No doubt, those who carried them off by force committed sin; but to hold their descendants in slavery does not seem unjust; since they were born into a condition which they cannot change."[14]

Kenrick's answer to this question exemplifies the fact that Catholic moral theologians up to his day had accepted the principle that there were just titles to the ownership of persons as slaves and that the morality of slavery depended on the possession of such a just title. Among such "just titles" were the capture of "enemies of the faith" in war and enslavement as punishment for grave crimes. The absence of such a just title explains the condemnation by Pope Gregory XVI of the "enslavement of innocent people" that provided the basis of the slave trade across the Atlantic. Kenrick agreed that "those who carried them off by force committed sin," since they had no just title to do this. But for their descendants another title came into play: that children born of a slave woman were the property of her owner. Neither Kenrick nor other Catholic moralists of his day were asking the question whether there really could be any just title for the ownership of one human person by another. Some did try to evade this question by claiming that the slaveholder did not really own the persons of his slaves, but only their labor and its fruit. Among other problems with this artificial solution was the accepted principle that the slaveholder owned the fruit of his female slave's womb.

It was only in the course of the nineteenth century that a radical change took place in public opinion regarding the institution of slavery, which resulted in its abolition, first in Europe and then in North and South America. Bernhard Häring has explained this change in the following way.

> At all times there have been unacceptable flaws and shortcomings in the existing socio-economic order, but only a critical age brings the situation to full consciousness. The question is one of diagnosis and therapy. The lack of a radical diagnosis leads to an inadequate approach to therapy, alleviating only the symptoms without removing the causes.... Only under the pressure of the humanist movement and changing socio-economic conditions did slavery become a *conscious* social problem calling for radical therapy to remove the causes by absolutely abolishing and by proclaiming the equal dignity and right to freedom of all people. For believers, it is humiliating to know how irrelevant in this social process was the contribution of the official church and the theologians.[15]

The question at issue between Judge Noonan and Cardinal Dulles is whether now, when more than a century has passed since slavery was abolished in most of the world, the Catholic Church has officially condemned the institution of slavery as gravely immoral. Noonan found a condemnation of slavery in a document of the Second Vatican Council, in the *Catechism of the Catholic Church*, and in statements made by Pope John Paul II. Noonan first invoked the council's Pastoral Constitution on the Church in the Modern World, which in no. 27 included slavery in a list of social ills it called *"probra"* (shameful, infamous). Noonan commented: "'Shameful' was not the strongest of theological epithets. It was weaker than 'evil,' and much weaker than 'intrinsically evil.' Nonetheless, put in the same box with homicide and genocide, slavery was comprehensively condemned."[16]

His second witness is no. 2414 of the *Catechism*, which says: "The seventh commandment forbids acts or enterprises that for any reason—selfish or ideological, commercial or totalitarian—lead to the enslavement of human beings, to their being bought, sold and exchanged like merchandise, in disregard of their personal dignity. It is a sin against the dignity of persons and their fundamental rights to reduce them by violence to their productive value or to a source of profit." Noonan found this text less than satisfactory, since it condemned acts that lead to enslavement, rather than the institution of slavery as such.

While Noonan recognized that neither Vatican II nor the *Catechism* had explicitly condemned the institution of slavery itself as morally evil, he was satisfied that Pope John Paul II did explicitly condemn it on two occasions. The first papal statement was made on February 2, 1992, on the island of Gorée, Senegal, where France had once collected slaves for its Caribbean colonies.

There, in the former "House of Slaves," John Paul said: "It is fitting that there be confessed in all truth and humility this sin of man against man, this sin of man against God."[17] The second papal statement was made in the Encyclical *Veritatis splendor*, in which Pope John Paul II quoted the list of things that *Gaudium et spes* had called "infamous" and described them all as "acts which are intrinsically evil."[18] Judge Noonan is satisfied that by declaring slavery to be intrinsically evil, Pope John Paul has condemned "the intrinsic character of a relationship in which one person bought, sold, mortgaged, and transferred another person without regard to that person's will or education or vocation, in which the one owned was a chattel of the owner."[19] In other words, he is convinced that there has been a reversal of the Catholic moral tradition that, while it had condemned the unjust enslavement of innocent people and the abuse of slaves, had never condemned the institution itself by which one person could lawfully be the property of another.

Cardinal Dulles focused his critique of Noonan's thesis on the conclusions he had drawn from those two statements of Pope John Paul II. With regard to what the pope had said at the House of Slaves in Senegal, Dulles commented: "If we look up the quotation, we will find that the pope is here speaking of the slave trade, which had repeatedly been condemned. Far from changing the doctrine, John Paul is explicitly reaffirming the position of Pope Pius II, whom he quotes as having declared in 1492 that the slave trade was an enormous crime, *magnm scelus*."[20] With regard to the inclusion of slavery in the list of things that John Paul II called "intrinsically evil," Dulles observes that the list includes such things as subhuman living conditions and degrading conditions of work, and whatever holds for slavery would have to be said of those things as well.[21] I agree with Dulles here and would add that to describe those things as "acts which are intrinsically evil," one would have to mean the sinful acts that reduce people to such conditions. From this, it would follow that Pope John Paul has not clearly gone beyond what previous popes had condemned, namely, the unjust enslavement of innocent people. I think Dulles is correct in arguing that it is not evident that in *Evangelium vitae* John Paul II has condemned the institution of slavery itself as intrinsically evil. He further insists: "Neither the *Catechism of the Catholic Church* nor the *Compendium of the Social Doctrine of the Church*, in their discussions of slavery, speaks so absolutely." Dulles concludes: "For all these reasons, Noonan's case for a reversal of doctrine is unconvincing."[22]

I think it is true that the Catholic Church has not yet explicitly declared slavery in itself, as a social institution, to be gravely immoral. However, I suggest that there is another way of proposing the question whether there has been a reversal of the long-standing Catholic tradition that held the institution of slavery to be morally unobjectionable. One has to remember that this meant teaching and believing that there was nothing morally wrong in itself about one person owning another person as a slave; having the right to the fruit of the slave's labor with only food and shelter as compensation; the right to decide what education, if any, the slave would have; the right to the ownership of the slave's children; the right to sell one's slaves and their children to another person; and so forth. What I will argue is that even though it is not certain that John Paul II has condemned the social institution of slavery as intrinsically evil, the long-standing tradition that slavery was morally acceptable has been effectively reversed by the development of Catholic doctrine on the dignity of the human person. In other words, I contend that the affirmation by the Catholic Church of the dignity of the human person, and of the inalienable rights that follow from that dignity, has made it logically impossible to maintain that the Catholic Church still considers morally unobjectionable the social institution that authorizes the buying, selling, and ownership of human persons as slaves.

I shall document the affirmation by the Catholic Church of the dignity of the human person, and of the inalienable rights that follow from that dignity, from the official teaching of the church as expressed in documents of the Second Vatican Council, in the *Catechism of the Catholic Church*,[23] and in the *Compendium of the Social Doctrine of the Church*.[24]

In the section of *Gaudium et spes* in which Vatican II described slavery as infamous, it also named it among things that are "offenses against human dignity" (27). In the previous section, it had said: "There is a growing awareness of the sublime dignity of human persons, who stand above all things and whose rights and duties are universal and inviolable." Among those rights it named: "the right freely to choose their state of life and set up a family, the right to education, work, to their good name, to respect, to proper knowledge, the right to act according to the dictates of conscience and to safeguard their privacy, the right to just freedom, including the freedom of religion" (26). It is obvious how many of those rights were denied to slaves and how grievous was the offense against human dignity by their denial. The council drew the practical conclusion: "It is for public and private organizations to be at the service of the dignity and destiny of humanity; let them spare no effort to banish every vestige of social and political slavery and to safeguard basic human rights under every political system" (29).

I would call attention to the fact that here the council had spoken of a "growing awareness of the sublime dignity of human persons." This "growing awareness" was also affirmed in the very first sentence of the council's Declaration on Religious Freedom (*Dignitatis humanae*), which said: "People nowadays are becoming increasingly conscious of the dignity of the human person" (1). In the same vein, having said that "revelation makes known the dignity of the human person in all its fullness," it went on to say that the demands of this dignity "have become more fully known to human reason through centuries of experience"(9). The idea that there has been a development in people's recognition of their human dignity is also expressed in the statement that "the leaven of the Gospel has long been at work in people's minds and has contributed greatly to a wider recognition by them in the course of time of their dignity as persons" (12).

While it is true that in *Dignitatis humanae* the council was explicitly concerned with religious freedom, it also spoke of the more universal demands of the dignity of the human person, as when it said: "The common good of society consists in the sum total of those conditions of social life which enable people to achieve a fuller measure of perfection with greater ease. It consists especially in safeguarding the rights and duties of the human person.... The protection and promotion of the inviolable rights of the human person is an essential duty of every civil authority" (6).

The Catechism of the Catholic Church has a chapter titled "The Dignity of the Human Person" that contains the following statements: "The dignity of the human person is rooted in his creation in the image and likeness of God" (1700). "By virtue of his soul and his spiritual powers of intellect and will, man is endowed with freedom, an 'outstanding manifestation of the divine image'" (1705). "Freedom is exercised in relationships between human beings. Every human person, created in the image of God, has the natural right to be recognized as a free and responsible person. All owe to each other this duty of respect" (1738). The *Catechism* does not mention slavery in this context, but it is obvious that slavery, of its very nature, denies to human persons their natural right to be recognized as free persons. As we have seen, the *Catechism*, in no. 2414, treated the question of slavery in such a way that its statement can be interpreted to mean that it did not condemn slavery as such but the enslavement of innocent people, something that several popes had condemned long ago. On the other hand, in the same place, the *Catechism* described practices to which slaves are inevitably subject, such as "being bought, sold and exchanged like merchandise," as done "in disregard for their personal dignity." It hardly needs to be said that such treatment is a denial of the respect that all owe to other human persons.

The *Compendium of the Social Doctrine of the Church* was drawn up at the request of Pope John Paul II by the Pontifical Council for Justice and Peace to provide a concise and up-to-date overview of the social teaching of the Catholic Church. This social teaching had been expressed in documents of varying magisterial authority, from council documents and papal encyclicals to documents issued by offices of the Roman Curia and papal addresses to particular audiences.

On the basis of these documents, the *Compendium* sets forth the fundamental elements of the church's social doctrine. I believe that the following citations further substantiate my claim that the long-standing tradition that slavery was morally acceptable has been effectively reversed by the development of Catholic doctrine on the dignity of the human person and the rights that follow from it.

The foundational role that the dignity of the human person plays in the current social doctrine of the Catholic Church is brought out in the following citations from the *Compendium*:[25]

- "The Church . . . intends with this document on her social doctrine to propose to all men and women . . . an integral and solidary humanism capable of creating a new social, economic and political order, founded on the dignity and freedom of every human person." (19)
- "The dignity of the human person is the foundation of all the other principles and content of the Church's social doctrine. . . . In the course of history and with the light of the Spirit, the Church has wisely reflected within her own tradition of faith and has been able to provide an ever more accurate foundation and shape to these principles, progressively explaining them in the attempt to respond coherently to the demands of the times and to the continuous developments of social life." (160)
- "The movement toward the identification and proclamation of human rights is one of the most significant attempts to respond effectively to the inescapable demands of human dignity. The Church sees in these rights the extraordinary opportunity that our modern times offer, through the affirmation of these rights, for more effectively recognizing human dignity and universally promoting it as a characteristic inscribed by God the Creator in his creature." (152)
- "The roots of human rights are to be found in the dignity that belongs to each human being. This dignity, inherent in human life and equal in every person, is perceived and understood first of all by reason. The ultimate source of human rights is not found in the mere will of human beings . . . but in man himself and in God his Creator." (153)

That the Catholic Church esteems the right to freedom as primary among the human rights that are rooted in human dignity, is evident in the following citations:

- "All social values are inherent in the dignity of the human person, whose authentic development they foster. Essentially, these values are truth, freedom, justice, love." (197)

- "Freedom is the highest sign in man of his being made in the divine image and, consequently, is a sign of the sublime dignity of every human person. . . . Every human person, created in the image of God, has the natural right to be recognized as a free and responsible being. All owe to each other this duty of respect. The right to the exercise of freedom . . . is an inalienable requirement of the dignity of the human person." (199)
- "The value of freedom, as an expression of the singularity of each human person, is respected when every member of society is permitted to fulfil his personal vocation . . . to choose his state of life and, as far as possible, his line of work. . . ." (200)

The following text shows that the Catholic Church now sees the denial of the right of a human person to freedom as a "social sin":

- "Social is every sin against the rights of the human person . . . every sin against the freedom of others, every sin against the dignity and honor of one's neighbor." (118)

While one does not find in the *Compendium* an explicit condemnation of the institution of slavery as an example of social sin, the following references to slavery make it clear that it is seen as a prime example of the violation of human rights and human dignity:

- "The solemn proclamation of human rights is contradicted by a painful reality of violations . . . the spreading on a virtual worldwide dimension of ever new forms of slavery such as trafficking in human beings. . . ." (158)
- "The Church's social doctrine condemns the increase in 'the exploitation of children in the workplace in conditions of veritable slavery.' This exploitation represents a serious violation of human dignity, with which every person, 'no matter how small or how seemingly unimportant in utilitarian terms,' is endowed." (296)

I believe that these citations from documents of the teaching authority of the Catholic Church provide more than sufficient proof that the long-standing Catholic tradition that viewed slavery as morally acceptable has been reversed by the Catholic Church's recognition of the inalienable dignity of the human person and the right to freedom that is primary among the human rights demanded by that dignity. At the same time, I believe one must say that until now this reversal by the Catholic Church of its traditional judgment with regard to the morality of the institution of slavery is rather implicit than explicit.

This is not the case, however, with regard to the reversal of the Catholic tradition according to which the government of a Catholic nation had the right and duty to use its coercive power to prohibit the profession of beliefs the church judged to be heretical. The Second Vatican Council, in its Declaration on Religious Freedom (*Dignitatis humanae*), made the following statement that makes it clear that the Catholic Church now rejects the use of coercive power to prevent people from professing their religious beliefs, whatever they may be.

> This Vatican Synod declares that the human person has a right to religious freedom. This freedom means that all men are to be immune from coercion on the part of individuals or of social groups and of any human power, in such wise that in matters religious no one is to be forced to act in a manner contrary to his own beliefs, nor is anyone to be restrained from acting in accordance with his own beliefs, whether privately or publicly, whether alone or in association with others, within due limits. The Synod further declares that the right to religious freedom has its foundation in the very dignity of the human person, as this dignity is known through the revealed Word of God and by reason itself. The right of the human person to religious freedom is to be recognized in the constitutional law whereby society is governed. Thus it is to become a civil right. (2)

The council acknowledged that "in the life of the People of God as it has made its pilgrim way through the vicissitudes of human history, there have at times appeared ways of acting which were less in accord with the spirit of the gospel and even opposed to it. Nevertheless the doctrine of the Church that no one is to be coerced into faith has always stood firm" (12). If one were to ask why it is only now that the church has recognized that coercive power should also not be used to prevent people from professing religious beliefs of which the church disapproved, an answer is suggested by the council's statement: "The leaven of the gospel has long been about its quiet work in the minds of men. To it is due in great measure the fact that in the course of time men have come more widely to recognize their dignity as persons, and the conviction has grown stronger that in religious matters the person in society is to be kept free from all manner of human coercion" (12). I understand this to mean that the development of Catholic doctrine regarding human dignity and the rights that are based on it has brought about the reversal of a tradition that is now recognized as having denied a freedom founded on human dignity.

In his review of Judge Noonan's book, Cardinal Dulles says that on this question there has been a change in teaching that might be called, in the language of John Paul II, a "necessary and prudent adaptation."[26] Dulles interprets it to mean that "the Church has applied the unchanging principles of the right to religious freedom and the duty to uphold religious truth to the conditions of an individualist age, in which all societies are religiously pluralist. Under such circumstances, the establishment of religion becomes the exception rather than the rule. But the principle of noncoercion in matters of faith remains constant."[27] It seems to me that it is far more than a "prudent adaptation" when the principle of noncoercion of consciences in matters of faith is finally understood to exclude the coercion the Catholic Church practiced and authorized for centuries toward people suspected or guilty of heresy.

I have written a book about another Catholic tradition to which the Second Vatican Council gave an interpretation that differed remarkably from the interpretation given to it by medieval popes and councils: I speak of the doctrine that there is no salvation outside the Catholic Church.[28] The medieval understanding of that doctrine was graphically expressed by the Council of Florence in 1442 in the profession of faith it prescribed for the Jacobites, which said: "The Holy Roman Church firmly believes, professes and preaches that no one remaining outside the Catholic Church, not only pagans but also Jews or heretics or schismatics, can become partakers of eternal life; but they will go to the eternal fire prepared for the devil and his angels, unless before the end of their life they are joined to it."[29] Vatican II, on the contrary, made it clear that the only persons who would be excluded from salvation for not belonging to the Catholic Church are those who, knowing full well that membership in the Catholic Church was necessary for their own salvation, would still choose not to belong to it.[30] For everyone else, salvation is possible without actual membership in the Catholic Church, provided they correspond with the grace that God does not fail to make available to them through other means.[31] Among such means of grace, the council mentioned the other Christian churches and ecclesial communities, saying that the Holy Spirit uses them for the salvation of their members.[32] One can hardly deny that here a long-standing Catholic tradition has undergone profound change.

I shall now mention two particular Catholic traditions that are currently undergoing such rethinking and reassessment as to indicate that they are in the process of being changed. The first of these is the long-standing belief that infants who die without having been baptized will never share the supernatural happiness of Heaven but will instead enjoy a state of natural happiness called Limbo. There are really two beliefs here: the more fundamental one is that the state of original sin into which infants are born involves inherited guilt, which deserves punishment unless the guilt is removed either by baptism or by the desire of it. Pope Innocent III, in 1201, explained that the punishment that is due to the inherited guilt of original sin alone is the privation of the beatific vision of God.[33] Since infants are not capable of the desire of baptism and hence cannot be saved by such a desire, the conclusion was drawn that infants dying unbaptized would not enjoy the supernatural happiness of Heaven. The other belief, which was shared by St. Thomas Aquinas, is that such infants would enjoy a state of happiness in harmony with their natural spiritual faculties; this came to be known as Limbo. The magisterium has never declared the Limbo solution to be the true one, but it defended it against the Jansenists who claimed that it was heretical.[34] It has certainly been a long-standing Catholic tradition.

However, during the past half-century, a number of Catholic theologians have suggested answers to the question of how infants could be freed from the guilt of original sin without actually receiving the sacrament of baptism. While none of these answers has been generally accepted, there is a broadly shared sense that the Limbo solution is not really in harmony with our more fundamental belief in the goodness and mercy of God. It would now seem that this view is reaching the status of a consensus in the Catholic Church. That this is the case can be seen in what one finds in the *Catechism of the Catholic Church*, where it speaks of children who have died without baptism. It makes no mention of Limbo. Rather, it says: "the Church can only entrust them to the mercy of God, as she does in her funeral rites for them. Indeed, the great mercy of God . . . and Jesus' great tenderness toward children . . . allow us to hope that there is a way of salvation for children who have died without baptism."[35] That Pope John Paul II shared this view is clear from what he said, toward the end of his Encyclical *Evangelium vitae*, when he addressed himself to women who have had an abortion. Encouraging them to humility and repentance, he said: "The Father of mercies is ready to give you his forgiveness and his peace in the Sacrament of Reconciliation. You will come to understand that nothing is definitively lost and you will also be able to ask forgiveness from your child, who is now living in the Lord."[36]

Another example of a Catholic tradition that is undergoing change is one that has been not only a matter of belief but also a matter of practice by the popes themselves when they were the sovereigns of the Papal States. It has to do with the use of capital punishment. In the past, the Catholic moral tradition has justified the death penalty as a means to protect society from the danger that those guilty of crimes like murder would commit more such crimes if they were allowed to live. This reason was also believed to justify the death penalty for heresy and for witchcraft, on the grounds that obstinate heretics and persons who were believed to be in league with the devil would continue to cause great harm to Christian society if they were not put to death. The tradition that saw capital punishment as a just penalty for obstinate heresy or for witchcraft was set aside several centuries ago, along with the tradition that justified the use of torture to compel persons to confess themselves guilty of such crimes.

The recent development on this issue has to do with the question whether the need to protect society from the danger that criminals will commit more crimes continues to justify capital punishment, in view of the capacity of modern states to protect society without recourse to the death penalty. Pope John Paul II expressed his judgment on this issue in his Encyclical *Evangelium vitae*, where he said:

> On this matter [of the death penalty] there is a growing tendency, both in the Church and in civil society, to demand that it be applied in a very limited way or even that it be abolished completely. The problem must be viewed in the context of a system of penal justice ever more in line with human dignity and thus, in the end, with God's plan for man and society. The primary purpose of the punishment which society inflicts is to redress the disorder caused by the offence. Public authority must redress the violation of personal and social rights by imposing on the offender an adequate punishment for the crime, as a condition for the offender to regain the exercise of his or her freedom. In this way authority also fulfills the purpose of defending public order and ensuring people's safety, while at the same time offering the offender an incentive and help to change his or her behavior and be rehabilitated. It is clear that, for these purposes to be achieved, *the nature and extent of the punishment* must be carefully evaluated and decided upon, and ought not go to the extreme of executing the offender except in cases of absolute necessity: in other words, when it would not be possible otherwise to defend society. Today, however, as a result of steady improvements in the organization of the penal system, such cases are very rare, if not practically non-existent.[37]

I would call attention especially to two points in the pope's statement. First, this problem must be viewed in the context of a system of penal justice ever more in line with human dignity. Second, recourse to capital punishment is not justified if there is another way of preventing the criminal from committing further crime. A long-standing tradition is undergoing change for two reasons, both of which reflect progress in human society: spiritual progress in the sense of a growing respect for human dignity, shown also in the way that criminals are treated, and material progress in the increased ability of states to protect their citizens from dangerous criminals without recourse to the death penalty.

This leads me to some reflections on factors that have brought about the recognition that some long-standing traditions in the church were not authentic expressions of the Word of God as handed down in the teaching, life, and worship of the church but were really human traditions. As Karl Rahner observed, there have been human traditions in the church that were unquestioned and existed for a long time and nevertheless became obsolete as a result of cultural change. A cultural change, a shared human development toward a greater respect for the dignity and rights of persons, is a key factor in making obsolete what had been long-standing Catholic traditions regarding the moral acceptability of slavery and the obligation of Catholic rulers to prevent the propagation of heresy. While it took an amazingly long time for this to happen, it has finally become a common conviction that it is gravely offensive to the dignity and rights of human persons to be the property of others or to be deprived of their freedom to follow their conscience in religious matters. Growth of respect for human dignity has surely been a major factor in the rejection of the use of torture by the church and by many governments. While it is perhaps too soon to speak of a consensus in the Catholic Church that capital punishment is incompatible with human dignity, there is, I believe, growing agreement with the judgment of Pope John Paul II that a system of penal justice must be ever more in line with human dignity and that a criminal should be executed only if this is really necessary for the protection of society.

Another factor that has led to change is the application of what Vatican II called the hierarchy of truths: the recognition that some truths stand closer to the foundation of our faith than do others. I would see this principle operative in the changes that have taken place with regard to the traditions that excluded non-Christians and unbaptized infants from salvation. The necessity of baptism for salvation is an important truth of faith. But it is not so close to the foundation of our faith as is the truth of God's love and mercy and his universal salvific will.

There is no doubt that during the many centuries when Catholics were taught that adults who died outside the Catholic Church would go to Hell and that infants who died unbaptized would go to Limbo, Catholics believed in God's mercy and in his universal salvific will. But evidently there was no general recognition of any incompatibility between those beliefs and the exclusion of the unbaptized from eternal salvation. What has happened in modern times is the growth of a conviction among Catholic theologians that the exclusion of the unbaptized from salvation is incompatible with God's universal salvific will and that this latter truth is so close to the foundation of our faith that there must be a way to understand the fate of the unbaptized that does not conflict with it. Gradually, this conviction has become generally shared by the faithful and confirmed by the magisterium. So we are dealing with a case of the development of doctrine, in this case not affirming a doctrine, as took place with regard to the Immaculate Conception, but questioning the long-standing tradition about the exclusion of unbaptized infants from Heaven.

The final point I wish to make is that the same gift of the Holy Spirit that enabled the Catholic faithful to reach a positive consensus on the doctrine of the Immaculate Conception is likewise inclining them toward a consensus that the tradition about Limbo is not consonant with what we believe about God's mercy. This gift of the Holy Spirit is the sense of faith, which Vatican II describes as a supernatural gift aroused and sustained by the spirit of truth, which characterizes the people of God as a whole. It is by virtue of this sense of faith, the council goes on to say, that God's people "clings without fail to the faith once delivered to the saints, penetrates it more deeply by accurate insights, and applies it more thoroughly to life."[38]

Here I shall focus on the idea that the supernatural sense of faith enables the people of God to arrive at accurate insights into what they believe. In this context, one can invoke St. Thomas Aquinas's notion of connaturality. He applies to the believer's capacity to make right judgments about matters of faith what he says more generally about a virtuous person's capacity to make right judgments about matters pertaining to virtue. He says that the practice of a virtue, such as chastity, creates a certain "connaturality" with what is proper to that virtue, so that a truly chaste person will instinctively recognize whether something is in accord with chastity or contrary to it. So also, he says, the divinely infused "light of faith" brings it about that faithful people assent to what is in accord with their faith and reject what conflicts with it.[39]

I conclude that what St. Thomas calls the "light of faith" and what Vatican II calls the "sense of faith" will lead the people of God not only to arrive at positive insights into what they believe but also to reject what is not consonant with their faith. Hence I would identify the sense of faith as the key factor that explains how the whole body of the Catholic faithful, including the theologians and the magisterium, were able to arrive at a consensus that certain beliefs and practices that had been long-standing traditions in the Catholic Church were not in harmony with more fundamental truths and therefore do not really belong to authentic Catholic Tradition.

I end with a question about the possible application of this principle in the future. Let us suppose that as the Catholic Church continues, with rare exceptions, to ordain to the priesthood only single men who pledge to remain celibate, at some point in the future it will be obvious that the continually declining number of priests is causing an ever greater number of the Catholic faithful to be deprived of the weekly celebration of the Eucharist. Will reflection on this situation, in the light of the sense of faith, lead to a consensus that whatever value the Catholic tradition of requiring priests to be celibate may have had in the past, this tradition is now in conflict with a fundamental element of Catholic faith and practice and must be set aside?

NOTES

1. R. F. Trisco, "Meyer, Albert Gregory," *New Catholic Encyclopedia*, 2nd ed., 15 vols. (Washington, DC: Catholic University of America, 2002), 9:589.

2. *Acta Synodalia Concilii Vaticani Secundi*, III/3, 150–151 (my translation).

3. Joseph Ratzinger, "The Transmission of Divine Revelation," in *Commentary on the Documents of Vatican II*, ed. Herbert Vorgrimler (New York: Herder & Herder, 1969) 3:184–185, 193.

4. P. C. Rodger and Lukas Vischer, eds., *Fourth World Conference on Faith and Order*, Montréal 1963 (New York: Association Press, 1964), 50.

5. Ibid., 52.

6. Ibid.

7. "Declaration on the Question of the Admission of Women to the Ministerial Priesthood" (*Inter insigniores*), *Origins* 6, no. 33 (February 3, 1977): 517–524, at 522.

8. Karl Rahner, "Women and the Priesthood," in *Theological Investigations*, 20:37–38.

9. Ibid., 45.

10. John T. Noonan, *A Church That Can and Cannot Change* (Notre Dame, IN: University of Notre Dame Press, 2005).

11. Avery Cardinal Dulles, "Development or Reversal?" *First Things* (October 2005): 53–61.

12. Apostolic Constitution, *In Supremo Apostolatus fastigio*, December 3, 1839. Denzinger-Schönmetzer, *Enchiridion*, 2745–2746.

13. Francis Patrick Kenrick, Archbishop of Baltimore, *Theologia Moralis* (Malines, Belgium: Dessain, 1860), 1:164 (my translation).

14. Ibid., 1:167.

15.Bernhard Häring, *Free and Faithful in Christ* (New York: Seabury, 1978), 3:306–307.

16. Noonan, *A Church That Can and Cannot Change*, 120.

17. Ibid., 122.

18. John Paul II, Encyclical *Veritatis splendor*, no. 80.

19. Noonan, *A Church That Can and Cannot Change*, 6.

20. Dulles, "Development or Reversal?" 56.

21. Ibid., 57.

22. Ibid.

23. *Catechism of the Catholic Church*, 2nd ed., rev. in accordance with the official Latin text promulgated by Pope John Paul II (Città del Vaticano: Libreria Editrice Vaticana, 1997).

24. Pontifical Council for Justice and Peace, *Compendium of the Social Doctrine of the Church* (Dublin: Veritas, 2005).

25. The numbers that follow the citations refer to the numbered sections of the *Compendium*.

26. Dulles, "Development or Reversal?" 60.

27. Ibid.

28. Francis A. Sullivan, S.J., *Salvation outside the Church? Tracing the History of the Catholic Response* (New York: Paulist, 1992).

29. Jacques Dupuis, ed., *The Christian Faith in the Doctrinal Documents of the Catholic Church*, 7th ed. (New York: Alba House, 2001), no. 1005, p. 421.

30. *Lumen gentium* 14.

31. *Lumen gentium* 16.

32. Decree on Ecumenism (*Unitatis redintegratio*), 3.

33. Denzinger/Schönmetzer, *Enchiridion Symbolorum*, no. 780.

34. Ibid., no. 2626.

35. *Catechism*, no. 1261.

36. *Evangelium vitae*, no. 99. There can be no doubt that Pope John Paul wrote the sentence we have quoted. It is certainly in his encyclical as it was originally published by the Vatican Press. However, it is not in the official Latin text published in *Acta Apostolicae Sedis*. In its place, the following sentence has been substituted: "You can commend your child with hope to the same Father and His Mercy." (AAS 87 (1995) 515.) Since this emendation was made while Pope John Paul II was still living, one can presume that he agreed to the change. What he had said in the encyclical suggested that the mother could be sure that her child was now enjoying the vision of God. It seems that he must have agreed that the mother should rather be encouraged to hope that this was the case.

37. *Evangelium vitae*, no. 56.

38. *Lumen gentium*, no. 12. (Translation by Joseph Gallagher in edition of the Documents of Vatican II by Walter Abbott, S.J.)

39. *Summa theologiae* 2a 2ae, q.2, a.3, ad 2.

5

Something There Is That Doesn't Love a Law

Canon Law and Its Discontents

John P. Beal

In the twenty-five years since a revised Code of Canon Law was promulgated by primatial act of Pope John Paul II, ordinary Catholics, and even many non-Catholics, have had more exposure to the intricacies of canon law than most people had during the entire sixty-five years the 1917 Code of Canon Law was the primary law governing the Catholic Church. Canonical penal law has been discussed frequently in media reporting on sexual abuse of minors by Catholic priests, and lawsuits stemming from this abuse have created a cottage industry for canon lawyers to serve as expert witnesses testifying about what canon law does and does not say about sexual offenses and their prosecution. Canon law governing the ownership and administration of church property has figured prominently in bankruptcy cases involving Catholic dioceses, in efforts of dioceses to restructure themselves civilly to shield church entities from tort liability, in occasional public conflicts between bishops and parish trustees, and in less than occasional revelations of embezzlement or misappropriation of church funds. At a more personal level, about 40,000 couples per year have experienced the tender mercies of the canonical judicial process as they seek declarations of nullity of their failed marriages, and thousands more have struggled with the canonical administrative process as they have sought to save their parishes from closure or merger, to retain beloved pastors, or to effect the removal of those who have worn out their welcome.

Despite this widespread exposure, ordinary people, whether Catholic or not, often experience canon law as remote from their normal experience of legal and moral norms. This experience of the remoteness of canon law from the everyday life of the faithful is not, however, unique to the early years of the twenty-first century. Already in the fourteenth century, Geoffrey Chaucer could, without fear of seeming implausible to his readers, use the fictional papal dissolution of the marriage of Walter and Griselda in "The Clerk's Tale" to parody the canonical annulment process as "a fiction, obtained as an adjunct to a hoax."[1] Today, many observers of the workings of canon law both inside and outside marriage tribunals would concur with Chaucer's "unspoken implications" that its operations "are the magical product of an incomprehensible process in which legal reasons play no part and [clerical] discretion is absolute."[2]

Canon Law and Its Discontents

Of course, canon law is neither the first nor the only legal system to suffer the slings and arrows of outraged, and sometimes outrageous, critics. From Dick the Butcher's simple solution to the injustice that often masqueraded as royal justice ("The first thing we do, let's kill all the lawyers")[3] in Shakespeare's *Henry VI* to Kafka's grotesque depiction of the administration of justice in a bureaucratic state in *The Trial*, secular legal systems have frequently been pilloried for protecting the interests of the privileged at the expense of real justice for the many, and lawyers have been the object of disdain and the butt of countless jokes. American culture has been particularly inhospitable to law and lawyers. Although commentators as early as Tocqueville have noted that Americans have long displayed a quasi-religious reverence for the law in the abstract and felt "a sort of paternal love for it,"[4] they have also exhibited considerable disdain for law in the concrete and even glorified the outlaw.[5] At the root of this ambivalence toward law is a tendency, deeply rooted in the American psyche and articulated first in terms of eighteenth-century moral-sense philosophy and later in the quintessentially American philosophy of pragmatism, to distinguish, and at times divorce, the head, the faculty for scientific knowledge, from the heart, the faculty for moral sentiments. When compared with the benevolence, friendship, and justice that flow from the heart, law, which is "pre-eminently an affair of the head," is often experienced as inauthentic, artificial, inhumane, and, at times, dishonest.[6] It is not surprising, therefore, that canon law has fared no better in the popular imagination than its secular counterparts. Indeed, since religious faith is often considered the most deeply personal of the habits of the heart, canon law, which claims the right to regulate religious behavior and to grant or deny access to God through the sacraments, can easily seem not only remote from, but at times an obstacle to, authentic religious experience.

The Catholic Church has not been immune to the destabilizing impact of the cultural storms that have been buffeting Western societies since the 1960s. These upheavals with their often antinomian tendencies brought into the open a systematic crisis of law both in society and in the church. In society, analysts have tended to characterize this crisis of law as the wrenching but inevitable growing pains accompanying the evolution of the legal system toward greater responsiveness and participation.[7] Of course, not all have taken such a sanguine view of the direction in which Western law seems to be evolving. Church officials frequently have expressed alarm at the uncoupling of positive law from its roots in the natural law and its resulting permissiveness, especially in the areas of sexuality and family life. Thus, the former president of the Pontifical Council for the Interpretation of Legal Texts complained:

> In this second half of the 20th century religious agnosticism and
> moral relativism in the Western world are leading to a type of
> democratic society that is predominately materialistic and permissive,
> one that shuns demands, not only those of the transcendental and
> religious truths regarding man's eternal destiny, but also the
> elementary demands of natural morality. . . . The reasonableness of the
> law, therefore, is no longer seen to depend on whether laws respond to
> objective truths and values, which is what law ought to protect in order
> to guide social behavior in a proper direction and avoid a return, a
> regression to a society of savages.[8]

Since members of the church are immersed in the culture of their time, those inclined to view the evolution of secular law as regression are also prone to complain "that this general contempt for the law which is affecting secular society has also crept into some areas of ecclesial society, as if by osmosis"[9] and to blame this polluted atmosphere for so poisoning the minds and hearts of the faithful that they have difficulty appreciating the importance of law in the church.

This tendency to blame the secondhand smoke from the body politic for the ailments of the body ecclesiastic does not prevent general recognition that canon law has undergone its own internal crisis in the years since that other defining event of the 1960s, the Second Vatican Council. The revision of the Code of Canon Law was already much needed in 1959, when Pope John XXIII announced his plan to revise the code at the same time he announced his decision to convoke an ecumenical council. This revision was even more

desperately needed by 1965, when the council had finished its work of changing the ecclesial landscape. By the time the winds of aggiornamento had
abated, however, much of what had been the law of the church had disappeared
or at least fallen into desuetude, "and the Church found herself in practice, if
not in theory, in a state of *anomia* or lack of law."[10]

The legal vacuum was filled in 1983, when John Paul II promulgated a
revised Code of Canon Law "as a great effort to translate the...conciliar
doctrine and ecclesiology into *canonical* language"[11] and thereby "to create
such an order in ecclesial society that, while assigning the primacy to love,
grace and charisms, it at the same times renders their organic development
easier both in the life of the ecclesial society and the individual persons who
belong to it."[12] For some, the appearance of this "legislative *corpus* that is up to
date and sure, and responds to the ecclesiological doctrine and disciplinary
requirements of Vatican II"[13] was sufficient to overcome any lingering effects
of the postconciliar crisis of law in the church. Indeed, for those who hold this
position, since the appearance of the revised code, "we should be speaking,
rather than of a 'crisis *of the law*,' of a 'crisis of *living according to the law*.'"[14] This
crisis of living according to the law is not, they contend, the result of defects in
the law itself but of bishops who have "an insufficient knowledge of the laws of
the Church or [do] not insure that they [are] properly respected and applied,
perhaps in the name of that false pastoral spirit,"[15] and of faithful whose
consciences are "deformed by a liberal-agnostic concept of freedom [that]
would turn into a justification of subjectivity without limits, that is of a false
freedom which would put a person outside the law of the Church."[16]

Whether a "crisis of the law" or a "crisis of living according to the law" is the
more apt way to describe the current situation of canon law, there can be little
doubt that a crisis atmosphere still prevails, even twenty-five years after the
promulgation of a revised Code of Canon Law. It may be comforting to point
the finger of blame for this situation on dark external forces in contemporary
culture, and there is certainly much in modern culture, including its legal
culture, that is profoundly out of harmony with the gospel. Nevertheless,
blaming outsiders for the current malaise can relieve canonists of the burden
of critical introspection about why many of the faithful who would bridle at the
suggestion that their consciences have been deformed by a liberal-agnostic
concept of freedom and not a few bishops who cannot easily be described as
pastoralist demagogues still find the revised canon law remote, baffling, and, at
times, forbidding.[17]

If contemporary Catholics find canon law remote from their everyday
experience of legal norms, it is because canon law simply is *not* like the other
legal systems with which they deal on a regular basis. This disconnect between

their experience of canon law and their experience of law in ordinary life was not always the case. From canon law's emergence as a discipline in its own right with Gratian's *Decretum* in the twelfth century until the nineteenth century, it developed in constant interaction with the secular systems of law and patterns of government in which it was immersed. Indeed, for more than half a millennium, it was simply assumed that canon law and secular law would mutually interact and influence one another. And so they did. The church

> has never stood wholly aloof from the world, uninfluenced by the legal and political presuppositions of the societies in which it has existed. But nor has the Church ever been a mere passive entity, molded by external secular sources. In the shaping of Western institutions down the centuries she has given more than she has received.[18]

Canon law and secular law differed, of course, in their contents and in the spheres of life they sought to regulate, and the demarcation of the spheres of competence of the two laws has never been undisputed.[19] Nevertheless, for a long time, the two laws shared enough common principles, procedures, and practices that someone who felt at home in one system could feel at home in the other as well. This interaction and interpenetration of the two laws came to an end in the modern era, "when vast Catholic populations became irrevocably committed to political democracy at a time when the Roman see had committed itself to the improbable task of governing a world-wide Church through the institutional apparatus of a petty baroque despotism."[20]

The discomfort of many contemporary Catholics when confronted with canon law has less to do with individual provisions of the Code of Canon Law than with the way the system of canon law functions, the way it feels when they try to live inside it. Brian Tierney's pithy but tart description captures two principal sources of this discomfort: the existing system of canon law unfolds against a backdrop that is, frankly, baroque, and its internal dynamic is, if not despotic, at least paternalistic.

A Baroque "Social Imaginary"

Laws and legal systems do not exist in a social vacuum. They are deeply embedded in conceptions of what constitutes a just moral order in society, conceptions that are widely shared but rarely articulated.[21] Since such "social models" often become perceptible only as the background against which the law is interpreted and applied and is widely shared not only by lawyers and other elites but also by ordinary members of society, it is not inappropriate to call them, as Charles Taylor does, "social imaginaries,"

> the ways people imagine their social existence, how they fit together with others, how things go on between themselves and their fellows, the expectations that are normally met, and the deeper normative notions and images that underlie these expectations.[22]

Although modern Western systems of law differ greatly among themselves, they are all conceived and function as projects for "realizing an association of free and equal citizens"[23] and share a common social imaginary. Taylor summarizes the main lines of this modern social imaginary in four points:

1. Society is a gathering of multiple "unencumbered" selves, that is, individuals "whose personal [identities are] established prior to and independent of [their] ends, history and communal relationships,"[24] and the social order structured and guaranteed by law serves the instrumental purpose of securing the mutual benefit of these individuals.[25]
2. Since political society is brought into existence as an instrument for securing these individuals the needs of ordinary life and, thereby, "the conditions for their existence as free agents," differentiations in status, power, and authority are evaluated solely on the basis of their effectiveness in achieving these ends. Hierarchical organizational structures are purely functional and have no necessary or ontological status.[26]
3. The service society provides to individuals "is defined in terms of defense of individuals' rights. Freedom is central to these rights," as is attested by the assumption that the legitimacy of society depends on the consent of those bound by it.[27]
4. "These rights, this freedom, this mutual benefit is to be secured to all participants equally," although what constitutes "equality" can vary widely from one society and legal system to another.[28]

Although this modern social imaginary has been articulated in a variety of forms and subjected to multiple improvisations or "redactions," every modern Western society and legal system somehow embodies and elaborates on its central tenets. Indeed, the price a legal order must pay for its legitimacy in the eyes of its subjects is effective protection of the fundamental rights of individuals, including the right of all society's members to participate in a meaningful way in the adoption of laws and policies that limit the scope of their freedom.[29] A principal source of the sense of remoteness that many contemporary Catholics experience when confronted with canon law is the fact that the social imaginary that provides the background against which canon law is played is not modern but baroque. Key elements of the modern social imaginary not only are not central to the social imaginary in which the canonical system is inscribed but also are, in many ways, antithetical to it.

The Priority of Community over Individuals

The social imaginary in which canon law is embedded does not begin with unencumbered individuals who join together to fashion a society in which they can freely pursue their own views of what is good for themselves and for the ecclesial society as a whole, but with an ecclesial order that is already endowed with its own history, tradition, social geography, and allocation of roles and that provides the indispensable matrix for nurturing the truly human flourishing of individual persons. Since this order is given in divine revelation, it preexists, both historically and ontologically, the individuals who at any particular moment are incorporated into the church. The immediate purpose of canon law, therefore, is not to construct a just ecclesial society but to conserve and foster the existing one. While the law is not indifferent to the welfare of individual members of society, its primary aim is to promote the common good of the ecclesial community as the nurturing environment in which alone individuals can achieve their true good. However, this good of individuals consists not in maximizing their temporal prosperity, happiness, or even autonomy, but in maximizing their virtue, both natural and supernatural. Just as in the Aristotelian-Thomistic framework, the ultimate end of the law of society is to make people good, so in the church "the salvation of souls is the supreme law."[30] Thus, canon law is concerned with humankind "as it makes its way toward life eternal" and "the order it introduces into human life is its marching orders."[31]

Hierarchical Order, Not Functional but Ontological

Canon law has shown a predilection for articulating its social imaginary in Aristotelian and Thomistic categories and language whose organic paradigm and metaphors have seemed to fit well with a church understood as the body of Christ. For premodern social imaginaries, ancient, medieval, and baroque alike,

> Society was seen as made up of different orders. These needed and complemented each other, but this didn't mean that their relations were mutual, because they didn't exist at the same level. Rather they

formed a hierarchy in which some had greater dignity and value than others.[32]

Although most people today have left this premodern social imaginary behind, it remains the one in which canon law is embedded. Thus, much of canon law is devoted to spinning out the implications of the church as the body of Christ in which head and members and members among themselves are structured in mutual relationships of hierarchical complementarity.

The most salient differentiation within the body of Christ is that between the ordained and the nonordained. In virtue of the sacrament of orders, some members of the faithful "are consecrated and designated, each according to his grade, to nourish the people of God, fulfilling in the person of Christ the Head (*in persona Christi Capitis*) the functions of teaching, sanctifying, and governing."[33] The other members are laity to whom "a secular character is proper and peculiar" and whose "special vocation" is "to seek the kingdom of God by engaging in temporal affairs and directing them according to God's will."[34] Despite the fact that the Second Vatican Council clearly intended its identification of the "secular" character and vocation of the laity to be merely descriptive of the typical situation of the lay faithful, it has become, especially in the teaching of John Paul II, an ontological definition of the lay state.[35] The proper sphere of activity of the ordained is the church; that of the laity is the world. Within the church, the ordained are the active subjects of the church's teaching, sanctifying, and governing functions, which they exercise in the name and in the person of Christ the head of the church, while laypeople are the passive subjects of the church's ministry. Just as the ordained should leave the affairs of the world to the laity unless unusual circumstances require their intervention, so the laity should cooperate with but not take on functions proper to the ordained except in situations of special need, especially situations where ordained ministers are lacking.

Like baroque monarchies of an earlier age, the Catholic Church has learned to justify its hierarchical structure and allocation of functions on the pragmatic ground that it is essential for maintaining unity in faith and discipline.[36] Nevertheless, this hierarchical differentiation is not merely instrumental and functional but normative and ontological.[37] Unlike in the secular world, where form follows function, function necessarily follows form in the church.

> It is crucial to this ideal that the distribution of functions is itself a key
> part of the normative order. It is not just that each order should
> perform its characteristic function for the other.... No, the
> hierarchical differentiation itself is seen as the proper order of things.
> It was a part of the nature or form of society.[38]

The Priority of "the Right" over Rights

Since the social imaginary in which canon law is embedded views the church community as the essential environment for the genuine flourishing of individuals, it gives primacy to the promotion and fostering of the common good of that community. As the theologian formerly known as Joseph Ratzinger explained,

> The fundamental right of the Christian is the right to the whole faith. The fundamental obligation that flows from this is the obligation of everyone, but especially the Church's ministers, to the totality of the unadulterated faith.... All remaining freedoms in the Church are directed towards and subordinate to this fundamental freedom.[39]

In fact, during the regime of the 1917 code, many influential canonists held that, since canon law was a law for public order only and was concerned solely with the *utilitas Ecclesiae*, it had no place for individual (subjective) rights.[40] Thus, at the time of the promulgation of the revised Code of Canon Law in 1983, much emphasis was given to its articulations of "the duties and right of the faithful and particularly the laity" as elements of "the *newness* of the new Code" and its vision of "the true and genuine image of the Church."[41] With the passage of twenty-five years, it has become apparent that this "newness" of the revised code is not as new as it first appeared. Although the revised code goes much further than the 1917 code in articulating the rights of the faithful, these rights fall considerably short of the sort of "fundamental rights" guaranteed by the constitutions of modern states.

Canon law continues to operate in "a universe of duties" in which "rights" function less as legitimate claims on which an individual can rely than as "privileges" conceded by ecclesiastical authority but revocable or subject to being abridged or ignored when substantive reasons of theology, morality, or expediency so dictate. The exercise of rights by the faithful is subject to careful monitoring and restriction by ecclesiastical authorities. In addition to restrictions written into the articulations of particular rights themselves, canon 223 stipulates:

1. In exercising their rights, the Christian faithful, both as individuals and gathered together in associations, must take into account the common good of the church, the rights of others, and their own duties toward others.
2. In view of the common good, ecclesiastical authority can direct (*moderari*) the exercise of the rights that are proper to the Christian faithful.

In this climate, many, if not all, rights of individuals are seen as strictly correlated with, if not actually derived from,[42] their duties and, therefore, as defeasible for failure to comply with their corresponding duties. Thus, the broad obligation of the faithful "to maintain communion with the Church even in their own manner of acting"[43] has been construed as restricting their right to join associations and hold meetings[44] to the right to join associations with which the local bishop is sympathetic, as many members of Voice of the Faithful have discovered to their distress; the exercise of the right to receive the sacraments[45] can be limited by the minister's judgment that a person is not properly disposed;[46] and the exercise of the right to marry[47] is subject to a judgment by a church authority that nothing stands in the way of its valid lawful celebration.[48]

Remedies for alleged violations of rights by church authorities are neither well developed nor effective. Since church tribunals lack jurisdiction in such disputes, the only remedy available is hierarchical recourse to the ecclesiastical superior of the one whose action is being challenged. This procedure for recourse is designed more for ensuring hierarchical control over inferior officials than for protecting rights.[49] Consequently, to use Ronald Dworkin's term, the "trumps" in the canonical system are not the rights of individuals but the pastoral discretion of the church authority.[50]

Structured Inequality

Prior to the Second Vatican Council, canonists were virtually unanimous in describing the church as a society of unequals in which the clergy governed and the laity were governed. Bowing to the teaching of the council, canon 208 now asserts: "From their rebirth in Christ, there exists among all the Christian faithful a true equality regarding dignity and action by which they all cooperate in the building up of the Body of Christ according to each one's condition and function."[51] However, this assertion of the equality of the faithful is subtly undermined by the qualification "according to each one's condition and function," which reinscribes it in a baroque social imaginary dominated by hierarchical complementarity. The equality of the faithful is undermined not so much by the fact that the church is not structured as a one man, one vote democracy but by the fact that there is no structured reciprocity between the hierarchy and the faithful. The church structured in canon law is

> one whose administration is almost entirely withdrawn from the
> control of its members. The relations between hierarchy and faithful
> are a one-way street: of the governors over against the governed, of the

teachers over against the taught and of the celebrants [of the liturgy] over against the spectators.[52]

It is difficult to speak meaningfully of equality in a society in which "the laity, who represent the overwhelming majority of the baptized, are carefully kept aloof from the decisions of some importance which affect them."[53]

For those imbued with the baroque social imaginary, promulgation by the competent hierarchical authority and conformity with the divine positive and natural laws are sufficient for establishing the legitimacy of canon law. For those imbued with a more modern social imaginary, however, canon law's indifference to individual rights and lack of mechanisms for ensuring participation in decision-making processes raise serious questions about this law's legitimacy.

Benevolent Despotism at Its Best

Predominance of Substantive over Formal Rationality

Max Weber identified the striving toward increased rationality as one of the critical factors in the evolution of Western law. Although his use of the term *rationality* is not always unambiguous, Weber distinguished two forms of rationality of particular relevance for the evolution of law: "substantive" rationality and "formal" rationality. Substantive rationality is "a manifestation of man's capacity for value-rational action."[54] The aim is "to find a type of law which is most appropriate to the expediential and ethical goals of the authorities in question."[55] Substantive rationality differs from and can sometimes conflict with "formal" rationality, whose aim is "achieving that highest degree of formal juridic precision which would maximize the chances for the correct prediction of legal consequences and for the rational systematization of law and procedure."[56] Formal rationality attempts to resolve problems instrumentally by reference to abstract and universal laws, norms and regulations applied impartially to everyone without exception. In procedure, formal rationality seeks to structure decision making to maximize accuracy in fact finding and precision in applying the law; in content, it strives to distill the law into abstract principles so that the legal system can function "like a technically rational machine."[57] However, since the abstract principles of formally rational law cannot take into account individual differences and circumstances and often enshrine the interests of the economically dominant class, they can often lead to results that offend popular senses of substantive justice.[58]

From the time of Gratian until fairly recently, canon law evolved in constant interaction with the systems of secular law in which the church was immersed and so shared in their striving toward both substantive and formal rationality. As Max Weber noted, canon law "was much more rational and much more highly developed on the formal side than the other cases of sacred law"[59] and "became indeed one of the guides for secular law on the road to rationality."[60] For example, canon law took the lead in replacing the system of proof by oaths, ordeals, and other quasi-magic methods with the more rational and reliable system of proof by evidence and concordant witness and, in criminal law, in displacing the accusatorial system that laid the burden of prosecuting and proving crimes on their victims with the inquisitorial system, which placed responsibility for criminal prosecution in the hands of a public authority. Moreover, it was the canonical notion of the moral or juridic person that provided the inspiration for the development of the notion of corporations in secular law, and canon law was in the forefront of overcoming often irrational and locally varying customs with universal legislation by rational enactment.[61]

However, there have always been limits to how far ecclesiastical authorities were willing to allow canon law to proceed along the path of formal rationalization. On the one hand, because of its highly abstract character, formal justice "must time and again produce consequences which are contrary to the substantive postulates of religious ethics or of political expediency"[62] and "infringe on the ideals of substantive justice."[63] Hence, the guardians of the canonical tradition have recoiled from these consequences and the system that produced them. For them, "the self-contained and specialized 'juridical' treatment of legal questions [characteristic of formal justice] is an alien idea, and they are not interested in any separation of law and ethics."[64] On the other hand, "formal justice is . . . repugnant to all authoritarian powers, theocratic as well as patriarchic, because it reduces the dependency of the individual upon the grace and power of the authorities."[65]

As a result of this tension between substantive and formal rationality, canon law represents something of a halfway house along the road from premodern to modern law, too oriented by the cluster of values represented by the gospel and classical natural law to pursue formal rationality to its logical conclusion in what Habermas calls "bourgeois private law" and Nonet and Selznick call "autonomous law,"[66] but too far along the path to formal rationality to turn back the clock completely.

The Codes of Canon Law of 1917 and 1983 have been the high-water marks of canon law's tendency toward formal rationality. Commentators have often noted that the drafters of the 1917 code (and by default those of the 1983 code) took as their model and inspiration the Napoleonic Code and its many imitations in nineteenth-century Europe.[67] And the similarity of the church's codes to these nineteenth-century paragons of formal rationality cannot be gainsaid.

Perhaps no area of canon law exhibits the relentless logic of formal rationality as much as canonical marriage law, the part of the law that touches most directly and intimately the lives of laypeople. Here two thousand years of Christian teaching and living are distilled into abstract, universally applicable principles, which are applied with a ruthless logic according to a hyperrational judicial process only a skilled lawyer can navigate. Max Weber would not be surprised that this most formally rational area of canon law is also the one whose application and development have historically been entrusted largely to professional jurists, the Roman Rota at the level of the Holy See, and diocesan tribunals staffed by canon lawyers at the level of the particular church. Nor should it be a surprise that this is also the area where the remoteness of the law's impersonal and abstract principles from the lived experience of the faithful is most palpable to ordinary people.

Despite the admiration of their drafters for the great nineteenth-century codifications and despite pronounced tendencies toward formal rationality within them, the church's two codes are actually more closely related to the patriarchal codifications of secular law in the era of enlightened despots than to codifications of the era following the French Revolution. In other words, in both form and content, the church's codes look more like the Prussian *Allgemeine Landrecht* of 1794 than the German *Bürgerliche Gesetzbuch* of 1896. A telltale sign of the real provenance of the codes is their interweaving of strictly rational legal norms with didactic theological assertions, ethical admonitions, prudential counsels, and spiritual exhortations, the same sort of potpourri that was characteristic of earlier patriarchal codifications.[68] While one of the primary and most prominent functions of modern secular codifications has been their efforts to lay out clearly and precisely the rights of citizens, rights took a back seat to duties in patriarchal codifications. In these codes, "the 'law' is primarily a universe of duties."[69]

Within the "universe of duties" delineated in the codes, formal rationality has made only limited headway. It predominates in the realm of "private law," where the law itself has been distilled to a high degree of abstraction and where disputes are resolved pursuant to a highly formalized and logical judicial procedure. In practice, however, this procedure is applicable only to marriage nullity cases, very rare contract and property cases, and penal cases. This tendency toward formal rationality is not irreversible, however. In response to public outrage at the failure of bishops to punish priests who had sexually abused minors, church authorities have moved to relax the requirement that the highly rational and formal but cumbersome judicial process be followed when dismissing (popularly, but inaccurately, referred to as "defrocking") clerics and to allow for the imposition of penalties through an administrative process, or sometimes no process at all. As this change in direction illustrates, when push comes to shove, substantive rationality will trump formal rationality in canon law. Like other patriarchal systems of law, although the canonical system is "rational in the sense of adherence to fixed principles, it is not so in the sense of a logical rationality of its modes of thought but rather in the sense of the pursuit of substantive principles of social justice of political, welfare-utilitarian, or ethical content."[70]

This central role of substantive rationality helps to explain why formal rational law has never made the same inroads in the church's "public law" that it has in "private law." Church authorities have adamantly resisted the infiltration of formal rationality into the canonical administrative process, where few formal criteria constrain the discretion of church administrators to pursue the common good as they see it and few procedural requirements prevent them from doing so expeditiously. Although the maxim *"quod principi placuit legis vigorem habet"* had its origins in classical Roman law, it has had a long life in the canon law of the Catholic Church. Since procedural regularity and transparency have never been as highly valued in canonical administrative law as they have in secular administrations, the actions and decisions by pastors, bishops, and other administrative authorities can often seem more than a little arbitrary and capricious to those who have learned to expect a high degree of formal rationality in administrative decision making.

Paternalistic Administration

Because of its affinities to the patriarchal forms of codification, canon law tends to take the form of what Nonet and Selznick call "repressive law"[71] but what, in a church context, might better be termed paternalism, in which neither the rights of the faithful nor the formal standards and procedures of the law itself provide much of a brake on the discretion of church authorities.

A BLURRED DISTINCTION BETWEEN LAW AND ADMINISTRATION. Unlike most modern secular states, canon law has no separation of powers. While legislative, executive, and judicial functions can be distinguished, these three powers are united in the office of the Roman pontiff for the universal church and in the office of the diocesan bishop for the particular church. Since the overriding concern of church governance is the good order and common good of the church, legal rules serve to give a patina of legitimacy to the exercise of governance power, but the use of these rules is qualified by criteria of substantive justice and expediency.[72] Like other patriarchal systems, canon law tends to collapse the law into administration, "not in the sense that all administration would assume the form of adjudication but rather in the reverse sense that all adjudication takes the form of administration" in which decisions are made according to the authority's "free discretion in the light of considerations of equity, expediency, or politics."[73]

Subordinate officials see themselves as, and in fact are, ministers of the Roman pontiff or local bishop and as relatively pliable instruments of papal or episcopal policy. Although the official position of the codes is that canon law is to be interpreted and applied according to clear, formally rational principles,[74] what prevails in practice is a form of interpretation that pays lip service to the letter of the law but gives free rein to the demands of substantive justice, morality, and expediency. This sort of results-oriented jurisprudence is reminiscent of the "legal realism" that once had a wide following among American lawyers,[75] except that legal realism sought to overcome the rigidity and inequities of formally rational law while church practice seeks to avoid them altogether. When canonists proclaim the superiority of canon law over secular law because it is not infected with "positivism," they are usually referring to the formally rational constraints on official discretion in secular law.

A REGIME OF "DUAL LAW." All the faithful are morally bound by the precepts of divine natural and positive law, but the higher one rises on the church's hierarchical ladder, the more one is entitled to wear the positive ecclesiastical law as a loose garment. The Roman pontiff is legally bound even as the supreme legislator of the church by divine law as authoritatively interpreted by the magisterium and by the unwritten constitution of the church known traditionally as the *status generalis Ecclesiae*.[76] However, he is not legally bound by merely ecclesiastical law. He is free to abrogate it, change it, dispense himself from its observance, or even ignore it,[77] even though morally he may be bound to set a good example for the rest of the church by observing the law. Legal "rules remain weakly binding" even at lower levels of the ecclesiastical hierarchy.[78] Norms containing unequivocal precepts and those touching on core theological principles will be strictly enforced against pastors, bishops, and even cardinals, but, when the norms have a measure of elasticity, great deference will be accorded to official discretion.

Most of the legal obligations of bishops, pastors, and other ecclesiastical officeholders are framed in general terms, often more exhortatory than preceptive and, even when preceptive, phrased in the subjunctive mood, which suggests more a weak "ought" than a strong "must." The code's lists of duties of officeholders often read more like homilies than like job descriptions that could provide the basis for serious performance evaluations. Their rather general language leaves church authorities with broad discretion to determine how best to carry out the duties of their offices. Since all lines of accountability point upward in canon law, only hierarchical superiors are competent to judge whether their subordinates have adequately fulfilled the obligations of their offices or abused their powers. Bishops, pastors, and other officeholders are accountable for their stewardship to those who appointed them, not to those they serve. The faithful may express disgruntlement about the shoddy performance, nonfeasance, and malfeasance of their pastors and even bishops to their hierarchical superiors, but superiors are free to give these complaints as much or as little weight as their discretion dictates when deciding whether to retain, remove, or discipline their subordinates. In the absence of genuine reciprocity between the governors and the governed, the latter are reduced in fact, if not in theory, to dependence on the paternal benevolence of the former.

The law takes little note of those at the lower end of the hierarchical pyramid. Long ago, Ulrich Stutz observed that, in the 1917 code, "The Church is the Church of the clergy" in which "the laity appear to enjoy only the rights accorded to protected residents, while the clergy enjoy full citizenship."[79] Although laypeople enjoy something more than an honorable mention in the 1983 code, it takes a considerable stretch of the imagination to say that the Christian faithful are the "real protagonist" of the revised law, as some claim.[80] Unfortunately for those at the bottom of the hierarchical pyramid, the failure of canon law to anchor their juridic status with secure and enforceable rights institutionalizes their dependency on the benevolence of their hierarchical superiors. The logic of legal codifications explicitly or implicitly privileges the secular model of a "perfect society," according to which the church is a means to an end.[81] The end is the salvation of individual souls, and the means the spiritual goods of the church, especially the Word of God and the sacraments, administered by the clergy. "Over against the clergy, who represent the institution and administer the goods of salvation, there are only individual Christians. The starting point is found in the individual to be saved . . . and not in the Church, sacrament of salvation."[82]

Ironically, the internal dynamic of codification has led canon law into a spiritual individualism every bit as "radical" as the individualism the magisterium is wont to criticize in secular society. By structuring the church along the axes of an "active" clergy and a "passive" laity, the code risks introducing "a conceptually insurmountable cleavage between the hierarchically structured society and the community through which we understand the 'we' of Christians (and not the laity)."[83] When this split is taken to its extreme, the church can easily begin to resemble a spiritual welfare state in which the clergy administer the spiritual goods of the church to the dependent faithful, and the law, supplemented by a generous dose of clerical discretion, provides the criteria for distinguishing the "deserving" from the "undeserving" faithful.[84]

Such a climate provides a fertile breeding ground for clericalism, not only the crass clericalism that privileges the position and interests of the clergy over those of the rest of the faithful but also the more corrosive clericalism that

> exalts the respect in which the Church is a hierarchy spreading out from Pentecost to all corners of the earth at the expense of the respect in which it is the community of the faithful offering its life to God—a life in which the whole creation is more and more integrated. . . . What is often forgotten is the respect in which the Church is a community where none is less necessary than any other, the sense in which the Church is made by its members and grows with them.[85]

PREVALENCE OF "LEGAL MORALISM." Like any legal system that prizes substantive rationality and largely resists the blandishments of formal rationality, canon law has rejected the strict segregation of law and morality that is characteristic of most modern systems of law. As a result, the code contains numerous provisions that are primarily moral in character. Some of these enunciations of moral principles have been translated into juridic language, but others have not. In addition to these explicit articulations of morality in the code, morality provides the atmosphere that surrounds canon law. Indeed, one of the aims of canon law is "to create such an order in the ecclesial society that, while assigning the primacy to love, grace, and charisms, it at the same time renders their organic development easier in the life of both the ecclesial society and the individual persons who belong to it."[86] Thus, the law and those who are charged with its execution are not indifferent to the moral climate of the ecclesial community or to the infractions of the moral law by its individual members.

In addition to their role in shaping and administering the church's legal system, the Roman pontiff and the bishops in communion with him are teachers of faith and morals. Although the ecclesiastical magisterium has rarely spoken infallibly in matters of morality, the faithful are not free to ignore or to dissent from its noninfallible moral teaching.

> Although not an assent of faith, a religious submission (*obsequium*) of the intellect and will must be given to a doctrine which the Supreme Pontiff or the college of bishops declares concerning faith or morals when they exercise the authentic magisterium, even if they do not intend to proclaim it by a definitive act.[87]

A similar *obsequium* is due to the authentic magisterium of bishops, whether they propose this teaching as individuals or as episcopal conferences.[88] Since the boundaries between the realms of morality and law are rather porous, it is rather easy for church teaching to leach from one domain into the other. In fact, one prominent school of canon law holds that the mere fact that the church's magisterium has recognized a moral norm as part of divine natural law is sufficient to establish that norm as part of the church's juridic order, even without any subsequent or accompanying act of promulgation.[89]

Although this position has been hotly disputed by other canonical schools, it has not prevented moralism from leaking into the legal arena in practice. Perhaps the best known example of this leakage occurred during the 2004 presidential campaign, when several bishops announced that Democratic candidate John Kerry would be barred from the reception of Holy Communion in their dioceses because he was "obstinately persisting in manifest grave sin."[90] The manifest grave sin in question was not dissent from the church's teaching on the immorality of abortion (Kerry had publicly proclaimed his personal opposition to abortion) but his refusal to support the public policy positions advanced by the church's magisterium to stem the tide of abortion. In short, Kerry's "sin" was disobedience, the refusal of religious *obsequium* to the ordinary teaching of the magisterium.

In a legal order like canon law where there is no very bright line between law and morality, disobedience becomes the paradigmatic offense. Following Durkheim, Nonet and Selznick have observed:

> Perhaps the most fertile ground for legal moralism is communal morality, that is, morality cultivated to sustain a "community of observance." In this context group identity is defined by common adherence to a detailed code of conduct that sharply separates members from outsiders and serves as a continuing affirmation of loyalty and solidarity. Disobedience is betrayal, an offense against the community as such, and its gravity bears little or no relation to whether or how seriously particular interests are injured.[91]

While no society, religious or secular, can long survive without some measure of communal morality,[92] heavy-handed legal moralism replaces the dynamic of teaching and learning with the dynamic of command and control. When the reciprocity inherent in the process of teaching and learning is short-circuited, neither genuine consent nor consensus can emerge in ecclesial society.

Conclusion

The discomfort many of the faithful feel about canon law is a reflection of the fact that canon law is still embedded in a baroque social imaginary that most of them find bewildering and that is quite paternalistic in the way it deals with "the simple faithful." One can, of course, view this nagging sense of the illegitimacy of canon law among a broad segment of the faithful as further evidence of the deformations wrought by "a liberal-agnostic concept of freedom." However, the erosion of the baroque social imaginary and distaste for paternalism has been encouraged, perhaps inadvertently, by the church itself.

Since the nineteenth century, the church has been active in mobilizing the faithful to restore Catholic life where it had been disrupted by the French Revolution, to protect it where it was threatened by Kulturkampf, and to build it from scratch where it had never existed before, as in the New World. Whether it was to raise funds to build and maintain churches and parish plants, to found and operate educational and charitable institutions, to organize a network of social service agencies, to protect Catholics from the dangers of drifting away with a web of social and fraternal organizations, to march on behalf of civil rights or an end to abortion, or to foster deeper piety and devotion,

> the Catholic Church has unavoidably been in the business of mobilizing..., organizing and recruiting people into membership organizations with some definite purpose. But this means new forms of collective action, created by the participants themselves; and this has no proper place in the ancien régime model. Gradually content began to break through form.[93]

More recently, the church has been active in mobilizing the faithful not just for causes outside the church or peripheral to its life and mission, but for activities central to its mission. The church's teaching mission from its prestigious universities to its smallest parish religious education programs is largely in the hands of dedicated laypeople; outside of seminaries and a few clerically dominated institutions, the church's liturgical life, the principal form in which its sanctifying mission is carried out, depends critically on the active cooperation of a host of talented "lay ministers"; even church governance, long the last bastion of clerical monopoly, has been infiltrated by lay professionals, either as members of parish, diocesan, and episcopal conference staffs or as members of advisory boards and councils. Once mobilization has begun, it is terribly difficult to stop.

The church's hierarchy has also contributed to the erosion of the baroque social imaginary in which canon law is embedded by making defense of human rights the linchpin of Catholic social teaching. Since John XXIII but especially during the pontificate of John Paul II, respect for human rights has become the central criterion by which the church judges the justice of societies and political regimes. After placing itself in the vanguard of the champions of human rights, the church cannot avoid a certain amount of blowback. As John Paul II recognized:

> The task of the church, and her historical merit, of proclaiming and defending man's fundamental rights at all times and places, does not exempt her but, on the contrary, obliges her to be a *speculum iustitiae* [a mirror of justice] before the world.[94]

While the church needs to be discriminating and at times selective when it incorporates rights into its life and law, a decent respect for the opinions of humankind requires it to offer an apologia for its departures from the sort of standards for rights and their protection to which it holds the rest of the world.

Not all of canon law's discontents can be blamed on dark outside forces or disobedient members of the church. There are internal tensions and contradictions within the law itself that the promulgation of a new code not only cannot paper over but also has inevitably exacerbated. As Charles Taylor has observed, the church has had difficulty "seeing how contradictory the goal ultimately is, of a Church tightly held together by a strong hierarchical authority, which will nevertheless be filled with practitioners of heartfelt devotion."[95]. Resolving that contradiction will require not more nervous scolding of the wayward, but a concerted effort to offer a gentle and respectful, but cogent and consistent, account of the reasons for this hope of ours.[96]

NOTES

1. John T. Noonan, *Power to Dissolve: Lawyers and Marriage in the Courts of the Roman Curia* (Cambridge, MA: Belknap, 1972), xiii.

2. Ibid.

3. William Shakespeare, *Henry VI, Part II*, act iv, scene 2, line 76.

4. Alexis de Tocqueville, *Democracy in America* (New York: Harper Perennial, 1988), 1: 241.

5. See Michael J. Himes, "Reflections on American Attitudes toward Law," *CLSA Proceedings* 46 (1984): 63–92.

6. Ibid., 74–78.

7. See Gunther Teubner, "Substantive and Reflexive Elements in Modern Law," *Law and Society Review* 17 (1983): 239–285. Nonet and Selznick view the "crisis" as part of the process by which the internal dynamics of "autonomous" law break out of formalism into more purposive and participative "responsive" law. See Philippe Nonet and Philip Selznick, *Law and Society in Transition: Toward Responsive Law* (New Brunswick, NJ: Transaction, 2001), 71–72. Luhmann attributes the crisis to the incapacity of the existing system of positive law to perform its function of systematically stabilizing

normative expectations as the transition from a stratified to a functionally differentiated society is realized. See Niklas Luhmann, *A Sociological Theory of Law* (Boston: Routledge and Kegan Paul, 1985), 103–158, and *Law as a Social System* (Oxford: Oxford University Press, 2004), 211–229, 423–463. Habermas views the crisis of law as the symptom of the crises of rationality, legitimacy, and motivation afflicting advanced capitalist societies and straining toward a new proceduralist paradigm of law that transcends both the formal and the materialized paradigms of law. See Jürgen Habermas, *Legitimation Crisis* (Boston: Beacon, 1975), 33–94, and *Between Facts and Norms: Contributions to a Discourse Theory of Law and Democracy* (Cambridge, MA: MIT Press, 1998), 427–446.

    8. Julián Herranz Casado, "Renewal and Effectiveness in Canon Law," *Studia canonica* 28 (1994): 24–25.

    9. Ibid., 25.

    10. Ibid., 27.

    11. John Paul II, apostolic constitution *Sacrae disciplinae leges*, January 21, 1983: A.A.S. 75 (1983): xxx. Emphasis in the original.

    12. Ibid., xxix–xxx.

    13. Herranz Casado, "Renewal," 28.

    14. Ibid., 22. Emphasis in the original.

    15. Ibid., 29.

    16. Ibid., 28.

    17. See Hervé-Marie Legrand, "Grâce et institution dans l'Église: les fondements théologique du droit canonique," in *L'Église: Institution et Foi*, ed. Jean Monneron (Brussel: Publications des Facultés Saint-Louis, 1984), 139–140.

    18. Brian Tierney, "Medieval Canon Law and Western Constitutionalism," *Catholic Historical Review* 52 (1966): 16.

    19. Rémi Brague, *The Law of God: The Philosophical History of an Idea* (Chicago: University of Chicago Press, 2007), 141–143.

    20. Tierney, "Medieval Canon Law," 15.

    21. "Among legal scholars expressions such as 'social ideal' or 'social model' and even 'social vision,' have become generally accepted ways of referring to those implicit images of society inscribed in a legal system. Such expressions refer to those implicit images of one's own society that guide the contemporary practices of making and applying law. These images or paradigms provide the background for the interpretation of the system of basic rights." See Jürgen Habermas, "Paradigms of Law," in *Habermas on Law and Democracy: Critical Exchanges*, ed. Michel Rosenfeld and Andrew Arato (Berkeley: University of California Press, 1998), 13. See also Habermas, *Between Facts and Norms*, 388–391.

    22. Charles Taylor, *Modern Social Imaginaries* (Durham, NC: Duke University Press, 2004), 23.

    23. Habermas, "Paradigms," 13.

    24. David Hollenbach, "A Communitarian Reconstruction of Human Rights: Contributions from the Catholic Tradition," in *Catholicism and Liberalism*, ed. R. Bruce Douglass and David Hollenbach (New York: Cambridge University Press, 1994), 130.

    25. Taylor, *Modern Social Imaginaries*, 19–20.

26. Ibid., 20.

27. Ibid., 20–21.

28. Ibid., 22.

29. Jacques Lenoble, "Law and Undecidability: Toward a New Vision of the Proceduralization of Law," in *Habermas on Law and Democracy*, 42.

30. 1983 *Codex Iuris Canonici*, c. 1752.

31. Brague, *The Law of God*, 142.

32. Taylor, *Modern Social Imaginaries*, 11.

33. 1983 *Codex Iuris Canonici*, c. 1008.

34. *Lumen Gentium*, §31.

35. On this misinterpretation of *Lumen gentium* that now seems to have become its official interpretation, see Klaus Mörsdorf, "Das konziliare Verständnis vom Wesen der Kirche in der nachkonziliaren Gestaltung der kirchlichen Rechtsordnung," in *Schriften zum kanonischen Recht* (Paderborn, Germany: Ferdinand Schöningh, 1989), 490–492; and Joseph Komonchak, "Clergy, Laity, and the Church's Mission in the World," *Jurist* 41 (1981): 298–349.

36. Charles Taylor, *A Secular Age* (Cambridge, MA: Harvard University Press, 2007), 412–413.

37. Underscoring the ontological nature of the division of roles and functions in the church is the sometimes polemical point of frequent reiterations of the principle of *Lumen gentium*, §10 that the ministerial priesthood of the ordained and the common priesthood of all the faithful differ "in essence and not only in degree."

38. Taylor, *The Modern Social Imaginary*, 11. A society in which hierarchical complementarity is part of the natural order of things meshes well with the culture of the *bella figura* that prevails in some sectors of the church. On the one hand, the *bella figura* requires supporting beleaguered officeholders, even when they have acted imprudently or been negligent, if failing to do so would discredit the office itself. Direct affronts to the law or hierarchical authority will be met with the full force of the law in all its fury. Direct confrontation is avoided if it would cause an authority to lose face, even though inaction may mean continued substandard or even incompetent performance. On the other hand, the culture of the *bella figura* "can have a surprising tolerance for human failure, but [it] will defend the law tenaciously at the level of principle." This aspect of the *bella figura* lies behind the old adage that, in the church, it is easier to receive forgiveness than permission. See John Allen, *All the Pope's Men* (New York: Doubleday, 2004), 127, 100–106.

39. Joseph Ratzinger, "Freedom and Constraint in the Church," in *Church, Ecumenism and Politics* (New York: Crossroads, 1988), 202.

40. See Pio Fedele, "Il problema del diritto soggettivo e dell' azione," in *Discorso generale sull'ordinamento canonico* (Padua, Italy: CEDAM, 1941), 158–170. This approach to law, characteristic of patriarchal codifications, tends to reduce individual "rights" to expectations of the fulfillment of duties by public officials. Weber explains: "Or the prince would issue 'regulations' concerning general directives for his officials. Such regulations mean that the officials are directed, until the receipt of further directives, to order the concerns of the subjects and to settle their conflicts in the manner indicated.

In that situation the prospect of an individual to obtain a certain decision in his favor is not a 'right' of his but rather a factual 'reflex,' a byproduct of the regulation, which is not legally guaranteed to him. It is the same as in the case where a father complies with some wish of his child without thinking, however, that he had bound himself to any formal juristic principles or fixed procedural forms." See Max Weber, *Economy and Society* (Berkeley: University of California Press, 1978), 2:843–844.

41. John Paul II, apostolic constitution *Sacrae disciplinae leges*, January 25, 1983: A.S.S. 75 (1983): xxx. Emphasis in the original.

42. On the priority of duties over rights, see Paul Hinder, *Grundrechte in der Kirche: Eine Untersuchung zur Begründung der Grundrechte in der Kirche* (Freiburg, Germany: Universitäts Verlag, 1977).

43. 1983 *CIC*, c. 209, §1.

44. Ibid., c. 215.

45. Ibid., c. 213.

46. Ibid., c. 843, §1.

47. Ibid., c. 1058.

48. Ibid., c. 1066.

49. See James H. Provost, "Rights of Persons in the Church," in *Catholicism and Liberalism*, 312: "In short, the system is inadequate and has been recognized as such by various authors. Despite the emphasis on rights in the early pages of the codes, the section dealing with the vindication and protection of rights leans heavily in favor of administrators and institutional concerns rather than the rights of the Christian faithful."

50. SeeRonald Dworkin, *Taking Rights Seriously* (Cambridge, MA: Harvard University Press, 1978), 90–94, 364–368.

51. See *LG*, §32.

52. Legrand, "Grâce et institution," 148. Although Legrand was reflecting on the church structured by the 1917 code, the revised code has not made a notable advance in overcoming this lack of reciprocity. See Charles Wackenheim, "L'influence des modèles juridiques sur la théologie catholique," *Review de Droit Canonique* 39 (1989): 31–41.

53. Wackenheim, 41, "L'influence."

54. Stephen Kalberg, "Max Weber's Types of Rationality: Cornerstones for the Analysis of Rationalizations in History," *American Journal of Sociology* 85 (1980): 1155: "Substantive rationality *directly* orders action into patterns. It does so, however, not on the basis of a purely means-end calculation of solutions to routine problems but in relation to a past, present, or potential 'value postulate.' Not simply a single value, such as positive evaluation of wealth or of the fulfillment of duty, a value postulate implies entire clusters of values that vary in comprehensiveness, internal consistency, and content."

55. Weber, *Economy and Society*, 2:810.

56. Ibid.

57. Ibid., 2:811.

58. Ibid., 2:812–814.

59. Ibid., 2:828.

60. Ibid., 2:829.

61. Ibid., 2:829–830.

62. Ibid., 2:812.

63. Ibid., 2:813.

64. Ibid., 2:811.

65. Ibid., 2:812.

66. Nonet and Selznick, *Law and Society*, 54: "The chief attributes of autonomous law may be summarized as follows: 1. Law is separated from politics. Characteristically, the system proclaims the independence of the judiciary and draws a sharp line between legislative and judicial functions. 2. The legal order espouses the 'model of rules.' A focus on rules helps enforce a measure of official accountability; at the same time, it limits the creativity of legal institutions and the risk of their intrusion into the political domain. 3. 'Procedure is the heart of law.' Regularity and fairness, not substantive justice, are the first ends and main competence of the legal order. 4. 'Fidelity to law' is understood as strict obedience to the rules of positive law."

67. See Stephan Kuttner, "The Code of Canon Law in Historical Perspective," *Jurist* 20 (1968): 139–140: "In the course of the Church's history no legislation had ever been enacted which completely absorbed all preceding discipline and formally abolished all previous collections. The *Codex* was the first to do this. . . . The historical explanation of this phenomenon must be sought in the methodological which shaped the Code . . . , principles which place the Code close to—indeed insert it in—the long line of civil law codifications of the nineteenth century. From the *Code Napoléan* to the German *Bürgerliches Gesetzbuch*, the nineteenth century witnessed the triumph of *Begriffsjurisprudenz* and of conceptual juridical abstraction. With an absolute trust in the ideal of the abstract formula, jurists sought to arrive at an almost mathematically constructed, impeccable system of legislation; a rational aggregate of all juridical norms, each reduced to the most absolute formulation and conceived as completely set apart from the concrete social situations which in life are the mainsprings of law itself. There is no doubt that Gasparri and his collaborators in 1904 had a profound admiration for these civil codes. From the start of their preliminary discussions they were determined to cast the law of the Church in canons and articles *ad formam recentiorum Codicum*." See also Legrand, "Grâce et institution," 155: "Soulignons donc que, comme toute oeuvre humaine, celle-ci est fille de son temps: par son positivisme et son individualisme, le Codex est à bien des égards la dernière codification du grand siècle de la bourgeoisie, qui se clôt, dans le sang et les armes, au moment meme où celle-là est prmulgué."

68. Max Weber, *Economy and Society*, 2:857: "The occurrence of numerous provisions of a merely didactic or ethically admonitory character gave rise to many doubts as to whether or not a particular provision was really meant to constitute a legally binding norm." On the struggle of canonists to deal with the problem of the multiplicity of "literary forms" incorporated into the Code of Canon Law, see Ladislas Örsy, *Theology and Canon Law: New Horizons for Legislation and Interpretation* (Collegeville, MN: Liturgical Press, 1992), 53–58.

69. Weber, *Economy and Society*, 2:856: "The universality of one's 'darndest debt and duty' (*verdammte Pflicht und Schuldigkeit*) is the main characteristic of the legal order, and its most notable feature is a systematic rationalism, not of a formal but of that substantive kind which always is typical of such cases."

70. Weber, *Economy and Society*, 2:844.

71. Nonet and Selznick, *Law and Society*, 29–52.

72. Ibid., 34–35.

73. Weber, *Economy and Society*, 2:844–845. This collapse of law into administration also meshes well with the culture of the *bella figura*, in which the priority is placed on conflict resolution that finds "face-saving compromises that allow all sides to feel like they had prevailed" without "resolving underlying problems or making a stand on matters of principle." See Allen, *All the Pope's Men*, 103. Whatever its merits, this sort of conflict resolution can only be satisfying for those fortunate enough to get a place at the bargaining table. Those at the lower end of the hierarchical pyramid tend to find themselves on the outside looking in when these compromises are brokered.

74. See 1983 *CIC*, cc. 1–28.

75. See Brian Leiter, "American Legal Realism," in *The Blackwell Guide to the Philosophy of Law and Legal Theory*, ed. Martin Golding and William Edmundson (Oxford: Blackwell, 2005), 50–66. Something quite like this approach is discussed by Nonet and Selznick, *Law and Society*, 73–113, as "Responsive Law," and by Ronald Dworkin, *Law's Empire* (Cambridge, MA: Harvard University Press, 1988), 147–150, 151–175, as "pragmatism."

76. See Yves Congar, "Status Ecclesiae," in *Droit ancient et structures ecclésiales* (London: Variorum Reprints, 1982), 3–31.

77. The popes have, for example, rather regularly ignored the law when they have nominated more cardinals than the law allows.

78. Nonet and Selznick, *Law and Society*, 35. For example, diocesan bishops are bound by universal laws of the church. They cannot dispense themselves from the observance of procedural, penal, or constitutive laws, but they can dispense themselves from observance of most universal disciplinary laws, as well as of their own laws and those enacted by episcopal conferences and particular councils.

79. Ulrich Stutz, *Der Geist des Codex Iuris Canonici* (Stuttgart, Germany: F. Enke, 1918), 83–88.

80. Eugenio Corecco, "Aspects of the Reception of Vatican II in the Code of Canon Law," in *The Reception of Vatican II*, ed. Giuseppe Alberigo, Jean-Pierre Jossua, and Joseph Komonchak (Washington, DC: Catholic University of America Press, 1987), 264.

81. Legrand, "Grâce et institution," 146–148. Legrand points out that the substitution for "perfect society" of more "progressive" imagery such as "the Church for others" does not fundamentally change this means-end schema. See Legrand, "Grâce et institution," 152. Nor does the interjection of heavy doses of *communio* language alter the underlying dynamic of codified law. At times, the invocations of *communio* do little more than "exploit it ideologically, covering with its spiritual and mystical connotations an ecclesiological theory and an ecclesial practice that do not differ

substantially from the old *societas perfecta* notion." See Joseph Komonchak, "Concepts of Communion. Past and Present," *Cristianismo nella storia* 16 (1995): 339.

82. Legrand, "Grâce et institution," 152.

83. Ibid., 153.

84. See Nonet and Selznick, *Law and Society*, 45.

85. Charles Taylor, "Clericalism," *Downside Review* 78 (1960): 174–175.

86. John Paul II, apostolic constitution *Sacrae disciplinae leges*, xxix–xxx.

87. 1983 *CIC*, c. 752.

88. 1983 *CIC*, c. 753.

89. Javier Hervada Xiberta and Pedro Lombardia, "Introduction to Canon Law," in *Exegetical Commentary on the Code of Canon Law* (Chicago: Midwest Theological Forum, 2004), 1:20: "Thus a simple magisterial statement or universal reception by the *sensus fidei*—as a point of faith—is sufficient for an unknown or disputed norm in divine law to have an immediate historical efficacy; it must then be accepted by the faithful and by the hierarchy as a juridical norm. For a little-known divine norm, a magisterial statement sets the content depending on the degree of knowledge reached at any moment in history and makes present the 'constitutional will to obey it.' But it does not presuppose or require any act of reception *ex novo* by the authorities."

90. 1983 *CIC*, c. 915. For a defense of the canonical appropriateness of the application of this canon in the cases of Senator Kerry and other public figures holding similar views, see Raymond L. Burke, "Canon 915: The Discipline Regarding the Denial of Holy Communion to Those Obstinately Persevering in Manifest Grave Sin," *Periodica* 96 (2007): 3–58.

91. Nonet and Selznick, *Law and Society*, 47.

92. As Charles Taylor has pointed out, even in avowedly secular societies, citizens share oral and spiritual insights rooted in a common "background picture." See Charles Taylor, *Sources of the Self: The Making of the Modern Identity* (Cambridge, MA: Harvard University Press, 1990), 3–24. In a similar vein, see Jürgen Habermas, "Pre-Political Foundations of the Democratic Constitutional State," in *The Dialectics of Secularization: On Reason and Religion*, ed. Florian Schuller (San Francisco, CA: Ignatius, 2006), 19–52.

93. Taylor, *A Secular Age*, 445.

94. John Paul II, allocution "ad Decanum Sacrae Romanae Rotae et eiusdem Tribunalis Praelatos at Auditores ineunte anno iudiciali," February 17, 1979: *A.A.S.* 71 (1979): 423.

95. Taylor, *A Secular Age*, 466.

96. 1 Peter 3:15.

6

A Teaching Church That Learns?

Discerning "Authentic" Teaching in Our Times

Gerard Mannion

Magisterial Malaises: Introductory Remarks

The life of the Roman Catholic Church has been blighted by divisions and disagreements in recent decades, and too often it has made headline news for all the wrong reasons. Such is well known. One particular set of issues is linked to the majority, if not all, of the problems the church has faced in these times. This is the understanding and exercise of church teaching authority (i.e., magisterium), in relation to which several developments of concern have arisen. Few pretend that it is the most exciting or energizing series of debates, and its discussion necessitates a degree of density. A more restrictive understanding and exercise of magisterium has emerged. There has been a renewed impetus to centralize matters upon Rome. Disagreement, dissent, and even discussion pertaining to "official" teaching on many issues have been dealt with in a stern fashion.

Because such developments have cumulatively influenced and shaped many aspects of Roman Catholic ecclesial life, teaching, formation, and theological inquiry, numerous Catholics today appear to have assimilated such an understanding of magisterium and accept such an exercise of the same as something both normative and apparently "traditional," despite the existence of considerable evidence to the contrary. This apparent conception of magisterium one finds in a wide range of locations, from official pronouncements from Rome, as well as from individual bishops and episcopal conferences, to discourse in theological journals and books, to discussions in the media and in the vitriol poured out against supposed "liberals" in the blogosphere: "*the* Magisterium" has become a concept that has generated as much controversy, division, and fear as it has misunderstanding.

In the main, theological discussions of such developments pertain to the reception of and appropriate response to what is termed "official" or "authentic" teaching today and who is authorized and/or competent to identify what counts as such.[1] Further issues emerge pertaining to wider questions of authority, governance, accountability, the role of the Catholic theologian and the notions of dissent, disagreement, and "creative fidelity" to such perceived official or authentic teaching. Questions concerning conscience, reception of doctrine, and *sensus fidelium* are recurrent themes in such debates.

This chapter, in the main, is about how the faithful, particularly theologians, understand and relate to church teaching authority. In broader terms, it seeks to discuss how the dynamics of authority, tradition, and dissent might be reenvisioned for postmodern times in a positive fashion. Kevin T. Kelly tells us: "Teaching authority, when properly exercised, empowers. It helps people to have a better understanding of the truth."[2] This chapter seeks to explore the implications of such an understanding of magisterium.

We begin by setting the scene with a consideration of the issue of assent to church teaching and move toward a discussion of its supposed converse, dissent. With such an example of the nature and scope of the confusions and problems in hand thus furnished, we next turn to explore how we might clarify our understanding of the differing types of church teaching and the authority they thus carry. These issues are core to many of the divisions in the church today. Then we explore further alternative strategies, suggestions, and resources for understanding and exercising magisterium in these times. Finally, we draw together our considerations toward the end of clarifying how we might best identify, perceive, and receive "authentic" (i.e., *authoritative*) church teaching in our times.

A core argument of this chapter is that the church desperately requires a more existentially oriented and humble (both in existential and epistemological terms) account of what the quest for Christian truth entails and, therefore, an understanding and exercise of magisterium complementary to this. Such a quest is a journey, a shared quest that proceeds in a tentative fashion. It is not a quest for certitude. The words of the former master of the Dominicans, Timothy Radcliffe, seem particularly apposite to the various debates we will encounter in what follows:

there is no short cut to the truth. Being truthful takes time. The role of the Magisterium is, or ought to be, to ensure that the Church takes the necessary time. It needs to pose tough questions when new views are articulated, not because of a fear of change or as "doctrinal enforcers," though that may sometimes be necessary, but to ensure that in the search for truth we do not take lazy short cuts and grab at premature and inadequate answers. The role of the Magisterium is to keep us talking, thinking and praying about what is central to our faith, as we journey towards the one who is beyond all words.[3]

Radcliffe's words help focus our attention on how the understanding of our faith and the role of magisterium should be oriented toward salvific practice, as opposed to being preoccupied in the main with laws and precepts. I wish to suggest that magisterium, like tradition itself, should be understood more as process than anything else. And a process that must, by necessity, involve the wider church as opposed to a restricted group of officeholders in particular *positions* of authority. Such authority itself only comes from the wider church and is held by such officeholders in trust. The task, then, is to discern more constructive ways for "Doing the Truth" in our times.

Assent and Its "Discontents": Understanding and Evaluating Magisterium Today

The Christian faith obviously rests on a core set of beliefs and practices. As a religion of revelation, these core beliefs and practices are connected with truths that Christians believe have been disclosed by God, most distinctly in and through the person of Jesus Christ. The church passes on, makes sense of, and bears witness to these beliefs and practices through its teachings, its doctrines. Obviously, it is well known that the Catholic Church claims that some of its teachings have been reached and set down with the gift of infallibility. Yet the term brings with it so much baggage and leads to a great deal of misunderstanding. We will not delve into those deep debates here except to point out that the sense of "infallibility" essentially refers not to any personal charism held by particular officeholders in the church as such; rather, it is an articulation of the belief that the Holy Spirit assists or maintains the church in its quest to understand, bear witness to, and put into practice the fundamental truths of the gospel.

In its ongoing attempts as fulfilling such a mission, Catholics give special place to both scripture and tradition, the latter encapsulating the ongoing task of making sense of revelation and of those core beliefs and practices. They also hold to the summaries of the core beliefs in the creeds and in other authoritative texts and documents that have emerged at various points throughout history, such as the teachings of key church leaders and theologians, the Code of Canon Law, and the Catechism of the Catholic Church.

So it is upon the church entire and not any particular member of it that this gift of the spirit is bestowed. The meaning of this gift (or promise, if one prefers) being, namely, that the truth of the gospel will be maintained and will endure. But even with that gift, the church still has to make sense of and explain the truths of the gospel for every age and discern how best to bear witness to them and put them into practice in each distinctive age and context. There are some teachings that appear to be so closely related to those divinely revealed truths, so universally assented to across time and space in the life of the church and that seem so important to the life and faith of the church, that they are understood to be teachings that should be held in perpetuity. They concern the fundamentals of what Christians believe to have been revealed, either directly or indirectly.[4] The existence of God is a most obvious primary example. Such teachings are those said to have been taught with the charism of infallibility.

Other teachings are most important to the understanding and safeguarding of those fundamental teachings. These, also, can sometimes be said to enjoy that gift of having been reached with the guidance of the Holy Spirit.[5] But then there are many other teachings, a number of which might relate to this second group to varying degrees, that carry significant weight and authority in the church but are not understood to be preserved from error or beyond reform or being reversed altogether. The technical term for this type of teaching is that it is said to have been taught with the "ordinary" teaching authority.

Obviously, there have been many debates throughout the history of the church about which teachings fall into which categories and what the appropriate response of Catholics to these teachings should be. In the main, a degree of respect is required for all teachings. But where the debates go from here is upon a long and winding journey, the end of which recent contributions make clear has yet to be reached.

The church is blessed with a number of gifted canon lawyers, moral theologians, and ecclesiologists, among others, who, in a patient, meticulous, and faithful spirit, hold developments in church teaching and their reception (or otherwise) up to close scrutiny. From their work, we can gain much inspiration with regard to seeing beyond the polarization generated by events and debates concerning magisterium, particularly those since the 1970s. It is important to underline the fact that, like most approaches to the contemporary situation that are constructive, positive, and forward-looking, such thinkers are certainly not afraid to learn from the past.

One of the foremost thinkers in the church of such character is Francis A. Sullivan, S.J., who, now in his ninth decade, has sought, in a faithful, objective, and fair-minded spirit, to articulate the nature of magisterium, as well as thereby illuminating the exercise and interpretation of the "official" magisterium in recent times. Fundamentally, for Sullivan, the concept of magisterium relates to that belief held by Christians across the ages and differing branches "that the Church of Christ is maintained in the truth of the gospel by the Holy Spirit."[6]

So it is important to appreciate that from this belief flow all manner of questions in relation to how the church entire comes to know, understand, live, and promote that truth. These questions eventually bring us to more specific matters of magisterium, but the latter concept does not come before broader questions concerning the faith, its transmission, and the doctrines that articulate both.

Thus in Sullivan's 1985 study, the very first chapter concerns "The Infallibility of the People of God,"[7] chapter 2 concerns "Magisterium" as a concept in itself,[8] and only after this chapter does Sullivan turn to questions concerning what some term the "hierarchical" elements and manifestations of magisterium. Sullivan works toward a consideration of the very relationship between theologians and magisterium in the church as a final chapter. Since the publication of that widely read monograph, Sullivan has devoted a great deal of time and energy to exploring these questions further still, particularly to trying to help the faithful understand the nature of magisterium itself better, and especially to trying to encourage greater mutual understanding and so better relations between theologians and Rome. In general, Sullivan has tried to enlighten people with regard to the precise scope and limitations of the various aspects and forms of teaching authority, as well as of differing types of teaching that, in themselves, hold differing levels of authority.

So, to consider but one key example of such contributions. Sullivan believes that when assessing the content, worth, and binding authority of any church document that sets down an aspect of the *ordinary* magisterium,[9] we should ask five particular questions. First, who is the teaching addressed to? Second, what *kind* of teaching is it? Third, what *kind* of document is the teaching contained in? Fourth, what particular level of magisterial authority is employed in the teaching? And, fifth, what sort of *language* is employed in the teaching?[10] As Sullivan states, while "popes have sometimes used language, in encyclicals or other letters addressed to the whole church, which has indicated their intention to settle a question that was disputed among Catholics,"[11] history suggests that, more often than not in their pronouncements, popes have *not* intended their language to be taken as "closure" on the subject matter in hand.

But problems have occurred in recent decades because many within the church still do not seem to be able to distinguish between the different gradations of church teaching and hence to identify the requisite response to such teachings. At times, this leads some teachings to be accorded greater authority than they actually merit, and if such a teaching relates to subject matter fraught with difficulties or that has proved the subject of differing interpretations, debate, and indeed controversy, then a misleading impression might be given that there is somehow a distinctive and final "official" Catholic position on that subject matter, when the reality might be something less settled altogether. Many suggest that some of this confusion has been exacerbated by the impressions in part generated by documents and pronouncements emanating from Rome itself in recent times.[12] The understanding of magisterium that has entered popular consciousness—both within and without the Roman Catholic Church—has compounded these problems.

One document that led to a great deal of confusion and debate in relation to the latter task was the new "Profession of Faith" released in 1989.[13] Indeed, this example opens up a wider debate relating to several key issues pertaining to magisterium in the contemporary era in general. To these we now turn.

Shifts in the Typologies of "Catholic Truth"

To provide some background in relation to this Profession of Faith, it should be noted that its significance is, in itself, ultimately concerned with the requisite authority pertaining to different types of church teaching. Indeed, there are, in the main, three types of teaching with which this document and a later commentary from the Congregation for the Doctrine of the Faith (CDF) upon it,[14] along with a 1998 papal motu proprio, *Ad tuendam fidem*[15] (which made particular changes to canon law in relation the same) are all concerned. Of additional relevance here is the 1990 CDF document, *Donum veritatis*, which offered an official interpretation of the new manner in which Catholic teaching authority was being categorized in Rome.[16] Collectively, these documents and the responses to them offer a vivid illustration of the tensions and divisions between Catholic theologians and Rome that have grown in the last four decades.

A variety of explanations have been offered concerning these shifting sands in the authority of particular categories of teaching. Christoph Theobald, for example, helps explain the shift that has taken place here by reference to some useful imagery. He suggests that we can divide Christian teachings into "three baskets of truth," and the situation brought about by the changes in relation to the *Professio* and the implications of *Ad tuendam fidem* negotiates a subtle shift of certain teachings (or "truths") from a lesser to a greater status of authority.[17] First are those truths of faith deemed to be revealed (what he calls the "first basket of Catholic truths"). Next are those doctrines relating to faith and morals that are "necessary for keeping and presenting faithfully the deposit of faith" (basket two). A "third basket of truths" are those teachings of the bishops and the pope that are furthest away from the "centre of revelation."[18]

Richard Gaillardetz, with the typical clarity that is his gift in such debates, abbreviates the three categories to "dogmatic teaching, definitive doctrine, and authoritative, non-definitive doctrine."[19] John Allen also offers a schematization, teachings pertaining to truths "Divinely revealed," teachings "Definitively proposed," and those that are exercises of the "Authentic Ordinary Magisterium."[20] The late Avery Dulles also offered his own threefold categorization in relation to the *Professio* and also the levels of assent required for each in an attempt to explain the purpose of *Ad tuendam fidem* and its wider magisterial context.

That profession recognized three levels of Catholic teaching: revealed truths infallibly taught as such by the magisterium, definitive Catholic teachings on matters of faith and morals intimately linked with revelation, and authentic but nondefinitive Catholic teaching. Corresponding to these three levels of teaching are three kinds of adherence: the assent of faith, firm acceptance, and "religious submission of will and intellect." The Code of Canon Law [hitherto] provided for the first and third levels. It prescribed automatic excommunication for culpable heresy and liability to "just penalties" for those who obstinately reject even non-definitive Catholic teaching. But the code said nothing specific about the second case. Should it be treated in the same way as the first or the third, or in some intermediate way?[21]

Although scholars employ different terminology, essentially they are referring to the same categories of teaching, as laid down by Theobald (and which correspond to the categories we outlined in general at the outset).[22] Collectively, such commentaries thus help identify significant issues that have emerged.

First, there have been various disagreements concerning the second and third "baskets of truths" (as Theobald described them) into which church teachings have been arranged in recent times. Suffice to summarize here that much debate was generated concerning whether such documents placed significantly greater restriction upon the work and freedom of intellectual inquiry and speech of Catholic theologians—more specifically, whether the implications of the same documents meant that theologians could no longer freely discuss certain issues as "Rome had spoken" and the matter was deemed closed. In particular, many feared that teachings were now being presented as having been "definitively" taught when, at best, some of these teachings are still considered by many to be open to further debate.[23] I.e., this has resulted in what Gaillardetz calls "authoritative, non-definitive doctrine" (Theobald's basket 3) being considered to hold the authority of teachings deemed "definitive doctrine" (basket 2).

Second, concerns were raised that the central Roman authorities or, in the main, the CDF appeared to be usurping the authority of what is termed the ordinary universal magisterium in order to actualize such changes.[24]

Third, a whole host of further complications and confusion were introduced by a rather wide ranging, imprecise and one has to say loose employment of the term 'definitive' in documents issuing from Rome and in statements from ecclesial leaders.

So the key question became whether such moves accorded an infallible "tone" to certain teachings hitherto seen as *noninfallibly* taught doctrines. The important point to remember here is that to *declare* something as holding the status of "definitive doctrine" is not equivalent to *making* it so. Perhaps encapsulating the issue at the heart of these concerns, Hermann J. Pottmeyer professed his considered judgment that *Ad tuendam fidem* confirmed and further demonstrated that a "new *form* of papal teaching" has come to the fore in recent years—namely, one that seeks to define certain teachings as having been taught infallibly, but to define them as such via a *fallible* process.[25]

Hence, in the opinion of many, developments illustrated by the *Professio* and, perhaps in particular, *Ad tuendam fidem* after it offered examples of an increasing strategy to seek closure or to declare consensual agreement where it was far from clear such had actually been achieved. As many of the teachings involved concerned contentious issues, it is fair to say that those who believed that such constituted attempts to short-circuit the necessary processes toward establishing the rightful path that Catholic teaching should take on various matters in these times did so with some justification.[26]

Space here does not permit an exhaustive treatment of all these debates, but essentially disagreement by theologians with particular interpretations emerging from Rome in recent decades has become an increasingly fraught business, as "dissent" from these interpretations has become a forbidden position in the eyes of the CDF, just as the perceived orthodoxy and faithfulness of theologians deemed to be worthy of the title Catholic has been increasingly policed anew. Assent has been demanded to an ever-growing number of propositions and Roman interpretations. Room for genuine debate and discussion has been squeezed out.

These problems have persisted as others in the church have increasingly seemed to find greater comfort in an all-or-nothing mentality with regard to church teaching authority or at least with regard to the thrust of a particular group of teachings concerning issues of contestation in recent decades. Catholics in general appear to be less clear now with regard to which teachings actually demand assent (and not just a "religious submission") than perhaps ever before.

One of the key problems is that "official" discourse pertaining to the understanding and exercise of magisterium in recent decades has been almost exclusively unidirectional in character: Rome has sought to impose as normative its own contemporary interpretation and practice. This not only accentuates divisions within the church but also creates something of a Catch-22 situation whereby magisterium is what those responsible for asserting a contentious notion of what it is, say it is.

These considerations thus far affirm the need for further open debates and reflection upon magisterium today. There are many alternatives to a uniform, authoritarian understanding of magisterium, attention to which might help to enhance the life and mission of the church in these times. But some further tools are needed to help overcome the difficulties. Indeed, the conversations that need to take place today must involve the participation of the widest possible variety of groups and individuals throughout the church, as opposed to being pronounced from the center. In such a spirit of mutuality, let us next consider a few additional positive potential proposals and ways forward for the understanding and exercise of magisterium in our times.

Exploring the Dynamics of Authority, Tradition, and Dissent

A perusal of an essay by Ladislas Örsy's from 1987,[27] obviously also composed prior to the drawing up of those documents issued by the 'official' magisterium, which for some, as we have observed, have proved contentious, might well have enlightened the character and tone of such documents in a number of ways.

> The inevitable conclusion is that, when the question arises, how far a
> point of doctrine proclaimed by the magisterium is binding, the only
> way to find out is not by invoking precise definitions (which do not
> exist) but by referring its content to our ancient traditions, by
> examining critically the source of that pronouncement, and weighing
> carefully the authority behind it.[28]

Örsy's perspective here adds further support to the carefully crafted arguments put forward in numerous writings by Sullivan. But the problem that remains is that, at least in relation to what is taken by most to be the official level, this is not how the process of magisterium has been understood in recent times.

Now some might suggest that by here focusing on particular documents and certain debates, one might fall into the trap of more centralizing tendencies. That is to say, by focusing on such official teaching, the interpretation given here could be said to be reinforcing the understanding of it that currently prevails and hence of what counts as dissent from it. Here, dissent is perceived solely in pejorative terms.

In response, due acknowledgment should of course be given to the arguments of those such as, for example, Kevin Kelly, Linda Hogan, Bernard Hoose, Nicholas Lash, and Joseph Selling[29] that terms such as *dissent* need to be avoided and that the whole language game pertaining to 'official' teaching and dissent from it should be resisted and dismantled. Indeed, Hoose and Kelly both suggest that the notion of dissent described in curial documents of recent decades is one of which it would be difficult to find one genuine example.[30] Kelly himself believes the term even misrepresents the very positive critical stance that theologians are often obliged to take in relation to teaching authority: "The term 'dissent' has no feel for all that is positive in such a position—respect for tradition, shared responsibility for the Church's mission in the world. It does not express the respect for teaching authority in the Church which motivates someone adopting this kind of stance."[31] However, as will become evident, while respecting so many of the insights shown in the arguments put forth by these and other scholars, I find myself more in sympathy with the interpretation offered by Charles E. Curran that dissent—or at least what many perceive by this term—can be (and throughout history demonstrably has been on a frequent basis) a necessary, positive, and, indeed, loyal stance to adapt in relation to certain church authorities and teachings. It is, then, part of tradition itself. As such, there is little to be gained from dressing dissent up as something else. Dissent can be the most appropriate response when faced with the dilemma that a particular teaching or interpretation of a teaching is being afforded an authority and weight that it does not, or even should not, truly hold.

But first, particularly given the evident confusion generated by the issuing of those church documents discussed previously, let us consider some particular ways in which we might today go about trying to follow the advice of those such as Örsy and Sullivan.

Rehabilitating Clearer Distinctions in Gradations of Authority

One example of an alternative strategy that has been proposed, of late, is the rehabilitation, in a form appropriate to our time, of the notion of "theological notes."[32] The concept, of course, returns us to our earlier discussions, for it

refers to the degree of authority that a theological statement, thesis, or proposition was issued under. The "notes" essentially qualify the requisite authority
and appropriate response to particular categories of teaching. Typically, the
theological manuals of the past would give a definition, explanation, example,
censure to be applied for the denial of such teaching, the effect of the latter, and
then perhaps some further remarks and guidance.

Hence the notes, which became systematically defined and increasingly
applied following the post–Council of Trent era of Roman orthodoxy and even
more so following the neoscholastic revival of the nineteenth century, served
the function of allowing the identification of, first, those things deemed to be
part "of the faith" (i.e., connected to divine revelation, including both those
things solemnly defined as such and not); second, those things perceived to be
closely related to or "bordering" on the faith; third, things considered as
"theologically certain"; and fourth, matters felt to be "probable opinion."[33]
Between such categories, still further "qualifications" have been offered. Francis Sullivan has illustrated how, since the demise in the neoscholastic system
(which was obviously centered on the employment of the notes), it has been
notoriously difficult to ascertain the theological consensus (or lack thereof) in
relation to any particular doctrine.[34]

So we are returned to threefold schemes[35] and, of course, there are clear
links here with the aforementioned baskets of truth and the attempts to outline
these and the assent due to them in the church documents we have discussed.
But although some might argue that such documents and the canonical revisions they introduced constitute, in themselves, an updating of the theological
notes, that is not how many commentators in the relevant fields have perceived
such changes. On the contrary, we might again underline the fact that, particularly with regard to the employment and interpretation of the various categories
of teaching in those Roman documents from the late 1980s and late 1990s
onward, there has seldom, if ever, been more confusion and less clarity with
regard to differing categories of church teaching and assent.

Indeed, in this period of what has been termed the "battle for the council,"
Harold Ernst suggests that renewed reflection on the notes would allow the
transitional nature of Vatican II to be better appreciated, thereby providing a
consistent hermeneutical principle for interpreting its documents today. This
method of procedure proves complementary to Sullivan's model of discernment; indeed, Ernst draws on the work of Sullivan at key stages of his own
essay. Ernst also concurs that the key issue pertaining to debates surrounding
magisterium today relates to the need for *consistency* in qualifying the authority
of differing teaching statements, and the literature addressing these debates,
some prime examples of which we have mentioned here, indicates how it is

precisely such that is missing from the recent "official" understanding and exercise of magisterium.[36]

As with Ernst's emphasis here on the "continuing need in theology for a means of evaluating the authority of doctrinal statements"[37] and our earlier discussion of Sullivan on weighing the documents of the magisterium, as well as Örsy's sentiments, Richard Gaillardetz has also argued for a "clearer presentation of the gradations of authoritative church teaching."[38] In Gaillardetz's judgment, there are necessary changes the church should introduce to rectify these problems. First, it needs to rely less on formal authority, which leads to a theology of magisterium more influenced by canon law than by ecclesiology, whereby "Obedience to Church office supersedes obedience to truth. The theologian and the ordinary believer are expected to respond to the authority of the officeholder more than to the authority of what is taught."[39] Thus, for Gaillardetz, the arbitrary closure of debate cannot replace genuine argument and dialogue.[40] This is because such arbitrary guillotining of discussion does not persuade, but rather leads to the diminishment of the church's teaching authority.[41]

So the solution as proposed in relation to the theological notes and related proposals, at least as I understand it, would not be to go back to the rigid scholastic formulation, but rather to embrace the need for clear gradations and a more expansive understanding of the varieties and forms (and hence authority) of church teaching in our times.

Hence thus far, we have encountered much support for the view that the assent due to statements and pronouncements of the various aspects of ecclesial magisterium is dependent on the manner in which they were formulated, how they were formulated, by whom, and for what purpose.[42] But would such a renewed attention to the theological notes prove sufficient to address the contemporary problems pertaining to magisterium?

Retrieving a Sense of "Hierarchy of Truths" and the "Dialogical Imperative"

Although it may seem somewhat obvious, it is telling that today one needs to reiterate more vociferously than has been expressed in recent periods of ecclesiological debate that there can be no justification for blurring the distinctions between teachings of differing authority and significance, nor for demanding equal assent to each and every aspect of ecclesial teaching. As Ernst laments, the danger in doing so is "that interpreters of doctrine lose their ability to discriminate among propositions, and the theoretically many gradations of doctrinal authority collapse into a 'zero-one' dichotomy."[43]

Yet this, unfortunately, would appear to be the situation in which many Catholics find themselves today. For this reason, I believe a renewed attention to something like the theological notes alone would not be enough. Indeed, trying to reach agreement with regard to what is actually in accord with differing categories of the notes (however revised) and trying to decide which teaching and theological opinions related to which specific notes would cause just as much, if not even greater, disagreement as the three baskets we have considered throughout this chapter. And at this point, it is apt to recall that one of the main difficulties with the recent understanding and exercise of Catholic magisterium is the *overlapping* form of the three baskets mentality that has become prevalent in recent decades.

Something significant changed, and those changes have not been helpful to the church as it goes about trying to fulfill its mission.[44] Many wider ecclesiological conversations and reforms need addressing in relation to these changes, as we will consider in what follows.

I do not wish to disagree that a renewed emphasis on the theological notes might very well be one way forward that could prove fruitful. However, to my mind, such could only do so in tandem with due attention to the great intra- (Roman) Catholic as well as ecumenical and interfaith promise offered by the notion of "hierarchy of truths."[45] A renewed and clearer understanding of the various gradations of church teaching authority, if combined with the latter notion, could offer much hope that the construction of a more engaging, dynamic, and less restrictive understanding of magisterium for these and future times is genuinely possible.

Such might well allow considerably more variation—and so debate in the church—than the form of the threefold formula applied in the *Professio fidei* and its subsequent interpretation and application. Such would prove problematic only to those who believe (contra so much of the Catholic tradition and history of the church) that only the central church authorities in Rome can lay claim to the authority to declare which truth belongs to which basket. The history of Catholic tradition clearly demonstrates that the journey toward discerning the truth has never been so easy and straightforward as such a model might suggest.

The scholastic tone of the notes and related canonical discussions, as we have here seen exemplified in the discussions pertaining to the *Professio* and *Ad tuendem fidem*, can often elicit greater confusion among the wider faithful. But the sense that some truths pertaining to the faith are of greater significance and carry greater and more enduring weight than others is more readily intelligible and helpful and open to ecumenical engagement in its scope.

I would suggest that if the church is to wean itself off any unhealthy and counterproductive overreliance on formal authority and indeed on the exertion of power, this will require an engagement in full and proper consultation with the church's own richly resourced theological community and the widening of conversations pertaining to magisterium throughout the church entire. The "dialogical imperative" that characterized so much of not only the spirit but also the (documentary) letter of Vatican II, needs to be rekindled.[46] What is further called for is a renewed understanding and practice of the incremental nature of all processes that carry Catholics along the path toward discernment and recognition, as well as lived experience of and commitment to truth.[47] What people frequently perceive, in negative terms, as dissent, can actually prove a fundamental part of this path and of these processes. So, taking up the challenge of that call to dialogue, let us turn to consider some further resources to shape alternative and constructive ways forward for the church of the future.

Principles for Discerning an Alternative Understanding and Exercise of Magisterium for Our Times

First of all, we should take heart from a most encouraging counterbalance to more divisive developments in recent years, namely that never before has magisterium been discussed so widely by so many lay Catholics and nonjurists alike. But this does not mean we can sweep the contentious issues under the carpet. So what additional considerations might help inform future efforts toward ensuring magisterium is exercised more collaboratively by the people of God for the service of the church as a whole? These times call for magisterium to move in the direction of a virtuous as opposed to a vicious circle. Today's church requires proposals for a renewed and existentially, ecclesially, and indeed ecumenically empowering ecclesiology and thus magisterium.

There are many studies that point towards the numerous and potentially life-denying fault lines in the recent understanding and exercise of magisterium. The exclusively pejorative understanding of disagreement with 'official' teachings (the notion of dissent) along with increased centralization and authoritarianism are key examples, as we have touched upon here. Such fault lines have further and considerable implications for the entire life of the church and especially so for the vision of Vatican II. They thus relate to much wider ecclesiological issues than even the broad field of magisterium (thankfully a number of these issues have been also been articulated by various other scholars).[48]

However, this in itself means that the resources from across the church's treasure trove of tradition can therefore be utilized in the service of overcoming these contemporary difficulties. In particular, the resources of Catholic tradition in the areas of social teaching, moral theology, and canon law can all be turned to for inspiration here.

The simple reason this is so is that authority emerges out of that tradition and stands in direct relation to it. To continue a central line of argument that this chapter seeks to offer, such resources might help us in today's church to appreciate anew the fact that what is often termed dissent has been seen to shape, refine, and develop church teaching, and sometimes, ultimately, it has even led to certain aspects of teaching being jettisoned altogether.[49] Thus dissent can prove to be fundamental to teachings in the church of the highest authority.[50] And the opposite of decentralization can be truly life giving to the church universal.[51] Let us briefly consider some of these resources, albeit painting in broad, general strokes, and touch on a few key areas that offer rich promise for further consideration.

Participation: Resources from Social Teaching

If a dynamic and collaborative understanding and exercise of magisterium is to prevail, then a truly dialogical and conversational commitment on the part of ecclesial authorities will need to become ever more the norm. We would thus do well to reflect on and further embrace the ecclesial life-giving principles of the Catholic *social* tradition,[52] for example, the principles of collegiality (which, of course, has much wider applications than the college of bishops alone),[53] subsidiarity,[54] and coresponsibility.[55] Above all else, the principle of participation (which embraces these and so many other principles) can and should become a fundamental part of discourse concerning magisterium.[56] And note that these principles themselves each became an increasingly important part of the Catholic social tradition in no small measure due to the exercise of what would today most probably be termed an attitude of dissent. In addition, the cumulative meaning of church teaching points to the fact that each and every one of the faithful is actually a part of the church's magisterium, to somewhat turn Pius IX's infamous saying on its head.

Hence here I am seeking to emphasize that magisterium is and should be understood in a fashion that is analogous to the ways in which we seek to understand wider aspects of (shared) human life in general. In human life, there will be exhilarating highs and very deep and dark low periods. There will be great hopes, achievements, and moments of bliss, insight, charity, and wider aspects of love. There will forever be change—often for good and sometimes for ill. But life is never about seamless transition without struggle from one period to the next. And it is never flawless or perfect, no matter how much we strive after such perfection. So if, where helpful, we could seek to understand and exercise magisterium in an analogous fashion to those ways in which we try to make sense of life itself or of our shared existence, our debates may move forward in a less divisive fashion. Many hands make light work on this shared journey. Involving as many of the community as possible and listening to voices rather than dictating from preconceived conclusions offer a significantly more positive and harmonious way forward for the Catholic communities across the globe.[57]

Provisionality: Resources from Moral Theology

Our considerations thus far have also collectively pointed toward the need for discussions pertaining to the contemporary magisterium to embrace a renewed and transformed appreciation and understanding of the provisionality of much Catholic teaching (or, to recall Radcliffe's words, understanding the truth takes time). Of course, in relation to ethical questions, the retrieval of such an understanding has been one of the most positive developments in *moral* theology in the second half of the twentieth century. Retrieving much insight from the thought of Aquinas here, such a notion became prevalent again through the work of major Catholic ethicists such as Charles E. Curran and has been termed by Margaret Farley as "the grace of self-doubt."[58]

This reminds us further how and that our means of ecclesial discernment (moral, social, and otherwise) are processes. The *imposition* of teaching of whatever authoritative gradation can only be contrary not simply to the gospel but to the fundamental character of both faith and assent alike (and hence can never constitute an example of authentic magisterium).

Thus I would suggest that any effective understanding and exercise of magisterium in these contemporary times must free itself from any pretense to omniscience, for, in reality, the character of its exercise in recent times would on occasion appear to hold more in common with the 'view from nowhere' genre. In other words, far from being grounded in fundamental and universally agreed upon traditions (whether diachronically or synchronically understood), pronouncements in recent decades have, at times, appeared to claim an authority that transcends context, culture, and history alike. And yet ecclesial authority is inescapably rooted and shaped by each of these factors. The popularized version of such an understanding of magisterium has mutated into ever-vindictive and judgmental forms.[59]

Such arguments are further supplemented by analogous sentiments expressed by Joseph Selling.[60] Here speaking in relation to morality, Selling believes that official pronouncements *cannot* form the sole basis of teaching; rather, the lived experiences of the people of God must be allowed to inform magisterium itself. Echoing our earlier considerations, he states that "the authority to teach in the area of morality within the context of the believing community is intimately tied to the matter being taught."[61] Selling's consistently stressed point is something also echoed in the writings of those such as Farley and Curran (and, of course, Aquinas himself): all hold that the further one gets from revelation, the less certain the value and lasting significance of the teaching.[62] Indeed, what is required is a greater engagement with the genuine depth and breadth of the natural law tradition and its methodological foundations, as opposed to those more rigid, absolutist, and legalistic conceptions of natural law that have found favor in many parts of the church in recent times, including Rome.[63]

Furthermore, an appreciation of the fact that the natural law tradition does not stand in isolation from other ethical modes of discernment, such as virtue theory, would enhance dialogue on magisterium across the church. Such an approach offers much to draw all such thinking together in a fashion where pastoral matters can be better wedded to moral and ecclesiological thinking. So the focus here would be not on what we must do or obey but on how we should aspire to live and to be, and in a way that is always attentive to specific contexts. Indeed, in general this chapter is an attempt to contribute to the shaping of a "virtue ecclesiology," whereby the life of the church literally is in greater harmony with the love and vision of the gospel it preaches.[64] Examples of virtues that might be especially valuable for the church to nurture in these times are openness, honesty, truthfulness, a willingness to enter into dialogue, and humility, both existential and epistemological.

Thus particular insights from moral theology from the second half of the twentieth century should be allowed to influence contemporary ecclesiological and thus canonical and governmental debates and decisions, along with those resources from the especially relevant field of Catholic social thought. All might be here utilized as resources to inform and move forward such debates and hence to foster more positive and collaborative practice throughout the church in general.

An overt focus on aspects of canon law alone, combined with further entrenchment of the renewed centralization of ecclesial authority and a more formal/normative ecclesiology, can only take debates so far and indeed risks taking such discussions down a futile cul-de-sac or, at best, perpetuating circular discussions that, in the end, leave the conversation partners as far apart from one another's positions as ever. But before drawing to a conclusion, it is first important to stress that we cannot and should not forget canon law either, for it might also have riches to offer anew.

Retrieving the "Blessing of Law": Resources from Canon Law

Other contributions to this volume have offered important and constructive critiques of the nature, failings, and also future potential of canon law. So M. Cathleen Kaveny and John P. Beal in particular explore a rehabilitation of manualist casuistry and denounce the baroque and clericalist-hierarchical social imaginary behind modern canon law, respectively.[65] Beal speaks of the remoteness of canon law from the everyday life of the faithful. Following the existential emphasis throughout this chapter, I wish to consider how the contemporary church might recast its understanding and practice of canon law in order that all might more fully recall that, following the New Testament especially, law is not the key end in itself; rather, the local community and its internal relations and its relationship with God are. Hence what I would wish to add to those other voices is to emphasize that virtue must shape law and its practice rather than vice versa.

A thought-provoking reflection upon the riches of the canon law tradition and a positive reminder of what law is for and what law is about can be found in a powerfully evocative essay by the Irish jurist and Dominican theologian, Joseph Kavanagh, who spent many years in Rome, and even more in the Caribbean, before returning to the Priory at Tallaght, Dublin. He takes as his starting point the line from Seamus Heaney's poem "The Settle Bed" that "there is nothing given that cannot be reimagined." I believe this has empowering connotations in relation to the very heart of tradition, along with the development and emergence of doctrine.[66] Kavanagh decries the "kind of laziness, when answers are sought simply through the formula of the law, as though the lawmaker's role is simply to provide solutions and dispense the community and the individual from wrestling with the complexities of their world."[67] He thus helps illustrate that a more open vision of magisterium, such as that we seek to sketch in this chapter, can prove fully consistent with fundamental tenets of the historical Catholic tradition of canon law itself. By implication, more negative understandings of magisterium might actually be identified as being out of step with the spirit and function of canon law.

Recalling the acute awareness of such dangers (of which Pope Paul VI himself was mindful), Kavanagh laments when legislators try to claim exclusive ownership of the right to interpret law and in doing so compound the failings of all in the church who "abdicate responsibility for wrestling with the demands of each situation."[68] Kavanagh urges the church to be empowered through the restoration of "critical memory" in order to help move forward the struggle for the vision of Vatican II, for such empowering memory will bring to mind the diversity that challenges us all both within and without the church. This again evokes a vivid image of the process of tradition.

Echoing the focus on the importance of reception and of the participatory and dialogical sense of magisterium outlined here, Kavanagh finds particular wisdom in Gratian's twelfth-century dictum concerning the reception of law: "'laws are instituted when promulgated; confirmed when approved by the users' (leges instituuntur, cum promulgantur, firmantur, cum moribus utentium approbantur)."[69] Note that Kavanagh makes it explicitly clear that Gratian does not here undermine legislators in the slightest. Rather, and in harmony with affirming the authority of the legislator, he simply allows that a community has the right and indeed duty to decide if and when a particular law might not apply in its case. Here I think the debates concerning the "battle for the council" and the requisite postconciliar moral, pastoral, doctrinal, and ecclesiological struggles are all brought into sharper focus. This chapter has suggested that the common denominator to many of the difficulties surrounding each area of ecclesial life is the understanding and exercise of magisterium in play at particular times and in particular contexts and situations.

Pertinently, and echoing our sentiments on the treasures of moral and social doctrine, particularly the notion of a virtue ecclesiology, Kavanagh also links a retrieval of the connection between law and fostering the common good, as well as the thus necessary retrieval of a healthy understanding of reception, with the retrieval of virtue theory and particularly its Thomistic forms.[70] He notes that "between the law and the action there is a process in which the law's *ordinatio* interacts with other factors to help bring about a prudential decision."[71] Likewise, Kavanagh echoes the importance of Farley's "grace of self-doubt" in his call for a greater application of the virtue of humility to lawmaking,[72] and he places particular emphasis on a further retrieval of the principle of equity and of the application of *epikeia*,[73] and thereby, contra much thinking in certain quarters in recent decades, on the indispensable role, indeed, the "supremacy," of conscience. And what does this bring to mind but the very essence of what too many reject in these recent times as "mere" dissent?

What draws all this together for Kavanagh is the Vatican II notion of the church as the people of God journeying together along the pilgrim way.[74] Thus we return to the dynamic interrelation of authority, tradition, and dissent. Pilgrims on a journey together bear common responsibilities toward one another and must also trust one another, and hence for Kavanagh, also, the notion of subsidiarity should be embraced as a keystone of church administration, just as there needs to be "a radical revision of the manner of Episcopal appointment."[75] This further underlines the importance of social doctrine in forging a more open vision of magisterium. And as a footnote to this "blessing," it is important to remember that canon law already contains numerous provisions for a more dialogical and participatory understanding and exercise of authority.[76]

Bringing Teaching Authority and Freedom into Right Relation

All the rich resources from the social, moral, and canonical realms of the Catholic tradition point toward an understanding and exercise of magisterium that brings authority and freedom into right relation. Indeed, I would suggest that due attention to human freedom (including freedom of conscience and freedom of theological inquiry and thus freedom to dissent from institutional interpretations and teachings when deemed necessary), as opposed to any focus on power and enforcement, presents by far a more fruitful strategy for defending and commending the faith. Questions concerning authority, teaching, and so magisterium have obvious existential significance both in individual terms and in social terms. The understanding and exercise of magisterium have a profound influence on how Christians, collectively and personally, strive to be faithful to the gospel in their being-in-the-world—the world that is, of course, God's own creation.

Any understanding and exercise of magisterium that debilitates human flourishing within the church and within the wider society and across the global communities that constitute the human family must therefore be deemed to be problematic at best and counterevangelical (literally, working against the gospel) at worst. Such would be deprived of "authenticity" and thus authority in any genuine sense at all. How would we ever recognize genuine authority without the principle of participation playing its part in the process of magisterium and without dissent itself? It is all the more disappointing, then, to see how, in its responses to the challenges of the postmodern age, the understanding and exercise of the 'official' magisterium in recent decades have, all too often, in effect been world-renouncing and existentially debilitating. As John L. McKenzie has argued, "When authority recognizes freedom, authority has that unique security which comes from the free consent of those who are subject to authority; their power is merged with its own."[77] In agreement with McKenzie that there is a healthy and productive tension between freedom and authority (might we even label this tension "dissent" for shorthand?), it is my hope that dialogue throughout the church leads to a wider acceptance of the fact that the nature of ecclesial authority can and ought only be understood within the context of freedom—a maxim that therefore calls for a reexamination of fundamental ecclesiological concepts and ecclesiastical practices.

"Authentic" Teaching in Our Times

How might we draw together the numerous reflections considered in this chapter? It is frequently pointed out that the most correct translation of *magisterium authenticum* is not "authentic" teaching but rather "authoritative" teaching. While acknowledging this, perhaps we might, in this context at least, retain the use of the word *authentic* for reasons that I hope have begun to emerge as the cumulative argument in this chapter has unfolded.

In short, this chapter has sought to set forth in a cumulative fashion some grounds for the case that the only truly authoritative Christian teaching is that which is faithful to the gospel mission of being oriented toward human flourishing and hence the path toward closer union with God, namely, salvation. What this entails in practice is that truly authoritative teaching is that which is existentially liberating and empowering; it values and enhances human freedom and the wider participation of all in the church in the processes that constitute magisterium (for such correctly refers only to the function and not the functionaries of authoritative teaching).

Thus such teaching respects, perhaps above all else, the principles of participation and subsidiarity as nonnegotiable tenets of prime importance to the life and mission of the church. Both draw together the social, moral, and canonical aspects of the faith and, of course, are in themselves a means by which authority and freedom are brought into proper relation. This is opposed to any erroneous understanding of magisterium that might confuse raw power with true authority and hence mistake authoritarianism with authority. Such erroneous understandings of magisterium rely on increasing centralization and attempt to short-circuit many of the traditional processes essential to the achievement of truly authoritative teaching. They can thus be debilitating and detrimental to the corporate life of the church and hence of all the faithful alike. They do not serve well that gospel mission of enhancing human flourishing.

In other words, erroneous understandings of magisterium do not facilitate the living out of authentic human existence-in-community. Both in personal and social terms, such understandings of magisterium are existentially inauthentic, just as they are bereft of true and genuine authority, which, as we have sought to suggest, is inseparably bound up with human freedom and flourishing and thus with authentic human existence.[78] I hope this wordplay, of sorts, will prove constructively illuminating in helping to demonstrate that the church cries out for a more existential and virtuous, as opposed to a primarily disciplinary, understanding and exercise of magisterium for these times.

The Abiding Value of Magisterium . . . and of Faithful Critique as Integral to Its Authenticity

None of the foregoing is to denigrate magisterium in the slightest. On the contrary, such suggestions are aimed toward enhancing the effectiveness of magisterium for these times and beyond and thus equally toward enhancing the respect and assent afforded it. As Thomas P. Rausch rightly states, "One of the greatest strengths of Catholicism is precisely its teaching office, its magisterium, which allows the Church to reinterpret and occasionally to correct its tradition when confronted with new questions. The Catholic tradition is a living tradition, not a dead one."[79] But that is all the more reason to commend an understanding of the fact that "not every theological critique of a belief, practice, or tradition is an attack on the Catholic tradition itself, tradition with a capital 'T.'"[80]

Again recalling Radcliffe's words at the outset, it does seem beyond doubt that, in recent times, some in the church have rushed toward shortcuts to the truth, as if such were possible. Numerous theologians in the church, out of love for the church, respect for its teaching and tradition, dedication to its mission, and a desire to serve the truth, have found it necessary to offer alternative hermeneutical and dialogical contributions to those put forth in recent decades by certain curial and hierarchical officials and set down in certain documents from the 'official' magisterium. These should be considered part of the necessary and indispensable processes of doing the truth that the church needs in these times, perhaps more than in many other eras.

Attempts to redefine the boundary markers of what constitutes acceptable or orthodox and what is classed as dissenting Catholicism reflect those shifts in the self-understanding of the institutional church center that we have seen emerge gradually over the past four decades or so. But the category mistake of absolutizing the institution itself at the expense of the people of God, whose living out the faith actually constitutes the reality of the Catholic Church, should not go unchallenged.

Rightly channeled and ordered, dissent can carry a moral authority all its own. The church stands in need, then, of a reminder that theologians also bear witness. Such witness has often proved unsettling to those in positions of secular and ecclesial power alike. Nonetheless, positive change and development in the church and theology alike almost always involve such a process of bearing witness.[81] Indeed, there are countless examples of times when dissent in the church has proven to be a virtuous act in itself, and here we can draw numerous parallels beyond those sketched admirably by John Henry Newman, such as the laity defending the Christological doctrines during the Arian controversy (over and against their bishops).[82] Indeed, Hermann Häring reminds us, with a more striking passage still, of this surprising virtue that can be life-giving to the church:

> Models for dissent? . . . let us recall the great *Christian prototype*: Jesus of Nazareth, who paid for his protest with a heretic's and insurgent's death. Only against this background can we confess him to be the Risen One and the Son of God. Ever since, dissent in his name has had a unique dignity so long as it follows the words given to Peter: "Follow me!" (John 21:22)[83]

By their very nature, faith and theology belong together but are not the same thing. Faith is the assent to the gospel message that Christianity proclaims, and as St. Anselm in his *Proslogion* argued (and, of course, Augustine before him), the point is not to seek understanding in order to believe but to believe in order to understand. The very business of theology is the business of faith seeking understanding.[84] But if what constitutes the faith can be rigidly defined prior to the pilgrim's journey toward understanding, then there is no longer any meaningful role for theology in the process—something that some overt forms of Christian fundamentalism have proclaimed. Faith must involve the subjective aspects of the human person in order to *be* faith. After all, faith cannot, by definition, be something set in stone. "Defending the faith" should not be about prescribing in precise terms how it must be lived in all places at all times, for such would deny that faith is a living entity, which is why it has endured for so long. It withers and dies when its vitality is threatened.

And if theology is rightly perceived as faith seeking understanding, then it is obvious that theology and hence the teaching it helps shape and inform and indeed revise, develop, and sometimes revolutionize cannot be about fixed positions and intransigent absolutes. Rather, both should point to a shared journey toward the truth, that truth which Christians call God. Our reflections here suggest that a rightful privileging of the Vatican II ecclesiology of seeing the church as the pilgrim people of God captures this sense of a shared journey perfectly.

Concluding Remarks

Lest we forget, St. Thomas Aquinas, whom the Roman Catholic communion reveres as the Angelic Doctor of the church, had his works condemned by representatives of that same church's magisterial authorities. His books were burned. But times change. Perspectives change. Antonio Rosmini Serbati's work, which has experienced the fluctuating fortunes of being approved and condemned at various points since the nineteenth century, until Joseph Ratzinger and the CDF sought to rehabilitate him once and for all in 2001,[85] demonstrates the fluctuating fashions at the official level of magisterium in a vivid and comprehensive manner. We must never forget that even judgments of the 'official' magisterium may—in the course of time—come to appear misguided, misinformed, and even not infrequently mistaken. Reception must remain a fundamental part of the processes of magisterium, and what is often termed dissent might be simply the litmus test of the true authoritative status of a teaching and hence its standing in relation to the journey toward the truth.

In conclusion, then, "creative fidelity" or, if one prefers, "loyal dissent" is an ecclesial virtue that steers between two extremes: on the one hand, centralizing and legalistic intransigence that is debilitating to the vitality of ecclesial existence, as well as to the change and development necessary to the life of the church, and at the opposite extreme, a drift toward total disregard for the rich traditions of the church in favor of an out-and-out relativism and slide toward a pick-and-mix postmodern individualism. The virtuous mean in between, which, of course, like every virtue, must always be context-attentive, is recognizing the provisionality of much church teaching because of the need to engage in various processes of dialogue and discernment and to understand that the shared journey toward the truth is an ongoing journey that will necessitate development, change, and sometimes a complete reversal of direction.

Dissent is simply another name for the virtue of having the courage to own one's convictions or doubts openly and honestly. Dissent can be the utmost form of a religious submission of will and intellect and of assent to the truth of the faith itself. And as ecclesiastical history demonstrates in abundance, the practice of such a virtue often comes with a heavy price, hence the witness borne by its practitioners is all the more worthy of our admiration and gratitude.

We live in a time that can prove to be a most wonderful learning opportunity for the church. But if dynamics of authority, tradition, and dissent point toward anything, it is this: only a church that *learns* from its own mistakes, past and present, from the voices of its own faithful, from its own theologians, from its various and disparate episcopal and ecclesial contexts, from those of other churches, of other faiths and of no faith, indeed from the wider human experiences in general, can truly teach with genuine authority. But of course, to say such is but to reaffirm the fundamental messages of Vatican II, itself a council both of retrieval of tradition and of renewal.

NOTES

1. The term "the official magisterium" will be employed here when referring to conceptions that center on the role of the "official" church authorities, particularly Rome, to distinguish them from broader understandings. The primary considerations relate to what (and not "who") magisterium is and who can and should exercise it.

2. Kevin T. Kelly, "Serving the Truth," in *Dissent in the Church*, Readings in Moral Theology 6, ed. Charles E. Curran and Richard A. McCormick, 478–483 (New York: Paulist, 1988), 480.

3. Timothy Radcliffe, "How to Discover What We Believe," *Tablet* (January 28, 2006): 13.

4. The technical term here is the "direct" object of magisterium.

5. Here some complex debates concern whether or not this category concerns what is called the "secondary objects of infallibility."

6. Francis A. Sullivan, *Magisterium* (Dublin, Ireland: Gill and Macmillan, 1985), 2.

7. Ibid., 4–23.

8. Ibid., 24–34.

9. I.e., noninfallible, but not to be confused with the ordinary and universal magisterium. The latter, the church teaches, can indeed carry the charism of infallibility.

10. Francis A. Sullivan, S.J., *Creative Fidelity* (London: Gill and Macmillan, 1996).

11. For example, Sullivan astutely notes that this final question has particular relevance to the tone of language employed in *Ordinatio Sacerdotalis* (a document reserving ordination to the priesthood to men alone); ibid., 22.

12. And also by the method employed in composing such documents and the manner in which particular church documents and official statements are used as "sources" to justify more rigid interpretations of teaching on numerous matters, regardless of the differing authority pertaining to these sources.

13. "Profession of Faith and Oath of Fidelity" (March 1, 1989). Available online.

14. Joseph Ratzinger and Tarcisio Bertone, *Commentary on the Profession of Faith's Concluding Paragraphs*, July 16, 1998, *Tablet* (July 11, 1998): 922.

15. John Paul II, *motu proprio, Ad tuendam fidem* (May 18, 1998).

16. Thus *Donum Veritatis* ("Instruction on the Ecclesial Vocation of the Theologian") set down definite parameters to what constitutes legitimate areas of inquiry for Catholic theologians, as well as limiting the levels of permissible disagreement with official church teaching ("dissent" is not an option). Hence the document "officially ratifies the extension of authority introduced in the second paragraph of the Profession of Faith" and different responses were to be outlined corresponding to different forms of teaching. William C. Spohn, "The Magisterium and Morality: Notes on Moral Theology 1992," *Theological Studies* 54 (1993): 95–111, at 99. See also Francis A. Sullivan, "The Theologian's Ecclesial Vocation and the 1990 CDF Instruction," *Theological Studies* 52 (1991): 51–68. It was *Donum Veritatis* that articulated the highly controversial "new" category of teaching known as "definitive doctrine" (which is, nonetheless, *not* irreformable). We should also mention a further document from 1990, *Ex Corde Ecclesiae*, a papal document on the nature and role of a Catholic university, which would lead to further scrutiny of the "orthodoxy" of Catholic theologians in many countries.

17. Christoph Theobald, "The 'Definitive' Discourse of the Magisterium: Why Be Afraid of a Creative Reception," in *Unanswered Questions*, ed. Christoph Theobald and Dietmar Mieth, *Concilium* (1999–2001): 60–69; citations used here taken from an abridged version in *Readings in Church Authority*, ed. Gerard Mannion, Richard Gaillardetz, Jan Kerkhofs, and Kenneth Wilson (Aldershot, England: Ashgate, 2003), 112–118.

18. Ibid., 114.

19. Richard R. Gaillardetz, "The Ordinary Universal Magisterium: Unresolved Questions," *Theological Studies* 63 (2002): 454.

20. John Allen Jr., *Pope Benedict XVI* (London: Continuum, 2005), 290–291.

21. Avery Dulles, "How to Read the Pope," *Tablet* (July 25, 1998): 967.

22. Obviously, they correspond to understandings of teaching set down in canon law and the Roman documents mentioned previously, which in themselves relate to the various earlier attempts at categorization. Where disputes arise is in relation to which teachings belong to which category, as we shall see.

23. Concerning some of the confusion pertaining to what teachings should be bracketed under which category, one might add to the existing evocative imagery in play with reference to the impression created by a magician who presents three cups and then places an object underneath one of the cups, before swapping them around very swiftly to reveal the object seemingly under a different cup.

24. Normally understood to refer to the collective teachings of the pope and bishops dispersed throughout the world.

25. Hermann J. Pottmeyer, "Auf fehlbare Weise unfehlbahr? Zu einer neuen Form päpstlichen Lehrens," *Stimmen der Zeit* (April 1999): 233–242; English trans. "Fallibly Infallible? A New Form of Papal Teaching," with commentary by James S. Torrens, in *America*, April 3, 1999, 19–20. Sullivan, it should be noted, did not believe the document was especially controversial but rather a routine tidying up of some anomalies in canon law.

26. The commentary on the *Professio* was criticized for going even further than these documents in generating controversy. Ratzinger offered examples such as the ordination of women, teaching on euthanasia, and the validity of Anglican orders as all being teachings that demanded unconditional assent.

27. Ladislas Örsy, "Magisterium: Assent and Dissent," *Theological Studies* 48 (1987): 473–497.

28. Ibid., 480.

29. E.g., Linda Hogan, *Confronting the Truth: Conscience in the Catholic Tradition* (London: DLT, 2000), 165–190; Bernard Hoose, "Authority in the Church," *Theological Studies* 63 (2002): 115–119; Nicholas Lash, "Waiting for the Echo," *Tablet* (March 4, 2000): 309–310. Selling's contribution is considered later in this chapter.

30. See Hoose, "Authority in the Church," 116, citing Kevin Kelly, *New Directions in Moral Theology* (London: Geoffrey Chapman, 1992), 150. (Kelly's work is also influential upon Hogan's study.)

31. Kelly, "Serving the Truth," 480. But note Kelly also offers a much more positive understanding of the *function* of what is termed dissent in "The Learning Church," 473–478.

32. A particularly creative attempt at doing so in recent years is by Harold E. Ernst, "The Theological Notes and the Interpretation of Doctrine," *Theological Studies* (2002): 813–825, whom we take as our example of such a constructive attempt here. We also consider the broader ranging specialist work in this field of Richard R. Gaillardetz, discussed later in this chapter. A classic textbook formulation of the pre–Vatican II type of approach, originally published in 1952, is found in Ludwig Ott, *Fundamentals of Catholic Dogma* (Rockford, IL: Tan, 1974), e.g., 1–10.

33. Ernst and others list still further gradations, but the most significant ones have thus been listed.

34. E.g., Sullivan, *Creative Fidelity*, 103–107. Note that one should not confuse the "theological notes" with the "notes" employed by John Henry Newman, *An Essay on the*

Development of Christian Doctrine, which appeared first in 1845. Newman was actually devising his own sevenfold system of judging what constitutes a legitimate "development" in doctrine ("Notes of Genuine Development"). Naturally, it has relevance to our debate here, as we shall touch upon, but the more traditional sense of "theological notes" actually deals with the authority of a teaching itself and the assent required in relation to it. Newman's employment of the term is not to distinguish between differing gradations of authority but rather to distinguish between legitimate additions to the store of Christian doctrinal tradition or otherwise. Obviously, such pertains to the "authority" of any teaching that results from such developments, but not in exactly the same way as the scholastic notes approached the issue. Newman only actually spoke of "notes" as opposed to "tests" of doctrinal development in the third edition in 1878, decades after he became a Roman Catholic and some years after he had been reflecting on the implications of Vatican I. Newman was essentially testing a hypothesis (on the validity of the Roman Catholic church and the truth of its teachings). Thus Newman means something quite different in terms of function when he refers to notes. The later Ernst believes Newman's contribution here is more analogous to the notion of the "hierarchy of truths" that emerged in later theological discourse, particularly at Vatican II; see Ernst, "The 'Hierarchy of Truths' in the Thought of John Henry Newman," *Irish Theological Quarterly* 70, no. 4 (2005): 307–330, at 321. We discuss the concept of hierarchy of truths in more detail later in this chapter. Suffice to say at this juncture that I believe much of Newman's thought is indeed more conducive to this ecumenically more promising notion than a more rigid redeployment of the "theological notes."

35. As noted, here I have abbreviated the notes down to the three main categories for the sake of not just space but in relation to the wider debates we are considering in this chapter. The key debate here is whether the recent understanding of magisterium in Rome offers too little distinction between different teachings and too few categories.

36. For Ernst, although the system of "notes" was *proposition* based and the language employed throughout much of the Vatican II documents sought to move away from neoscholastic categories to fulfill the pastoral intentions of the council, it nonetheless seems to be the case that most of the council fathers continued to operate according to commonly known and accepted assumptions with regard to the system of theological notes. See Ernst, "The Theological Notes," 819ff.

37. Ibid., 813.

38. Richard R. Gaillardetz, *Teaching with Authority: A Theology of the Magisterium in the Church* (Collegeville, MN: Liturgical Press, 1997), 289–293.

39. Ibid., 290–291.

40. Ibid., 291.

41. Ibid., 291–292. Cf., Jayne Hoose, "Dialogue as Tradition," in *Moral Theology for the 21st Century: Essays in Celebration of Kevin Kelly*, ed. Julie Clague, Bernard Hoose, and Gerard Mannion, 57–66 (New York: Continuum, 2008).

42. Reprising much of Sullivan's proposals concerning the ordinary magisterium.

43. Ernst, "The Theological Notes," 823–824.

44. Cf. Gerard Mannion, "'Defending the Faith': The Changing Landscape of Church Teaching Authority and Catholic Theology—1978–2005," in *The Vision of John Paul II: Assessing His Thought and Influence*, ed. Gerard Mannion, 78–106 (Collegeville, MN: Liturgical Press, 2008).

45. Cf., for example, *Unitatis Redintegratio*, §11: "When comparing doctrines with one another, they should remember that in Catholic doctrine there exists a 'hierarchy' of truths, since they vary in their relation to the fundamental Christian faith."
See also Francis A. Sullivan, *Magisterium*, 117–118, and his *Creative Fidelity*, 93.
The concept of "hierarchy of truths," along with that closely related to it from the Anglican and Protestant traditions of "adiaphora," is discussed and utilized to great ecumenical insight in Roger Haight, *Ecclesial Existence*, vol. 3 of *Christian Community in History* (New York: Continuum, 2008), esp. 7, 10, 216–217. Since the 1980s, a particular and limiting interpretation of the concept "hierarchy of truths" has emerged from Rome.

46. Cf., particularly in relation to the centrality of dialogue to the legacy of Vatican II, Mannion, *Ecclesiology and Postmodernity: Questions for the Church in Our Time* (Wilmington, DE: Michael Glazier Books, 2007), chapters 5–7, 105–172.

47. For an excellent extended study on the notion of ecclesial dialogue, see Bradford Hinze, *Practices of Dialogue in the Roman Catholic Church* (New York: Continuum, 2006). The numerous works pertaining to magisterium by Gaillardetz, as already briefly illustrated, also call for such dialogue and offer sound systematic foundations for why such is necessary.

48. To name but two examples, Gaillardetz, *Teaching with Authority*, esp. 275–293, and Paul Lakeland, *The Liberation of the Laity: In Search of an Accountable Church* (New York: Continuum, 2003) and also his *Catholicism at the Crossroads. How the Laity Can Save the Church* (New York: Continuum, 2007).

49. A familiar example here is to compare the Catholic understanding of the Jewish faith from the teaching of the Council of Florence with that in the teaching of the Second Vatican Council.

50. The doctrines pertaining to the divinity of Christ and how lay dissent eventually helped to overcome the Arian denials of Christ's divinity offer the most obvious example.

51. As, for example, the long and rich history of the emergence of religious orders helps illustrate.

52. The numerous works of Charles E. Curran prove instructive in many ways, just two informative examples of which are "Responsibility in Moral Theology: Centrality, Foundations and Implications for Ecclesiology," in *Who Decides for the Church? Studies in Co-Responsibility*, ed. James A. Coriden, 113–142 (Hartford, CT: Canon Law Society of America, 1971), and "What Catholic Ecclesiology Can Learn from Official Catholic Social Teaching," chapter 6 of his *The Living Tradition of Catholic Moral Theology*, 134–159 (Notre Dame, IN: University of Notre Dame Press, 1992).

53. In this chapter, we will not find space to treat the concepts of *sensus fidelium* and reception explicitly in their own right. But it will be evident that both notions are presupposed as being important to the sense of magisterium here being commended,

and the principles from social, moral, and canonical theological explorations we discuss are naturally mindful of both such concepts.

54. The principle of subsidiarity helps strike a healthy balance between smaller and larger social institutions, e.g., between a local community and the state. Social tasks are best carried by those closest to the situation at hand. This principle means, basically, that no larger body or institution (e.g., a government) should take away from (or unnecessarily interfere in) a smaller body, institution, or community the functions that such a smaller body or community can best fulfill for itself.

55. Cf. n. 54 Coresponsibility entails that there is a collective sense of duty, empowerment, and responsibility for the life and "health" of the church and its mission, structures, and authority.

56. E.g., cf. *Gaudium et Spes* §65. All human beings have the right to play as full as part as possible in their communities and to enjoy the benefits of freedom that others enjoy. A problem here, of course, is that some believe that Catholic social teaching does not actually apply within the church itself. To name but one recent study of particular relevance to the call for greater participation across the church, and an incisive study of theological and ecclesiological breadth and depth alike, see Bradford Hinze, "The Reception of Vatican II in Participatory Structures of the Church: Facts and Friction," in Canon Law Society of America, *Proceedings of the Seventieth Annual Convention*, Kansas City, Missouri (October 13–16, 2008), 28–52.

57. Concrete proposals here would involve the greater use and genuine empowerment of more inclusive structures of dialogue and governance at every level of the church.

58. See Margaret Farley, "Ethics, Ecclesiology and the Grace of Self-Doubt," in *A Call to Fidelity on the Moral Theology of Charles E. Curran*, ed. James J. Walter, Timothy E. O'Connell, and Thomas A. Shannon (Washington, DC: Georgetown University Press, 2002). For Curran, perhaps the most succinct and moving account of his thought is provided in his own memoir: Charles E. Curran, *Loyal Dissent* (Washington, DC: Georgetown University Press, 2006). For a discussion of both Farley and Curran on these insights and of the interrelation between ethics and ecclesiology in recent times in general, see Gerard Mannion, "Act and Being in the Church," in *Christian Community Now: Ecclesiological Investigations*, 109–134 (New York: T&T Clark, 2008), and also Gerard Mannion, "After the Council: Transformations in the Shape of Moral Theology and the Church to Come," *New Blackfriars* (March 2009): 232–250. See also a variety of related discussions in Lisa Sowle Cahill's contribution to this present book, "Moral Theology after Vatican II."

59. This is one reason that the thoughtfully constructive proposals of M. Cathleen Kaveny in this book ("Retrieving and Reframing Catholic Casuistry"), while most welcome, might be complemented with a greater emphasis on how profitable it would be today to encourage a further updating of aspects of the *method* of casuistry found in some manuals of moral theology (the manual tradition and casuistry not being one and the same thing), particularly because of the ahistorical and acontextual approach that the manual tradition at times encouraged. Kaveny's proposals concerning the need to understand the emergence of a tradition and the parallels she draws with common

law are especially welcome. But we must also keep in mind the implications of the fact that the manuals emerged out of contexts and social imaginaries that have long since disappeared. Here John P. Beal's chapter ("Something There Is That Doesn't Love a Law: Canon Law and Its Discontents") offers much additional food for thought.

60. Cf., e.g., Joseph Selling, "Magisterial Authority and the Natural Law," *Doctrine and Life* 47 (1997): 334–342; "The Authority of Church Teaching on Matters of Morality," in *Aiming at Happiness: The Moral Teaching in the Catechism of the Catholic Church*, ed. F. Vosman and K.-W. Merks, 194–221 (Kampen, Netherlands: Kok Pharos, 1996); and "Authority and Moral Teaching in a Catholic Christian Context," in *Christian Ethics: An Introduction*, ed. Bernard Hoose, 57–71 (London: Cassell, 1998).

61. Selling, "Authority and Moral Teaching in a Catholic Christian Context," 68–69. Selling is offering an alternative to the "three baskets of truth" system of authoritative teaching currently prevalent, as Bernard Hoose summarizes in his own discussion of Selling's work in "Authority in the Church," 114.

62. E.g., Selling, "Authority and Moral Teaching in a Catholic Christian Context," 64.

63. C.f. Gerard Mannion, 'Collective Discernment in Medicine and Theology– Recent Developments from an (Ecumenical) Roman Catholic Perspective', in John Elford and D. Gareth Jones (eds.), *A Glass Darkly; More Discussions in Medicine and Theology*, New International Studies in Applied Ethics Series, (Peter Lang, 2010), 81–110.

64. Again, Lisa Sowle Cahill's chapter, "Moral Theology after Vatican II," offers numerous informative and constructive contributions in relation to developments in both natural law theory and virtue ethics. Elsewhere, I have addressed such an application of virtue ethics in Mannion, *Ecclesiology and Postmodernity*, 175–222.

65. See note 59.

66. It also complements Beal's focus on social imaginaries.

67. Joseph Kavanagh O.P., "The Blessing of Law," in *Watchmen Raise Their Voices: A Tallaght Book of Theology*, ed. Vivian Boland O.P., 197–206 (Dublin, Ireland: Dominican, 2006), 199. In addition to Kavanagh's contribution, alongside the work of Beal and Kaveny, further constructive examples include the canon law contributions in Leo J. Donovan, ed., *Cooperation between Theologians and the Ecclesiastical Magisterium* (Washington, DC: Canon Law Society of America, 1982); the works of James A. Coriden, such as *The Rights of Catholics in the Church* (New York: Paulist, 2007); and also Ladislas Örsy, *The Church: Learning and Teaching* (Wilmington, DE: Glazier, 1987) and *Receiving the Council: Theological and Canonical Insights and Debates* (Collegeville, MN: Michael Glazier, 2009). The various works of Gaillardetz are also relevant here.

68. Kavanagh, "The Blessing of Law," 199.

69. Ibid., 200, citing Gratian, *Decretum*, D4, C.3.

70. Here see Jean Porter, *The Recovery of Virtue* (London: SPCK, 1990), and, again, Mannion, *Ecclesiology and Postmodernity*, 175–222.

71. Kavanagh, "The Blessing of Law," 203.

72. Ibid., the essential thrust of pp. 202–205, following this by commending attention to the "Humour That Liberates," 205–206.

73. I.e., the principle by which one might discern when a law may be *disobeyed* and the related principle of equity. Cf. the discussion in Richard M. Gula, *Reason Informed by*

Faith (New York: Paulist, 1989), 257–259. Obviously, this again brings into play the principle of participation.

74. Kavanagh, "The Blessing of Law," 202.

75. Ibid.

76. Here cf., again, for example, Coriden, *The Rights of Catholics in the Church*.

77. John L. McKenzie S.J., *Authority in the Church* (London, Geoffrey Chapman, 1966), 163.

78. Cf. Mannion, *Ecclesiology and Postmodernity*, 105–123, especially122–123.

79. Thomas P. Rausch, *Reconciling Faith and Reason: Apologists, Evangelists and Theologians in a Divided Church* (Collegeville, MN: Michael Glazier, 2000), 19.

80. Ibid.

81. Here cf., in particular, Julie Clague, "Moral Theology and Doctrinal Change," in *Moral Theology for the 21st Century: Essays in Celebration of Kevin Kelly*, ed. Julie Clague, Bernard Hoose, and Gerard Mannion, 67–79 (New York: Continuum, 2008), and also Clague's forthcoming *Catholic Tradition and Moral Change*.

82. John Henry Newman, "The Orthodoxy of the Body of the Laity during the Supremacy of Arianism," in *On Consulting the Faithful in Matters of Doctrine*, ed. John Coulson (London: Rowman and Littlefield, 1985), part 3, 109ff.

83. Hermann Häring, "The Rights and Limits of Dissent," in *The Right to Dissent*, ed. Hans Küng and Jürgen Moltmann, in *Concilium* 158 (1982): 106.

84. Here notwithstanding the elements of *Donum veritatis* on the subject of faith, vis-à-vis the role of the theologian.

85. Rosmini was subsequently beatified in 2007.

7

Moral Theology after Vatican II

Lisa Sowle Cahill

This chapter focuses on moral theology in the United States, with connections to other social contexts and to the development of moral theology prior to the council. "Moral theology" since the mid-twentieth century has been increasingly integrated with "social ethics" and Catholic social thought, has become more biblical in its inspiration and sources, has become sensitive to change and historicity, and has become the province of lay theologians as well as clergy. These changes have had varied and sometimes contradictory consequences on several levels, including the interpretation of "natural law," the prospect of "dissent" from magisterial teaching, and the public and political engagement of moral theology.

For the generation of Catholics who were adults at the time of Vatican II, these changes created challenges to the church's moral authority, which some tried to bolster by reaffirming traditional norms, and others tried to dislodge by arguing for revisions. For "millennial" Catholics, debates about ecclesial authority and dissent are not central to understanding Catholicism or to defining Catholic identity. Instead, the authority of traditional teachings, as well as of moral and devotional practices, depends on power to inspire spirituality and create community.

The relations among moral theology, social ethics, biblical and historical influences, and changing social and cultural contexts of moral theologians themselves will be considered along three trajectories: Vatican II and its aftermath (*Humanae vitae*); natural law, moral realism, and public social ethics; and "millennial generation" moral theology. These trajectories are not so much sequential phases as gradually emerging and interdependent trends, although their appearance or at least time of greatest prominence reflects the order in which they are treated. The effects on these trends of postmodern philosophy,[1] of feminist theology, of liberation theology, and of the John Paul II phenomenon will also be discussed, though certainly not comprehensively.[2]

Vatican II and Its Aftermath (*Humanae vitae*)

Viewed at a distance of four decades, the most pervasive and prominent characteristic of moral theology after Vatican II has been development of the discipline's social and historical dimensions. These are two sides of the same coin, insofar as both express the reconnection of moral analysis to particularity of agency and perspective, including religious membership. Personal moral agents are better appreciated to exist in social contexts, be shaped by social relations, and be accountable within social institutions. Such contexts, relations, and institutions exist diachronically, or across time. Hence sociality and interdependence entail the historicity of morality and moral knowledge. Revisionist moral theologians embrace these developments. Traditionalist moral theologians deny any substantial impact on magisterial teaching, but official teaching has in fact adapted significantly under their influence.

Before the council, theology and teaching concerning government and economics ran on a track parallel to but rarely crossing that of personal morality, especially in the area of sexuality. John Mahoney argues that the two sides of moral theology became disjointed partly as a result of the church crackdown on Jansenism and the centralization of diminishing Vatican authority during a time of increasing secularization in Europe.[3] Stringent norms became the rule in personal, especially sexual, matters, while more flexibility and an inductive method of knowledge obtained in the political arena. The same pope, Leo XIII, who instigated moral theology's neoscholastic treatment of personal ethics, by encouraging the revival of Aquinas, also wrote the first of the modern papal social encyclicals, *Rerum novarum* (1891). Moral theology and social teaching were generally treated as separate departments. Further, although the doctrine of creation was regarded as the basis of the natural law, the natural law method of moral theology in both areas was largely disconnected from the Bible and faith or spirituality.

Post–Vatican II Catholic thinkers follow a common critique of Enlightenment reason, insofar as they view the moral self, its commitments, and its

obligations as socially constituted and see knowledge as socially and historically mediated. In culture and philosophy, a historicizing trend gained traction at
least a century earlier, through the writings of figures like Rousseau, Hume,
and Marx. In the Catholic Church, the trend was at first firmly resisted, then
tacitly incorporated via "personalist" philosophy and the adoption in moral
theology of a "gospel identity." A landmark work uniting Bible and ethics was
Bernard Haring's *The Law of Christ*.[4] Moreover, as laypeople entered graduate
programs in theology after the council and took up theological vocations, the
content of moral theology began to reflect their experiences and even to be held to
the criterion of experience. Since the council, moral theology has been increasingly understood in terms of social contexts, practices, and institutions and to
have a history that is reflected in its content. This obviously has the potential to
undermine magisterial pronouncements claiming universal authority.

The Council and *Humanae vitae*

The council itself already foreshadows the integration of the social, the historical, and the religious with the moral and focuses new attention on the realities
of lay Catholics. *Gaudium et spes*, the document most concerned with moral
issues, opens by tying the mission of the church to "mankind and its history"
(no. 1).[5] Discussing the problem of birth control, *Gaudium et spes* observes that
"certain modern conditions" can interfere with the "harmonious" arrangement
of marriage and family life. Moreover, by emphasizing that the church scruti-
nizes "the signs of the times" "in the light of the gospel" (no. 4), and by
repeatedly bringing the gospel to bear on the traditional problems of moral
theology, as well as on those of social ethics, *Gaudium et spes* refers moral
theology to an ongoing historical tradition of beliefs, interpretations, and
practices that are understood to affect the analyses and recommendations
given (e.g., nos. 32, 58, 72).

Historian Stephen Schloesser, S.J., has remarked that the council documents' frequent allusions to the "unity" of mankind are in fact belied by the
actual conflicts and fragmentations of the mid-sixties, for example the Vietnam
War, the Cold War, the fairly recent memory of the Holocaust, continuing anti-
Semitism, and worldwide struggles for the recognition of the civil rights of
oppressed and colonized peoples. In the face of such realities, the council
offered a "panegyric" to unity, an exhortation to people of faith and to all people
to rise above divisions and address fundamental questions of human meaning
and purpose. "The council's call for the Church to be a 'humanizing' force was
an ethically necessary response to a century that had been, in Nietzsche's ironic
phrase, 'human, all too human.'"[6]

One may note in addition, with Jose Casanova, that this message represented a decisive rebuttal to the secularization thesis that as a result of modernization, religion must necessarily become more privatized and more marginal to public and social concerns. Instead, "religious institutions and organizations refuse to restrict themselves to the pastoral care of individual souls and continue to raise questions about the interconnections of private and public morality."[7] This movement can be seen in the appropriation of prophetic biblical categories such as "the poor," "the powerless," and "the disinherited" to summon support for social revolutions;[8] it can also be seen in recent North American political activities of the religious right, of mainline churches invested in progressive causes, and more recently of evangelical churches urging action on the environment and global poverty. A question or problem that results is the integration or reconciliation of the specifically religious identity of public churches and their members with their broad social and political appeal for moral consensus to back reform.[9] This problem will be addressed further in the next section.

Considering the effects of Vatican II on so-called personal morality, it is evident not only that the Roman Catholic Church has here, too, exercised its public, political voice and influence (e.g., on "pro-life" issues and on gay marriage) but also that its rhetorical style is again a panegyric to unity taking its cue from actual pluralism and fragmentation in popular attitudes and practices. Precisely because its moral authority was under challenge, the Roman Catholic magisterium moved to reassert the reasonableness and self-evidence of its stances on sex, abortion, and, a bit later, physician-assisted suicide. In the context of the culture wars over women's roles and the limits of permissible sexual activity, *Humanae vitae*, the 1968 encyclical of Paul VI reinforcing the Catholic ban on artificial contraception, became a disproportionate focus for the renegotiation of moral theology in the half-century following Vatican II. Compared with other pressing topics of recent decades, like the Vietnam War, the nuclear weapons standoff, global economic development, or even a U.S. divorce rate rising to 50 percent, the use of birth control by married couples would seem to pale in importance. Nonetheless, no other issue has so defined opposing Catholic positions on authority, tradition, and dissent.

In *Humanae vitae*, the purposes of sex are not derived solely from the physical potential for procreation or from the fact that this is one of the purposes of the institution of marriage. The argument reflects a changed cultural perception of the "meaning" of sex. The encyclical and its defenders try to make the argument that procreation is tied to the love of the marriage partners, and hence to their own personal fulfillment and good, in an ineliminable and inviolable way. *Gaudium et spes*, *Humanae vitae*, writings of John Paul II, and their various theological advocates argue that sex in marriage is a type of "total mutual self-gift" of which openness to procreation is an indispensable part. In this way, they reposition as serving the personal relationship of a couple a moral teaching about sex that was originally developed in an era when sexual passion was considered dangerous if not sinful, women were seen as destined primarily for childbearing and as subordinate to men, and marriage was valued primarily as a guarantor of family life socially ordered and controlled to produce heirs. While the "panegyric to unity" of *Gaudium et spes* on social issues left the definition of forms of compliance open to further specification, the panegyric of *Humanae vitae* defined the terms of unity quite specifically. In fact, the proclamation of absolute norms based on supposedly absolute and universal sexual experiences and values was itself part of the rhetorical invocation of unity.

It is important to register the "personalist" element introduced in the modern magisterium's rendering of sexual "nature." Personalism emphasizes the moral subject and interpersonal relationships as key to a complete and holistic ethics and to an adequate reading of moral responsibility.[10] It leads to a view of natural law that is oriented by the ultimate fulfillment of the person in all his or her relationships, personal and social. This accommodation reflects a greater historical malleability of moral teaching about sex than the magisterium has been willing to concede in theory. It is influenced by modern concerns with the subject, subjectivity, and self-fulfillment (not necessarily to be equated with selfishness). Throughout the twentieth century, in modern industrialized and postindustrial cultures, popular and philosophical understandings of identity, meaning, and responsibility have become increasingly centered on the modern self and its encounter with other selves or "the other." Reflexive interiority and intersubjectivity are regarded as constituting the authentic sphere of morality and its ultimate referent, even if morality is also oriented to an objective good or goods and realized in community or society.

Charles Taylor develops "a portrait of modern identity" focused on "modern inwardness, the rise of the ethic which affirms ordinary life and puts great emphasis on equality and benevolence, and the articulating of the expressivist understanding of agency with its attendant emphasis on the creative imagination."[11] In such an outlook, moral values and judgments have reference above all to personal "authenticity"[12]—freely embraced convictions, integrity, virtue, and respect for other, equal selves. Taylor also notes that in the 1960s, sensuality, sexuality, and intimacy came to be seen as essential to authentic self-fulfillment. Contributing factors were greater equality for women, women's entry into the workforce, and the availability of effective contraception. The sexual revolution rehabilitated sensuality as good in itself and introduced an ideal of equal male-female partnership, a sense of "'transgressive' sex as liberating," and "a new conception of one's sexuality as an essential part of one's identity."[13] The resulting changes in sexual mores reflect the influence of several moral themes that are just as prominent in the post–Vatican II papal teaching on sexual morality as in the culture as a whole, at least from Paul VI to John Paul II. These include the importance of discovering one's true and authentically fulfilling sexual identity, the goal of equality, the revaluation of the body and sexuality, and the overcoming of divisions between mind and body, reason and feeling.[14] Of course, in magisterial teaching, these elements are brought together in a counterrevolution against any forms of sexual "transgression."

Those dissenting from *Humanae vitae*, like Curran, actually concur in its personalism and its modern take on the meaning of sex. They do not necessarily reject the idea of natural law. However, they are deliberately historically minded and think that if sex is put in a larger view of agency and relations, the moral conclusions will change. They emphasize that *Gaudium et spes* sees morality as centered on "the dignity of the human person," and sexual morality as likewise conformed to "the dignity of the person and his acts" (no. 51). If the dignity of the whole person, including his or her personal and intersubjective relationships, becomes the moral baseline, then older prescriptions that privileged and protected procreative heterosexual marriage are endangered. From the new standpoint, the dignity of the person must include individual contexts and needs. Within marriage, it refers to the totality of the whole relationship over time and to the quality of the sexually expressed love spouses share. The needs of couples and families can sometimes override the good of procreation; the best ways to respect competing goods must be discerned diachronically and inductively.

What is required is a historically developing interpretation of what nature and nature's good demand, given that humans are reasonable, free, historical creatures. Sexual morality is governed neither by biological capacities and drives nor by societal interest in regulating reproduction, but by personally fulfilling sexual expression and intimacy. It is important to incorporate the experience of married couples in determining the morality of artificial contraception. Charles Curran lost his position at Catholic University for advocating change in teaching on the basis of marital experience and of growing "historical consciousness" and has continued to be a strong advocate of the legitimacy of "faithful dissent" from the magisterial position on this issue.[15]

On the other side, Germain Grisez claims that *Humanae vitae* is not only authoritative but infallible. With the legal scholar John Finnis, he launched a "new natural law" theory, arguing that certain basic goods are self-evident and absolute. These goods permit no compromise in light of individual or social experience. Among them are life and marriage. Procreation is included under life and is seen as the culminating meaning of marriage; no extenuating circumstance can justify its deliberate elimination from an act of sexual intercourse. (This theory will be discussed in the next section.) Those favoring *Humanae vitae* assert that natural law is universal and unchanging and, in regard to sex, prescribes and proscribes acts absolutely, based on the essential purposes of human sexuality: to procreate and to express the interpersonal love of the (heterosexual, married) partners. In principle, the demands of the natural law are apparent to reason; however, in cases of confusion or difficulty, the church has the authority to interpret the natural law and the obligation to promulgate its results.

After Vatican II, increased references to scripture, to "gospel values," and to a faith orientation lent a renewed evangelical vigor to moral theology, even though moral theology ostensibly also retains its basis in reason and natural law. The council had urged—in a document on the education of priests—that the "scientific exposition" of moral theology "should be more thoroughly nourished by scriptural teaching."[16] Yet the biblical coloring did not immediately seep down into the foundations on which the specifics of sexual and medical ethics were still being assessed. The real battles shortly to be fought over postconciliar moral teaching would remain focused on natural law–based definitions of absolute norms and "intrinsically evil acts," especially and originally contraception. Indeed, if moral theology had really been formed by the New Testament, control of sex would never have remained so central to the Catholic moral vision. Both "sides" of the debate claimed to best address the problems of contemporary cultures, and both made adjustments in their message that reflected changing historical circumstances and attitudes. But while the "traditionalist" side advanced under a rhetoric of continuity and unity, the "revisionist" side explicitly acknowledged and endorsed change and "historical consciousness" as new components of postconciliar moral theology and revised natural law thought and hence rejected the authority of several traditional norms.

Catholic theologians writings about sex (and other moral issues) after the council paid attention not only to biblical and ecclesial authority but also to the authority of evidence drawn from the natural and social sciences. One factor was certainly the modern trust in scientific evidence as more reliable and less ideological than philosophies and religions; another was the fact that, in opening the windows of the church to the "modern world," *Gaudium et spes* at once undermined the speculative bases of the old natural law system and suggested new paths to the validation of moral claims.

Critics of *Humanae vitae* and related teachings still assumed the general normativity of procreative, heterosexual, permanent marriage but wanted to justify more exceptions. In pursuit of this end, they adduced various kinds of empirical and experiential evidence to argue that the rhythm method does not work very well, that sex is psychologically necessary to the health of a marriage, that sexuality and the need for sexual expression are deeply rooted in the human personality, that sex is not always "naturally" procreative, that conception does not happen in a "moment," that sexual orientation is not a matter of choice, and so on. On the one hand, the defenders averred that morality is not validated by surveys and polls. Yet on the other, they also resorted to empirical and experiential backings for their versions of natural law. For example, nonmarital sex is always "dishonest" and "not fulfilling," homosexuals can change and/or live fulfilling celibate lives, the individual genotype is irreversibly formed at conception, natural family planning (NFP) couples have better relationships, and the truly liberated and feminist woman finds artificial contraception invasive and offensive. An illustration from legal philosopher Robert P. George:

> in order for a choice to engage in sex to be respectful of the basic,
> intrinsic goods of persons, this choice must: (1) respect the integration
> of the person as bodily with the person as intentional agent; and (2)
> constitute a choice to participate in the real and basic good of marital
> union, rather than to induce in oneself and one's partner(s) a merely
> illusory experience of interpersonal unity... if sexual acts do not
> consummate or renew marriage, they involve either self-
> alienation... or constitute the pursuit of a merely illusory
> experience... the abuse of sex is a degradation of persons.[17]

Early Modifications of Natural Law Thinking

In the wake of the council and *Humanae vitae*, debates about sexual ethics, medical ethics, and other areas still conceived officially as matters of personal morality presented numerous challenges to ahistorical norms focused on individual behavior. Indeed, they revealed these norms themselves to have a history and to be insufficiently flexible to meet the changing values and needs of new contexts.[18] "Proportionalism" (a liberalizing interpretation of double effect) was a response to these developments that insisted that the morality of individual acts cannot be decided without reference to circumstance and, by extension, to histories. Proportionalism still takes for granted the essential authority of natural law principles; the question is how to interpret and apply them more flexibly. Proportionalism's proponents viewed it as a necessary development of tradition, while its adversaries portrayed it as unacceptable "dissent" from norms forbidding "instrinsic evil."[19] The proportionalist debate is an early manifestation of the gradual historicization of postconciliar moral theology, a process that in the later decades of the century would incorporate scripture and spirituality more fully and lead as well to more serious and extensive questioning of the natural law method and its purported universalism.

Despite what I regard as its legitimate insights into the relevance of context, the proportionalist critique was limited by the fact that it continued to rely on a framework of neoscholastic principles that were developed to avoid or at least reduce contextual pluralism and to guarantee clear and certain knowledge of results. Even with revisions, this system could not adequately handle the emerging mid-century convictions that contexts, circumstances, and histories make a difference to moral "objectivity" and that judgment is to a significant degree perspectival. Feminist theologies, liberation theologies, and social approaches to bioethics were to break the limits of this mold.[20]

Indeed, theologians interested in ethics and politics were increasingly to define their work as feminist, liberationist, and social, even when it dealt with topics like sex, marriage, family, reproductive technologies, abortion, and stem cell research. Today, the feminist maxim, "the personal is political" represents the way many Catholic moral theologians approach sex and gender issues, as well as questions of access to and use of health care and other formerly "personal" decisions.[21] Moreover, U.S. Catholic theologians who are Latino, African American, or Asian American do not differentiate moral theology from systematic theology and biblical theology in the same way as more traditional authors. They virtually always put a political edge to their theological work, without separating personal from social categories. Their voice in Catholic theology has grown since the council and will increase in decades to come.[22]

The introduction of a historical consciousness in Catholic moral theology did more than undermine the authority of certain specific sexual norms. As is evident in the transition of moral thought from neoscholastic principles through proportionalism to a more thoroughly social and contextual approach, moral reason was itself being perceived in a new way: as contextual, communal, inductive, and modest. On one level, this new model of reason is but a return to the Thomistic model of practical reason as concerned with "contingent matters" and hence as flexible and fallible in its grasp of particular moral truths.[23] It need not in principle call into doubt the reality and accessibility of truth. Yet, on another level, skepticism about the objectivity of moral knowledge and the generalizability of religious and moral claims encourages a view of moral reasoning as particularistic and nonuniversal. Consequently, even in

Catholic moral theology, some thinkers portray moral reason as radically relative to communities, to social contexts, and to limited practical agreements on the good and the good life.[24] In its religious or theological forms, contextual reasoning is sometimes reconnected to objective truth via a concept of revelation that grounds communal knowledge in a transcendent, supernatural source.[25] This move helps the churches and theology get a critical distance from modern liberal culture and its supposed universals of freedom, autonomy, and rights. It also shores up the framework of transcendent meaning that "secular" culture has pushed aside.[26] But at the same time, it diminishes the plausibility of a religious and theological presence in ethics and politics, as well as the possibility of making claims about justice and rights that transcend cultural limits. This had led to markedly different schools of thought about the theoretical foundations of moral theology and about its relation to the public sphere.

Natural Law, Moral Realism, and Public Social Ethics: Under Stress

Variations in natural law thinking are responsive to wider cultural and philosophical developments. In the United States, Catholicism, like other religious traditions, has interacted with "liberal" North American culture and politics, with postmodern epistemological caution, and with the globalization of economic interdependence and communication.

Modern Catholic social teaching typically confronts these realities with the categories of the dignity of the person, the common good, and the global common good, now complemented by religious themes stressing humanity's transcendent origin and destiny, and the "preferential option for the poor." Catholic teaching about personal morality after Vatican II begins similarly by establishing supposedly nonnegotiable aspects of the human good (e.g., sex as heterosexual, procreative, and "mutual self-gift") and then links these to supporting social conditions (e.g., legal protection of the institution of marriage and the exclusion of gay unions, abortion, and artificial birth control). In both the personal and the social spheres, personal dignity and the common good usually are advocated (certainly by the magisterium) as values confirmed equally by the gospel and the natural law. They are presented as relevant to the public sphere, domestically and internationally. Yet any retrieval of the natural law tradition encounters huge obstacles in the global pluralism of values and politics, the many cultural and philosophical critiques of liberal universalism, the drive of Catholics and members of other faith traditions to reclaim particularistic identities and communities, and the pervasive influence, culturally and intellectually, of postmodern and postcolonial philosophies and political theories.

Five Models of Catholic Natural Law and Public Ethics

Catholic moral theology has developed a variety of different, even opposing, responses. First are fairly modest adjustments of natural law in light of historical consciousness that came into play shortly after the council. By and large, internal Catholic debates about *Humanae vitae* in the 1970s and 1980s did not pose any truly radical questions about the reality of a common human nature, discernible by reason, despite the conditioning of historical change. They were postmodern only in a soft sense, not in the sense of a thoroughgoing rejection of objective truth, knowledge, and judgment. The distinctive gospel values and the inspiration of faith that were increasingly incorporated into Catholic moral theology after Vatican II were not at first perceived to threaten the premise of a common or "natural" and reasonable human morality. Although this morality is now understood in a more holistic or "personal" way, it is still considered objective and, in its essentials, culture transcendent. Church documents advising policy makers on the family, gay marriage, or infertility treatments make this clear.

Those who disagreed with some specific points of teaching still accepted the basic model. Hence it is all the more remarkable that they called down such vehement rejection by adversaries and the magisterium and that they them-selves readily granted that they were promoting "dissent" from authority rather than "development." Charles Curran suggests a "relationality-responsibility" ethics that he claims has been developing gradually in Catholic social teaching, that is even represented in the 1994 *Catechism of the Catholic Church*,[27] and that is equally or more apropos of sexual morality. The outcome is not a relativiza-tion of moral truths to idiosyncratic relationships, yet moral truth does refer to multiple natural dimensions of human sexuality:

> The sexual faculty should never be absolutized and seen only in itself but in its relationship to the person and the person's relationship to others. Thus in the matter of artificial contraception for spouses, the good of the person or the good of the marriage relationship justifies interfering with the faculty or its act. A relationality-responsibility model logically calls for a number of changes in the contemporary hierarchical sexual teaching.[28]

The rejoinder of those who want to defend that teaching is usually to propose a version (or versions) of natural law that can accommodate a full, nonphysicalist reading of authentic personhood, while still asserting that traditional Catholic sexual norms are required and validated by the new personalist vision and hence retain their authority. They want to exclude Curranlike revisions of sexual teaching in the name of timeless continuity, but they in fact revise the terms of that teaching as they interact with mid-century philosophies and culture. Some of these defensive approaches refer back to the "natural law" of Thomas Aquinas.

Their key argument is that respect for embodied personhood requires not violating some physical capacities or ends that are asserted to be so closely tied to personal fulfillment or flourishing that no set of circumstances could justify suppressing, overriding, or redirecting them. The main example is the necessary relationship of sexual acts respecting the "procreative structure" of intercourse to genuine sexual love and hence to the moral integrity of sex. Human nature is argued to include or require both a natural sexual structure and a certain kind of relationship between sexual partners. Enhanced by modern insights, Thomas's natural law ethics of sex is still useful in presenting chastity as the expression of personal sexuality in a way that is intelligent, free, and responsible for procreation and care of offspring; that expresses marital friendship through sexual union; and that "contributes to authentic human flourishing."[29]

A second and very influential line of reinterpretation, "the new natural law," affirms the authority of the magisterium's norms but gives them a different philosophical defense, more indebted to Kant than to Aquinas. The new natural law purports to identify goods to guide human action without reference to any inductive or experience-based theory of human nature. With this move, the theory exempts its claims about human goods from any accountability to empirical evidence or confirmation. Instead, it resists historicizing moves in moral theology after the council by turning resolutely to ahistorical and a priori foundations—a novelty in Catholic tradition. For instance, Robert P. George, whose take on sexual ethics was cited earlier, follows the "new natural law theory" originally developed by Germain Grisez, Joseph M. Boyle, and John Finnis. In this theory, practical reason is directed by intrinsic first principles that are not derived from any other knowledge.

These principles direct human action toward basic, equal, incommensurable, and inviolable goods or purposes: human life (including health and procreation), knowledge, aesthetic appreciation, play and all skilled performances, self-integration, practical reasonableness, justice, friendship, religion, and marriage.[30] These goods are supposedly known "in noninferential acts of understanding in which we grasp possible ends or purposes as worthwhile for their own sakes."[31] This theory already reveals an awareness, on the part of those who want to defend *Humanae vitae*, that "old" natural law theory is very vulnerable to accusations that it misrepresents the human sexual experience of many people and the "meaning" of sex in many cultures and subcultures. That critique is deflected by eliminating the relevance of actual experience to the foundations of morality.

Around the turn of the century, new philosophical and cultural sensibilities began to make even more decisive inroads in the Catholic consensus that "reason" and "natural law" could be historicized at the epistemological level (morality is known inductively and progressively, with formulations being open to revision), without threatening its ontological objectivity (moral knowledge may often be tentative, but objective truth does not change in its essentials, only in its particular applications). Catholic thinkers and movements in a third line of interpretation reflect the general distrust of any kind of universal reason, whether defined in neo-Thomistic or Kantian terms. They take the moral and epistemological emphasis off individual nature, flourishing, and reasoning capacity, which had been the basis for moving to "the social nature of the person" and then to the nature of universal participation in the common good. They place the emphasis instead on formative communities of identity with distinctive traditions. In so doing, they move away from modern liberalism, as well as from the assumptions of most post–Vatican II natural law debates. They do not deny (with strong postmodernisms) that truth is available but understand it to be so only within communities based on revelation, formed by the gospel, and guided by authoritative narratives and the virtues they entail.

The philosopher Alasdair MacIntyre and the Protestant theologian Stanley Hauerwas have been important shapers of this more radically historicizing trajectory. In *After Virtue*,[32] MacIntyre argued that modern moral discourse is incoherent because interlocutors have no shared idea of the good with which to adjudicate competing claims. He proposed that moral discourse makes sense only within shared traditions, including practices internal to those traditions, goods internal to the practices, and virtues defined in relation to the goods, as the qualities that orient agents to the latter. Borrowing eclectically from MacIntyre, Aquinas, and the Mennonite theologian John Howard Yoder, Hauerwas built an enormously influential "narrative ethics" around the idea of the church as a "community of character" that forms virtues to serve the good of discipleship as revealed in Jesus Christ. The church tells the story of Jesus Christ through its practices, and it is this story and not reason or experience that defines what Christian moral faithfulness means. For example, obedience to the cross of Christ demands nonviolence as a nonnegotiable demand.[33] Hauerwas neither thinks this view of life will be persuasive to those outside the Christian community nor thinks that it will have any significant impact on liberal society and politics. It is a countercultural way that defines a distinctive community faithful to its own traditions and the vision of reality they embody.

Hauerwas claims that Thomas Aquinas, Catholic social tradition, and the writings of John Paul II support his views.[34] There is a resonance between his call for a faithful living of the Christian story and the "gospel values" approach developed from Vatican II to *Evangelium vitae*.[35] Yet it is hard to envision a complete convergence as long as one keeps in mind the long-standing and current commitment of the Catholic Church and its moral theologians to bring its values to bear on public policy and law and especially its efforts to increase equality and justice for peoples in the developing world. In any event, Hauerwas's thought has proved a source of inspiration for many younger Catholic scholars, several of whom have been his students at Duke (including Emmanuel Katongole, David McCarthy, Therese Lysaught, Kelly Johnson, William Cavanaugh, and Michael Baxter). Many of these, however, give their social ethics a justice orientation in collaboration with other agencies and groups in government and civil society, a dimension that is missing in the thought of their mentor.[36]

Also taking cues from MacIntyre, Catholic scholar Jean Porter interprets the scholastic natural law tradition of the Middle Ages as an expression of a particular theological tradition, rather than as evidence that there are moral values and obligations that underlie or transcend all such traditions and that are recognizable across traditions.[37] In *Nature as Reason*, she argues that there is no philosophical defense of human rights and that such a defense depends on a theological worldview.[38] In this work, Porter seems dubious about the commonality of human nature across cultures and about whether moral knowledge is at some level universal, premises that were key to traditional moral theology and to the debates in the immediate aftermath of the council.

But not all historically oriented reconstructions of natural law have gone this route. Above all, Catholic moral theologians who are committed to social justice discourse, especially in a global environment, search for ways to validate a common morality without underplaying legitimate differences in perspective and interpretation. This makes up a fourth revision of natural law tradition. David Hollenbach urges intellectual and social "solidarity" across a global "network of crisscrossing communities." He proposes a "dialogic universalism" that does not rely on incontrovertible claims, abstract first principles, or deductive lists of goods. Despite the absence of such guarantees, it is still possible to achieve incremental knowledge of just global arrangements and the kinds of evolving infrastructures that may be needed to move toward greater justice in the international environment.[39]

Taking a similar approach to sex and gender, Margaret Farley typifies the post–Vatican II, feminist, internationalist approach to moral theology as social ethics. In particular, sex and gender ethics can in no way be divorced from the social conditions that shape gender norms and define acceptable sexual behavior. Farley proposes a framework for sexual morality that prioritizes personal and interpersonal freedom; unity of body, spirit, and moral agency; and mutual respect. Anecdotal accounts and generalizations about human sexual experience are important to her, as is evidence from the natural and social sciences about the realities of sex and gender. Her approach is flexible regarding specific kinds of sexual behaviors but suggests a moral baseline for sexual relationships: "only a sexuality formed and shaped with love has the possibility for integration into the whole of the human personality."[40] She integrates her sexual ethics into an ethics of gender and of social justice, considering just and unjust institutionalizations of sex worldwide and the pervasive reality of gender discrimination and violence.

The inductive, dialogical, collaborative, and culturally differentiated approach to a common morality exemplified by Hollenbach and Farley is also reflected in some varieties of philosophical and political communitarian thinking in North America. The major difference is that the latter are not explicitly religious in sources or orientation, hence not ultimately versions of moral theology. Yet some of these political communitarians are Catholic, including Charles Taylor and Michael Lacey. These communitarians draw on traditions of philosophical pragmatism, participatory democracy, and local social activism to mount a critique of liberal individualism. They advocate a sense of social responsibility, often in tandem with a "progressive politics" of social justice that is quite consonant with modern Catholic social teaching, though presented in nonreligious terms. Although Charles Taylor's *Sources of the Self* might be interpreted as epistemologically very close to Alasdair MacIntyre's nonfoundationalist account of virtue, Taylor expressly affirms moral realism and practical reason oriented by goods that are real and shared. This is so, even if arguments about goods have to begin with disagreements about particular accounts of goods in particular moral horizons.[41] (Jean Porter may be moving in this direction as well.)[42]

The primary founder and leader of the communitarian movement in U.S. political philosophy and political activism, Amitai Etzioni, argues that there is "a core of self-evident truths," and giving it a public voice will result in "a world better than it would be otherwise."[43] According to the website of the Communitarian Network, founded by Etzioni to combat the corrosive effects of "excessive individualism" on the public sphere and "the moral fabric of society," the protection of individual rights must be paired with a sense of civic responsibility.[44] According to its self-description, the Communitarian movement prizes individual liberty within a democratic society, seeks "balances between individuals and groups, rights and responsibilities, and among the institutions of state, market, and civil society," and starts with the renewal of civil society.[45] One theme of recent Catholic social teaching, that government has a responsibility to ensure that material and economic rights are assured to the extent necessary to secure just and universal participation in the common good, seems largely absent from the communitarian agenda. Communitarianism reminds liberalism what is required for its realization, rather than modifying its basic framework.

However, the Roman Catholic scholar Michael Lacey (who does see liberalism and Catholicism as "compatible")[46] agrees that "public bureaucracies are tools for the pursuit of justice and the common good" and decries the fact that a third of the wealth in the United States is held by 1 percent of the households.[47] Lacey and his coauthor, William Shea, see communitarianism as attractive to "Catholics who take seriously the social teachings of the church (the natural-law tradition on family and social justice, subsidiarity, public responsibility for the social and economic safety net)."[48] They endorse what they regard as the commitment of the Catholic tradition to "universal values" that are "real," as well as John Paul II's virtue of social solidarity.[49] Lacey supports and expands the resources of politically progressive yet realist natural law thinking through an interpretation of American pragmatism that capitalizes on what he thinks is the moral realism of its original founders. "The struggle to shape the natural inclinations and tendencies of human nature in light of ideals latent in them is the basic stuff of pragmatist ethics," but these ideals are realized only as a socially embedded self engages in "a process of interpretation, linking past and future in the present, and dealing incessantly with what is happening."[50] The interesting alliance between pragmatism and Catholic moral theology provides a fruitful axis on which to make natural law ethics more inductive, collaborative, and flexible, while connecting it with an indigenous philosophical school that can lend credibility to natural law in U.S. academic culture. Post–Vatican II moral theologians will recognize that the interpretive process of the socially embedded self includes religious identity and the relevance of that identity to "what is happening." The challenge this poses is the preservation or cultivation of the public presence and global message of traditional natural law, in unison with newly heightened religious self-consciousness.

A fifth response to the post–Vatican II interest in community as the locus of moral knowledge is very important: virtue ethics. This model overlaps at points with the others. Better, it might be said that virtue ethics can develop within each of the other models, depending on how virtue is understood to relate to the community, the human good or goods, religious faith, and so on.

MacIntyre, Hauerwas, and Porter (in some major works) all defend a Christian virtue ethics that to some extent limits the knowledge of objective moral truth to the religious community. MacIntyre at least is open to the interpretation that truth is grounded nowhere other than in historical human communities. (As theologians, Hauerwas and Porter affirm the certitude of revealed truth more clearly.) But virtue theory, including Christian virtue theory, is internally pluralistic. Some points of difference are whether virtue is an end in itself or refers teleologically to goods the agent pursues; how virtue builds on and correlates human characteristics such as reason, will, emotion, and embodiment; whether virtue theory is a unique and stand-alone account of morality or either a version of teleology and/or deontology or a moral theory component that is interdependent with other items (like goods, principles, and action-guiding norms); whether some virtues and their related goods hold for humans in general or are entirely internal to communities; and whether general virtues and goods, if there are any, may be known reliably from particular standpoints.[51]

I take virtue to mean, with Aquinas, a disposition to act in a characteristic way (a habit)—specifically in a way that leads us to real goods whose concrete meaning we discern inductively and communally, using practical reason.[52] As a general proposition, the resurgence of virtue ethics in Catholic moral theology shares this realist bias, but one important way in which versions differ is the degree to which they connect virtues and formative practices within faith communities to responsibility for social structures and peoples beyond the immediate community and even beyond Christianity. Before taking that up, it is first important to appreciate the distinctive contributions of virtue ethics and begin to understand why it is so appealing in contemporary North American culture.

Stephen J. Pope notes instructively that a good deal of the attraction of virtue ethics lies in the attention it permits to human interconnectedness. For Christians and others who are tired of expressive individualism, the virtue framework offers a way to bring morality back from the brink of solipsistic self-regard, and reconnect it with relationships. "'Relationships' are not just a matter of idiosyncratic preferences but, rather, reflect the deeply social nature of the person." A Thomistic virtue ethic, according to Pope, resists "an individualistic view of freedom" centered on "the unencumbered self" who wants to be "left alone" by others. True virtue "coheres with a view of the self as connected to, interdependent with, and responsible for others."[53]

For religious authors, connection, interdependence, and responsibility are referred first and foremost to the religious community or church. Thus, in addition to recovering a sense of communal belonging, virtue ethics is also a vehicle that encourages the integration of biblical faith, liturgies and other religious practices, and spirituality and transcendence with Catholic morality and moral theology. Virtue ethics allows for a full and round appreciation of the historical nature of agency; the agent's material and embodied identity; the interdependence of belief, action, and theory; and the recasting of all of these in light of a Christian or Catholic worldview. In Catholic theology, natural or cardinal virtues such as prudence, justice, fortitude, and temperance are transformed by love of God and unity with God, by knowledge of the divine will and trust in the divine promises of salvation and renewal, and by confidence that moral relations themselves can be transformed through the eschatological power of God's reign. In other words, the natural virtues are affirmed but taken into new forms by the theological virtues of charity, faith, and hope.

Some of the most compelling renditions of Christian virtue ethics' practical, communal, and pastoral qualities have been offered by James Keenan, S.J.[54] Keenan's *Works of Mercy* defines and displays the meaning of virtue in practices of the imprisoned, the homeless, the hungry, the sick, and the bereaved; it interfaces with recent traumas such as the terrorist attacks of 9/11 and the church sex abuse crisis; it connects the practice of virtue to Christian liturgical celebrations; and it opens Christian virtue to global responsibility by taking up the AIDS crisis, a problem to which Keenan has devoted another long book.[55] And by organizing, arranging to fund, and convening a 2005 international conference of Catholic moral theologians, whose extremely diverse cultural perspectives and challenges are collected in a volume of papers,[56] Keenan again attests to the importance of connecting virtue ethics not only to local Christian fellowship but also to Catholic social ethics and to global justice issues in all their frightening variety and urgency. In my view, the connection of interpersonal morality, faith, community, and virtue to Catholic social teaching is a distinctive contribution of Catholic moral theology since Vatican II. But it may be a weakening connection in the minds of post–Vatican II Catholics and even in some portraits of virtue.

"The Millennial Generation": Younger Catholics and Catholic Theologians

The post–Vatican II generations have not grown up with the strong sense of Catholic cultural identity that characterized Irish, Italian, Polish, German (and so on) "ethnic" Catholics in their parents' and grandparents' formative years. Nor were they formed with a 1960s confidence in the transformative possibilities of participatory democracy in society and church. They are more disillusioned with or cynical about national programs for moral and social transformation at home and abroad and more interested in membership in local communities that support spirituality and a sense of belonging. Some embrace Catholic teaching about sex and marriage[57] or the more antiestablishment aspects of Catholic social teaching[58] as a way of standing up against individualism, consumerism, militarism, and other modern forms of "the Constantinian temptation" (in Yoder's phrase).[59]

Sharing in countercultural "Catholic" ways of life intentionally referred to divine and supernatural realities helps create identity, bond community, and nurture a worldview that can hold its own against the "immanentism" of "a secular age." In the "immanent frame" Charles Taylor finds so pervasive in North America and Western Europe (though somewhat less so in the United States), individualism, instrumental rationality, and overconfidence in the judgments of natural science are central planks. These are powerful eroders, not only of experiences of the ineffable and transcendent but also of communities of personal relationship that endure over time.[60]

Young Catholics have an incredible interest in a post–Vatican II type of spirituality and community that bypasses the issues of the sixties. They seek an alternative to today's widespread cultural fragmentation and insecurity. Margaret O'Brien Steinfels comments that changes in church and society "have left younger Catholics not with a sense of solidity and rootedness, but with a fear of permeability and shallowness."[61] According to one young author, "Those of us in our twenties and thirties ... saw unprecedented changes in the familial, political, social, and economic structures that, for the first time in U.S. history, make it likely that society's young members might not be better off than their parents. While nearly half of us experienced the divorce of our parents ... we also experience divorce between ourselves and our world."[62] Younger Catholics are, for the most part, not particularly invested in the battles over church authority on targeted moral questions that so consume the Catholic culture warriors who came of age around Vatican II. A young theologian finds "endless politicization around key issues (abortion, birth control, women's ordination and others)" to be the salient characteristic of the church's post–Vatican II public life. He comments that for many of his generation, John Paul II is the tradition's consummate representative.[63] What this pope represents to them is not ecclesial control over dissenting theologians but personal holiness and an appeal to the world's cultures and relations to grasp life and hope over death and despair.

Some recent studies of younger Catholics help explain how and why their theological peers are responding to this ethos. According to sociologist Dean Hoge, what young Catholics think is really essential to being Catholic is neither adherence to nor dissent from authority, but contact with God through the sacraments and "charitable efforts toward helping the poor." This is supported somewhat less strongly by the conviction that "God is present in a special way in the poor."[64] Since the council, there is a general trend to think that laypeople should be involved in decision making. A newer study, the core of which is presented in chapter 10 of this book, confirms this and also notes that "the younger the Catholic, the less importance he or she gave to the Church's involvement in activities directed toward social justice."[65] Of Catholics in general today, 84 percent put "helping the poor" among "very important" priorities, while "Church's involvement" in "social justice" activities was ranked as high by only 47 percent. The sacraments, daily prayer, and Catholic devotions (Eucharistic adoration, the rosary) were all ranked as important by greater numbers of people.[66] Latino Catholics think similarly. However, somewhat higher percentages rank daily prayer and the church's involvement in justice activities as very important.

The authors also conclude that younger Catholics are less attached to the church as an institution than their elders.[67] Robert Wuthnow confirms a similar phenomenon among young non-Catholic Americans (ages 20–45). After college, the churches fail to provide support systems for young people that they find vital and attractive.[68] Yet small Christian communities are a growth area in Catholic parishes; according to the authors of *American Catholics Today*, "we have experienced impressive small Christian communities on certain college campuses and find them hopeful for the Church."[69]

These trends are no doubt very complicated, and I am not a social scientist. Nevertheless, they suggest three things to me. First, young Catholics are looking for a sense of transcendent spirituality and religious community, which they find in liturgy and devotions, especially when they are small-scale or sponsored by voluntary organizations; and in the fellowship of small, intensive, face-to-face peer groups. Second, while part of their practical identity is liturgical and devotional, another part is personal service to the poor, preferably also within voluntary organizations with a religious dimension. Third, compared to their parents, young Catholics are less interested in or confident about institutions, including the church. Hence, they seem not to care much about church advocacy for social justice. They are less likely to make their own the traditional commitment of Catholicism to engage with social institutions and work for just structures in society as a whole. This would cohere well with the notorious disinclination of young Americans to vote or otherwise become involved in the political process. Young people, including Catholics, went to the polls in great numbers in November 2008 to elect President Barack Obama and his message of hope. It remains to be seen whether Obama's successful grassroots campaign has inspired long-term social commitment and political activism in the younger generation.

Finally, social scientists identify a loose and even "individualist" attitude of young Catholics—like their non-Catholic peers—toward inherited sexual norms. What Hoge regards as the biggest generational shift for millennials (born in 1979 or later) is the belief that sexual morality is more situational than older generations see it.[70] There is a return of some young Catholics and young Catholic theologians to parts of Catholic tradition on sex, especially John Paul II's "theology of the body." Interestingly, while the students and young theologians I know are accepting of gay people, they are critical of casual sex and divorce and are looking for ways to understand and explain the importance of sexual commitment. This may be a reaction against cultural permissiveness that has gone too far in the subculture of the hook up and friends with benefits. Even from my limited interactions, at my own and other Catholic institutions, with students, other faculty, campus women's organizations, the Boston College Church in the Twenty-First Century Center, and student life staff, I can affirm that this culture is indeed pervasive. It is also tacitly and sometimes overtly sexist. There is widespread dissatisfaction with it, among students and adults alike.[71] This helps explain the attraction of many to the theology of the body, with its promise to rebut sexual nihilism with a more fulfilling discipline grounded in the deep meaning of sexual experience and even a celebration of the body.[72]

In the widely cited "Here Come the Evangelical Catholics," William Portier expresses admiration for a "new breed" of college-age theology students, who may not be the majority but who are gaining strength. I have taught some of these, too. They are neither liberal nor conservative and are attracted to Catholic lay movements like the Catholic Worker. "These students are interested in Catholic-specific issues. They want meat. They love the Pope [John Paul II]. They are pro-life. They do service trips during breaks and gravitate toward 'service' upon graduation."[73] They are "discovering" Eucharistic adoration, wear John Paul II T-shirts, travel to World Youth Day, switch easily between MTV and Mother Angelica, and adopt evangelizing strategies from Campus Crusade or InterVarsity fellowship.[74] In my experience, they are also blithely unaware of local Catholic bishops and their teachings and, like most other Catholics, are selective about which of the papal teachings they actually put into practice. Economic teachings might be sidelined, for example, while teachings on sex, abortion, or war are embraced. Rather than trying to reform the institution, they seek out satisfying faith-sharing groups. They support gender equality, but many are willing to overlook gender inequity in the Catholic Church, as long as they have access to charismatic and affirming local clergy.

A report by and for young Catholics on trends among their peers observes that,

> In our rapidly changing world more and more Catholic students searching for a greater sense of security and unambiguous identity, are attracted by a growing emphasis on the absolute authority of tradition and of the "magisterium" demanding obedience from all of the faithful. As part of this, many "new movements" with a restorationist spirituality are attracting many young people. Some of these have a fundamentalist or evangelistic character.[75]

I would only add that for many, "the absolute authority of tradition" is in fact not accepted on all issues. In addition, the creation of a like-minded community and a strong Catholic identity are more important than obedience to authority as such. Ultimately, I question whether what is at stake is the norms' authoritative source, rather than that they define values and practices that adherents find existentially meaningful at the personal level.

The emphasis on personal meaning and community belonging can be at odds with long-term commitment to the larger church or society. Catholic young adult leaders in lay movements have themselves identified as a problem the fact that events like World Youth Day "often lack elements of critical reflection and action and channels for deepening the engagement of youth in the Church and the world between such events."[76] This is in contrast to earlier youth movements such as Catholic Action, where students were to develop piety and "spread the faith" but were also specifically mandated to educate themselves for action by undertaking debates, participating in discussion clubs, and visiting "a nearby home Indian or Negro mission" and making "a survey of the needs."[77] This intentional and critical social link even in pre–Vatican II Catholic culture, along with developments like Dorothy Day's Catholic Worker and the founding of the Maryknoll lay missionaries, readied the laity to engage Vatican II renewal with the movements for civil rights, peace, and democracy that were simultaneously gaining ground in society.[78]

As I was completing work on this chapter, I met for lunch with an advisee, a very bright undergraduate in an elite academic program at Boston College. This student shared with me his appreciation for Benedict XVI's *Jesus of Nazareth*, which interprets the meaning of the biblical "kingdom of God" to be the historical possibility of a personal relationship with the transcendent God.[79] This young man is also a member of a campus group, the Thomas More Society, that sponsors weekly adoration of the blessed sacrament, followed by pizza gatherings and the occasional speaker. He told me about a recent presentation by a young married couple who promoted John Paul II's "theology of the body." Far from an angry young conservative, my undergraduate friend is a likable, low-key person interested in service and in the lay Catholic movement Sant' Egidio. When I inquired about his opinion of events going on in the 2008 presidential primary elections, he replied that he wasn't much interested in politics. When pressed, he offered that he liked Mike Huckabee (evangelical Republican candidate) but had not registered to vote.

Three days later, I participated in Sunday Mass at my local parish. Afterward, a student from the parish's Catholic high school stood up to request donations for an April vacation service trip to build homes in the Dominican Republic. She expressed her hope to show "love and compassion" to some of the "millions" who live in poverty—eating, praying, worshipping, and living "by their side" for a week. This would be a "spiritual journey" to "truly love ourselves and bring this spiritual wealth home to our own community." Although the pasta dinner sign-up forms later distributed mentioned "learning the reality of third world poverty," the global causes of poverty and opportunities first-world Catholics might find to reduce them had apparently not crossed this student's horizon. I mustered the presence of mind to record her phrases on the back of an envelope as I sat in shock in the pew, feeling very Vatican II.

While few in the Vatican II generation doubted the reality of the supernatural realm to which their Tridentine Mass and Marian devotions had directed them, they welcomed a break from claustrophobic piety and its more repressive moral expressions. As globalization set in for real in the U.S. popular consciousness, Vatican II Catholics were energized to meet it by social encyclicals that called them to a new sense of responsibility for "the wretched of the earth."[80] The Catholic culture in which the millennial generation has come of age is far different. Its children are seeking purpose and direction in the face of dizzying moral options and a global economic downturn curtailing options for education and career. Feelings of insecurity understandably abound. Yet "small Christian communities" with their internal narratives, spiritualities, and virtues must not become cut off from the political commitment of the modern Catholic social tradition. Nor is it acceptable, from a Catholic viewpoint, to undertake service to the poor mainly as a step in one's own spiritual growth. That is but a religious version of an "ethic of authenticity" that holds the self true to its deep yearnings but remains indifferent to the common good and the structural conditions that furnish "enriching" service opportunities.

Millennial moral theologians (those in graduate programs and taking up faculty positions in the first decade or two of the new century) are developing strategies to combat the more pernicious leanings of the Catholic identities they might find in their students. An introduction to a collection of their essays observes that they have already grown up thoroughly immersed in "the world." They do not signal a "retreat" from it just because they seek to build a strong Catholic identity and a cache of Catholic wisdom before tangling with the world's challenges.[81] But these theologians are not interested in revisiting old debates over sex and gender, absolute norms and proportionalism, or church authority and dissent. Their vision is guided by "attention to virtue, character, and moral psychology," by "a desire to order diverse experiences within the Christian tradition," and by "a longing for lives of Christoform holiness and witness."[82]

Millennial theologians seek specifically religious reasons for the moral positions they adopt, as well as practices that enable concrete moral formation. Some of their scholarly forays thus identify such things as Eucharistic community, community-based service learning, home schooling, practices of voluntary poverty, and lay preaching as essential to the vocation of a moral theologian and to the educational process that he or she is able to activate for students. Yet they also identify Catholic social teaching and even natural law as political resources for the economy, consumer culture, the environment, and war and peace.[83] As moral theologians, they are aware of and committed to Catholic social tradition. My only concern is that, just as Vatican II–era Catholics took solid spiritual formation for granted and failed to convey it clearly enough to their children, so millennial-era theologians may take the connection of spirituality to political engagement for granted and fail to convey it clearly to students too prone to read Catholic identity in terms of personal needs for fulfillment, connection, and security. It is thus encouraging to read that "the life of the church, the witness of the saints, and the practices of devotion are sites of justice, necessary aids to other works of justice, and witnesses to the rest of the world of what God's peace looks like."[84]

What Thomas Massaro observes about new directions in Catholic social teaching is equally true about Catholic moral theology in general at the beginning of the new century. Moral theology is "personalistic," assuming the dignity and freedom of the person, along with the person's indispensable connection to others through social relationships and institutions. Catholic moral theology also exhibits a well-warranted "humility before the data of social analysis" and of all kinds of reliable empirical investigations into the human reality. An "awareness of social sin" gives a dose of realism to calls for social reform. It also reminds us that "the Cross" is a symbol of enduring relevance to the enterprise of moral theology.

Finally, Catholic moral theology today is public theology and thus concerned about its "credible witness." While not giving up the call to be prophetic and countercultural, Catholic moral theology aims to convert the imaginations, motivations, and practices of the cultural public in which and to which it also speaks. Religious narratives, stories, symbols, and practices can no longer be excluded from public processes, although moral theology and social ethics must search out ways to speak broadly of human goods, the common good, and just structures. Catholic moral theology intends to shape national and international attitudes about life, rights, technology, poverty, and war, as well as a distinctively Catholic consciousness. Unfortunately, the church risks incredibility because of the deficiencies of its teaching and practice on such items as gender, internal church organization, and employment policies.[85]

To this we must add the credibility gap that results when "official" church spokesmen emphasize the primacy of narrowly defined "pro-life" issues over every other dimension of human rights, justice, and the common good. In June 2007, the president of the Pontifical Council for Justice and Peace repudiated any Catholic support for Amnesty International on the grounds that the organization did not oppose abortion for women and girls who had been raped. With no apparent word endorsing the human rights of victims of sexual violence or decrying situations of oppression that provoke abortion, the Vatican representative condemned the evil of an attack on "an innocent child in the belly of its mother."[86] In 2008–2010, the U.S. Catholic bishops were much more vocally opposed to candidate Obama, then President Obama, on abortion than they were in support of his signature domestic issue, health care reform. This is despite the fact that they have supported a right to health care since at least 1993 (*Resolution on Health Care Reform*) and that in the 2007 voting guide, *Forming Consciences for Faithful Citzenship*, they called health care reform an "urgent national priority."[87]

Certainly pro-life commitments are important to Catholic moral theology and to Catholicism's public engagement. However, they cannot be divorced from other issues of violence, poverty, access to medical care, and availability of resources to foster a decent life for all. As his papacy progressed, Benedict XVI spoke out with increasing frequency for social justice issues. A landmark is his 2009 encyclical *Caritas in veritate*, composed in the face of the global economic crisis. His World Day of Peace Message 2009 addressed world poverty, while the 2010 message called for action on the environment.[88] Would that all bishops, the media, and Catholic theologians across the generations might join in giving these priorities the attention they deserve.

In the new millennium, Catholic moral theologians will be building up communities of faith and practice that aim to embody Christian discipleship at both the personal and the social levels. They see moral theology as an intellectual and practical vocation. It is also an ecclesial vocation. But their notion of "ecclesial" is not formed primarily in reference to "authority" and "tradition" as institutionally defined and centered in Rome, the episcopacy, "official" teaching, or "dissent" therefrom—the foci of controversies in the Vatican II generation. Rather, "church" is first and foremost a local reality that connects believers ("disciples") with the scriptures, with saints and theologians of the past, and even with the pope as a symbolic point of unity and, ideally, a moral and spiritual beacon. Beyond this, or as a result of it, the church is a space in which to renew identity and instill virtues and practices of faith and justice. From the church, moral theologians can turn to confront twenty-first-century dilemmas of violence, poverty, and politics with renewed commitment and faith. Perhaps moral theology's greatest challenge will be convincing its lay audience that, even given economic insecurity and terrorist threats at home, and the intransigence of global problems abroad, the Christian moral vocation is still to engage the world actively for justice, with courage and in hope.

NOTES

1. The term *postmodernism* has a variety of meanings and is hard to pin down. I am using it to refer to the philosophical position and cultural sense that universal experiences, values, and knowledge are very difficult to defend in the face of historical change and global pluralism. "Although diverse and eclectic, postmodernism can be recognized by two key assumptions. First, the assumption that there is no common denominator—in 'nature' or 'truth' or 'God' or 'the future'—that guarantees either the One-ness of the world or the possibility of neutral or objective thought. Second, the assumption that all human systems operate like language, being self-reflexive rather than referential systems—systems of differential function which are powerful but finite, and which construct and maintain meaning and value" (Elisabeth Deeds Ermarth, "Postmodernism," in *Routledge Encyclopedia of Philosophy* at www.rep.routledge.com/article/N044? ssid=64697189&n=1#). Jean-François Lyotard gave the term philosophical currency with *The Postmodern Condition* (1979), but John Courtney Murray had already in *We Hold These Truths* (1964, 133) asserted that "the quest for unity-amid-pluralism has assumed a new urgency in the mind of post-modern man."

2. For the improvement of this chapter, I am much indebted to my faculty colleagues and doctoral students in the Boston College Ethics Doctoral Seminar, February 8, 2008. Colleagues whose specific points have been incorporated here are James Keenan, David Hollenbach, Ken Himes, Stephen Pope, and millennial theologians Meghan Clark, Jeremy Cruz, Matthew Sherman, Nick Austin, and Kevin Ahearn, the last four of whom generously provided me with additional materials after the seminar meeting.

3. John Mahoney, S.J., *The Making of Moral Theology: A Study of the Roman Catholic Tradition* (Oxford and New York: Clarendon and Oxford University Press, 1990).

4. Bernhard Haring, *The Law of Christ: Moral Theology for Priests and Laity*, trans. Edwin G. Kaiser (Westminster, MD: Newman, 1961).

5. *Pastoral Constitution on the Church in the Modern World* (*Gaudium et spes*), in *Catholic Social Thought: The Documentary Heritage*, ed. David J. O'Brien and Thomas A. Shannon, 166–237 (Maryknoll, NY: Orbis, 1998). See also Kenneth R. Himes, ed., *Modern Catholic Social Teaching: Commentaries and Interpretations* (Washington, DC: Georgetown University Press, 2005).

6. Stephen Schloesser, S.J., "Against Forgetting: Memory, History, Vatican II," *Theological Studies* 67 (2006): 319.

7. Jose Casanova, *Public Religions in the Modern World* (Chicago: University of Chicago Press, 1994), 5.

8. Ibid., 4.

9. Kristin Heyer, *Prophetic and Public: The Social Witness of U.S. Catholicism* (Washington, DC: Georgetown University Press, 2006).

10. Personalism is a somewhat amorphous school of thought, with both Catholic and Protestant expressions (e.g., "Boston Personalism" at Boston University). In addition to John Paul II, a leading Catholic representative is Jacques Maritain (*Integral Humanism: Temporal and Spiritual Problems of a New Christendom*, trans. Joseph W. Evans (New York: Scribner's, 1968), and *The Person and the Common Good*, trans John J. Fitzgerald (London: Geoffrey Bles, 1948).

11. This summary of Charles Taylor, *Sources of the Self: The Making of Modern Identity* (Cambridge, MA: Harvard University Press, 1990) is offered by Taylor himself in "Reply to Commentators," *Philosophy and Phenomenological Research* 54, no. 1 (1994): 203.

12. Charles Taylor, *The Ethics of Authenticity* (Cambridge MA: Harvard University Press, 1991).

13. Charles Taylor, *A Secular Age* (Cambridge, MA: Harvard University Press, 2007), 502.

14. Ibid.

15. Charles E. Curran, *Loyal Dissent: Memoir of a Catholic Theologian* (Washington, DC: Georgetown University Press, 2006); *Catholic Moral Theology in the United States: A History* (Washington, DC: Georgetown University Press, 2008).

16. *Optatam totius* (*Decree on Priestly Formation*), no. 16.

17. Robert P. George, *In Defense of Natural Law* (Oxford: Clarendon, 1999), 162.

18. An extremely useful guide to names, events, writings, and intraecclesial issues of the times before and after Vatican II is Curran's *Catholic Moral Theology in the United States: A History*.

19. See Richard A. McCormick, S.J., and Paul Ramsey, eds., *Doing Evil to Achieve Good: Moral Choice in Conflict Situations* (Chicago: Loyola University Press, 1978); Charles E. Curran and Richard A. McCormick, S.J., eds., *Moral Norms and Catholic Tradition* (New York: Paulist, 1979); Bernard Hoose, *Proportionalism: The American Debate and Its European Roots* (Washington, DC: Georgetown University Press, 1987); and William E. May, *Moral Absolutes* (Milwaukee, WI: Marquette University Press, 1989).

20. See Aline Kalbian, "Where Have All the Proportionalists Gone?" *Journal of Religious Ethics* 30 (2002): 3–22. Kalbian argues that social ethics, including feminist ethics, took over the landscape and drove the proportionalists out of business. I think

another factor is that the proportionalists were already onto the fact that all personal ethics is circumstantial and even social; hence the trajectory they spearheaded broke the bounds of the traditional principles of moral theology, and a thoroughly social orientation to ethics was required.

21. Christine Gudorf, *Body, Sex, and Pleasure: Reconstructing Christian Sexual Ethics* (Cleveland, OH: Pilgrim, 1994);Margaret A. Farley, *Compassionate Respect: A Feminist Approach to Medical Ethics and Other Questions* (New York: Paulist, 2002); Cristina Traina, *Feminist Ethics and Natural Law: The End of the Anathemas* (Washington, DC: Georgetown University Press, 1999);Charles A. Curran, Margaret A. Farley, and Richard A. McCormick, eds., *Feminist Ethics and the Catholic Moral Tradition* (Mahwah, NJ: Paulist, 1996).

22. Two among dozens of possible examples are Roberto S. Goizueta, ed., *We Are a People! Initiatives in Hispanic American Theology* (Minneapolis, MN: Fortress, 1992); and Maria Pilar Aquino and Maria Jose Rosado-Nunes, eds., *Feminist Intercultural Theology: Latina Explorations for a Just World* (Maryknoll, NY: Orbis, 2007). Latino theology especially is sure to gain prominence with changing U.S. demographics.

23. Thomas Aquinas, *Summa Theologiae*, I–II.Q 94.4, "Whether the Natural Law Is the Same in All Men," trans. Fathers of the English Dominican Province (New York: Benziger Brothers, 1947).

24. Alasdair MacIntyre, *After Virtue: A Study in Moral Theory* (Notre Dame, IN: University of Notre Dame Press, 1981). Postmodernism is famously difficult to define, trace, and assess. Here it shall be treated in a very limited way.

25. H. Richard Niebuhr, *The Meaning of Revelation* (New York: Macmillan, 1960).

26. Charles Taylor, *A Secular Age* (Cambridge, MA: Harvard University Press, 2007).

27. Curran cites *Catechism of the Catholic Church* (Liguori, MO: Liguori, 1994) n. 2483, p. 595, where a lie is defined as wrong, not because it violates the faculty of speech, but because it violates responsibility to someone who has a right to know the truth.

28. Charles E. Curran, *The Catholic Moral Tradition Today: A Synthesis* (Washington, DC: Georgetown University Press, 1999), 82.

29. John S. Grabowski, *Sex and Virtue* (Washington, DC: Catholic University of America Press, 2003), 82.

30. See Germain Grisez, *The Way of the Lord Jesus, Volume One: Christian Moral Principles* (Chicago: Franciscan Herald, 1983). The items on the list vary somewhat throughout writings of new natural law theorists.

31. George, *Defense of Natural Law*, 85.

32. Alasdair MacIntyre, *After Virtue*.

33. Stanley Hauerwas, *Peaceable Kingdom: A Primer in Christian Ethics* (Notre Dame, IN: University of Notre Dame Press, 1983).

34. Stanley Hauerwas and Jana Bennett, "Catholic Social Teaching," in *The Oxford Handbook of Theological Ethics*, ed. Gilbert Meilaender and William Werpehowski, 520–537 (Oxford: Oxford University Press, 2005). Bennett is one of Hauerwas's Catholic students.

35. John Paul II, *Evangelium vitae (Gospel of Life)*, 1995. Available on the Vatican Web site (www.vatican.va/holy_father/john_paul_ii/encyclicals/documents/hf_jp-ii_enc_25031995_evangelium-vitae_en.html).

36. This is especially true of William T. Cavanaugh's *Torture and Eucharist: Theology, Politics, and the Body of Christ* (Oxford: Blackwell, 1998).

37. I find Porter to have been ambivalent on the possibility of a common morality, and her views may be changing. Her early treatment of virtue ethics, *The Recovery of Virtue: The Relevance of Aquinas for Christian Ethics* (Louisville, KY: Westminster John Knox, 1990), is more sympathetic than later works such as *Natural and Divine Law: Reclaiming the Tradition for Christian Ethics* (Ottawa, Canada: Novalis, 1999) and *Nature as Reason: A Thomistic Theory of the Natural Law* (Grand Rapids, MI: Eerdmans, 2005). In "The Search for a Global Ethic" (*Theological Studies* 62 [2001]: 105–121), she seems to see universal ethics as requiring a set of principles and norms that all can agree to more or less in the abstract, then rejects such a possibility as philosophically and culturally untenable. My question is whether this is the only possible way to view the defense of a common or global ethics (" Toward Global Ethics," *Theological Studies* 63, no. 2 [2002] 324–344). Yet in a later essay, Porter defends "a naturalistic account of ethics," in which morality is "an expression of human nature, broadly construed to include the needs, desires, physical and psychic constitution, and patterns of behavior and activity characteristic of us as a kind of creature existing in nature" ("Moral Ideals and Human Nature," in *Universalism vs. Relativism: Making Moral Judgments in a Changing, Pluralistic and Threatening World*, ed. Don Browning [Lanham, MD: Rowman & Littlefield, 2006], 60).

38. Porter, *Nature as Reason*, 371: "I have yet to see a persuasive philosophical argument, developed on grounds that would be compelling to all, for a doctrine of human rights, and this inclines me to the view that a theoretical defense of human rights must ultimately rest on theological grounds."

39. David Hollenbach, S.J., *The Common Good and Christian Ethics* (Cambridge: Cambridge University Press, 2002), 229.

40. Margaret A. Farley, *Just Love: A Framework for Christian Sexual Ethics* (New York: Continuum, 2006), 173.

41. Charles Taylor, "Reply to Commentators," *Philosophy and Phenomenological Research* 54, 1 (1994): 205–206, 208.

42. See note 36.

43. Amitai Etzioni, "Self-Evident Truth (Beyond Relativism)," in *Universalism vs. Relativism*, 30. Etzioni's major work on communitarianism is *The New Golden Rule: Community and Morality in a Democratic Society* (New York: Basic Books, 1996).

44. The Communitarian Network, sponsored by George Washington University, along with an Institute for Communitarian Policy Studies (www.gwu.edu/~ccps/about_us.html). The Network sponsors a quarterly journal, *The Responsive Community: Rights and Responsibilities*, available online at www.gwu.edu/~ccps/rcq/rcq_archives.html.

45. "The Communitarian Platform" at www.gwu.edu/~ccps/platformtext.html.

46. Michael Lacey and William Shea, "Catholics & the Liberal Tradition: Still Compatible," *Commonweal*, October 22, 2002. Lacey regards the social scientist Philip Selznick as a representative and able proponent of both the communitarian philosophy and the natural law; see "Taking Ideals Seriously: Philip Selznick and the Natural-Law Tradition," in *Legality and Community: On the Intellectual Legacy of Philip Selznick*, ed.

Robert A. Kagan, Martin Krygier, and Kenneth Winston, 67–81 (Lanham, MD, and Berkeley, CA: Rowman & Littlefield and Berkeley Public Policy Press, 2002). See also Philip Selznick, *The Communitarian Persuasion* (Washington, DC: Woodrow Wilson Center Press, 2002), with a foreword by Michael Lacey.

47. Ibid., 1.

48. Ibid., 7.

49. Ibid., 9.

50. Ibid., 45, 46.

51. Obviously, I trust, not all these problems will be dissected here. For discussions, see Roger Crisp and Michael Slote, eds., *Virtue Ethics* (New York: Oxford University Press, 1997); Stephen Darwall, ed., *Virtue Ethics* (Malden, MA: Routledge, 2003); Stepehen M. Gardiner, ed., *Virtue Ethics, Old and New* (Ithaca, NY: Cornell University Press, 2005); Joseph J. Kotva Jr., *The Christian Case for Virtue Ethics* (Washington, DC: Georgetown University Press, 1996); and William C. Spohn, "The Return of Virtue Ethics," *Theological Studies* 53, no. 1 (1992): 60–75.

52. See Thomas Aquinas, *Summa Theologiae*, I–II.Q 55, "Of the Virtues, As to Their Essence," trans. Fathers of the English Dominican Province (New York: Benziger Brothers, 1947). Especially in contemporary appropriations of Aquinas for virtue ethics, reason is not understood apart from communities or from emotions and other dimensions of the embodied and social self.

53. Stephen J. Pope, "Expressive Individualism and True Self-Love: A Thomistic Perspective," *Journal of Religion* 71, no. 3 (1991): 392–393.

54. See James F. Keenan, S.J., *The Works of Mercy: The Heart of Catholicism*, 2nd ed. (Lanham, MD: Rowman & Littlefield, 2008); *Moral Wisdom: Lessons and Texts from the Catholic Tradition* (Lanham, MD: Rowman & Littlefield, 2004); *Virtues for Ordinary Christians* (Kansas City, MO: Sheed and Ward, 1996); and James F. Keenan, S.J., and Joseph Kotva Jr., *Practice What You Preach: Virtues, Ethics, and Power in the Lives of Pastoral Ministers and Their Congregations* (Franklin, WI: Sheed and Ward, 1999).

55. James F. Keenan, S.J., ed., *Catholic Ethicists on HIV/AIDS Prevention* (New York: Continuum, 2000).

56. James Keenan, ed., *Catholic Theological Ethics in the World Church* (New York: Continuum, 2007).

57. David Matzko McCarthy, *Sex and Love in the Home* (Norwich, England: SCM. 2001); Jennifer J. Popiel, "Necessary Connection? Catholicism, Feminism and Contraception," *America*, November 27, 1999, 22–25; and, in part, Julie Hanlon Rubio. See also the Web site of Feminists for Life at www.feministsforlife.org/.

58. Michael Budde and Robert Brimlow, eds., *The Church as Counterculture* (Albany: State University of New York Press, 2000); Tom Beaudoin, *The Cost of Economic Discipleship: U.S. Christians and Global Capitalism*, Santa Clara Lecture (Santa Clara, CA: Santa Clara University, Department of Religious Studies, 2001).

59. John Howard Yoder, *The Original Revolution: Essays on Christian Pacifism* (Scottdale, PA: Herald, 1971), 146.

60. See Taylor, *A Secular Age*, 542, 578–580, 590–591.

61. Margaret O'Brien Steinfels, "The Unholy Alliance Between the Right and the Left in the Catholic Church," *America*, May 2, 1992, 380

62. Jeremy Langford, "In Their Own Words," *Commonweal*, November 23, 2001, 13.

63. Tom Beaudoin, "Beginning Afresh: Gen-X Catholics," *America*, November 21, 1998, 11. See also Thomas P. Rausch, "Another Generation Gap: Some Younger Theologians Seem Uncomfortable," *America*, October 14, 2002, 12–15.

64. Dean R. Hoge, "How Laity See the State of American Catholicism," in *Common Ground Initiative Report*, March 3, 2007, 6. See also Dean R. Hoge, William D. Dinges, Mary Johnson, and Juan Gonzales, *Young Adult Catholics: Religion in a Culture of Choice* (Notre Dame, IN: University of Notre Dame Press, 2001).

65. William V. D'Antonio, James D. Davidson, Dean R. Hoge, and Mary L. Gautier, *American Catholics Today: New Realities of Their Faith and Their Church* (Lanham, MD: Rowman & Littlefield, 2007), 25.

66. Ibid., 24.

67. Ibid., 149–150.

68. Robert Wuthnow, *After the Baby Boomers: How Twenty- and Thirty-Somethings Are Shaping the Future of American Religion* (Princeton, NJ: Princeton University Press, 2007).

69. Ibid., 151.

70. Hoge, "Laity," 3.

71. See Donna Freitas, *Sex and the Soul: Juggling Sexuality, Spirituality, Romance, and Religion on America's College Campuses* (Oxford: Oxford University Press, 2008).

72. See David Cloutier, "Heaven Is a Place on Earth? Analyzing the Popularity of Pope John Paul's Theology of the Body," and William Mattison, "'When They Rise from the Dead, They Neither Marry nor Are Given to Marriage': Marriage and Sexuality, Eschatology, and the Nuptial Meaning of the Body in Pope John Paul II's Theology of the Body," in *Sexuality and the U.S. Catholic Church: Crisis and Renewal*, ed. Lisa Sowle Cahill, 18–31, 32–51 (New York: Crossroad, 2006). See also *Josephinum Journal of Theology* 14, no. 2 (2007), focus issue on "Sexual Ethics 40 Years after *Humanae Vitae*." For writings of the pope, see John Paul II, *Man and Woman He Created Them: A Theology of the Body*, ed. Michael Waldstein (Boston: Pauline, 2006).

73. William L. Portier, "Here Come the Evangelical Catholics," *Communio* 31 (2004): 37, available at www.communio-icr.com/articles/PDF/portier31-1.pdf.

74. Ibid., 55.

75. International Young Catholic Students and the International Movement of Catholic Students (IMCS-Pax Romana), *IMCS and IYCS Paper on Integral Education*, drafted and edited by Kevin Ahearn, 24 August 2003, 3.

76. Ibid.

77. Sister Rosaria, PBVM, "Student Crusaders for Catholic Action," *Catholic Action* 23, no. 5 (May 1941), reprinted in *Prayer and Practice in the American Catholic Community*, ed. Joseph P. Chinnici and Angelyn Dries (Maryknoll, NY: Orbis, 2000), 168.

78. See Joseph P. Chinnici, OFM, *Living Stones: The History and Structure of Catholic Spiritual Life in the United States* (New York and London: Macmillan and Collier Macmillan, 1989).

79. Joseph Ratzinger, *Jesus of Nazareth: From the Baptism in the Jordan to the Transfiguration*, trans. Adrian J. Walker (New York: Doubleday, 2007).

80. Frantz Fanon, *The Wretched of the Earth*, trans. Constance Farrington (New York: Grove Weidenfeld, 1963).

81. David Cloutier and William C. Mattison III, "Introduction," in *New Wine, New Wineskins: A Next Generation Reflects on Key Issues in Catholic Moral Theology*, ed. William C. Mattison III (Lanham, MD: Rowman & Littlefield, 2005), 5, 9.

82. Ibid., 11.

83. See also David Matzko McCarthy and M. Therese Lysaught, eds., *Gathered for the Journey: Moral Theology in Catholic Perspective* (Grand Rapids, MI: Wm. B. Eerdmans, 2007), from which some of these examples are taken.

84. Kelly S. Johnson, "Catholic Social Teaching," in *Gathered for the Journey*, 234.

85. Thomas Massaro, S.J., *Living Justice: Catholic Social Teaching in Action* (Franklin, WI: Sheed and Ward, 2000), 207–225.

86. Chris Middleton, "Perilous position for unborn," *Australian*, June 8, 2007, 16.

87. These documents can be obtained from the Web site of the United States Conference of Catholic Bishops at www.usccb.org/chronological.shtml and www.usccb.org/healthcare/official_documents.shtml.

88. These documents can be accessed on the Vatican Web site, www.vatican.va. For a discussion of these and other papal writings on social issues, see Lisa Sowle Cahill, "*Caritas in veritate*: Benedict's Global Reorientation," *Theological Studies* 71, no. 2 (2010).

8

Retrieving and Reframing Catholic Casuistry

M. Cathleen Kaveny

Introduction

For nearly five hundred years, Roman Catholic moral theology was
dominated by a mode of analysis that focused on specifying the
morally right—and the morally wrong—courses of action in a wide
range of specific situations faced by Christians of all walks of life.
Commonly known as "casuistry" because of its concern with specific
"events" or "cases," the method was not a purely theoretical exercise in
moral reflection or speculation. In fact, the very opposite was true. For
many centuries, Catholic moral theology was articulated, defended,
and developed in the course of producing "manuals" for confessors to
use in identifying and evaluating the sins confessed to them by
penitents seeking absolution in the Sacrament of Penance.[1] The
manuals grew in importance after the Council of Trent, which emphasized the necessity of confession for the forgiveness of sins.[2] The
practical stakes were high, because the confessors were concerned not
only with the temporal well-being of the penitents but also and primarily with their eternal well-being.

   Yet during a period of about ten years, 1960 to 1970, the decade of
the Second Vatican Council, the monopoly of the casuistical method
in Roman Catholic moral theology began to crumble. The next fifteen
years witnessed its fade from prominence, as many contributors to the
discipline began to explore a variety of different approaches. In a
nutshell, Catholic moral theology was no longer being written by

priests for priests, with the goal of preparing knowledgeable and judicious confessors.[3] It began to be written by laymen and laywomen, with a larger array of purposes, including the purpose of making a contribution to a broader academic discussion of theological and philosophical ethics.

The fading role of casuistry as the dominant mode of Roman Catholic moral theology can be seen most clearly in the annual "Notes on Moral Theology" section of the Jesuit-sponsored journal *Theological Studies*, arguably the premier American journal of Catholic theology. For thirty years (1965–1984), that section was authored solely by Richard A. McCormick, S.J., whose annual survey chronicled an ongoing international conversation among Catholic moralists about matters ranging from contraception and abortion to just war theory. McCormick developed his own position on these issues in the course of thinking with—and against—conversation partners equally interested in cases and controversies. The vast majority had the same sort of church-based training he did and operated within the same highly technical moral framework.

Both the content and the tone of the moral notes shifted substantially after McCormick relinquished primary responsibility for them in 1984.[4] First, the notes became more focused on academic discussion and less concerned with pastoral issues faced by priests and religious in the course of their ministry. Second, whereas McCormick's focus was an international body of literature produced largely by Catholic moralists, the focus of his successors has tended to be the scholarly materials produced by English-speaking academic ethicists, Catholic and non-Catholic, philosophical as well as theological. Third, and related, the governing methodological presuppositions shifted substantially. McCormick operated within the particular moral framework handed down over centuries by the moral manualists. While attempting to revise it substantially, most notably through his advocacy of proportionalism, he never abandoned it. In contrast, the methodological commitments of his successors, even the Jesuits, are far more pluralistic.[5]

In my judgment, the fate of the Catholic casuistical tradition in the notes is an accurate reflection of its fate in the broader American Catholic moral discussion. It is one voice, but by no means the only voice. Not surprisingly, traditional casuistry is not the dominant mode of moral reflection among Catholic moral theologians formed in the immediate aftermath of the council, many of whom are progressive. More interesting, however, it is also not favored among younger moralists formed during the papacy of Pope John Paul II. Although some are more conservative about doctrinal issues, their methodology tends to be more influenced by the late pope's phenomenological personalism than by the manuals of moral theology. The elaborate and sophisticated moral matrix used for centuries by Catholic moralists to evaluate human actions has been eclipsed, if not entirely supplanted, by other methods of moral analysis.[6]

I think that the time is ripe for a renewal of the Catholic casuistical tradition. Before proceeding any further, however, let me be clear: I am not advocating a return to the days when that tradition both monopolized Catholic moral discourse and failed to reflect critically on its own presuppositions and limitations. I am not pressing for a rigid application of the Thomistic casuistical framework in a manner blind to the strengths of all other approaches to moral reasoning. I am, however, suggesting that the Catholic casuistical tradition offers significant insights to a community committed to deliberating about difficult aspects of human life and the choices those difficulties press on us. While that tradition has its flaws, it cannot be entirely dismissed as a "legalistic" morality that is unresponsive to human welfare or human problems.[7] Appreciating its advantages, however, requires setting Catholic casuistry within a broader theoretical and historical context.

To facilitate renewed, albeit critical, interest in the Catholic casuistical tradition, I propose to draw on two sets of resources, one theoretical and one practical. The theoretical resource is the tradition theory of Alasdair MacIntyre, developed in his groundbreaking book, *After Virtue*,[8] and subsequent elaborations and modifications of his theory in books such as *Whose Justice? Which Rationality?*[9] and *Three Rival Versions of Moral Inquiry*.[10] For my purposes, the most crucial aspect of MacIntyre's theory is his insistence that moral traditions are not entirely captured by the two-dimensional, paper-and-ink reflections of scholars; rather, they are embedded in three-dimensional practices that are sustained over time by institutions and enacted by persons imbued with the appropriate character traits or virtues.

The practical resource is the Anglo-American common law tradition. In my view, it can provide us with a touchstone, a living example of how casuistry operates within the context of a well-functioning tradition. Having taught contracts, the quintessential common law topic, to first-year law students for more than a decade now, I have become increasingly aware of how case law—casuistry—is suspended within a broader set of institutions and practices that are constitutive of a well-functioning moral tradition. To understand case law and the values it serves, one has to understand its broader context in a three-dimensional way. In my judgment, the common law tradition offers us a living model of the tradition theory set forth by Alasdair MacIntyre.

Appreciating the benefits and liabilities of the Roman Catholic casuistical system requires more than simply reading the dry, dusty confessors' manuals. One must situate those manuals in the broader, three-dimensional context in which they were used, making explicit the practices whose goods they were intended to support and the institutions that sustained those practices. One has to account for the assumptions of those writing and reading the manuals, as well as the limited purposes for which they were written. Taken together, MacIntyre's tradition theory and the living example of the common law will assist us in accomplishing this task, to which I will devote the remainder of this essay.

My manner of proceeding will be as follows: In section one, I attempt to formulate a definition of *casuistry* that can account for not only the manualist tradition but also recent theoretical work on the topic and the phenomenon of case-based reasoning in the common law tradition. In section two, I show how MacIntyre's tradition theory and the common law can be used to give a broader account of the context in which good casuistry is practiced. In section three, I recast the Roman Catholic manualist tradition in an appropriate, broader context. In the fourth and final section, I reflect on the benefits and preconditions of reinvigorating the Catholic casuistical tradition in a methodologically self-conscious way.

Section One: What Is Casuistry?

The first question, of course, is how to define *casuistry*. In their influential book, *The Abuse of Casuistry*, Albert Jonsen and Stephen Toulmin set up casuistry in opposition to deductive moral reasoning.

> We inherit two distinct ways of discussing ethical issues. One of these frames these issues in terms of principles, rules, and other general ideas; the other focuses on the specific features of particular kinds of moral cases. In the first way general ethical rules relate to specific moral cases in a *theoretical* manner, with universal rules serving as "axioms" from which particular moral judgments are deduced as theorems. In the second, this relation is frankly *practical*, with general moral rules serving as "maxims," which can be fully understood only in terms of the paradigmatic cases that define their meaning and force.[11]

In my judgment, Jonsen and Toulmin posit too sharp a dichotomy between rule-based reasoning and casuistical reasoning. In large part, this dichotomy stems from their decision to use medical diagnosis as a model for moral reasoning. Based on this model, they argue that within the casuistical framework, ethical norms can have only provisional force; they are general guidelines or norms. In their view, the true engine of casuistry is not deductive reasoning, but rather analogy; one decides a new case by comparing its similarities and differences to a set of paradigmatic cases. They claim that a sense of tentativeness, even in deciding a particular case, is the hallmark of casuistry, as it is in diagnostic medicine. Both casuistry and "clinical inferences and conclusions—being substantive, timely, not formal, and atemporal—are presumptive, rebuttable, and open to revision in the light of fresh evidence."[12]

The theoretical difficulty with their analogy, of course, is that medical *diagnosis* is not centrally prescriptive; it is centrally descriptive and predictive. Physicians confronted with a difficult case are not attempting to say how bodies ought to choose to act; they are attempting to figure out how a particular human body has reacted under a particular set of circumstances and to *predict* how it will continue to react with and without specific medical interventions. Medical diagnosis is a matter of matching symptoms to probabilities in order to predict the future course of a patient's ailment; taken together, current symptoms and their likely progression constitute a "diagnosis."

In contrast, however, moral casuistry has an inescapable prescriptive element. Moral norms, whether standards or rules, are not statistical summaries of how bodies or minds do in fact behave in the vast majority of cases; they are action guides that make some claim of how thinking human persons *ought* to act in a particular case. Moralists are not centrally anthropologists predicting how particular human beings will react when insulted or challenged, complimented or supported by others. They see their task as discerning how particular human beings *ought* to react when insulted or challenged, complimented or supported by others. Furthermore, they attempt to assess degrees of objective wrongdoing and subjective blame when particular human beings fail to act as they ought. In short, they articulate moral norms and evaluate moral character.

The late Oxford jurisprudence scholar H. L. A. Hart highlighted an aspect of legal reasoning that helps distinguish the type of casuistry in diagnostic medicine from the type of casuistry involved in morality (and law). He pointed out that successfully resolving a hard legal case generally involves taking an "internal perspective" toward the normative system one is describing.[13] A medical diagnostician's judgment about what *should* happen to a particular patient cannot cloud his judgment about what will happen in this particular case. In contrast, a jurist or moralist's judgment about what should happen— how people should conduct themselves under particular circumstances—deeply affects his or her judgment about the moral requirement that actually binds in a given situation. In deciding how to extend a normative framework to cover a new case, good casuists are deeply conscious of the fact that they are not merely external observers but are actually participating in its ongoing maintenance and extension. Their judgments about what the casuistical system *should* require has a direct effect on what it *does* require.

Let me emphasize that I am not here arguing that norms are self-interpreting and self-applying; clearly, they are not. To apply the norm "thou shalt not kill," one needs to interpret the norm to specify the meaning of each of its terms, and any unstated exceptions. We must ask, for example, who is encompassed by the "thou," what counts as "killing," and whether the prohibition applies to soldiers in wartime. Furthermore, I am not denying the intimate relationship between facts and values; in fact, I am affirming it. I hold with MacIntyre that norms are coherently identified and applied against the background of a rich conception of human flourishing that is both descriptive and normative. A norm picks out certain facts as relevant, because it is embedded within a broader conception of human life that sees those facts as relevant in some way for how one ought to live one's life.

In addition to the theoretical difficulty, there is also a practical difficulty with Jonsen and Toulmin's definition of casuistry. When transferred to the realm of moral judgment, it appears to favor a form of undisciplined intuitionism. Any two cases have similarities and differences. While identifying them is important, it cannot exhaust the task of casuistry. It is always possible to point out similarities and distinguish differences in a way that supports one's preconceived notions of how a controversial case should be decided. The mere identification of similarities and differences does not answer why these particular similarities or differences ought to be morally relevant. For example, suppose Bob and Tom both cut ahead of a third person in the Starbucks line; Bob cuts ahead of Prince William, while Tom cuts ahead of a homeless woman. Is the identity of the displaced person a relevant difference to the moral analysis? Why? Because of rank (in the case of Bob)? Or because of gender (in the case of Tom)? To answer these questions, casuists must draw, tacitly or explicitly, on a broader, normative picture of right relations in society. Casuists are not moral intuitionists; if pressed, they can and should offer a normative account of what counts as morally relevant in the analysis of a case.

Acknowledging the theoretical and practical difficulties in Jonsen and Toulmin's account of casuistry helps us see why that account does not help us understand the manuals of moral theology. Centrally focused on application of norms, not upon analogy, the manuals are frequently organized according to the prohibitions and requirements contained in the Ten Commandments.[14] They also generally preserve, in form at least, the self-conception of interpreting and applying a commandment and its subsidiary norms to a given range of situations; their comparative case analysis takes place within a broader endeavor of interpreting and applying those norms. Furthermore, the authors of the manuals generally do not see themselves as engaged in an unstructured effort to evaluate cases for their similarities and differences, but as operating out of a fairly stable (if slowly evolving) sense of what circumstances are relevant to their moral analysis of a case.

Jonsen and Toulmin could reply by pointing to their distinction between the high casuistry of the manuals of moral theology of the early sixteenth century (e.g., John Mair's *Commentary on the Fourth Book of the Sentences*, 1509), which proceeded in an analogical manner between and among cases, and the later deductive application of principles to cases, including cases dealing with emerging situations (e.g., Francisco de Toledo's *Summa causuum conscientiae sive De instructione sacerdotum, libri septem*, 1598).[15] On this view, one might argue that high, sophisticated casuistry works by analogy; it is only low, workmanlike casuistry that applies rules to facts. I want to suggest, however, that there may be less conflict than initially appears between the methods of "high" and "low" casuistry. That possibility can be seen more clearly by shifting our touchstone for good casuistical reasoning from medicine to the legal realm. More specifically, in my judgment, the best contemporary touch- stone for well-functioning casuistry is not diagnostic medicine, as Jonsen and Toulmin maintain, but rather the Anglo-American common law.

Like the Catholic manualist tradition, the common law tradition takes factual particularities seriously. At the same time, it often understands itself as articulating, sharpening, and refining rules and standards that are meant to guide human behavior in a way that leads to the flourishing of the community. Some controversies—in fact, the vast majority—are settled by what looks like a mechanical, deductive application of rules to facts. These are the ordinary cases, the meat-and-potatoes of legal dispute resolution. Not every case, how- ever, is ordinary. There are times when a more searching inquiry is needed. In these cases, analogical reasoning, a triangulation of the facts in the new case between the facts in settled cases, plays a large role in deciding the case. Even in these circumstances, however, rules are not left behind entirely. Very often, judges proceed by probing the deeper meaning of the rule to articulate its rationale, the tacit assumptions of its operation, and the limits of its reach. Good moralists addressing specific cases operate in the same way as good common law judges. In discussing the application of the natural law, for example, Aquinas notes that wise men would recognize that the generally applicable rule requiring the return of deposits to their owner must admit of an exception in cases where the owner is a traitor or other enemy to the country.[16]

Can we formulate a definition of casuistry that captures what is involved in the best of both the common law and Catholic moral theology, and in particular the relationship between rules and facts? Drawing on my own experience with the common law as well as moral theology, I would emphasize that the process of casuistical reasoning is complicated; it is not completely captured either by the linear process of applying rules to facts or by the analogical process of drawing comparisons between factual circumstances. The black-letter law—the rules—matter, but the facts shape the way a rule is understood, not merely by justifying an exception at the margins, but more integrally by affecting the breadth, depth, reach, and strength of a rule. Facts make a rule multidimensional.

Because casuistical reasoning is multidimensional, it cannot be graphed linearly or even on a two-dimensional x-y axis. One cannot realistically expect to formulate a completely exhaustive series of rules with well-defined exceptions. Different aspects of a superficially similar situation—including character, place, and circumstance—can combine in different ways to yield different judgments. Sometimes, the most important question is not how to apply the rule, but which rule to apply, which in turn depends on how one frames the question, which in turn depends on how one perceives the total constellation of the facts in light of all relevant norms. Ultimately, the successful resolution of hard cases requires judgment—the judgment of one who is *phronimos tō nomō*—one who is wise with respect to the moral law. This aspect of the definition, I believe, captures something of what is involved in "high casuistry," whether legal or moral.

At the same time, it is important not to go too far in this direction. More specifically, it is essential to remember that not all cases are hard cases; in fact, in a well-functioning legal or moral system, most cases ought not to be hard. If the norms are formulated appropriately in a well-functioning casuistical tradition, they will provide reliable guidance for the majority of situations. The rule picks out the salient features of the case, there are no weighty countervailing features, and the appropriate decision becomes clear. Sound rules have a robust "focal meaning": they are framed with a range of cases in mind, and most cases that arise fall within the frame.[17]

So what is casuistry, at least at its best? I would define it as normative reflection on what course of action is to be taken in a particular case or class of cases, which (i) takes into account the interplay between principles, rules, and particular factual circumstances; (ii) understands the tacit or explicit factual and normative assumptions of applicable law (or other authoritative texts) and adjusts for the degree that they no longer hold true; (iii) recognizes the degree to which different resolutions of the case or class of cases may protect or threaten certain values that are not always compatible, such as justice, mercy, efficiency, and practicability; and (iv) understands that all the relevant factors are to be understood against a background view of human flourishing, both individual and communal, that is rarely, if ever, fully articulated. I hope the next section makes this definition plausible.

Section Two: Integrating Theory and Practice—MacIntyre on Tradition and the Common Law

Many definitions of casuistry suggest that it simply involves straightforward application of the relevant law to the facts of a case. They imply that the practice of casuistry is akin to following a recipe. Moreover, they convey the impression that casuistry is an isolated practice, capable of being understood and applied without reference to a broader setting. In fact, the practice of casuistry is not akin to following a recipe. Nor is it an isolated and esoteric type of moral reflection. As a practice, casuistry is only intelligible within a broader social and institutional context, the essential components of which are well described by Alasdair MacIntyre's tradition theory. More specifically, in *After Virtue* and subsequent books, MacIntyre argues that a moral tradition is "an historically extended, socially embodied argument, and an argument precisely in part about the goods which constitute that tradition."[18]

The goods constituting a tradition are not free-floating. They are embedded within the constitutive social practices of that tradition. In turn, practices are sustained through time by institutions created by a society for that purpose. We can see the intimate relationship between practices and institutions in contexts we do not normally associate with morality. The practice of music, for example, is sustained by institutions such as Suzuki Music Schools, the New England Conservatory, and the New York Philharmonic.

What, then, are virtues? According to MacIntyre, virtues are the habits of character that enable persons thinking and acting within the context of a moral tradition to appreciate the *goods internal to the constitutive practices* of that tradition.[19] Obviously, then, the notion of "goods internal to practices" is key to understanding MacIntyre's theory. They are goods that one can appreciate fully only by participating in the practice in question and by acquiring some competency in that practice. A key mark of great competency, according to MacIntyre, is the internalized ability to assess what counts as excellence within that practice, both in one's own case and in the case of other participants in the practice. Acquiring this ability takes time, training, practice, and guidance by one who is more expert in the practice.

In contrast, "external goods," like money, physical pleasure, and power, are instrumental goods whose value does not depend on taking an internal view toward a given practice. One can appreciate them regardless of whether one appreciates the goods internal to the practice. For example, one does not need to have dedicated one's life to music to appreciate the value of winning a million-dollar prize from the American Music Society for the best original composition. External goods both sustain and threaten practices, as well as the traditions that they instantiate. External goods can sustain practices, by generating interest in the practices, as well as by supporting the institutions that allow them to continue over time. They can also threaten practices by eclipsing the internal goods in their attractiveness. If a musician begins to value fame and fortune more than the intrinsic rewards of creating beauty and order for the human ear to appreciate, he or she has been seduced by external goods. Moreover, he or she may well betray the internal goods of creating and appreciating music in order to obtain them. Those responsible for the institutions that sustain practices over time are particularly susceptible to the lure of external goods. As those familiar with the history of religious institutions and institutions of higher learning can attest, the pursuit of money, power, and security may prompt officials to misuse or ignore the very values they are ostensibly dedicated to preserving.

MacIntyre's theory suggests that a moral tradition cannot be understood by looking solely within the four corners of the books that give it the most explicit and pointed articulation. Here, the common law offers a good analogy. By reading the case reports in tort, contract, and criminal law, one does not acquire a full, systematic introduction to the positive goods, virtues, practices, and institutions of the Anglo-American legal tradition.[20] That is not the purpose of those texts. They are designed to be read by professionals, who are presumed to have the same training as those making the decisions. They take a great deal for granted, including a thorough background knowledge of the purposes and political values of the common law. They are written primarily for those who have acquired some competency in that tradition, who have developed some of its characteristic virtues, and have learned to appreciate the goods internal to its practices.

The case reports are limited in aim. Their purpose is to provide a record of how men and women who have been trained to appreciate the goods internal to the Anglo-American legal tradition settle cases in which norms have been violated by participants in some of its constitutive practices. Most of the reports deal with hard cases, where the application of the relevant norms is difficult for some reason, either because it is not obvious what a given norm requires in a particular case or because there appears to be a conflict between relevant norms. Finally, the purpose of these case reports is fundamentally practical, not theoretical. They give practicing lawyers a sense of what the law requires in concrete cases, offering them more information that can be helpful in counseling their clients.

Furthermore, in the common law, there are case reports, and there are case reports. The majority of cases filed in trial court can easily be placed under a settled legal rule. They are of immense concern to the persons whose lives they immediately affect, but of little to no broader legal interest. Not all cases, however, are routine. Some cases decided by courts of appeals do require more care in applying the law to the facts; some cases involve the interpretation of an ambiguous rule, the clash of rules or policies, or even the sense that an exception must be made for this case or class of cases. A subset of these cases in any field are groundbreaking; they are the cases that are excerpted and included in the casebooks studied by law students. In this subset one does see "high casuistry"—the subtle interplay between law and facts, the careful distinctions, the judicious resolution of tension between various rules.

Invariably, however, the new "rule of the case" gets tamed; it gets simplified and reduced to a series of abstract principles that can easily be applied to new facts. In contract law, this function is performed by the "Restatement 2nd of Contracts," which is produced by the American Law Institute, a body of eminent practitioners, jurists, and academic lawyers. Student study guides follow much the same procedure, articulating rules and applying them to skeletal facts. This bare-bones literature of rule-and-application resembles the "low casuistry" described by Jonsen and Toulmin, Keenan, and others. It would be a mistake, however, to see it as disconnected to "high casuistry." The two forms of literature merely serve different functions in the same broad moral practice of doing justice within the particular tradition. Difficult cases arise; they must be addressed with all the care we can bring to bear. If the resolution is sound, subsequent cases of that sort are then dealt with in a more or less routine way, by applying the newly articulated rule to the facts and by articulating an interpretation or an exception from time to time.[21]

Interpreting the case reports properly requires a significant degree of training for three reasons. First and most obviously, the professional jargon can be misleading to those who have not been initiated into legal discourse. Second, and more important, if taken by themselves, case reports provide a distorted picture, not only of the common law but also of the particular subject matter they represent. Case reports are autopsy reports, not MRIs of healthy human beings; they detail situations where one or more of the parties involved failed to act as they ought to have acted in their dealings with others. But the negative judgments do not stand on their own; they draw their force, tacitly or explicitly, from a positive vision of how persons ought to relate to one another.

Contract law furnishes the clearest example in the common law tradition of the relationship between the sad narratives of human failure frequently found in case reports and the positive set of activities the law aims to protect.

In a nutshell, the point of contract law is to enable people to make mutually beneficial promises to one another and to encourage reliance on those promises. Without the ability to make promises to sell, lease, or buy property, goods, and services and to rely on the promises made to us, our economy would come to a screeching halt. Thousands of contracts are made, performed, and modified every day. The percentage that are breached is small; the percentage that are litigated after breach is even smaller, and the percentage that make new law in a way that suits them for inclusion in appellate law reports (and a fortiori, student casebooks) is infinitesimal. The law of breach is only intelligible in light of the broader practices that contract law is designed to promote and protect. For example, a party may breach a contract if he or she does not conform to commercially reasonable standards regarding its performance.[22]

Third and finally, no area of the common law may be well understood without reference to broader societal values, social practices, and conceptions of flourishing. Contract law again furnishes a good example. Contract law is private law; in writing a contract, the parties essentially draft a law that governs some aspect of their interactions. It is precisely because our culture values autonomy so dearly (*auto* + *nomos*) that we are willing to devote the resources of the community to enforcing these private legal frameworks. To take another example, we in American society see a great virtue in creative fortitude, an ability to respond to life's unanticipated difficulties with ingenuity and optimism. The status of this virtue is reflected in how we expect the nonbreaching party to respond to a breach of a contract by the other party. The law does not encourage the nonbreaching party to act like a passive victim; the nonbreaching party is expected to take reasonable steps to mitigate damages by making other arrangements. Contract law reflects the broader maxim: "Don't cry over spilt milk."

What happens if we see Catholic casuistry and its associated literature as participating in a MacIntyrean tradition and model such a tradition on the Anglo-American common law? What happens, then, if we situate the Catholic casuistical literature more broadly within the Catholic tradition, and its constitutive institutions, practices, virtues, and goods? I now turn to this question.

Section Three: Catholic Casuistry as Part of a MacIntyrean Tradition

If we keep MacIntyre's tradition theory in mind, the first point that we need to emphasize is that the confessors' manuals do not *constitute* the entire Catholic moral tradition; they contribute to a part of it, and merely a limited part of it. To understand the Catholic moral tradition, one needs to take a sweeping look at its actual normative practices in all their fullness, as well as the virtues that allow one to appreciate the goods internal to those practices. We also need to examine the institutions that support those practices through time, while on occasion threatening them with an excessive concern for external rather than internal goods.

At its broadest, the Catholic Christian tradition attempts to instantiate the gospel—the good news of Jesus Christ, who came to redeem humanity from sin and death. Over the centuries, the church developed practices that allowed the faithful to grow in their identity as members of the body of Christ. Central was the reception of the seven sacraments, which absorbed the key events of a human life, from infant baptism to extreme unction, into the broader story of Christian redemption. The creation of a "thick" and seamless Catholic culture in many places facilitated the development of other practices, such as cults to particular saints tied to specific locales and devotions to the Virgin Mary. The theologian Hans Frei used to say to his students that precritical Protestants absorbed their world into the biblical text;[23] it would be true of Catholics to say that they absorbed their world into the sacramental life of the church, particularly the Eucharist. Before the Second Vatican Council, many Catholics were able to draw on a total Catholic world, which took for granted the truth of the big and smaller aspects of the great story of salvation.

Obviously, a full account of the constitutive practices of a Catholic Christian way of life would require a monograph. It seems to me, however, that one might profitably focus on the virtue of mercy and its associated works. Mercy is a virtue describing love of neighbor; in fact, Aquinas considered it the highest virtue by which we relate to other human beings.[24] The corporal works of mercy include feeding the hungry, giving drink to the thirsty, clothing the naked, sheltering the homeless, visiting the sick, visiting the imprisoned, and burying the dead. The spiritual works of mercy encompass converting the sinner, instructing the ignorant, counseling the doubtful, comforting the sorrowful, bearing wrongs patiently, forgiving injuries, and praying for the living and the dead.

Participation in the works of mercy enables people, with the essential help of divine grace, to develop key Christian virtues, particularly an actualized commitment to justice transformed and elevated by love, which in the modern era is nicely captured by Pope John Paul II's conception of solidarity. In his encyclical *Solicitudo Rei Socialis*, he writes that solidarity "is not a feeling of vague compassion or shallow distress at the misfortunes of so many people, both near and far. On the contrary, it is *a firm and persevering determination* to commit oneself to the common good; that is to say to the good of all and of each individual, because we are *all* really responsible for *all*."[25]

What are the goods internal to the practices of the works of mercy? It seems to me that they center around the increasing conformity of one's will to that of Christ, as one begins to treat others not merely according to the highest norm of justice, the Golden Rule ("Do unto others as you would have them do unto you"),[26] but according to the higher standard of charity, encapsulated in Christ's new commandment: "Just as I have loved you, you also should love one another."[27] As an individual's mind and heart become more and more conformed to Christ's, he or she becomes better able to grasp that all human beings are made in the image and likeness of God, no matter what their appearance or physical condition. By the term *grasp*, I mean not merely an academic ability to give academic assent to the proposition to that effect, but a practical ability to treat others in accordance with Christ's injunction, no matter how messy, difficult, or inconvenient it might be.

Over the centuries, the church has created, maintained, and reformed institutions to support the corporal and spiritual works of mercy. Hospitals, orphanages, charitable associations, and old age homes, many founded by religious orders, offered a stable context for the corporal works of mercy.[28] As parishes were founded in the United States, so were Catholic elementary and high schools. Catholic colleges came into existence to serve their graduates. Families organized their lives around the parish church and its activities. Historian of American religion John McGreevy has described the coherent world enveloping Catholic immigrants in the nineteenth and early twentieth century, created by an interlocking and mutually supporting set of church-related institutions, practices, and family life.[29]

What is the role of sacramental practices in this framework? From a sociological perspective, five sacraments integrate the milestones of life with the framework of Catholic belief: baptism marks the incorporation of a new child into the community; confirmation proclaims the willingness of those now (partially) grown children to affirm membership and its attendant responsibilities, holy orders or marriage celebrates the commitment to a vocation recognized and supported by the church; and the sacrament of the sick ("last rites") marks an individual's transition out of earthly existence and into eternal life. Two sacraments ensure the ongoing integration of an individual within the broader moral and spiritual framework of Catholic Christianity: the Eucharist, generally received in Sunday Mass, and the sacrament of penance, which was commonly sought by the faithful on a weekly or monthly basis.[30] The Mass reiterates the basic story of Christ's life, death, and resurrection, inculcating basic values and reinforcing the frame in which individual believers live their lives. The sacrament of reconciliation allows believers to situate themselves within that framework personally, by confessing transgressions, seeking instruction on morally dubious courses of action, and receiving absolution, penance, and encouragement to "go and sin no more."

Within a Catholic framework, however, the sacraments are not reducible to a purely sociological analysis. From a theological perspective, the sacraments offered faithful Catholics channels to seek and receive divine grace. The sacrament of penance heals the breach in our will wrought by original sin and restores us to an intimate relationship with God. If we follow St. Thomas, the moral life of a Catholic is also, in some sense, a mystical life—a participation in the very life of God. The natural law, according to St. Thomas, is a "participation" of the human mind in the eternal law—which is, in the final analysis, nothing other than God's own mind and will.[31] In making moral decisions, therefore, every human being draws upon a relationship to God, in a more or less imperfect way. Furthermore, the grace that, according to Aquinas, heals and elevates our will also confers a share in divine life. The "new law" is intimately associated with God's grace; it not only commands that we love our neighbor but also gives us the strength to fulfill what it commands. For Aquinas, the gift of God's grace is ultimately a gift of participation in God's own life.[32]

How should we situate the moral manuals within this broader account of constitutive practices and institutions of the Catholic moral tradition? In my view, by viewing their function as analogous to case reports in the Anglo-American legal tradition. Accordingly, the first point that we need to emphasize is that the confessors' manuals do not constitute—*and were never intended to constitute*—the entire Catholic moral tradition; they count as merely a limited part of it. They were never meant to describe the entire sweep of the normative vision of human flourishing in the Catholic worldview. They were meant to be helpful, practical guides, designed for a limited, professional audience—confessors—who, ideally, were already trained to appreciate the goods internal to the practices of Catholic Christianity and committed to assisting others in appreciating the same goods.

Like legal case reports, the manuals of moral theology also can be seen as pathology reports, as John Mahoney has noted.[33] They were meant to assist confessors in identifying the nature and the seriousness of the sinful acts brought to them by penitents, so that they could both impose an appropriate penance and propose an appropriate remedy for the harm caused by the sinner. If we see the manuals of moral theology as analogous in function to law reports, we will appreciate them for what they are, refrain from criticizing them for failing to be what they were never meant to be, and help them find their (limited) place within the broader framework required to understand the Catholic moral tradition. We can, in other words, contextualize the flaws of the genre. What are those flaws?

One commonly identified flaw is a certain hidebound resistance to new ideas. As Mahoney notes, the manualist genre saw itself as prizing conservativism and continuity, not innovation. He quotes the eminent English-speaking Jesuit moralist Henry Davis on this point: "'A writer on Moral Theology today must be indebted beyond measure to the labour of past writers, for the matter is one that has been treated with the greatest acumen and scholarship during well nigh three centuries, and there is no room for originality.'"[34]

Here, the practical focus of the manuals, like the practical focus of the common law system, gives us a way to evaluate the purpose of originality. Writing case opinions, like writing confessors' manuals, is not a purely speculative enterprise on the part of an individual moral luminary. It is rather, a practical endeavor, community based and oriented toward the common good. So originality is not to be prized for its own sake; the goal of the genre is not to demonstrate the sparkling brilliance of an isolated intellect, no matter how perceptive. The touchstone is the common good, understood in practical terms. The moral and legal prohibition against intentional killing of the innocent has served humanity well for centuries. An argument in favor of repealing it might be extremely original from a philosophical perspective, but that does not mean it should immediately be adopted by a wise judge or moralist.[35]

This does not mean, however, that there is no room for creativity in either the common law or the manualist tradition. If a new problem or controversy arises in the community, it must be addressed. Extending the normative tradition to encompass new questions requires a type of interstitial creativity that is not utterly unfettered but is disciplined and bounded by the fundamental commitments of the moral tradition.[36] For example, in the 1980s, many American courts needed to grapple with the novel phenomenon of surrogate motherhood. In one of the most famous contract cases of the twentieth century, the "Baby M" case, the New Jersey Supreme Court refused to enforce a surrogacy contract in which a woman agreed to terminate her parental rights before birth in exchange for payment, because such a transaction would violate state law against baby selling.[37] Analogously, the manualists developed the Catholic moral tradition when a need to address new problems arose. As modern medicine proved itself able to extend life in the eighteenth and nineteenth centuries, albeit with uncertain, painful, and sometimes expensive means, Catholic moralists began to consider when it was morally required to avail oneself of those means and when it was permissible to forgo them. So the distinction between "ordinary" (morally required) and "extraordinary" (not morally required) means of medical treatment began to take on added depth.[38]

In this context, Father Davis's caution against originality can be better understood: *If* (the qualification is important) the articulation of a moral law has long been found to be sound and serviceable, there is no need to reinvent the wheel. To do so would be to put one's own egoism ahead of the common good. Manualists, like appellate judges, expected their work to be *applied*, not simply studied. To call for the application of a new idea without a good reason to do so undermines predictability and thereby destabilizes the normative framework the manualists have committed their life to preserving and extending.[39]

Mahoney identifies three other flaws that have stemmed from moral theology's development in the context of confessional manuals. First, moral theology is preoccupied with sin. He writes:

> As a consequence of this commitment to spiritual pathology, the discipline of moral theology was to relinquish almost all consideration of the good in man to other branches of theology, notably to what became known as spiritual theology. But inevitably this study of Christian perfection was pursued in a rarified and élitist atmosphere more suited to those few who aspired to the life of the counsels, particularly in the religious orders, than to those laity in the world who would, it was considered, find it sufficiently challenging and formidable to attain even to salvation by observance of the Ten Commandments.[40]

Second, Mahoney states that moral theology tends to focus on the individual. Each person enters the confessional alone, taking responsibility for the state of his or her own soul before God.[41] He notes that this has led to an emphasis in the manuals on sexual sins. According to Mahoney, "this stress on the individual, with a view to his confession, is a reason why the Church's moral tradition has found it difficult to handle the idea of collective responsibility on a large scale."[42]

Third, Mahoney maintains that the manualist literature contributed to the legalism of Catholic moral theology: "the casting of moral theology for centuries as the handmaid of canon law has only reinforced the predominantly legal approach to morality which has dominated the making of moral theology through its close connection with a primarily penal theology of the Sacrament of penance."[43]

Although Mahoney takes pains to nuance and qualify his criticisms about the manualist tradition, those nuances and qualifications do not ultimately overcome his negative verdict. He admits, for example, that it can be argued that "the whole body of literature is professional, intended to help the general practitioner of the Sacrament to diagnose the spiritual ailments of his sick patients, and not intended for morbid reading by the general public."[44] Nonetheless, he maintains that the focus on sin is "inadequate and misleading in concentrating on, and in the process isolating and exaggerating, one aspect of the moral life, and so militating against any integrated and holistic view of man and his moral vocation."[45] Mahoney admits that the sacrament of confession developed the doctrine of cooperation with evil to investigate shared responsibility for wrongdoing but notes that this doctrine worked best when "the total number of participants is small."[46] Ultimately, it was not enough to overcome the individualism of the manualist framework. Finally, he emphasizes that the legalism of the focus on sin was often "accompanied by a confessional practice which is mercifully quite different."[47] At the same time, he maintains that the medicinal function of confession was systematically subordinated to its forensic function.[48]

It seems to me that Mahoney's nuances and qualifications have a much greater mitigating effect if we keep in mind the functional analogy between moral manuals and law reports. The latter, too, are a jargon-filled type of professional literature, meant for people who have already been inculcated with a particular specialized view of the subject matter. They, too, are largely focused on determining individual, personal responsibility.[49] They, too, are concentrated on sin, understood in secular terms as irresponsibility. In short, law reports have an important but limited focus and reach in the articulation of the broader values of our political and legal tradition. Most American lawyers would not think that they should be faulted for failing to accomplish more than their important but limited task. Most would not fault judges for their lack of creativity in either articulating or revising long-standing rights and obligations in the tradition.

Moreover, thinking about the role of moral manuals in comparison with legal cases allows us to get a better sense of why the moral manuals fell into disuse, if not disrepute, after the Second Vatican Council. First, the sacrament of confession fell into disuse; consequently, there was less need for guidance for confessors to use in hearing confessions. Second, and relatedly, after the Second Vatican Council, both the clergy and a newly energized, educated laity found themselves hungry for a broader, more positive discussion of Catholic moral life. Such a discussion called for explicit reflection upon the virtues, practices, and goods internal to the Christian life. Interestingly enough, at about the same time in the American legal realm, a parallel move was taking place in civil law, away from litigation and toward more positive and flexible forms of conflict resolution, such as arbitration.[50]

Third, it is indisputable that the manualist tradition was deleteriously affected by the controversy precipitated by *Humanae Vitae*,[51] a controversy that has shaped the discourse of Catholic moral theology in the West for the past forty years. Pope Paul VI rejected the majority report of his own blue-ribbon commission, which recommended that the church develop its teaching to permit married couples to use some form of artificial birth control under some circumstances. Instead, he took the advice of the minority, which recommended that all forms of birth control be deemed morally impermissible.[52] Many moralists in favor of revision took the rejection of the majority report as a sign of the ossification of the tradition; they viewed the highly public dismissal of Charles Curran from the Catholic University of America as confirmation of the view that the magisterium of the church viewed any argument for a revision of the tradition as a direct threat to its authority. The fact that the reaffirmation of the ban was so poorly received, even by practicing Catholics,[53] undermined the claims of the tradition to articulate a "natural law" approach to morality in principle accessible to all persons of good will.

Interestingly enough, the poor reception of the ban affected both progressive and conservative moral theology. Not surprisingly, some progressives who did not believe that the use of artificial birth control was always immoral abandoned the manualist tradition as too rigid and constraining for sound moral reflection.[54] More interesting, however, many conservatives, especially younger ones, attempted to preserve the ban, not by emphasizing its conformity with the universal moral law, but by situating it within the broader context of a distinctively Roman Catholic theology and marital spirituality indebted to John Paul II's "theology of the body."[55]

Fourth, many people who went into the study of moral theology after the Second Vatican Council were laypeople, not priests; consequently, they understandably did not see their vocation as making a direct contribution to the wise administration of the sacrament of confession as part of a larger vocation of the *cura animarum*. Many of them were trained at non-Catholic universities, and some did not have divinity degrees as a basis for their doctoral work.[56]

Consequently, their training inclines them to see their work as more analogous to that of scholars in cognate fields in the humanities, such as philosophy or history, than to that of scholars working in the professions such as ministry or law.

It is not, of course, that scholars bear no responsibility for the well-being of the subject areas they study. But the more one sees one's work as having direct bearing on the life or well-being of another, the less room there is for experimentation, innovation, and creativity. Because law includes different levels of engagement with practical issues, the analogy with law is again helpful. As a legal scholar, I am free to advocate the recognition of an innovative defense to the enforcement of a contract, based on theoretical concerns such as its intellectual elegance and coherence with the latest theories of neurobiology. As a lawyer representing a client accused of breaching a contract, however,

I am required to put forward the defense most likely to succeed on my client's behalf. In some cases, that may be the innovative defense; in others, the client is more likely to achieve the desired outcome if the lawyer follows a tried-and-true strategy. As a judge trying to decide whether to allow an innovative defense, I must consider the fit with other aspects of the case law and basic jurisprudential principles, as well as more pragmatic questions such as ease of application and likelihood of abuse.

In the foregoing pages, I have argued that the moral manuals do not present, and do not claim to present, the normative vision of Catholic Christianity in its entirety. Rather, they should be seen as playing a limited but essential role that is analogous to that played by case law in carrying on the Anglo-American legal and political tradition. What follows from this attempt to reframe the Catholic casuistical tradition? In my view, it offers the possibility of viewing the manualist tradition more sympathetically than has previously been the case. If we cease blaming the manualists for failing to do what they never intended to do, we may be more able to appreciate the real value of what they did accomplish. Both liberals and conservatives might find it worth their while to carry those accomplishments into very different cultural and ecclesiastical circumstances.

Section Four: Toward Critical Retrieval

I see two basic benefits of the manualist tradition of casuistry, one related to the community that it both presupposed and enabled, and the other related to the kind of discussion of moral issues that it fostered. Both of these are worth retrieving, although the form in which they are carried forward will probably be very different than in the past.

A Common Professional Context

The manualist tradition of casuistry was produced and sustained by a body of highly trained priests who saw themselves as engaged in a common task, despite their differences of language or culture. That task had a practical orientation, because the manualists recognized that their central focus was preparing priests to provide a certain type of pastoral care to the laity. At the same time, the manualists assumed that good priests would see themselves as distinguished from those whom they served by both their knowledge and their sensibilities.

The preparation for the priesthood was intense. Discussing Jean-Jacques Olier's *Traité des saints ordres*, which was the dominant account of priestly formation in both Europe and the United States from 1676 to 1966, Kenan Osborne

describes how the dedication to prayer, particularly saying the breviary and cele-
brating the Eucharist, took priority above the *cura animarum* in the life of a future
priest. Seminarians were ideally set apart from other young men their age to
prepare themselves for a life that was to some degree separate and apart from lay
people.[57] After high school (sometimes spent in a minor seminary) and college,
future priests studied Latin, Greek, and Hebrew; philosophy; scripture; church
history, dogmatic, moral, and pastoral theology; liturgy; and canon law. Moral and
spiritual training, in addition to prayer, was also a key part of the education; a
seminarian's life was closely regulated for sixteen hours a day.[58] The manualists
not only participated in this training, they were formed by it themselves.

The development of seminary education could easily be considered a precur-
sor to formal professional education more broadly. Today, the intensity and depth
of professional education of all stripes—medicine and law as well as holy
orders—aims to strip away the prior self-understanding of the student and
replace it with a professional identity.[59] The common training received by professionals, even those who attend different schools, creates a bond among them and
a sense of difference from laypersons who have not received such training. Like
lawyers, budding priests speak a jargon that virtually no one else understands,
they take for granted a certain set of canonical texts that virtually no one else has
read, and they reason in ways that are distinctive to their particular discipline. Like
lawyers, they undergo common practical experiences: budding lawyers participate in "trial advocacy programs" and budding priests prepare to administer the
sacraments, including the sacrament of confession. The study of law, like the
study of divinity, began to incorporate a serious practical or pastoral component
into the curriculum comparatively recently. It was assumed that the students
would acquire such skills in their first years on the job.

The intense common formation in professional life fosters a common
sensibility, teaches a common language, and inculcates a common set of
values. In the field of law, for example, there is a common set of core courses
that all lawyers will have taken and even a set of cases that all lawyers are likely
to have read. Furthermore, there is a common way in which American lawyers
have been trained to approach rules, facts, and circumstances. More specifically, they have learned how to reframe rules, to recast facts, and to render
circumstances more or less relevant. Knowing how to deal with those materials, how to maneuver with their concepts and facts, is part of what is meant by
"learning to think like a lawyer."

It strikes me that this common formation and common language is no
longer present, or at least no longer as strongly present, in the field of contemporary moral theology. Some Catholic moralists are trained in Catholic programs;
others are not. Some Catholic programs are staffed partly or mainly with professors

who studied at non-Catholic programs. There is no one dominant method in Catholic moral theology; instead, there are several methods that do not employ the same terminology. Most American Catholic moralists will have read Aquinas and Augustine, but reading Aquinas with Stanley Hauerwas at Duke is not the same as reading Aquinas with James Keenan, S.J., at Boston College. Furthermore, the official documents on moral theology issued by the Vatican tend to employ a language drawn from the manuals that most American-trained Catholic moralists were not taught to parse and interpret in their graduate education. An unfamiliarity with the technical jargon and characteristic modes of speech of official church documents can on occasion result in overreading them or misreading them. This observation is not meant to cast aspersion on the Curia; the interpretive difficulties associated with jargon are not unique to the Vatican's documents. The same is true when those untutored in the terminology of constitutional law read a case from the U.S. Supreme Court.

Because they have not all received the same basic type of training, the sense that American Catholic moralists are engaged in a common project may have become attenuated over the years. This attenuation can be seen in three areas. The first has to do with the nature and presuppositions of their research, which tends to be greatly influenced by where they did their doctoral work. Precisely because Catholic moralists were trained at different places, the problems they see themselves called to work on vary significantly, and the theoretical presuppositions they bring to those projects vary widely as well.

The second has to do with how they understand the purpose of their work. Many Catholic moralists find their identity primarily as academics; they see their work as contributing to general understanding without necessarily having a direct impact on how others live their lives. In contrast, when judges (and law clerks) write opinions, they know that the parties (and others) will be bound to follow their directives regardless of whether they agree with them. My sense is that the attitude of Catholic manualists who knew they were writing for confessors would have seen their work as more analogous to that of judges and law clerks than to that of academic moralists.

The third has to do with the sense that the moralists trained before the Second Vatican Council had of a broader connection with the world church. Many did their training in Rome; most were fluent in several European languages, as well as Latin. Despite new resources such as the Internet and the greater ease of international travel, it can seem as if the geographic horizons of American Catholic moralists are smaller than they used to be before the council.

What, if anything, can be done to foster a larger, more integrated conversation among Catholic moralists? What can be done to create a common basis of experience and knowledge? I see some signs of promise. A group of younger

Catholic moral theologians has begun meeting together on an annual basis to share their work and reflect on their vocation as Catholic moralists. They refer to their group as "New Wine, New Wineskins." Their meeting seems designed to find ways for lay Catholic moralists to develop some sense of their identity in— and responsibility for—speaking to and for the members of the body of Christ.

Moreover, Boston College's Professor James Keenan, S.J., recently organized a spectacularly successful international conference, Catholic Theological Ethics in the World Church, held in Padua, Italy, in 2006.[60] Arguably, the strong participation from the developing world, as well as from Europe and North America, offers the possibility of conversation far broader than that enabled by the manuals.[61] A second conference is planned for 2010; a Web site and monthly updates allow communication in the meantime.[62]

It seems to me, however, that a more organized and concerted approach might be in order. How can we give the benefits of a common professional identity to Catholic moralists who were not trained for the priesthood and who received their scholarly training in non-Catholic settings? How can we encourage all Catholic moralists to be conversant in the tradition, even if they take very different stances on it? After all, a common basis in a textual tradition makes possible not only agreement but also productive disagreement. A good example of the latter can be found in the pages of *Theological Studies* in the ongoing debates between Richard McCormick, S.J., John Connery, S.J., and others over how to understand a human act, the morality of contraception, and other topics.[63] It strikes me that the University of Notre Dame or Boston College (or perhaps the Institute of Advanced Catholic Studies) could run a summer program for advanced graduate students in moral theology, introducing them to the manualist tradition and encouraging them to reflect on the professional dimensions of their work in service to the church.

Such a project would cultivate the seed sown by the "New Wine, New Wineskins" movement described previously. It would encourage young moralists to ask themselves the following questions: Who is their audience? Solely other academics? Administrators of Catholic health care facilities and schools? How do they describe the way in which they are accountable to the tradition and what such accountability means?[64] Moreover, it would also provide an opportunity for an introduction to the terminology and the mind-set of Catholic moral theology, whose astute practitioners in the United States are not all academics.[65]

A More Constructive Approach to "Dissent"

Any attempt to retrieve and reinvigorate the Catholic casuistical tradition must grapple not only with the various sociological factors that led to its decline (such as the increase in the number of lay moralists and the increasing disuse of the sacrament of confession) but also with internal aspects of the tradition that may not be suitable for the contemporary context. One such aspect, in my judgment, is the way in which those responsible for carrying on official teaching handle dissenting opinions. Needless to say, this issue took center stage in the wake of *Humane Vitae*, as the case of Charles Curran vividly exemplified. After much back-and-forth with the Vatican, Curran was forced to leave the Catholic University of America because of his dissenting position on the contraception question and other related questions.[66]

In both moral theology and in the common law, there is a "magisterium" that makes judgments about competing views of what the tradition in question means or requires in a particular case or set of cases. From the perspective of tradition theory, this is all to the good. In a living tradition that purports to bind its adherents, some form of authoritative interpretation is virtually indispensable. Those responsible for the articulation and implementation of a normative tradition have a responsibility to distinguish between sound and unsound articulations and developments of that tradition.

Nonetheless, the necessity of an authoritative magisterium that provides resolution to some disputed questions does not entail a particular approach to handling authors and positions that dissent from that resolution. Over the centuries, the Roman Catholic tradition developed an elaborate and interlocking system for ensuring uniformity in matters of faith and morals. Most theologians, including moral theologians, were priests; they could be required to submit their material to their local ordinary to receive a *nihil obstat* and an imprimatur before publishing it. Indeed, theological material could not be published by Catholic presses (controlled by the church) unless it received such confirmation of orthodoxy. Seminaries were prohibited from carrying suspect material in libraries or teaching it in classrooms, except for the limited purpose of refuting it. The faithful were prohibited from reading theological material that did not pass the scrutiny of diocesan censors (or indeed, other material on the now-defunct Index of Forbidden Books). The Sacred Congregation for the Doctrine of the Faith could investigate controversial theological materials and compel their authors to recant or revise controversial positions on pain of being silenced or even losing their teaching positions.

As the highly public cases of Charles Curran, Hans Küng, and Roger Haight, S.J., demonstrate, these procedures are still in use in the post–Vatican II era, at least in some situations. As measures that took root in a preliberal, pre–information age context, where censorship was a common activity on the part of both church and state, they were effective and understandable, if not ultimately defensible. In the contemporary context, however, a program of silencing and censorship can have very little legitimacy or effectiveness. Most Western societies have endorsed the view that the truth is best achieved, not through censorship of ideas, but through vigorous engagement and debate. An attempt to "protect" the truth by silencing the opposition is likely to seem both disingenuous and counterproductive. Moreover, censorship is of questionable effectiveness in this era of Amazon.com and the Internet as a whole, which makes the worldwide dissemination of controversial positions easier than ever. Finally, in today's context, the application of procedures such as censorship and silencing will inevitably involve inequities. The church has sufficient power to act against priests or nuns but not against laypersons, whose tenure in most institutions is normally not dependent on being a theologian in good standing with the local ordinary.

Is there a way for the church's magisterium to exercise real authority—real judgment about theological matters in a way consistent with the contemporary context and contemporary values pertaining to the pursuit of truth? I believe there is, although working through what it would be like is beyond the scope of this chapter. Let me make two observations. First, even in a free society, there ought to be no obstacle to the magisterium in expressing the judgment that a particular theological position or argument is not consistent with the tradition (although humility in making this judgment is obviously a desideratum).

Second, especially in a free society, learned, honest, dissenting opinions ought not to be viewed as dangerous to the common good of the tradition they propose to advance. Such opinions ought to count, even if they cannot be allowed to win the argument. On this point, the common law tradition may provide a helpful model.[67] When an appellate court issues a judgment, the majority opinion determines the interpretation of the law, controls the ultimate resolution of the case, and sets the precedential value of the case. The dissenting opinions, however, are not erased; in fact, they are published along with the majority opinion. This practice not only acknowledges the fact that both majority and dissenting judges are ultimately loyal to the same tradition but also institutionally expresses a welcome confidence and humility. The confidence of the judges in the majority is demonstrated by the fact that they do not fear contradictory analysis appearing alongside their own. Their humility appears in their recognition that later courts may find the dissent more helpful and persuasive as a justification for either qualifying the majority opinion or overruling it altogether.[68]

Disciplined Focus on Particularity

Why ought we to care about retrieving and engaging the tradition of moral casuistry embodied in the manuals of moral theology? What can be gained, apart from a mere connection with the past? What can the manuals teach us? How can we refurbish the mode of analysis in which they specialize to assist the church in our times? I believe that there are three reasons that the manuals continue to be worth our time and attention, which can be summed up by saying that they encourage a disciplined focus on the particularity of human lives and human actions.

First, the manuals' elaborate taxonomy of a human action recognizes the complexity of moral reflection. Following Aquinas,[69] who was himself following Aristotle, the manualists distinguished between the object of an act (*finis operis*), the agent's motive in acting (*finis operantis*), and the circumstances in which the action was performed (*quis, quid, ubi, quibus auxillis, cur, quomodo, quando,* and sometimes, *materia circa quam*—who, what, where, with what means, why, how, when, and sometimes, about what matter). The manualists, like Aquinas, held that an act had to be acceptable in all respects for it to be morally permissible. One significant defect rendered it morally impermissible. The absolutism of the ultimate judgment, however, should not be allowed to occlude the nuance and texture available in the analytical framework. The human mind, heart, and will are not simple. People sometimes perform a good act for less than noble reasons (e.g., giving money to charity to gain business contacts) and a wrongful act for good reasons (e.g., euthanasia to spare a loved one suffering). The tradition supports more nuanced analysis than the bottom-line judgments seem to indicate.

Second, it seems to me that this disciplined but richly textured understanding of human action can be appropriated by theorists of virtue who want to move beyond general reflections on character to a detailed picture of how virtue operates in concrete circumstances. An expansive consideration of character, aim, motive, and circumstances leads naturally into narrative theory and, in particular, narrative theology.[70] The manuals' use of case studies had tended to be abbreviated. There is no reason that longer and more nuanced fact patterns cannot be employed to encourage readers (both professional and lay) to develop their capacity for moral insight and imagination. The casebooks used in law schools regularly include rich descriptions of facts as well as law; they encourage the students to recognize that moral discernment is not merely an application of facts to rules, but an interplay between them.[71]

Third, I think that a critical but appreciative reconsideration of the manuals can help us develop a richer picture of the intertwined relationship between moral insight and moral blindness in human life in general. Students of critical race studies and feminist scholars might find that working at the level of detail engaged in by the manuals adds insight to the manner in which false presumptions about human beings enter into the fabric of human society.

The manuals—and the tradition of casuistry that they carry forward—constituted a major part of the Roman Catholic moral tradition for five hundred years. They were sidelined in the emphasis on aggiornamento that immediately followed the Second Vatican Council, as moral theology explored new sources of wisdom and light. Now, it may be time to return to those dusty volumes and reintegrate them into our ongoing moral reflection.

NOTES

1. The best history is John Mahoney, *The Making of Moral Theology* (Oxford: Clarendon, 1987), chapter 1. As he details, there were confessors' manuals before the Council of Trent. There were also other forms of penitential books.

2. CANON VI: "Si quis negaverit, confessionem sarcramentalem vel institutam vel ad salutem necessariam esse iure divino; aut dixerit, modum secrete confitendi soli sacerdoti, quem Ecclesia catholica ab initio semper observavit et observat, alienum esse ab institutione et mandato Christi, et inventum esse humanum: an. s." Henricus Denzinger, *Enchiridion Symbolorum Definitionum et Declarationum de Rebus Fidei et Morum*, ed. Alfonsus Schoenmetzer, S.J., 34th ed. (Barcelona, Spain: Herder, 1965), para. 1706.

3. A fascinating new history of the change in the field is Charles E. Curran, *Catholic Moral Theology in the United States: A History* (Washington, DC: Georgetown University Press, 2008). In a phone conversation, Father Curran told me that the manual most in use in the United States before Vatican II was produced by an Austrian Jesuit, H. Noldin, S.J., with other editors. See Noldin, *Summa theologiae moralis*, ed. A. Schmitt, 17th ed. (Oeniponte, Austria: Rauch, 1940). Other manuals associated with the Jesuits include Aloysius Sabetti, S.J., *Compendium theologiae moralis*, 34th ed., ed. Daniel Creeden (New York: Pustet, 1939). Like Sabetti, others updated the influential manual of Jean Piere Gury, S.J. See, e.g., Gury, *Compendium theologiæ moralis*, 34th ed., ed. Antonio Ballerini, S.J. (Cincinnati: Pustet, 1939).

The Dominicans produced Dominicus M. Prümmer, O.P., *Vademecum theologiae moralis: in usum examinandorum et confessariorum*, 6th ed., ed. Engelbert M. Münch (Barcelona, Spain: Herder, 1947) and Henri Benoît Merkelbach, O.P., *Summa theologiae moralis ad mentem d. Thomae et ad normam iuris novi* (Paris: Desclée de Brouwer, 1949). A prominent manual by an English Jesuit is Henry Davis, S.J., *Moral and Pastoral Theology* (New York: Sheed & Ward, 1946). The only manual written in English by Americans is John A. McHugh and Charles J. Callan, *Moral Theology: A Complete Course Based on St. Thomas Aquinas and the Best Modern Authorities* (New York: J. F. Wagner, 1929).

4. In 1985, McCormick was joined by three other scholars: two Jesuits (David Hollenbach, S.J., and John Langan, S.J.) and one laywoman (Lisa Sowle Cahill). Since that time, a number of scholars (including me) have made contributions to them in areas of their scholarly expertise.

5. Some drew upon other aspects of the Catholic tradition than casuistry; David Hollenbach, S.J., for example, integrates Catholic social teaching into a methodology

designed to identify, protect, and promote human rights. Others incorporate influences from other religious traditions into their approaches; Lisa Sowle Cahill's approach to sexual ethics is indebted not only to the Catholic tradition but also to the influence of the eminent Protestant ethicist James M. Gustafson, with whom she studied at the University of Chicago. While casuistical reflection is not entirely absent from the Moral Notes (thanks in part to the important contributions of James Keenan, S.J.), it by no means can be said to dominate them.

6. See William C. Mattison III, ed., *New Wine, New Wineskins: A Next Generation Reflects on Key Issues in Catholic Moral Theology* (Lanham, MD: Rowman & Littlefield, 2005).

7. Mahoney maintains that the manualist literature contributed to the legalism of Catholic moral theology. "[T]he casting of moral theology for centuries as the handmaid of canon law has only reinforced the predominantly legal approach to morality which has dominated the making of moral theology through its close connection with a primarily penal theology of the Sacrament of penance" (Mahoney, *The Making of Moral Theology*, 35). The charge of "legalism" is a slippery one; it can have more than one meaning. See M. Cathleen Kaveny, "What Is Legalism? Egelhardt and Grisez on the Misuse of Law in Christian Ethics," *Thomist* 72 (2008): 443–485.

8. Alasdair MacIntyre, *After Virtue* (Notre Dame, IN: University of Notre Dame Press, 1981).

9. Alasdair MacIntyre, *Whose Justice? Which Rationality?* (Notre Dame, IN: University of Notre Dame Press, 1988).

10. Alasdair MacIntyre, *Three Rival Versions of Moral Inquiry* (Notre Dame, IN: University of Notre Dame Press, 1991).

11. Albert R. Jonsen and Stephen Toulmin, *The Abuse of Casuistry: A History of Moral Reasoning* (Berkeley: University of California Press, 1988), 23.

12. Jonsen and Toulmin, *The Abuse of Casuistry*, 43.

13. H. L. A. Hart, *The Concept of Law* (Oxford: Oxford University Press, 1961), 85–88.

14. See, e.g., Marcellino Zalba, S.J., *Theologiae Moralis Summa*, vol. 2: *Theologia Moralis Specialis: Tractatus de Mandatis Dei et Ecclesiae* (Madrid, Spain: Bibliotecha de Autores Cristianos, 1953). The fifth tract of the volume is on the Fifth Commandment; it has four chapters, on dominion over life and suicide, homicide, dueling, and war. The first chapter has two articles or subsections, one on dominion over human life and the other on suicide, mutilation, and the proper care for life. The second subsection defines suicide and divides it into categories of direct and indirect. Direct (i.e., intentional) suicide is always illicit, while indirect (i.e., an act committed while the agent foresees but does not intend to cut short his or her life) is sometimes permissible (or even required), sometimes not. Under the treatment of indirect suicide there are five applications to different factual circumstances. Among these are whether it is ever permissible or even required for a doctor, nurse, or priest to expose themselves to risk of death by visiting contagious patients (yes to both questions) and whether a virgin is permitted to kill herself in order to avoid rape (no).

15. I am here drawing on James F. Keenan, S.J.,'s discussion of the distinction in "Moral Theology," in *From Trent to Vatican II: Historical and Theological Investigations*,

ed. Raymond F. Bulman and Frederick J. Parrella (Oxford: Oxford University Press, 2006) 161–178.

16. St. Thomas Aquinas, *Summa Theologica*, II–II, q. 57, art. 2, rep. ob. 1.

17. Obviously, there is a question about what I mean by "most cases that in fact arise." Most cases of intentional homicide are covered by the rule that "it is wrong intentionally to kill another human being." Given the pedagogical function of the law, it seems to me that the set of cases that arise ought to include not only cases of homicide that occur and are prosecuted but also cases in which someone considered committing intentional homicide but was deterred by doing so by the fact that it violates both moral and legal norms.

18. MacIntyre, *After Virtue*, 207.

19. Ibid., 177–178.

20. One might well ask whether the English common law tradition, Protestant in its origins, will be accepted as a touchstone for the revision for Roman Catholic casuistry in the manner that I suggest. While it is beyond the scope of this chapter to make a detailed argument for the connection, let me suggest its outline: the eminent Anglican moralist Richard Hooker borrowed many of his casuistical categories from the Thomistic tradition. The Thomistic categories for the analysis of an act, themselves indebted to the Aristotelian tradition, made their way into the English common law tradition, where they can still be seen today. Murder, for example, is commonly defined as *intentional* homicide—acting with the immediate purpose (object) of taking another's life without legal justification. I do not deny, of course, that there is some dispute about the meaning of intention in the legal realm, no less than in the realm of Catholic moral reflection. See, e.g., M. Cathleen Kaveny, "Inferring Intention from Foresight," *Law Quarterly Review* 120 (January 2004): 81–107.

What about the canon law tradition, so ably critiqued by John Beal in this volume? The tradition of moral theology, in my view, is not quite as rigid as the tradition of canon law as he describes it. Moreover, contemporary canonists, such as my colleague John Coughlin, O.F.M., are attempting to situate the norms of canon law within a broader, positive framework supplied by the Catholic theological and sacramental tradition. See John Coughlin, O.F.M., *Law, Person, and Community: A Comparative Study of Canon Law and Secular Legal Theory* (New York: Oxford University Press, forthcoming).

21. See John T. Noonan Jr., *Persons and Mask of the Law* (Berkeley: University of California Press, 1976), chapter 4, for an account of how this process occurred with reference to *Palsgraf v. Long Island Railroad*, 248 N.Y. 339 (1928), the most famous tort case of modern times. As the appellate court construed the facts, they involved a woman who was injured by a freak accident while standing on a train platform. Conductors employed by the defendant railroad helped a man board a moving train; his package fell to the ground, and the fireworks it contained exploded. The explosion somehow toppled scales at the other end of the platform, injuring the plaintiff. Tamed by interpretive process, the case stands for the proposition that harm to the plaintiff must have been reasonably foreseeable by the defendant at the time of its action for the defendant to be liable for negligence.

22. Many provisions in Article II of the Uniform Commercial Code, which governs most transactions for the sale of goods, incorporate reference to the "usage of trade"—the standards to which merchants in a given community of buyers and sellers actually conform.

23. For an account of how the emergence of modern biblical interpretation greatly impeded the ability of believers to engage in this process, see Hans W. Frei, *The Eclipse of Biblical Narrative: A Study in Eighteenth and Nineteenth Century Hermeneutics* (New Haven: Yale University Press, 1974).

24. Aquinas, *ST*, II–II, q. 30, art. 4.

25. Pope John Paul II, *Sollicitudo Rei Socialis (On Social Concern)* (Boston: St. Paul, 1988), no. 38.

26. The Golden Rule is invoked in Matthew 7:12 and Luke 6:31.

27. John 13:34 (NRSV).

28. See, e.g., George C. Stewart, *Marvels of Charity: History of American Sisters and Nuns* (Huntington, IN: Our Sunday Visitor, 1994); John Fialka, *Sisters: Catholic Nuns and the Making of America* (New York: St. Martin's Press, 2003); Suzy Farren, *The Women Who Built Health Care in America* (St. Louis: Catholic Health Association of the United States, 1996).

29. John T. McGreevy, *Parish Boundaries: The Catholic Encounter with Race in the Twentieth-Century Urban North* (Chicago: University of Chicago Press, 1996). See also Jay Dolan, ed., *The American Catholic Parish: A History from 1850 to the Present*, 2 vols. (New York: Paulist, 1987).

30. See James O'Toole, "Empty Confessionals," *Commonweal*, February 23, 2001. A study by the National Opinion Research Center showed that the number of American Catholics participating in the sacrament of confession on a monthly basis declined from 38 percent to 17 percent from 1964 to 1974. In 2008, the Center for Applied Research in the Apostolate (CARA) conducted another survey. Only 2 percent of Catholics go to confession monthly; 45 percent do not go at all. Only 61 percent of weekly Mass attenders go to confession at least once a year. See CARA, "Sacraments Today: Belief and Practice among American Catholics" at http://cara.georgetown.edu/sacraments.html.

31. Aquinas, *ST*, I–II, qq. 91, art. 2, 93, art. 1.

32. Aquinas, *ST*, I–II, q. 110, art. 1.

33. "One should not expect more, this defence would claim, from the Summas or the manuals of moral theology in terms of spiritual good health than one does in terms of physical flourishing from textbooks of medical pathology" (Mahoney, *The Making of Moral Theology*, 29).

34. Ibid., 27, quoting, H. Davis, *Moral and Pastoral Theology*, 4 vols. (London: Sheed & Ward, 1935), vol. 1, pp. xviii–xvix.

35. Some act utilitarians might argue that the prohibition should be abandoned in favor of a rule that one ought to be permitted intentionally to kill the innocent if doing so would result in the greatest happiness for the greatest number.

36. "The judge, even when he is free, is still not wholly free. He is not to innovate at pleasure. He is not a knight-errant roaming at will in pursuit of his own ideal of beauty or of goodness. He is to draw his inspiration from consecrated principles. He is not to yield to spasmodic sentiment, to vague and unregulated benevolence. He is to exercise a discretion informed by tradition, methodized by analogy, disciplined by system, and

subordinated to 'the primordial necessity of order in the social life.' Wide enough in all conscience is the field of discretion that remains." From Benjamin N. Cardozo, *The Nature of the Judicial Process* (New Haven, CT: Yale University Press, 1921), 141.

37. *In re Baby M*, 109 N.J. 396 (1988).

38. The distinction still holds and today. See United States Catholic Conference, *Ethical and Religious Directives for Health Care Services*, 4th ed., directives 56 and 57, at www.usccb.org/bishops/directives.shtml#partfive.

39. Aquinas recognizes value in the stability of positive law: "Consequently, when a law is changed, the binding power of the law is diminished, in so far as custom is abolished. Wherefore human law should never be changed, unless, in some way or other, the common weal be compensated according to the extent of the harm done in this respect. Such compensation may arise either from some very great and very evident benefit conferred by the new enactment; or from the extreme urgency of the case, due to the fact that either the existing law is clearly unjust, or its observance extremely harmful." *ST*, I–II, q. 97, art. 2.

40. Mahoney, *The Making of Moral Theology*, 29.

41. Ibid., 32–34.

42. Ibid., 34.

43. Ibid., 35.

44. Ibid., 29.

45. Ibid.

46. Ibid., 34.

47. Ibid., 35.

48. Ibid., 33–34.

49. Corporations are treated as legal "persons," allowing them to have many of the rights and responsibilities of individuals.

50. For an interesting account, see Jerome T. Barrett and Joseph Barrett, *History of Alternative Dispute Resolution: The Story of a Political, Social, and Cultural Movement* (Edison, NJ: Jossey-Bass, 2004).

51. Pope Paul VI, *Humanae Vitae* (1968), at www.vatican.va/holy_father/paul_vi/ encyclicals/documents/hf_p-vi_enc_25071968_humanae-vitae_en.html. The literature on all aspects of *Humanae Vitae* and its reception is voluminous. A good place for Americans unfamiliar with the broader context of the debate to begin is Leslie Woodcock Tentler, *Catholics and Contraception: An American History* (Ithaca, NY: Cornell University Press, 2004). See also chapter 11 in this book.

52. See, e.g., Robert McClory, *Turning Point: The Inside Story of the Papal Birth Control Commission, and How Humanae Vitae Changed the Life of Patty Crowley and the Future of the Church* (New York: Crossroads, 1995).

53. See, e.g., "Beliefnet Poll: Catholics Observant, but Some Seek Change," April 16, 2008, at www.beliefnet.com/Faiths/Christianity/Catholic/2008/04/Beliefnet-Poll-Catholics-Observant-But-Some-Seek-Change.aspx. The poll shows that on the eve of Pope Benedict XVI's first visit to the United States, a "vast majority, 73.8 percent, do not believe that artificial contraception is sinful and 59.4 percent say that they have used artificial contraception." See also Jennifer Ohlendorf and Richard J. Fehring, "The

Influence of Religiosity on Contraceptive Use among Roman Catholic Women in the United States, *Linacre Quarterly* (May 2007): 135–143. The study shows, among other things, that on average, Roman Catholic women in the United States use contraception at the same rate as other American women.

54. See, e.g., Lisa Sowle Cahill, *Between the Sexes: Foundations for a Christian Ethics of Sexuality* (Minneapolis, MN: Fortress Press, 1985).

55. See Pope John Paul II, *Man and Woman He Created Them: A Theology of the Body* (Boston, MA: Pauline, 2006). Christopher West has popularized the approach; see his *Theology of the Body for Beginners* (West Chester, PA: Ascension, 2004).

56. In July 2008, I asked my research assistant to analyze the membership of the Catholic Theological Society of America: 132 members listed "moral theology" as a specialty, while 258 members listed "ethics." Of those who listed a specialty in moral theology, 37 received their doctoral degree from a non-Catholic institution; 4 before 1970, and 33 in 1970 or thereafter; 95 of those stating a specialty in moral theology received their degree from a Catholic institution, 14 before 1970 and 80 in 1970 or thereafter. Of those who listed a specialty in ethics, 78 received their doctoral training from non-Catholic institutions, whereas 180 received it from Catholic institutions. Who, then, is training future moralists in doctoral programs at Catholic universities? Of the 10 people specializing in Moral Theology/Christian Ethics at the University of Notre Dame, 9 have their doctoral degrees from non-Catholic institutions, while 1 has it from a Catholic institution. At Boston College, 6 of the 7 specializing in this field have degrees from non-Catholic institutions. Of the 5 specializing in this field at the Catholic University of America, in contrast, 1 has a degree from a non-Catholic university, whereas 4 have degrees from Catholic institutions.

57. Kenan B. Osborne, "Priestly Formation," in *From Trent to Vatican II: Historical and Theological Investigations*, ed. Raymond F. Bulman and Frederick J. Parrella (New York: Oxford University Press, 2006), 119.

58. A compact description is found in the *Catholic Encyclopedia*, "Ecclesiastical Seminaries," at www.newadvent.org/cathen/13694a.htm.

59. See Roger Finke and Kevin D. Dougherty, "The Effects of Professional Training: The Social and Religious Capital Acquired in Seminaries," *Journal for the Scientific Study of Religion* 41, no. 1 (2002): 103–120.

60. The plenary papers from the conference are available in James F. Keenan, ed., *Catholic Theological Ethics in the World Church* (New York: Continuum, 2007). Other papers can be found in Linda Hogan, ed., *Applied Ethics in a World Church* (Maryknoll, NY: Orbis, 2007).

61. See John Allen, "All Things Catholic," *National Catholic Reporter*, July 14, 2006, at www.nationalcatholicreporter.org/word/pfw071406.htm.

62. The Web site is available at "Catholic Theological Ethics in the World Church, Trento, Italy, July 24–27, 2010," at www.catholicethics.com/.

63. The best way into this literature is through the index to the two volumes of Richard McCormick's "moral notes." See Richard A. McCormick, S.J., *Notes on Moral Theology 1965 through 1980* (Washington, DC: University Press of America, 1981), and

Notes on Moral Theology 1981 through 1984 (Washington, DC: University Press of America, 1984).

64. Pope John Paul II attempted to raise many of the right questions in *Ex Corde Ecclesiae*, his apostolic constitution on Catholic universities, at www.vatican.va/holy_father/john_paul_ii/apost_constitutions/documents/hf_jp-ii_apc_15081990_ ex-corde-ecclesiae_en.html. In my judgment, what might have been a productive discussion became hopelessly sidetracked because of the mandatum issue.

65. My immersion in the terminology and the debates indebted to the manuals came not from my training at Yale, but from my participation in a working group on cooperation with evil sponsored by the Catholic Health Association (CHA) and organized under the presidency of Father Michael Place. The project is described at the CHA Web site. www.chausa.org/Pub/MainNav/News/HP/Archive/2007/11Nov-Dec/Articles/Features/hp0711l.htm.

66. For a personal account, see Charles E. Curran, *Loyal Dissent: Memoir of a Catholic Theologian* (Washington, DC: Georgetown University Press, 2006).

67. Needless to say, the common law courts do not have the same claim to divinely given authority that the Roman Catholic magisterium has; nonetheless, I think the disanalogy can be overcome by drawing on the careful work in development of doctrine stemming from John Henry Newman, especially that of John Noonan in the area of development of moral doctrine. See Noonan's *A Church That Can and Cannot Change* (Notre Dame, IN: University of Notre Dame Press, 2005).

68. In American law, the segregation cases are a good example of the importance of dissenting opinions. See *Plessy v. Ferguson*, 163 US. 527 (1896) (upholding the constitutionality of racial segregation in public accommodations on the grounds that the Constitution only requires that "separate but equal" facilities be provided to African Americans) and *Brown v. Board of Education*, 347 U.S. 483 (1954) (which recognized that "separate educational facilities are inherently unequal" and therefore that segregation in public facilities was a violation of the Equal Protection Clause of the Fourteenth Amendment to the Constitution). Justice John Marshall Harlan's sharp dissent to *Plessy* was vindicated in *Brown*; Harlan maintained that "our Constitution is color-blind, and neither knows nor tolerates classes among citizens."

69. Aquinas treats human acts most directly in *ST*, I–II, qq 1–21.

70. Charles Pinches has already begun this project; see his *Theology and Action: After Theory in Christian Ethics* (Grand Rapids, MI: Eerdmans, 2002).

71. Germain Grisez has produced a massive three-volume work that attempts to integrate the insights of the manuals with the teaching of the Second Vatican Council. See Germain Grisez, *The Way of the Lord Jesus* (3 vols.): *Christian Moral Principles*, vol. 1 (Quincy, IL: Franciscan, 1983); *Living a Christian Life*, vol. 2 (Quincy, IL: Franciscan, 1993); and *Difficult Moral Questions*, vol. 3 (Quincy, IL: Franciscan, 1997). The third volume considers two hundred case studies, some submitted by readers and some constructed by the author. It is well worth reading, although in my judgment its methodology functions too deductively. We do not see how the facts press on each other

and on the rules as much as we see how rules are applied to complicated facts. Moreover, Grisez's underlying moral theory, which focuses on the importance of not acting against one of a number of "basic goods," is to my mind quite problematic. Some of the goods, e.g., the good of marriage, seem defined rather arbitrarily, in a way that functions to justify and preserve the ban on contraception.

9

Magisterial Authority

Charles Taylor

The Question of Proper Scope

I see two main questions about the authority of the magisterium: what is its scope, and how should it be exercised? Obviously, these two are linked.

Let me start with the first question, that of the scope of this authority. We can find a short way of defining this with a phrase like "the deposit of faith handed down from the apostles." This is sometimes expressed as "matters of faith and morals." But the latter formula can already pose problems. Moral decisions not only require a firm grip on the most basic principles and goals, and these are indeed for a Christian shaped by faith, but also depend on some grasp of the situation in which these principles and goals are being applied. And this grasp of the situation cannot by the nature of things be derived from our faith. This does indeed deeply shape our perception of our situation, but the actual contours of the latter have to be properly perceived.

The difficulty leaps out: if the authority of the magisterium concerns the deposit of faith, this cannot suffice to determine authoritatively what we ought to do in a host of situations. Immediate consequences follow for how this authority ought to be exercised. It means that authoritative pronouncements on issues where contingent circumstances are crucial to our judgment cannot be taken as definitive, let alone "infallible."

Of course, there are glaringly clear issues, like torture and genocide, where a categorical condemnation is called for, but that is because this holds in any possible circumstances. These issues are important, but rare. And there is also the continual reminder, which our bishops should provide us, that certain acts are intrinsically wrong, even though the discernment that such acts have taken place may sometimes be disputed. I return to this later.

This limit has frequently not been respected by the magisterium of the Catholic Church. This is particularly glaring in recent centuries. Or perhaps we ought to say that it stands out more clearly as a transgression of an important limit in recent centuries, as we have become more aware of the variability of circumstances. Thus Pius IX's fulmination against liberalism, democracy, and human rights in the *Syllabus of Errors* stands out today as an illegitimate attempt to decide for all time questions that have to be constantly revisited. In fact, the situation is worse than that. Insofar as there are issues in this area that come close to being resolvable independently of circumstances, we would today class the importance of human rights in this category. Pius in our view came close to denying a universal truth.[1]

But in fact, it is wiser to be charitable and to appreciate how much of a threat the French Revolution and its aftermath seemed to be from the standpoint of the papacy, and how the loss of temporal rule seemed to condemn the popes to the kind of abject dependence that Pius VII had experienced at the hands of Napoleon. But even if we can sympathetically understand where this reaction was coming from, we can see that there was a culpable lack of awareness of the possibility that conditions could change—that, indeed, Catholics could work to change them—and hence that the trends of growing equality and democratization could be lived in a quite different fashion. Figures like Tocqueville and Lamennais were aware of this, as were their successors among the proto-Christian democrats of the end of the century, but they were frequently held back, even condemned by the blind historical panic of much of the hierarchy.

Have we learned this lesson? I'm not sure. I'm thinking, for instance, of how certain American bishops in recent elections have tried to virtually command their flock not to vote for Catholic politicians who wouldn't advocate outlawing abortion, even invoking the possible threat of excommunication of these politicians. I'm thinking of a Canadian bishop who tried similar tactics on the issue of legalizing gay marriage.

These clergy cannot see the limit they are overstepping. Let's look at the issue of abortion. Is there something wrong with abortion?[2] Yes. Should we try to reduce its incidence in our societies? Yes. But it doesn't follow (1) that outlawing it is the best way to achieve this latter goal (indeed, there is some evidence that the opposite is the case). And even if (1) were true, the issue remains (2) of how much this should weigh in the overall decision to vote for X or Y. What if the candidate who would outlaw abortion is a superpatriot, burning to engage in ill-advised wars? This kind of all-in judgment is of the essence of moral decisions in politics and lies beyond the domain of magisterial authority.

The Question of Limits

This raises deep issues about the way magisterial authority ought to be exercised. Do limits of this kind mean that clergy should remain silent on the questions that require this sort of contingent judgment? I don't think so. But before looking into this issue more deeply, I'd like to examine other kinds of limits, which have also been sometimes overstepped in recent years.

Take the issue of artificial birth control, where the modern stand of the magisterium was reaffirmed by Paul VI in *Humanae Vitae*. There are two kinds of limits here that are sometimes ignored. The first is evident in some of the justifications of the interdict. These fall back on a natural law type of argument, arguing from the basic finality of the sexual act. Now, reading natural law in this way—perhaps one might say even taking natural law as one's preferred moral philosophy—goes beyond the deposit of faith, which in other situations and contexts has been worked out with the aid of other concepts, with terms like, for instance, responsible stewardship. The limit transgressed here involves the sacralization of one philosophical language over other ones equally available for the articulation of Christian faith.[3]

This phenomenon was rampant in the decades prior to Vatican II, in particular during the antimodernist campaign. A particular historical version of Thomism (heavily criticized by some of the most creative minds in the tradition of Aquinas) was given virtually the status of dogma, and all dissentient voices were sidelined and often dealt with in the most heavy-handed fashion. We could call this move false sacralization, which involves identifying certain modes of thought, certain moral codes, or certain historical periods of the church's life as essential to the faith and consequently downgrading or even rejecting other philosophies, moralities, and periods. This goes against the spirit of Catholicism itself, which by its very nature is the faith of a universal church, at once at home in and alien to all times, ages and civilizations. It is very easy to fall into this error. We are falling into it all the time, outside the context of the faith, when we burrow into our ethnocentric judgments. But it got much worse for Europeans (in the broad sense, including us North Americans) in the period of world dominance by the West. We are just slowly recovering from this today (we hope). This is such an easy trap to fall into that we can't be too hard on those who succumb.

But we hold the church, rightly, to a higher standard, and it has often lived up to it to a surprising degree. Think of the great Jesuit missions in India and China. But still our church, along with the rest of European civilization, seems to have lost sight of the demands of Catholicism in the nineteenth century. We have to ask seriously whether it is a false sacralization, in the form of a too simple and direct reading of natural law, which accounts for the lapidary judgment that homosexual love is an "objective disorder." Or whether we aren't sacralizing certain historically based conceptions of gender identity when we conclude that women should not be ordained priests.

But to return to birth control, there are other arguments that don't depend on natural law. There is, for instance, an ideal of married sexual life, which has received some deep justification in John Paul II's theology of the body. This is an ideal of sexual life that deliberately sets aside artificial modes of contraception, that prefers abstinence to the use of these methods, and that accepts the limits this imposes on sexual life. This may be hard to understand in the context of contemporary sitcoms and consumer advertising, but we can recognize this as a spiritual discipline of bodily life. However, there is a real issue when this spiritual ideal is the basis for a general interdict on all practicing Catholics. The Catholic Church is the site of a great profusion of spiritual disciplines, a continual source of spiritual richness and even holiness. We do harm to these freely adopted rules if we treat them as laws. Their inner purpose is overshadowed, and they become the site of mindless brawls between the church and a confused permissiveness abroad in modern culture. The limit overstepped here is more like a category mistake, turning potential paths to holiness into conditions of admission, denaturing aspirations to make them laws. We see here a malign reflection of the fatal tilt toward legalism in the Western church over the centuries.

Respect for the Enigmatic

My claim here has been that our notions of magisterial authority have been tainted by a failure to observe certain limits. I've mentioned three sources of transgression: the failure to respect the contingency of the conditions of moral judgment, false sacralization, and legalism. There is a fourth source of transgression as well, a lack of reserve before the enigmatic. Our faith poses us several very deep enigmas: the problem of evil, the tension between the justice of God and his mercy, and the potential tension between our belief that our faith is true and the obvious fact that some very saintly and spiritual people don't share it. A very important part of the response to this is the recognition that we haven't (yet) got all the answers—and that we may never have them. We have to be able to dwell in uncertainty and ambiguity and yet be able to grow spiritually.

The last area I mentioned, that of ecumenical relations, is a very good instance. A certain relation can be built up in ecumenical exchanges. These can be real sites of spiritual growth. And yet the theoretical account of why this is so will elude us. In the past, we were always tempted to resolve the ambiguity too quickly: either refusing to recognize the spiritual stature of people of other faiths or watering down all faiths as just different external clothing on some very general spiritual stance. The first reaction breaks the contact with the other faiths; the second hides the real differences by washing out certain crucial defining features of our respective spiritual paths.

But the continued conversation that manages to avoid either of these evasions may make us nervous, hence some statements of the present pontiff on ecumenical exchange. "A real dialogue between religions is not possible without putting one's faith in parentheses," he claimed. It would be more prudent to dialogue about cultural differences. I want to stress right away that I am not saying that Benedict ought not to have said this. As we shall see later, I think we should concede to our clergy the right to be wrong. But of course, I don't agree, and I think there is here a denial or evasion of one of the central enigmas we live with. I should also add that this kind of intolerance of ambiguity is less a Catholic problem than one that has infected the tradition of Latin Christendom as a whole. Think of the ruthless logical thrust behind the Calvinist doctrine of double predestination. Better to embrace a monstrosity than to admit that there are unresolved enigmas.

Preempting Personal Duties

I have mentioned four kinds of transgression of limit: false sacralization, legalism, and the refusal of contingent conditions and of the enigmatic. We could find others, but these should suffice for the argument I want to make here. In fact, these refusals to respect limits tend to bring about a dispossession, a preemption of the Christian's capacity to work out by his or her own intellect and groping spiritual maturation, how to live the faith, do the right thing, reconceive his or her life, and live with its enigmas. At its worst, it can lead to an infantilization of the laity. This trend was always in massive contradiction with the fundamental Christian stress on conscience, and fortunately, the power of the spirit was frequently too strong to be hemmed in by these lead strings.

Many of the greatest pioneers of Catholic spirituality were targeted at one time or another by the Inquisition or the hierarchy, St. Teresa, St. John of the Cross, and Ignatius Loyola among them. The development of Western modernity had a paradoxical effect on the Catholic practices of authority. On one side, the rise of liberal legal regimes meant that some of the grimmer practices of persecution of heretics were no longer possible. The torture and execution at the behest of the church of the Protestant Jean Callas, decried by Voltaire, couldn't be repeated in the nineteenth century. But on the other side, the hierarchy, as I mentioned before, often saw in these liberal regimes a threat. The church frequently had a sense of being beleaguered in modernity.

The result was a series of attempts to mobilize the faithful, to make them resistant to the blandishments of liberalism. We see this, for instance, in nineteenth-century France, but we in Quebec lived our own version of the same response in the twentieth century. This response had a paradox built into it. The techniques of mass mobilization, the building of Catholic associations and political parties, and the organization of campaigns to mold public opinion—we can think of the campaigns around "l'Ordre Moral" in the first years of the Third Republic—are those of the modern, antihierarchical, eventually democratic world. There was inevitably a tension between the end and the means.

Of course, the Catholic Church has always had lay organizations: sodalities, guilds, and the like. But what was peculiar to the situation in the nineteenth and twentieth centuries was that they were operating in societies with a more and more modern social imaginary, in which independent voluntary associations and political parties played a bigger and bigger role. It proved impossible not to accommodate to this context. This eventually led to contextually determined abandonments of the alliance with thrones—especially where these regimes left no choice by attacking the church themselves, as in Germany under Bismarck—and also later to hesitant and localized abandonment of the alignment with employers, which opened the road for the beginnings of Christian Democracy, most notably in Belgium. These showed that the alienation of the working class was far from an ineluctable consequence of industrialization.[4]

But the exigencies of operating in the age of mobilization meant inevitably the loosening of clerical control as well. Trade unions and political parties had to be cut some slack if they were to be effective. The irony is reflected in an incident during the Kulturkampf, Bismarck's attack on the German Catholic Church. This attack sparked a strong sense of union and solidarity among German Catholics, in a sense doing the work of the church for it. As the archbishop of Köln was being dragged off to imprisonment, masses of faithful turned out and lined the streets, kneeling as he passed. This strong political demonstration of loyalty to established church authority had, however, necessarily another side. The continued political resistance could only be carried out by a political party, and in the long run, this gave greater and greater importance to its lay leadership.

But in the shorter run, the mobilization of a counterpower to the diverse national legal regimes strengthened ultramontanism and led to that apotheosis of papal power, the declaration of the dogma of papal infallibility in 1870. In the context of a mobilization against counterpowers, Liberal or Protestant according to the context, the firm adherence to papal leadership came to seem a criterion of loyalty to the cause. The context came to resemble the defense of certain national identities under threat: you don't break ranks over matters of private judgment when the survival of the tribe is at stake. And indeed, in a number of cases, like the one we lived in Quebec, national identity fused with Catholic allegiance—until the Quiet Revolution of the 1960s unraveled this synthesis. This was the era in which "error had no rights," wherever the church was in control. Where it was not, compromises had to be made, and appeals to freedom of religion were vigorously put forward. In the long run, this double standard couldn't be maintained. Church authority required mobilizing Catholics, and this mobilization ultimately fostered Christian democracy. Vatican II was the moment when the long rejection of liberal society was ultimately abandoned.

But some of the earlier mode of operation survives. In the final analysis, to recognize that freedom of conscience is a fundamental right, that it is an essential component of human agency, must require a recognition within the church itself that each Christian must be free to exercise his or her judgment in applying the gospel to contingent moral or political circumstances, in finding a language to articulate the faith, and to make whatever sense they can of the enigmas we live with and in. Each Christian can (and should) be part of the conversation from which the *consensus fidelium* will emerge. But if this is to be the case, then the magisterium can no longer claim definitive authority beyond the limits I described earlier. The often half-formulated threat of excommunication can't be held over the heads of Catholics who exercise this capacity of judgment, even in the highly ambiguous form that we see today, where the threat can't really be carried through in the face of the resistance of liberal society and the majority of Catholics. This ambiguous situation, which enrages rigorist Catholics, stands in the way of a healthy, open life of the mind in the Catholic Church.

But this situation is worse than ambiguous. It is unacceptable. A Christian is bound in conscience to follow his or her best judgment in deciding, say, how to vote. A supposedly definitive ruling by the magisterium that deviates from this judgment would be tantamount to a command to go against it and follow another, incompatible course of action. Our bishops could be in the anomalous position of commanding us not to do what we are in conscience bound to do. The judgment itself cannot be commanded; all we can be ordered to do is to go against it. A failure to respect the limits of church authority creates a morally impossible situation for everyone.

Christian Freedom

The current debate around magisterial authority is often confused because the issues are not clearly distinguished from other questions that are ultimately unrelated. In his profound and convincing encyclical, *Veritatis Splendor*, Pope John Paul II laid out the framework within which Christians seek to discern the moral guidance that is implicit in their faith. The moral law of the first covenant is to be fulfilled in following Christ and thus coming to accede to Christ's "indivisible love for the Father and for humanity" (*VS* para 14). Submission to God is not a limitation on human freedom. On the contrary, "human freedom and God's law are not in opposition; they appeal to one another" (*VS* para 17). In a sense, we first learn in following Christ what our freedom really consists in.

It follows that certain lines of thought, much explored in modern philosophy, are alien to Christian faith and are bound to distort it. Such are, for example, attempts to conceive human freedom as utterly distinct from God's will or theories that define moral rightness in terms of freely exercised human judgment. It follows also that certain widely canvassed modes of moral thinking in our world cannot really be accepted. A thoroughgoing consequentialism, for instance, which doesn't accept that any acts are intrinsically right or wrong but makes everything depend on a calculation of the contingent results of an action, can't do justice to the moral reality in which we live. It can't allow that certain kinds of acts, by their very nature, carry us away from the love of God and our neighbor, which is the ultimate landmark guiding us. As John Paul puts it, "There exist acts which per se and in themselves, independently of circumstances, are always seriously wrong by reason of their object" (*VS* para 80).

And he goes on to quote the Second Vatican Council:

> Whatever is hostile to life itself, such as any kind of homicide, genocide, abortion, euthanasia, voluntary suicide; whatever violates the integrity of the human person, such as mutilation, physical and

mental torture and attempts to coerce the spirit; whatever is offensive to human dignity, such as subhuman living conditions, arbitrary imprisonment, deportation, slavery, prostitution and trafficking in women and children; degrading conditions of work which treat labourers as mere instruments of profit, and not as free responsible persons: all these and the like are a disgrace, and so long as they infect human civilization they contaminate those who inflict them more than those who suffer injustice, and they are a negation of the honour due to the Creator. (cited from *Gaudium et Spes*, 27)

Now of course, the widespread reluctance to follow the teachings of the Catholic hierarchy often springs from deeply felt reluctance among our contemporaries to accept this vision of the moral life. The rejection of the church's teachings can spring from "subjectivism, utilitarianism and relativism" (*VS*, para 106) or "pragmatism and positivism" (*VS*, para 112). But these are not the only sources of resistance, even for those hostile to the church. The widespread attribution of opposition to the church's teaching to "relativism," which one often hears from today's Vatican, is another sign of its relatively weak grasp of the contemporary world.

And certainly these are not why many faithful Catholics demur from some of judgments of their bishops. On the contrary, there is widespread acceptance of the idea that we are on a journey, over the centuries, in which we hope that, guided by the Holy Spirit, we can better discern the path that our faith opens to us. But "we" here refers to the whole church. The journey is a long one, and we cannot go forward if we forget our past. And thus a crucial component of our understanding comes from tradition. But what is at any given time understood as tradition may need completion and correction to take account of realities hitherto underappreciated. And here is where the prophetic spirit plays a crucial role. Examples abound in our history. We have only to think of the relatively late realization of the unacceptability of slavery or the even more recent espousal of democracy and human rights, which is at the center of today's Catholic vision of the political world.

It is obvious that the magisterium plays a crucial role, though even here not an exclusive role, in reminding us of tradition, but the workings of the prophetic spirit can't be confined to one hierarchical level. We are all now the heirs of those Christian democrats who held on to their vision even when it was denigrated and condemned by a hierarchy that was blinded by its fears of an admittedly often hostile modern world. We cannot refuse prophetic insight, wherever it happens to be found, even if it emanates from outside the church altogether. For these reasons, I cannot see what justifies the flat statement of

John Paul, near the end of *Veritatis Splendor*: "Opposition to the teaching of the Church's Pastors cannot be seen as a legitimate expression either of Christian freedom or of the diversity of the Spirit's gifts" (*VS*, para 113). This flies in the face of our history, including that turn that allowed John Paul himself to become one of the great prophetic advocates of human rights in the twentieth century.

Teaching Without Threats

But what does all this mean for the exercise of magisterial authority? As I argued previously, it must not mean that popes, bishops, and other clergy should not give their views on these matters, transgressing the limits, if that is what they in fact think. We all need guidance, and we won't get the good kind if we try to silence all of the bad.

What is inadmissible, however, is a combination of two things: (1) trenchant answers to our questions about what we should do, how we should think of a question, or how to resolve (or remain in suspense before) an enigma, where these answers are (2) considered as rules of faith, that is, accepting them is considered a condition for being a Catholic in good standing. Of course, there are issues where an unequivocal stance can be taken, defining a condition of membership, if someone denies the Incarnation, or on the political level, proposes or, even more, practices genocide. But on a wide range of questions, bishops should be free, singly or collectively, to offer leadership, as long as declining this leadership doesn't carry the possible cost of excommunication.

That is the recommendation that seems to me right. But it could be taxed with unrealism. It might be thought to make too much of a break with the practice of recent centuries, even though it is more in keeping with the spirit of Vatican II than this practice itself is. The situation now is that the laity is split between very different stances. Some relate very positively to the older model of authority, which was relatively heedless of the limits discussed here. For them, this mode of clear binding authority is one of the main defining characteristics of the Catholic, as against other churches. Then over against them are others for whom the defining feature of the church is its sacramental life, and the exercise of this type of authority is more in the nature of a defect they have to live with.

The difference about authority coexists with a sense of a common sacramental life. A more modest proposal than the previous one might be to try to heal the rift, while opening a discussion about the nature of authority in the church, which is one of the objects of this book. It would involve accentuating the common life, to the point of struggling against the divisive judgments and actions that accentuate the alienation many feel. In this, the magisterium could be really helpful. In the climate that might thus be created, we could perhaps make some headway on the deep questions in dispute between us.

NOTES

1. "The right to religious freedom and to respect for conscience on its journey towards the truth is increasingly perceived as the foundation of the cumulative rights of the person." Cf. John Paul II, in his Encyclical *Veritatis Splendor*, para 31. He goes on to say: "This heightened sense of the dignity of the human person and of his or her uniqueness, and of the respect due to the journey of conscience, certainly represents one of the positive achievements of modern culture."

2. I put the issue in this way, rather than asking, Is abortion wrong? because the latter formulation may imply that it's always the same thing wrong with it. In reality, there are cases that come within a whisker of infanticide, and others that are very far removed and raise other issues. There is a certain discourse that assimilates all abortions to the former category that is as intellectually blunt as the diametrically opposed position of pro-choice.

3. See John Paul II's encyclical, *Veritatis Splendor*, para 29: "Certainly the Church's Magisterium does not intend to impose on the faithful any particular theological system, still less a philosophical one."

4. See Carl Strikwerda, "A Resurgent Religion," in *European Religion in the Age of Great Cities: 1830–1930*, ed. Hugh McLeod, chapter 2 (London: Routledge, 1995). For other interesting insights into Belgian Catholicism, see Vincent Viaene, *Belgium and the Holy See from Gregory XVI to Pius IX 1831–59: Catholic Revival, Society and Politics in 19th Century Europe* (Leuven: Brepols, 2001), 157–215.

SECTION III

Practical Limits

*Authority in the Lived Catholicism of American
Laity and Clergy*

10

American Catholics
and Church Authority

William V. D'Antonio, James D. Davidson, Dean R. Hoge, and Mary L. Gautier

One of the goals of our surveys[1] has been to describe the way American Catholics relate to the formal teaching authority of the Catholic Church. The church's teaching authority covers a broad range of moral and structural issues: some of the moral issues concern family and human sexuality; others concern war and capital punishment; still others concern social justice for the poor, aged, and persons otherwise neglected in human society. Structural issues have to do with the church's hierarchic governing structure and access to roles within it.[2]

The roots of the Catholic Church's claims to authority are found in the Gospels and the writings of Peter, Paul, and other apostles, often based on their own firsthand experiences with Christ. As the centuries passed, the church developed its teachings, beginning with the definitive teachings that emerged from the Council of Nicaea (325 C.E.), commonly known as the creed. Church authority was also built on its claims to apostolic succession, in this case citing the passage from the Gospel of Matthew 16:18: "Upon this rock [Peter], I will build my church." In its most formal sense, the church's claims to authority rest on the scriptures, apostolic succession, and tradition.[3] All indications from social research are that acceptance of the Catholic Church's moral authority has been diminishing since Vatican II.[4] To understand why this may be so, we look at the nature of authority in general and how it rises or falls throughout historical periods.

Measuring Authority

The most quoted sociological definition of authority is Max Weber's: "the probability that certain specific commands from a given source will be obeyed by a given group of persons."[5] This kind of *authority* refers specifically to voluntary obedience, in contrast to *coercion*, which connotes nonvoluntary obedience. Thus, the legitimacy of a leader's commands rests in the voluntary nature of the obedience of the followers.

Authority entails not merely a proclamation by a leader but also the probability that a follower or group of followers will accept the proclamation and obey it. Thus, authority becomes fully legitimate when it is claimed by a leader or office (in this case, the papacy) and the claim is accepted by the follower or followers (the bishops and the laity). In a free and democratic society, the legitimacy of authority ultimately rests in the hands of followers, who make their own decisions based on their perceptions of the leader, the office held by the leader, and the leader's justification for the claim. This is called rational-legal authority, and it is the foundation on which democratic society is based. Although the Catholic Church in the United States has become more and more a voluntary association as people choose to affiliate or leave, by its own admission it is grounded more in traditional than in rational-legal authority and is not a democratic organization in any sense in which that term has current meaning.

In earlier times in Catholic countries, religious claims were often backed by political force. To the extent that physical or psychological forms of coercion were used, the claimed authority lacked legitimacy, even though large numbers of Catholics may have acquiesced at least overtly. But today in Western societies, religious leaders cannot use force. They can only ask for voluntary obedience. The followers obey the teachings if they believe that the teachings are legitimate, justified, and true to the will of God as they understand that will. If the followers doubt the claims for whatever reason, including their own consciences, they feel free to follow their consciences as having supremacy over obedience.

In today's world, where claims of authority are expounded daily by all kinds of leaders and wannabe leaders, even within the Catholic Church, there is a growing gap between claims to authority and accepted authority. More authority is claimed than is accepted. To estimate the gap, one needs to know as much as possible about both claimed and accepted authority. In the case of the Catholic Church today, the claims to authority are found in the catechism of the Catholic Church, the encyclical letters of the popes, and the writings and public statements of the bishops. Theologians and philosophers may prepare formal statements for official use by popes and bishops, but the formal authority statements come from the bishops themselves.

For centuries, the hierarchy attended to its teaching responsibility by adhering to a monarchical style of leadership and governance, relying on a mix of traditional authority and deductive reasoning.[6] It developed moral positions deductively and disseminated them downward. The hierarchy in Rome and in local dioceses worked through the structures of parishes, schools, and other institutions to promulgate church policies and doctrines to the laity. Letters from Rome or from the local bishop were regularly read at Mass, and students at all levels of schooling were taught the church's position on moral issues.

But the Catholic Church was beset during the nineteenth and early twentieth centuries by events introduced by modern life.[7] The worldwide spread of democratic civil governance was accompanied by the gradual extension of suffrage to women, blacks, and other oppressed peoples. As a result, more people than ever, including Catholics, became accustomed to being part of decision-making structures, built on rational-legal authority. The dramatic growth in formal education, especially in the United States after World War II, enabled people to become more informed about issues affecting their lives, further undercutting systems of hierarchical, tradition-oriented governance. Administrative requirements for running bureaucracies, such as the need for input from accountants and financial advisers, made it difficult for a church elite to govern without consulting with laity. Premises of traditional church teachings were challenged by demographic trends, such as decreased fertility and increasing longevity. The fact that women, in particular, could expect to spend a significant portion of their lives without parenting responsibilities raised questions about the association between sex and family life. While Catholics continued to maintain strong ties to family and church, they were also becoming more and more a part of American society, with its emphasis on personal autonomy.

These experiences underscored the importance of certain values and their potential conflict with others. Catholics' success within a structure of religious pluralism supported principles of religious tolerance,[8] which challenged the mentality that had dominated the hierarchy for more than a century. Norms of self-fulfillment and individuals' rights burgeoned. As Greeley noted, the emphasis on personal autonomy was one of the century's most important cultural developments.[9] Professionalism and expertise gained in importance. A steadily growing population of Catholics was also becoming mainstream American.

When John XXIII succeeded Pius XII in 1958, American Catholics were ready to heed his call to open the windows of the church and let in some fresh air.

Pope John XXIII wanted Vatican Council II to revitalize and update the church, to bring it into the modern world. From 1962 to 1965, the council did so, as the body of more than two thousand bishops found middle ways between the most progressive and the most traditional forces. The council, in its documents, reaffirmed the joint authority of the bishops with the pope; it opened a biblical perspective toward the church; it made important changes in the liturgy, especially the use of the vernacular in the Mass; it encouraged ecumenical activity; it fostered episcopal leadership; for the first time, it emphasized the importance of conjugal love in marriage; it heralded freedom of religion and conscience; it encouraged active engagement with the larger social world; and it gave new emphasis to the laity as "the people of God, the body of Christ, and a community of faith." And most important, by all accounts these new teachings were widely accepted by the great majority of the American laity.[10]

In retrospect, the tumult in the wake of Vatican II should not have been surprising. The social structures needed to implement the changes made by the council were lacking. The documents themselves did not provide more than a general idea of how to bring about structural changes. On matters of moral authority, laypeople were encouraged to believe that they had freedom of conscience. For them, this has come to mean combining reason, faith, and experience to reach decisions on a wide range of moral issues.[11] The outcome of the tension between obedience and conscience was predicted forty years ago: "In the long run the laity will do what seems rational and practical, and whenever the Church is defending a tradition that cannot be sustained by reason, it will probably be ignored."[12]

We will always be left to wonder what might have been, had the encyclical *Humanae Vitae* incorporated the recommendation for change made by the great majority of the Papal Birth Control Commission rather than the reaffirmation of the traditional teaching by the minority that it did. The debate over birth control, and especially over the birth control pill, had become very public in the United States during the period 1960 to 1968, and American Catholics had come to expect a change in church teachings. No event of the twentieth century so challenged the teaching authority of the Vatican as the debate about birth control and the publication of the encyclical.[13] For the great majority of Catholics, Vatican II was a positive change, bringing the church closer to the modern world with its emphasis on rational authority and personal responsibility. In contrast, *Humanae Vitae* was seen as contradictory of the more open and self-responsible Catholicism. It was rejected by a majority of the laity and by a large number of priests and theologians. The U.S. bishops stood firmly with Rome; bishops in other countries took a variety of stands, some firmly with Rome and others citing the need to inform and follow one's conscience.[14]

The Growing Split between Conservative and Progressive Catholics

This historical overview outlines some of the major events that have helped to undermine what was until Vatican II a largely unchallenged church teaching authority. In the four decades since *Humanae Vitae*, there has emerged a spectrum of groups among American Catholics. On the far right is a conservative group, often identifying its position as being the only properly orthodox Catholic position as it "emphasizes the stability of the institutional Church. This group is concerned about the credibility of the Church and its persistence as a social institution. It is rooted in the traditional, hierarchical exercise of authority."[15] Its position is exemplified by the Reverend John Ford, one of the moral theologians on the Papal Birth Control Commission who was one of the four dissenters from the commission's report in 1965. He defended the church's teaching on the evil of contraception in these words:

> The church cannot change her answer because this answer is true.... It is true because the Catholic Church, instituted by Christ to show men a secure way to eternal life, could not have so wrongly erred during all those centuries of history.... The Church could not have erred...even through one century, by imposing under serious obligation very grave burdens in the name of Jesus Christ, if Jesus Christ did not actually impose those burdens.... If the Church could err in such a way...the faithful could not put their trust in the magisterium's presentation of moral teaching especially in sexual matters.[16]

On the other end of the spectrum are the progressive Catholics. According to Kennedy, they reflect the modern world with its emphasis on personal autonomy. They believe the locus of authority is within the believer—that God speaks through the experiences and reflections of individual Christians. From this perspective, Catholics must take personal responsibility for the faith and for living that faith in the world. This understanding of the Catholic faith in the modern world was contained in advice given by married Catholics in the Christian Family Movement to the Papal Birth Control Commission in 1965:

> God has created us to develop our talents to govern the universe and ourselves. Since medical research has learned a method of

intelligently controlling ovulation, it would seem reasonable for men
to use this knowledge for the good of their own family. Other
functions are intelligently controlled with no question as to the
morality of the use of a drug.[17,18]

The reality of American Catholics is that the groups at each end of the
continuum are small, with a majority of Catholics in the middle. In a test of
Kennedy's thesis, Davidson and Pogorelc found a majority of American Catholics (52 percent) in the middle; 12 percent on the conservative side; and 35
percent on the progressive side.[19]

Measuring the Acceptance of Claims to Authority

Is the church's authority accepted by Catholics today? To measure the level of
accepted authority is a different kind of task from finding and describing the
church's teachings, which are in the catechism, encyclicals, and pastoral letters.
Measuring accepted authority requires empirical measures of the degree to
which followers accept the teachings or commands.

Claims for authority may be either institutional or personal. A leader may
demand obedience based on his or her office or on personality or charisma.
Catholic leaders normally depend on the authority of office and remind the
faithful of the institution's history, traditions, and past claims to legitimacy.
When that is sufficient to induce obedience, the authority of leaders has been
strong, predictable, and stable. But if the followers lose faith in the institution,
any authority based on church office or tradition becomes shaky.

Claimed authority also varies in scope. A teacher may claim a wide or a narrow
domain. Similarly, the follower has conceptions of how broad the leader's authority
really is. This is the source of the frequently heard statement "I wish those priests
would stay out of politics and stick to religious things they know something about."
In turn, followers may make claims for their own authority when they find official
authority threatening their own beliefs. For example, we are currently witnessing
a strong move by conservative believers, both Protestant and Catholic, to challenge
the public schools' academic courses on biological evolution. These people are not
only challenging the claimed authority of the biology teachers but also making
a claim of their own for what they have called "creation science" or, more recently,
"intelligent design." They use the mechanisms of a democratic society (media,
public pressure on teachers, school officials) to achieve their goals.

An obvious case of the breakdown in accepted authority among Catholics
is that the vast majority of Catholic couples use some form of birth control,

which *Humanae Vitae* disallows, and the great majority do not see their behavior as sinful. Research has monitored the change in Catholic attitudes and behavior in this regard. In 1963, more than half of American Catholics accepted the church's teaching that contraceptive birth control was wrong; in a 1987 poll, only 18 percent said it was wrong.[20] A 1993 survey found only 13 percent of Catholics holding that conviction. In that survey, only 12 percent of Catholics under age fifty said they agreed with "all" church teaching on faith and morality; of those fifty and older, the figure was 28 percent.[21] The act of disobeying or simply ignoring a church pronouncement, especially when a person knows that millions of others are also doing it, creates alienation from the pronouncement itself.[22]

Further evidence that the authority of the Vatican was seriously weakened during the middle period of the twentieth century is in a series of polls asking American Catholics to agree or disagree with this statement: "Jesus directly handed over the leadership of His Church to Peter and the popes." In 1963, 86 percent agreed the statement was certainly or probably true; in 1974, 71 percent agreed; and in 1985, 68 percent,[23] a decline of eighteen points in a span of twenty-two years. Part of the change may be related to the acceptance of the right to freedom of conscience for all Catholics, written into the documents of Vatican II. Catholics increasingly look to their own informed consciences in deciding what they will believe, even on such fundamental teachings as the Petrine principle of church authority.

Other events besides Vatican II caused change. The political and cultural turmoil in the United Sates in the 1960s undoubtedly had an effect. The powerful experiences of those years heightened mistrust of all institutions among many Americans, especially the young. When the dissembling of national leaders and even presidents was revealed during the Vietnam era, when the duplicity of President Nixon came to light in the Watergate scandal, and when a president and other beloved national figures were assassinated, skepticism about government rose to new heights. Many people concluded that the whole system was rotten. They lost faith in government, and that faith has never returned to its pre-1970 level.

Finally, there is the split that occurred within the hierarchy of the American church in the 1980s. Following the public presentation of the Peace Pastoral in 1983, Cardinal Joseph Bernardin gave a series of public lectures in December 1983 and early 1984 in which he proposed that Catholic Church leaders open a national dialogue in the public arena on what he called a "Consistent Ethic of Life." This ethic would focus on life from conception to death. He believed that the church's teachings were strong enough to sustain a national dialogue. Conservative Catholics, led by Cardinal Bernard Law of

Boston, disagreed and insisted that conception was not open to discussion, saying that the church's position in opposition to abortion under any circumstances precluded including the prebirth period in the moral dialogue. Shortly thereafter, conservative Catholics, including bishops, began to criticize Catholic political leaders such as Governor Mario Cuomo of New York and Democratic vice presidential candidate Geraldine Ferraro, who said they were personally opposed to abortion but did not believe that they should impose their beliefs on others in a pluralistic society. Since 1984, this issue has been at the center of the split among Catholics in political and religious circles. For one group of Catholics, abortion is the litmus test for Catholic orthodoxy; for another group, it has become the focal point for the primacy of conscience.

Teaching Authority and the Growing Divide: Key Findings

To assess accepted authority by Catholic laity, we used two sets of survey questions. The first asked how important various elements of being a Catholic are felt to be. Table 10.1 includes the four elements of the series of twelve that the respondents rated as most important. It provides evidence that in some areas of teachings there is a high level of acceptance. Three of four Catholics in the 2005 survey said that the four teachings in table 10.1 were very important to them. All four are rooted deep in Catholic Church history, and we may say that they are accepted as basic or core elements of their faith. Even the youngest generation of Catholics, the millennials, accepts these teachings. Hispanics agree with European Catholics. The findings show that women were slightly more accepting of these beliefs than were men and that only with regard to the teaching of Mary as the Mother of God were the millennials significantly less accepting than the older generations. Although these teachings have deep roots, it is important that Pope John Paul II spoke out often about the importance of these core elements. These teachings had the same high level of acceptance in the 1999 survey. We have no comparable data prior to 1999.

Table 10.2 presents a different picture. It contains the four teachings lay Catholics considered least important of the series of twelve. Only four in ten Catholics said the church's teaching in opposition to abortion and the teaching authority claimed by the Vatican was very important to them. Also, only one in three said the teaching in opposition to the death penalty was very important, and only 29 percent said a celibate male clergy was very important. Lay Catholics did not see these teachings as important or central, even though Pope John Paul II taught them constantly. He was an outspoken opponent of abortion throughout his twenty-seven-year reign. In his later years, he also

TABLE 10.1. Catholics Who Say Specific Church Teachings Are Very Important to Them, by Gender, Ethnicity, and Generation, 2005 (in percentages)

	Total %	Gender		Ethnicity		Generation			
		Men %	Women %	Hisp %	Non-H %	Pre-VII %	VII %	Post-VII %	Mil %
Helping the poor	84	77	91	88	84	84	82	84	91
Belief in Jesus' resurrection	84	81	86	80	85	85	83	85	81
Sacraments	76	72	79	75	76	82	75	74	77
Mary as Mother of God	74	69	78	72	74	79	77	71	61

spoke out against the death penalty, made special pleas to American Catholics and U.S. governors to spare the lives of particular death row inmates, and even forgave the person who tried to assassinate him. He proclaimed the importance of the church's teaching role and defended the "gift" of the celibate clergy.

There were no gender differences on the latter teachings; men and women generally agreed. On only one item were Hispanics different from European Catholics; half of the Hispanics strongly agreed that the "Teaching Authority of the Vatican was very important to them." The differences were more significant across generations on three of the four items, revealing a gap between the older and younger age groups. With the four teachings in table 10.2, we see that church authority is not accepted on all teachings. Lay Catholics are making choices.

Catholics and the Locus of Moral Authority on Issues Relating to Human Sexuality

We also asked a series of questions on who should have the final say about issues involving sexual morality. We focused on five teachings that were the subject of ongoing discussion during the papacy of John Paul II and that have also been on the agenda in local and national politics: divorce and remarriage without a church annulment, contraceptive birth control, abortion, homosexual behavior, and nonmarital sexual relations. Throughout his world travels, John Paul II spoke loudly and consistently in condemnation of the five. Our surveys allow us to see how much authority American Catholics accord to

TABLE 10.2. Four Teachings Receiving the Least Acceptance by Catholics as Being Very Important to Them, by Gender, Ethnicity, and Generation, 2005 (in percentages)

	Total	Gender		Ethnicity		Generation			
		Men	Women	Hisp	Non-H	Pre-VII	VII	Post-VII	Mil
	%	%	%	%	%	%	%	%	%
Percentages saying very important to them:									
Teachings that oppose abortion	44	46	42	40	44	58	44	45	7
Teaching authority claimed by the Vatican	42	45	39	51	40	52	40	42	27
Teachings that oppose death penalty	35	33	37	41	35	38	34	34	39
A celibate male clergy	29	30	28	32	29	36	25	35	11

church leaders regarding these teachings. The following question was asked in 1987, 1993, 1999, and 2005:

> I would like your opinion on several issues that involve moral authority in the Catholic Church. In each case I would like to know who you think should have the final say about what is right or wrong. Is it the Church leaders such as the pope and the bishops, or individuals taking Church teachings into account and deciding for themselves, or both individuals and leaders working together?

Table 10.3 presents the overall trends on each of the five teachings, comparing the averages for church leaders, individuals, and both. In 1987, about one in three Catholics saw church leaders as the proper source of authority on the teachings of abortion, homosexual behavior, and nonmarital sex. By 2005, the percentages for church leaders on these teachings had declined to one in four. The percentages in 1987 looking to church leaders on divorce and remarriage (23 percent) and on birth control (12 percent) remained steady over time. The topic on which the 2005 respondents saw the least church authority was birth control; fewer than one in seven Catholics in 2005 saw church leaders as the locus of authority in that regard. Regarding contraception, support for individual conscience was highest (of the five teachings) in 1987, and it remained steady at 61 percent in 2005. In respondents' choice of "individuals," the only significant change over time occurred on one teaching—divorce and remarriage, which had an 11 percentage point increase toward individual moral authority.

Perhaps the most interesting finding was the number of respondents who said "both." (See table 10.3, bottom.) Large numbers of Catholics want dialogue

TABLE 10.3. Catholics Who Look to Church Leaders, Individuals, or Both, as Proper Locus of Moral Authority on Five Teachings Regarding Human Sexuality, 1987–2005 (in percentages)

	1987 %	1993 %	1999 %	2005 %
	Church Leaders			
Divorce and remarriage without an annulment	23	23	19	22
Practicing contraceptive birth control	12	14	10	13
Advocating choice regarding abortion	29	21	20	25
Engaging in homosexual behavior	32	26	20	24
Engaging in nonmarital sex	34	23	23	22
	Individuals (Themselves)			
Divorce and remarriage without an annulment	31	38	45	42
Practicing contraceptive birth control	62	57	62	61
Advocating choice regarding abortion	45	44	47	44
Engaging in homosexual behavior	39	39	49	46
Engaging in nonmarital sex	42	44	47	47
	Both			
Divorce and remarriage without an annulment	43	37	32	35
Practicing contraceptive birth control	23	26	23	27
Advocating choice regarding abortion	22	33	29	30
Engaging in homosexual behavior	19	30	25	28
Engaging in nonmarital sex	21	30	26	30

between individuals and church leaders.[24] On three of the five teachings (abortion, homosexual behavior, and nonmarital sex), the respondents increased their preference for dialogue. In these three cases, the increases came at the expense of moral authority of church leaders alone. By 2005, there was more support for both laity and church leaders working together than for church leaders alone.

Most notable is that the highest percentage of votes for laypeople and church leaders working together occurred over the teaching on divorce and remarriage without an annulment. Perhaps this change reflects the fact that in the past forty years many Catholics have experienced divorces among family and friends, leading them to more sympathetic attitudes and thus to desire a reconsideration of the church's traditional teaching on divorce. It may also be a reflection of the increased participation of lay professionals in diocesan tribunals involving annulments.

In the next section, we look at specific groups of laity using data from 1987 and 2005. The trend lines from 1987 to 2005 are constant, so there is no need to include the findings from 1993 and 1999. Also, we focus most of our attention on the acceptance of church leaders as the locus of moral authority, because their acceptance rates are the ones that suffered the most decline.

Gender and Moral Authority

Figure 10.1 compares Catholic men's and women's responses to questions on teaching about gender and moral authority. In 1987, there were no significant differences in their responses. Overall, between one in three and one in four Catholic men and women continued to see church leaders as the locus of moral authority on these teachings. For men, the findings remained stable over time except for a decline in support for the teaching on nonmarital sex. Women's acceptance of church leaders as the proper source of moral authority decreased for the teachings on abortion (down 7 percentage points), homosexual behavior (down 13 percentage points), and nonmarital sex (down 14 percentage points).

By 2005, the differences between men and women in terms of seeing the individual as the proper locus of moral authority had become significant on four of the five teachings: divorce and remarriage, 38 percent of men versus 45 percent of women; contraception, 55 percent versus 66 percent; abortion, 39 percent versus 49 percent; homosexual behavior, 39 percent versus 51 percent; and nonmarital sex, 41 percent versus 51 percent. Thus, over time women looked more to themselves and less to church leaders than did men (the data are not shown in figure 10.1).

Moral Authority across Generations

In 1987, we compared the three generations of Catholics and found that pre–Vatican II Catholics were most accepting of the claims of church leaders on all five of the teachings, with Vatican II Catholics in the middle, and post–Vatican II Catholics least accepting. The three teachings receiving the widest acceptance of church leaders by all three generations were nonmarital sex, homosexual behavior, and the opposition to abortion.

In 2005, pre–Vatican II Catholics were still the most likely to accept church leaders' claims; nevertheless, on four of the five teachings, their support had declined significantly. (See figure 10.2.) Whereas in 1987 more than four in ten senior Catholics accepted the claims of church leaders on abortion, homosexual behavior, and nonmarital sex, their acceptance level had dropped to three in ten by 2005. Among Vatican II Catholics, the acceptance rates remained more stable, ranging from a low of 11 percent (contraception) to 32 percent (homosexual behavior) in 1987 and declining significantly only with regard to nonmarital sex. Post–Vatican II Catholics also were basically stable from 1987 to 2005 in their acceptance of church authority. The millennials, making up only a small portion (9 percent) of the total sample in 2005, need

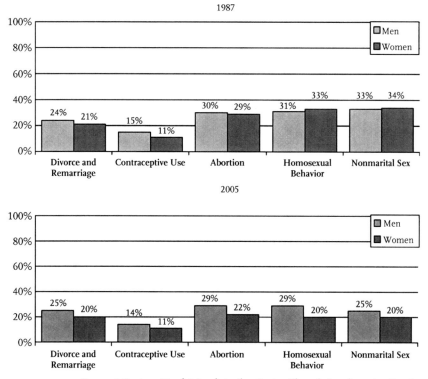

FIGURE 10.1. Percent Seeing Final Moral Authority in Church Leaders, by Gender: 1987 and 2005.

close watching in coming years, given their limited number in our survey. In summary, there was a decline in acceptance of church leaders within and across generations, with the long-term trends pointing toward further declines.

Catholics have increasingly seen authority in individual consciences. As the acceptance of church leaders as the locus of moral authority declines, individual authority increases (figure 10.3). There were increases between 1987 and 2005 regarding divorce and remarriage and homosexual behavior. The largest increase occurred among pre–Vatican II Catholics on their attitudes toward homosexual behavior and nonmarital sex. Vatican II Catholics turned to individual conscience on divorce and remarriage (up 16 points). Post–Vatican II Catholics changed little during the eighteen years.

The bishops have declared abortion to be the most important moral issue facing Catholics. Figure 10.4 depicts the differences in responses regarding the teaching on abortion for the pre–Vatican II and the post–Vatican II generations. The top two circles show that acceptance of church leaders as the proper locus of moral authority declined by nine percentage points, acceptance of individuals declined by three percentage points, and laity and church leaders

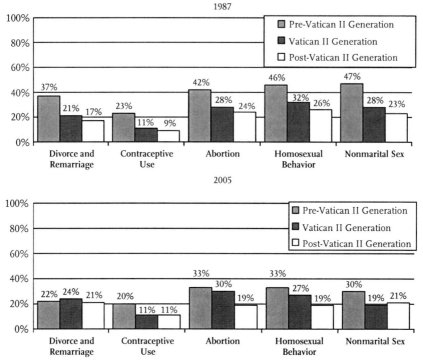

FIGURE 10.2. Percent Seeing Final Moral Authority in Church Leaders, by Generation: 1987 and 2005.

working together increased by 17 percentage points. Among the young generation of Catholics, acceptance of church leaders declined by five points, individuals increased by two points to 50 percent, and both working together increased by 5 points to 31 percent.[25] Thus, we find that three of ten of the oldest and youngest generation would like to see laity working with church leaders as the proper locus of moral authority. Similar findings resulted when we examined the responses of the high-commitment Catholics; an average of one in three said they would like to see leaders and laity working together. These results are at variance with church leaders, who state that these teachings are anchored in natural law and not subject to discussion of any sort.

In summary, acceptance of the church's teaching authority on these moral issues has declined across all generations of adult Catholics, as laypersons increasingly look to themselves. At the same time, a growing minority of Catholics, including the highly committed, would like to see moral authority teachings resting with both church leaders and individuals in some kind of dialogue. We will return to this finding in the concluding section.

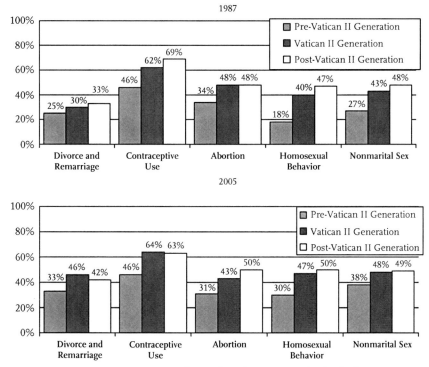

FIGURE 10.3. Percent Seeing Final Moral Authority in Individuals, by Generation: 1987 and 2005.

A Young Adult Talks about Moral Authority

Our interviews demonstrated how many young adult Catholics think about moral authority. Here, as an example, is an educated Catholic woman, age 33, of Polish ethnicity, whom we will call Kate. She grew up in Ohio, works as a lawyer, and was married three years ago. She exemplifies the complexities of many young persons' views, especially on moral questions.

INTERVIEWER Do you think it is almost always wrong, or not, to use condoms or birth control pills to prevent pregnancy?

KATE No, it is not always wrong. It's not always wrong because the consequences of unprotected sex can be ones that aren't desired. And I don't think it's wrong to have sex for pleasure. And it's certainly not wrong to use a condom when you're talking about nonconsensual sex. I don't think birth control is wrong. I just got married, so I'm thinking in terms of a couple making decisions, though I know it's not always in

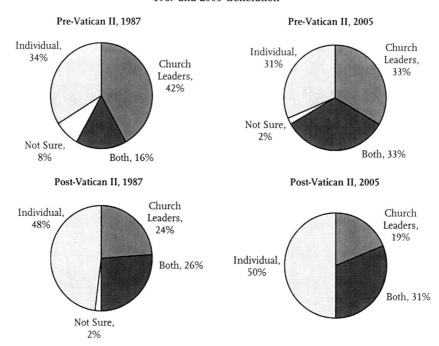

1987 and 2005 Generation

FIGURE 10.4. Percent Seeing Final Authority on Choice Regarding Abortion, by Generation: 1987 and 2005. Note: The post–Vatican II generation includes Millennials in 2005.

that situation—but, I think for a couple, it's okay to use birth control pills or condoms when they decide they don't want to risk pregnancy. I think it's very responsible to not bring a life into this world if you're not going to take care of it.

INTERVIEWER Maybe it depends on the circumstances.

KATE There are certain circumstances when it would be wrong to use birth control pills. Suppose you have a couple where the man is desirous to have children and the woman isn't, and she's using birth control without his knowledge. It would be dishonest. But that's an honesty question rather than whether those things are intrinsically wrong.

INTERVIEWER That raises another question. If the church says it's wrong, and you think it's not wrong, maybe that reflects back on the church's teachings.

KATE Yes, I think the church has that wrong.

INTERVIEWER So that raises another question. Maybe some of the other things it says are wrong, too.

KATE Yes, I think the church is wrong in a lot of the areas about sex. Even in the mainstream media, you hear what's coming out of the Vatican. I understand that these issues are not ones that they are going to budge on right now, especially premarital sex. The sex-outside-of-marriage issue is one that challenges a lot of young people in this country, and it's one that is forming a wedge between young people and the church.

INTERVIEWER Here is another question. Do you think that it is always morally wrong to terminate a pregnancy by having an abortion?

KATE No.

INTERVIEWER Would there be certain circumstances that would affect that?

KATE Well, number one, I think any abortion at all would be a sad thing. No matter what. I don't think abortion should be thought of as a birth control method. I think it should be a last resort in limited cases, in cases of rape or incest or endangering the mother's life. I saw an interesting sign on the subway. It said something like "Abortion is a reflection that society has not yet let women have their rights." That spoke to me. This issue bothers me personally. I know where the church stands on it, and I don't have any beefs with the church about it. But where it bugs me is that, like I said, I think abortion should be a last resort, and I would hope it would happen as infrequently as possible. But at the same time, I don't want anybody trying to restrict women's rights to have it done.

INTERVIEWER Do you think it is always morally wrong, or not, to engage in homosexual acts?

KATE I don't think it is. I just don't. I can't articulate why, I guess. It's like I'm kind of somewhat libertarian, like, I don't have much to say about what other people do, unless someone is harming one another or doing something against their will. If it's their business, it's their business. It's nice that some of the people find somebody to love in this short life. If people want to express themselves homosexually, be physical, and there's no love there, I suppose I don't have a problem with that either. I don't really like to say too much about what goes on in other people's bedrooms. It's just not my thing.

Kate accepts church authority in many other matters.

INTERVIEWER Some people say that laypeople should participate in selecting their parish priests. Do you agree with that, or not?

KATE No. I don't. Because it's not supposed to be a popularity contest. It's not a priority for me that laity have some say in selecting their priest.

INTERVIEWER Some people think that lay people should have a right to participate in deciding how parish income should be spent. What do you think?

KATE I don't think they should have a role in that. It should be up to the priest, on the theory that he's taking orders from somewhere else.

INTERVIEWER That is, you trust the system.

KATE I think I do.

Discussion and Conclusion

This chapter has focused on the teaching authority claimed by the Catholic Church. We reviewed the nature of the church's claims to authority over time and pointed out that during the course of our four surveys, 1987 to 2005, Pope John Paul II was a strong and firm advocate for the church's teaching authority. He carried his message to all corners of the earth. Whether it was encouraging Catholics to attend Mass more frequently, reclaiming the sacrament of reconciliation, or calling young people to personal lives of holiness and greater commitment to social justice, his voice was strong. He won widespread acclaim as the dominant religious leader of the last quarter of the twentieth century. Our surveys, which were done during two-thirds of his pontificate, provide a measure of the degree to which the church's teachings on these moral issues continue to be accepted by the laity.

There is continued high acceptance of the church's teachings on helping the poor, belief in Jesus' resurrection, the sacraments, and Mary as the Mother of God. However, support declined on issues like abortion, opposition to the death penalty, and a celibate male clergy. Over time, Catholics moved away from looking to church leaders as the appropriate source of moral authority and toward the individual. At the same time, a minority of Catholics (about 30 percent) stated that the appropriate source of authority should be both laity and church leaders working together. By 2005, more Catholics selected this option as the proper source of authority, rather than selected church leaders.

NOTES

1. The authors commissioned the Gallup Organization to carry out four surveys of American Catholics. The first survey took place in spring 1987 in anticipation of the second visit of Pope John Paul II to the United States. Subsequent surveys were carried out in spring 1993, 1999, and 2005. The first survey was paid for by the *National Catholic Reporter*, with additional funds from Rev. Andrew M. Greeley; the second survey also by the *National*

Catholic Reporter, the third by the Louisville Institute; and the 2005 survey jointly by the Louisville Institute and an anonymous donor. The *National Catholic Reporter* also provided funds for the third and fourth surveys and helped publicize them with supplements in the *NCR*. We are grateful to all the donors who have made these surveys possible.

2. Peter Steinfels, *A People Adrift: The Crisis of the Roman Catholic Church in America* (New York: Simon and Schuster, 2003); David Gibson, *The Coming Catholic Church: How the Faithful Are Shaping a New American Catholicism* (San Francisco: HarperSanFrancisco, 2003); Francis Oakley and Bruce Russett, eds., *Governance, Accountability, and the Future of the Catholic Church* (New York: Continuum, 2004); José Casanova, *Public Religions in the Modern World* (Chicago: Chicago University Press, 1994).

3. John T. Noonan, *A Church That Cannot Change: The Development of Catholic Moral Teaching* (Notre Dame, IN: University of Notre Dame Press, 2005).

4. Oakley and Russett's *Governance, Accountability, and the Future of the Catholic Church*, an edited book derived from a conference held at the Yale Law School in March 2003, recognizes that the current crisis in the church is part of a larger crisis that has brought "into question all forms of authority, secular no less than ecclesiastical." It addresses such central questions as (1) the historical antecedents to the contemporary hierarchical and centralized institution that is the church; (2) relevant theological perspectives on greater responsibility for the laity and clergy; (3) existing models of structures that would create greater participation and accountability, including financial accountability; and (4) features from the American experience of freedom and democracy that might prove either helpful or hurtful in efforts to encourage participation. The book is a clarion call for voice from those whose loyalty to the church in crisis means "speaking up, insisting on being heard and heeded," and acknowledging that action for change "requires a long-sustained effort" (201–202).

5. Max Weber, *The Theory of Social and Economic Organization* (Glencoe, IL: Free Press, 1947), 324.

6. Marcia L. Colish, "Reclaiming Our History: Belief and Practice in the Church," and John Beal, "Constitutionalism in the Church," in Oakley and Russett, *Governance, Accountability, and the Future of the Catholic Church*.

7. Gerald P. Fogarty, S.J., "Episcopal Governance in the American Church," in Oakley and Russett, *Governance, Accountability, and the Future of the Catholic Church*.

8. John Courtney Murray, *We Hold These Truths: Catholic Reflections on the American Proposition* (New York: Sheed and Ward, 1960).

9. Andrew M. Greeley, *The New Agenda* (Garden City, NY: Doubleday, 1973).

10. Andrew M. Greeley, William C. McCready, and Kathleen McCourt, *Catholic Schools in a Declining Church* (Kansas City, MO: Sheed and Ward, 1976).

11. Michele Dillon, *Catholic Identity: Balancing Reason, Faith, and Power* (New York: Cambridge University Press, 1999).

12. William V. D'Antonio, *The Layman in the Wake of Vatican II* (Notre Dame, IN: Ave Maria, 1966), 12.

13. Greeley et al., *Catholic Schools in a Declining Church*; Andrew M. Greeley, *The American Catholic: A Social Portrait* (New York: Basic Books, 1977); Andrew M. Greeley,

Crisis in the Church: A Study of Religion in America (Chicago: Thomas More, 1979); Jay P. Dolan, *The American Catholic Experience: A History from Colonial Times to the Present* (Garden City, NY: Image, 1985); Eugene Bianchi and Rosemary Ruether, *A Democratic Catholic Church* (New York: Crossroad, 1992); Thomas C. Fox, *Sexuality and Catholicism* (New York: Braziller, 1995); Garry Wills, *Papal Sin: Structures of Deceit* (New York: Doubleday, 2000).

14. Andrew M. Greeley, *The Catholic Myth* (New York: Scribner's, 1990); Kathy Coffey, "It's Time to End the Hypocrisy on Birth Control," *U.S. Catholic* (June 1998): 24–25.

15. Eugene Kennedy, *Tomorrow's Catholics, Yesterday's Church* (San Francisco: Harper and Row, 1988).

16. Robert McClory, *Turning Point* (New York: Crossroad, 1995), 110–111.

17. Ibid., 94.

18. On the other hand, Avery Dulles, S.J., argued that the cultural secularization that has created the progressive Catholicism has put Catholic orthodoxy under enormous pressure. He accepted that "in a secularized society such as ours, consistently orthodox Catholics will constitute a minority within their religious community." Still, he concluded that "orthodoxy rather than accommodationism [to progressive ideas and behavior] offers greater promise for the future" of the church. See Avery Dulles, S.J., "Orthodoxy and Social Change," *America* (June 20, 1998): 8–17.

19. James D. Davidson, *Catholicism in Motion: The Church in American Society* (Liguori, MO: Liguori, 2005).

20. "Research Report on 1987 Nationwide Poll #128," *Los Angeles Times*, August 14–19, 1987.

21. "How U.S. Catholics View Their Church," based on a *USA Today*/CNN/Gallup Poll, *USA Today*, August 10, 1993, 6A.

22. The degree to which the teaching against contraception is ignored was acknowledged by Father John McCloskey in his January 2006 newsletter to his predominantly conservative readers: "Unfortunately, but not surprisingly, Catholics tend to contracept at the same rate as the rest of the world." He went on to suggest that "one of the major issues for the Church in the decades ahead will be clarity as to who is considered a practicing Catholic and who is not. This may result in a smaller but much more fervent and evangelizing Church." See John McCloskey, "State of US Catholic Church at Beginning of 2006," *Spero News*, January 16, 2006, 11, at www.speroforum. com/site/article.asp?idCategory=34&idsub=127&id=2427.

23. Dean Hoge, *The Future of Catholic Leadership: Responses to the Priest Shortages* (Kansas City, MO: Sheed and Ward, 1987), 57.

24. When we first formulated this question in 1987, we offered only two options, church leaders or individuals. During the pretest period, many respondents said they would prefer a third option, namely, a dialogue between church leaders and Catholic laity. We added it as a third option and subsequently found that it gained support over time.

25. Given the small percentage of millennials, we use the post–Vatican II figures as being more reliable.

II

Souls and Bodies

*The Birth Control Controversy and
the Collapse of Confession*

Leslie Woodcock Tentler

The intra-Catholic debate over birth control came to a head in the mid-1960s, when the resulting impasse was properly labeled a "crisis." Another crisis, this one wholly unanticipated, was in the making by then as well. This latter crisis had to do with the sacrament of penance. More than 80 percent of American Catholics in the early 1960s went to confession on at least an annual basis, many frequenting the sacrament as often as once a month.[1] A devout elite went weekly. But by 1966, priests were reporting a suddenly diminished number of penitents—a problem that accelerated sharply in the years immediately following. By the mid-1970s, the sacrament of penance was widely described as being in a state of collapse. Given that more than half of American Catholics today say they "never" go to confession, one can confidently assert that the sacrament remains in a parlous condition.[2]

What did the crisis over contraception have to do with the collapse of confession? I personally doubt the validity of a once-popular proposition—that numerous Catholic adults, bitter over difficult confrontations in the confessional over birth control, abandoned the sacrament out of resentment. The lived experience of confession was simply more complicated than this formulation would suggest. It would be more accurate to say that contraception was the issue around which a substantial majority of Catholic adults came to a new understanding of sin and the nature of church authority. Confession as it was then practiced—swift, anonymous, governed by an act-centered moral logic—could not easily accommodate a psychologized and situational view of sin, which was what most Catholics eventually embraced. By the time the sacrament had been reformed, moreover, most Catholics appear to have decided that their moral lives were best adjudicated in the internal forum. Conscience, increasingly, was all. Confessors may inadvertently have encouraged this revolution in consciousness—and again, contraception was key. By the mid-1960s, significant numbers of younger priests, who probably heard the lion's share of confessions, had serious doubts about church teaching on contraception. They were no longer willing to take a hard line on the issue as confessors. The easiest solution—and it was taken by a great many priests after 1965—was to tell married penitents to consult their consciences.

Shortly after the issuance of *Humanae Vitae* (July 1968), contraception largely disappeared as a topic in Catholic public discourse, presumably because the encyclical made dissent far riskier for priests and theologians. The ultimate effect was to muzzle the clergy as credible sources of moral authority, at least with regard to sex. One can hardly speak intelligibly about sex to the world as we know it if one can't be honest about contraception. The clergy's silence further confirmed the laity in their newfound sense of moral autonomy, which may have been replicated among the young as a growing moral confusion. Catholics born since Vatican II seem to believe, if we can trust recent polls, that the church has little to offer them in the realm of sexual decision making. No wonder they seldom go to confession! The sacrament of penance in its preconcilar heyday was preeminently about sexual guilt and sexual sin. How could it have been otherwise in a world unacquainted with notions of "structural" sin and a moral tradition where every sexual lapse, no matter how seemingly minor, was objectively grave or "mortal"?

I want to explore this revolution in the Catholic moral imagination by doing three things. First, by way of preface, I will summarize what is known about the history of confession in the United States during the first half of the twentieth century.[3] It is important for our purposes to understand how relatively recent the disciplined practice of the 1950s actually was. Second, I will trace the evolution of the crisis over contraception from the early twentieth century into the 1960s and examine the ways in which the looming crisis played out in the confessional. Third, I will discuss, from an admittedly subjective perspective, the moral and psychological implications of the twin crises over contraception and confession and the ambiguous legacy they present to Catholics today. This chapter is largely based on research for my recent book, *Catholics and Contraception: An American History*, which includes extensive archival work, as well as broad reading in pastoral literature and lengthy interviews with fifty-six priests ordained between 1938 and 1963.[4] It is almost certainly conditioned by my own experience of marriage and parenthood, especially the journeys of my three children through their adolescent years.

Let us begin with the history of confession. This is a history based on very little quantitative data: even pastors who kept precise accounts of the communions distributed annually in their parishes seldom recorded the number of confessions. Mission preachers sometimes did, given that the number of confessions heard in the course of a mission was a principal measure of its success. But missions rarely took place in a parish more frequently than every other year, and they were proverbially the setting in which recalcitrant sinners—"big fish," in the parlance of mission confessors—returned to the sacrament of penance after a long absence. A few diocesan archives, including one I have researched extensively, include parish reports that estimate the number of persons who failed to make their "Easter duty" in a given year, which would nearly always have translated into a failure to confess annually.[5] (How a priest in a large urban parish, who could not have known all his parishioners by name or even necessarily by sight, would have come up with the numbers is something of a mystery.) By coupling such flawed and fragmentary documents with the testimony of priests and other informed observers, we can probably conclude that a substantial majority of American Catholics in 1900 confessed on at least an annual basis, as church law prescribes. A great many of them, however, do not seem to have confessed much more frequently than that.

By 1900, in most American dioceses, a campaign for frequent confession—monthly reception of the sacrament was typically encouraged—was already well underway. It received a major boost in 1905 from Pius X's decree on frequent communion, which encouraged the faithful to receive the sacrament weekly or even daily, and the same pope's 1910 decree lowering the age at first reception of the Eucharist to about seven. (The standard age hitherto in the United States had been twelve or thirteen.) The reception of communion was firmly linked to confession in the Catholic mind: those who confessed annually or semiannually generally received the Eucharist only once or twice a year. More frequent communion was widely understood to require more frequent confession. A lowered age at first communion, moreover, meant that children in Catholic schools could be trained from almost the outset of their school careers to the frequent reception of both sacraments. Monthly confession and communion was the norm for American children growing up in the 1920s, which presumably had some effect on their parents' behavior, as well as their own as adults. (Monthly devotions to the Sacred Heart and, somewhat later, to Our Lady of Fatima also had an effect, since they required the devotee to receive communion.) By the 1930s, a decade not just of economic crisis but visibly quickened Catholic devotionalism, at least in the United States, even the modal adult male was confessing on more than an annual basis—four times a year might be a sensible estimate. Notably devout Catholics by then—as ever, a disproportionately female population—typically went to confession once a week, as did priests and religious. The weekly ideal was consistently touted in Catholic sermons and pious periodicals.

What did more frequent confession mean for penitents and their confessors? For priests, the new pattern intensified an already heavy workload: fifteen or even twenty hours a week in the confessional and more at Christmas and Easter. Priests, with the possible exception of pastors, spent far more time hearing confessions than they did saying Mass.[6] (The Jesuit Joseph Schuyler estimated that the priests at the Bronx parish he studied in the late 1950s heard an average of average of 15,000 confessions a year.)[7] Long lines at the confessional—and such was invariably the case at Christmas and Easter—did mean that priests could not spend much time with individual penitents. The average confession probably lasted about two minutes, and some priests worried that the sacrament had in consequence taken on something of a mechanical quality. But most priests seem to have found deep satisfaction in their work as confessors. It was the priestly role for which they felt most adequately prepared, as Joseph Fichter discovered in a study done in the early 1960s.[8] Long lines of penitents, moreover, inevitably boosted priests' confidence in their capacity as moral authorities and spiritual guides. And they appreciated the sacrament's peculiar intimacy, which somehow triumphed over speed and anonymity. "I thought it was a tremendous compliment to a priest to have a person come in and talk to them like that, even though the screen was there," a Detroit priest told me in the course of my recent research.[9]

Deciphering the impact of frequent confession on lay penitents is more difficult. It makes a certain sense to assume that persons who confess annually are less scrupulous about sin and less troubled by guilt than persons who confess monthly or weekly. It would also seem plausible that those who confess annually are better able than more frequent penitents to distance themselves psychologically from church authority. But Catholics living in the United States in 1900, to pick a date at random, had been taught that confession was essential at the point of death. Heirs to a tradition with an intensely eschatological orientation, nearly all had been nurtured on a diet of the "four last things" (death, judgment, heaven, and hell), the reality of which was attested to by sources as diverse as the Baltimore Catechism and the rougher edges of mission preaching. Did such Catholics really believe that otherwise well-conducted persons would go to hell for an unconfessed sin like contraception, which did no apparent harm to anyone? Consider how quickly their descendants appear to have lost the fear of hell in the wake of Vatican II, when Catholic theology and culture abruptly moved to a this-worldly orientation. But whatever their private doubts and moral reservations, it seems unlikely—given the culture in which they lived—that most preconciliar Catholics thought it safe to assume that hell did not exist. This alone gave the church enormous authority in the lives of ordinary believers and endowed its machinery for the assured forgiveness of sins with an ultimate surpassing importance. Infrequency, moreover, did not necessarily diminish the emotional impact of confession—the sense of comfort, release, and spiritual cleansing that the sacrament sometimes afforded. One can readily imagine the opposite being true.

At the same time, frequent confession was uniformly regarded by the clergy as a powerful mode of religious discipline. Clerical literature by the very early twentieth century nearly always depicted those who confessed annually as spiritually tepid and, very probably, morally lax. Such was the experience of a young Detroit priest whose first assignment in 1938 took him to a working-class parish on the city's east side. A stubborn handful of his immigrant parishioners—"those old Belgians and Italians"—were accustomed to confess only once a year, which some of them did with remarkable dispatch: "Same as last year, Father." Naturally, they seemed to this very green priest— amused, in his old age, by their evasions—like hardened sinners.[10] Along with their bemused confessor, Father Ferdinand DeCneudt, I doubt that they actually were such. But at the very least, these men—and in DeCneudt's telling, all were male—had put themselves at a certain remove from clerical authority and expectations. They apparently lacked fluency in the language of self-scrutiny, if only for want of practice; did that in turn inhibit the close internal monitoring of thought and behavior that frequent confession was meant to achieve? Men like these, moreover, could hardly have had much psychic room for acute anxiety about the immediate state of their souls. Their God was presumably One for whom the intention to confess, whether at Easter or—if remotely possible—on one's deathbed, was sufficient for salvation. So common sense, along with the clerical proponents of frequent confession, should probably carry the day. Frequent confession was indeed apt to result in an increased consciousness of sin and greater deference to a clerically defined morality, which is not to say that it necessarily caused people to behave any better.

It made a difference, then, that the Catholic crisis over contraception—the subject to which we now turn—developed at a time when ordinary Catholics in the United States confessed frequently. When did that crisis begin to develop? I would argue for the very early 1930s. (No one doubts that it reached its apex in the mid-1960s.) On the last day of 1930, that inaugural year of a global depression, Pope Pius XI issued *Casti Connubii*, his encyclical on Christian marriage; in that encyclical, the pope articulated—clearly and forcefully—the church's ancient opposition to all forms of fertility control with the exception of mutually agreed upon abstinence. "Any use whatsoever of marriage, in the exercise of which the act by human effort is deprived of its natural power of procreating life, violates the law of God and nature, and those who do such a thing are stained by a grave and mortal flaw." The pope was motivated in part by the very recent decision of the Anglicans' Lambeth Conference to give a guarded blessing to marital contraception under certain well-defined circumstances. He was apparently also troubled by reports, principally from continental Europe, of confessors failing to admonish penitents they knew or suspected were practicing illicit modes of family limitation. He pointedly warned confessors against "conniving in the false opinion of the faithful" by neglecting to question married penitents or giving evasive answers to their queries about birth control.[11] *Casti Connubii* received unusually broad publicity in both the secular and religious press, where its reception was generally warm and respectful—in marked contrast, it might be noted, to the reception accorded *Humanae Vitae* in 1968. It would have been difficult for an American Catholic adult in the early 1930s never to have heard of it.[12]

Why was *Casti Connubii* so important? Precisely because the pope's anxieties were well placed: like their European brethren, American Catholics prior to 1930 heard relatively little about birth control, even in the confessional. Most American priests as late as the 1920s were governed by essentially Victorian standards, no matter that the society around them was in sexual matters changing rapidly. For men like these, and for the vast majority of their parishioners, contraception was emphatically not a topic for polite public discourse; contraceptive devices, indeed, retained for this not-inconsiderable population their long association with prostitution and other illicit forms of sex. It was thus extremely difficult to preach on marital morality at Sunday Mass, much less to preach frankly.[13] Nor was it easy to broach the subject in the confessional. Even in the 1920s, most American priests were apparently extremely cautious when it came to interrogating married penitents about their sexual lives. Some were accustomed to respond in cursory fashion even when the sin of contraception was actually confessed.[14] As for premarital instruction, it was typically hurried and mainly devoted to ensuring that both parties were canonically free to marry.[15] Only at missions were Catholics almost guaranteed hear a clear and vigorous condemnation of birth control, at least by the time of the First World War. Typically addressing congregations segregated by sex and sometimes by marital status as well, mission preachers had a freedom the parish clergy lacked. It probably also helped that they were itinerants and thus protected for all practical purposes from whatever resentment their preaching might stir up.[16]

The relative silence around contraception did not mean that Catholics were wholly ignorant of church teaching. Nearly all of them probably knew that their church regarded birth control as gravely sinful. (Until the 1930s, every state in the union had laws limiting or even prohibiting access to contraceptives.) But some, perhaps many, Catholics in this time of relative silence may not have grasped the absolute nature of their church's doctrine. Fragmentary evidence suggests that even reasonably devout Catholics sometimes thought that contraception was not mortally sinful in unusually hard circumstances: in the context of grinding poverty, for example, or a desperately sick wife. A well-regarded textbook of moral theology, published early in 1930, advised confessors not to disturb unfortunate penitents whose personal circumstances caused them to cling tenaciously to such a misconception. And many Catholics apparently believed that coitus interruptus, probably the most widely employed mode of fertility control in working-class families as late as the 1920s, was less seriously sinful than using a contraceptive device. Steadily declining Catholic birthrates also suggest that at least some Catholics had made personal peace with at least some forms of contraceptive practice.[17]

Casti Connubii signaled an end to the era of "good faith ignorance." Confessors were suddenly expected to be proactive: to question married penitents who gave reason for suspicion (or, for a time in the Archdiocese of Chicago, simply because they were married) and to condemn the sin in unyielding terms when it was confessed.[18] Birth control was increasingly the subject of Sunday preaching, particularly on the Feast of the Holy Family and during Lent. Such preaching was seldom graphic; preaching of that sort was still the province of parish missions, where the "shaming and degrading"— indeed, "vicious"—sin of contraception was regularly denounced.[19] But the laity heard about birth control in other venues, too. The 1930s saw the proliferation of a vivid Catholic pamphlet literature, where the teaching on contraception was conveyed in colloquial terms, as it was in a variety of Catholic periodicals.[20] The secular politics of birth control, moreover, meant that contraception and the laws governing access to it were the stuff of front-page news, as was Catholic opposition to the forces of liberalization, which now included a number of Protestant religious leaders.[21]

The new circumstances did not necessarily mean that Catholics conformed in greater numbers to church teaching. American birthrates remained at low ebb for most of the 1930s. But growing awareness of the teaching meant that disobedience was increasingly accompanied by guilt and even anguish.

The situation was difficult for priests, as well. "Every priest who is close to the people admits that contraception is the hardest problem of the confessional today," the Jesuit Joseph Reiner wrote from Chicago in 1933, when he was inclined to believe "that more than one half our married people use contraceptives."[22] Reiner saw reason for hope, however. Perhaps providentially—Father Reiner certainly thought so—the early 1930s witnessed the advent of the rhythm method, or family limitation by means of periodic abstinence from intercourse, a development made possible by new data on the timing of female ovulation. For men like Reiner, the rhythm method held out the possibility of "legitimate birth control" for Catholics—such, in fact, was the title of a 1934 pamphlet by Father John A. O'Brien—and thus an end to the suffering of their many penitents who were too poor or sick or emotionally depleted to welcome a baby every year.[23]

"Rhythm" was a staple of Catholic experience into the 1960s. Most laity turned against it then, asserting that the method was unreliable and—because it typically required abstaining from intercourse for at least ten days a month—subversive of marital happiness. Most priests eventually turned against it, too, in the sense that they ceased recommending the method to penitents. But rhythm was nonetheless of long-term significance. Church teaching would hardly have been credible to the laity without it, not once the church had begun to enforce that teaching vigorously. (The method, if employed conscientiously, would normally result in the more generous spacing of children.) Even more important, faith in rhythm made it possible for a reforming elite among the clergy to embrace a more positive theology of marriage—something for which, in twentieth-century circumstances, a reliable mode of fertility control was obviously necessary. Most Catholic writing on marriage in the 1930s assumed that marital sex was redeemed only by its procreative aspects; too much sex in marriage was widely regarded as dangerous to spiritual health. But by the late 1940s, a positive view of marital sex was moving into the Catholic mainstream. Far from being spiritually dangerous, marital sex was increasingly seen as a form of prayer—a means of union not just with one's spouse but with God.[24]

Catholic family life after 1945 was decisively shaped by this new understanding of marriage, especially in the rapidly growing middle class. The gospel of sacralized sex was preached in Catholic colleges, by diocesan family life bureaus, and especially by groups like Cana Conference and the Christian Family Movement—both founded in the later 1940s. (Young priests attached to Chicago's Pre-Cana organization, which provided workshops for the newly engaged, worried in the 1950s about sexual inhibitions among their young clients—the result, they assumed, of repressive socialization.) The new gospel was exceedingly attractive and fit neatly with period assumptions about marital happiness and sexual health. It found ready adherents among idealistic young couples in every region of the country, most of them now sufficiently affluent that larger-than-average families did not pose insuperable problems. Indeed, rueful veterans of groups like the Christian Family Movement (CFM) sometimes spoke in retrospect of the competitive natalism that prevailed in their circles. The larger the family, the holier the parents—or so it seemed at the time.[25]

Most Catholic couples, even in the domesticated 1950s, were not active in groups like Cana or CFM. But by their seemingly joyous example, the more ardent members of these organizations infused the teaching on contraception with an enhanced legitimacy. Perhaps that teaching couldn't be dismissed simply on the grounds that a celibate clergy knew nothing about the realities of marriage. They bolstered clerical morale as well. Birth control continued in the prosperous postwar years to be a persistent problem in confession. Marrying at earlier ages than ever before, young Catholics in the postwar period could plausibly anticipate a quarter-century of fertility. Not every Catholic family then was affluent; even the affluent could not necessarily afford to send eight or ten or twelve youngsters to college. Nor was every Catholic mother equipped with the physiology or the temperament required for successful nurturance of a very large family. So confessors heard plenty of anguished stories, in response to which they could offer only prayer and the rhythm method, which had frequently been tried by the penitent in question and found wanting. How good it was, in the dispiriting circumstances, to know couples whose obedience to church teaching had flowered forth in deepened faith and vibrant family living.

By 1960, according to a national fertility study, 38 percent of Catholics wives in their childbearing years were using—or had previously used—a means of family limitation forbidden by their church.[26] They tended as a group to be less educated than those in the sample who obeyed church teaching, in flat contradiction of demographic precedent. They also tended to be older. Evidently, many Catholics in this generation turned to forbidden modes of contraception only after having had several children. This would explain an otherwise puzzling phenomenon that several postwar studies documented: the tendency of married Catholics in their thirties and early forties to receive the sacraments less frequently than single Catholics and those in both younger and older age groups.[27] Confession was excruciatingly difficult for Catholics who regularly used birth control, since even gentle confessors had to ask for a "firm purpose of amendment"—a commitment to avoiding the sin in the future. Few confessors would grant absolution to penitents who did not at least promise to try. For a penitent with scruples about deception, it made eminent sense to confess as infrequently as possible and in a context where long lines made close questioning unlikely. The Saturday prior to Trinity Sunday—the final Sunday of the Easter season—was a favored time, at least according to Detroit's Monsignor William Sherzer: "There would be lines around the block coming to confession. And it would all be birth control."[28]

Some priests dismissed infrequent penitents like these in much the way their predecessors had done—as lukewarm Catholics whose spiritual tepidness was evidenced by their sinful behavior. But many more were troubled by the phenomenon, which they saw as a growing problem. Such infrequent penitents, whatever their current situation, had almost certainly been socialized into a more disciplined practice; typically the parents of several children, they had obviously lived for a time in obedience to church teaching. Had they not been effectively abandoned by their church at precisely the moment when most in need of grace and spiritual counsel? For many laity caught in this unhappy situation, the experience was indeed one of abandonment. "Our two priests know us only slightly," as a young mother articulated the problem in 1957, when she had opted for contraceptive use after six births in close succession. "This is a huge parish and they are overworked. I would tell them our problem but I know their answer already."[29] Like other Catholics in her increasingly common situation, she apparently accepted her church's right to dictate marital morality, even if that morality failed to square with the realities of modern marriage. Catholics who practiced contraception prior to the early 1960s typically received the Eucharist infrequently—at Christmas and Easter, perhaps, or even once a year, in mute acknowledgment of their church's authority. At the same time, their isolated state more or less forced them to begin thinking about the relationship of conscience to authority and experience to the building of moral systems.

Those Catholics who remained obedient to the teaching proved ultimately more subversive. It was they who fueled the explosion of dissent that went public in the United States in the waning days of 1963, when lay-edited *Jubilee* magazine carried two lay-authored articles challenging the logic and even the morality of the Catholic position on contraception, which were seconded by an unprecedented outpouring of readers' letters.[30] Public dissenters like these were highly educated, as the zealous "core Catholics" of the day—those hitherto wholehearted champions of the teaching—tended overwhelmingly to be. They were primed for dissent as of 1963 by a number of recent developments, including the advent of the anovular pill, popular anxiety over global population growth, and the unexpectedly progressive drift of the Second Vatican Council, still sitting in Rome. They had also been primed for dissent, however unwittingly, by their church's new emphasis on a personalist theology of marriage. If generous sexual communion was essential to a truly Christian marriage, as numerous postwar couples had been taught by their church, how could one justify the sexual abstinence that the practice of rhythm required, not to mention the anxiety that rhythm's uncertainties lent to every sexual encounter? (One young father, a veteran of rhythm, memorably evoked the latter: "Marital union was accomplished in fear, apprehension and, on occasion, tears.")[31] Increasingly, even devout married couples seemed to believe that rhythm was too damaging a mode of family planning to be truly moral. If marital sex was akin to prayer, what sense did it make to ration it?

The explosion of lay dissent surprised nearly every priest, even those involved in family life ministry. Priests knew in a general way that birth control was a problem for a great many adult Catholics. But they did not usually grasp—not existentially, at least—the depths of guilt and fear and despair that the problem brought in its wake. ("I had a very real sense of something within me that was dark and dead, as though a great light had been switched off and I was a walking shell of a body," as a military wife characterized her psychological state during a postchildbirth bout of contraceptive use.)[32] Nor were most priests sufficiently informed about female physiology to understand why rhythm was frequently undependable, especially during perimenopause or the aftermath of birth. One confessor, according to a respondent to a CFM survey in 1965, was "quite surprised to hear" that a nursing mother did not normally menstruate, the practice of rhythm being impossible in the absence of a menstrual cycle.[33] Once the laity began to speak publicly on the subject of contraception and hitherto docile penitents began to talk back, a good many priests were brought up short—sympathetic to the penitent's plight, in a growing number of cases, but suddenly without an authoritative response. It was exceedingly hard to invoke the church's teaching authority when an otherwise well-disposed penitent was challenging the very morality of the teaching in question.

Confessors responded as they had been trained to do—humanely, for the most part, but in terms of a highly legalistic system. Many expressed genuine sympathy for their troubled penitents. "I used to feel so sorry for some of those people who'd come in," as Monsignor Vincent Howard remembers it, regretting "the tension" he had of necessity to "force" into their lives. "What right do we have to do that?"[34] Most were willing to grant absolution after only the most minimal promises about amendment of life. Even penitents who fell repeatedly into the same sin evinced genuine contrition simply by coming to confession, or so many priests believed. Save in exceptional circumstances, the priest should always presume in favor of the penitent. In the words of an Irish moralist, writing in 1950 for an American priests' magazine: "The confessor can never be sure that there is no likelihood of future amendment. He may rather hope that the grace of absolution will enable the sinner at least to lessen the number of his falls, and that the grace of repeated absolutions, if he comes to confession regularly, will gradually win him entirely from the error of his ways."[35]

A confessor's kindness, however, could not dissolve the strictures of the system. Contraception was always a mortal sin, regardless of a penitent's motives or circumstances. "You were forced to confront people with an absolute," in the words of Monsignor William Sherzer, and this could be "terribly painful."[36] No matter how modest a confessor's demands when it came to a purpose of amendment, the penitent had to acknowledge his conduct as gravely sinful. The most devout laity, of the sort that peopled groups like CFM, had once regarded the teaching as hard but morally admirable—a noble embodiment of antimaterialism and a source of spiritual discipline. Many equally devout Catholics by the mid-1960s were inclined to regard it as a cause of moral mischief. "Cannot one sin by *having* a child," in the telling words of a father of five—a child for whom the parents were not physically, emotionally, or financially prepared?[37] Was it not gravely wrong to risk one's marriage in dogged obedience to a teaching that no longer made moral sense? Even feminist logic put in an appearance, at least among the college-educated young. Was it right to consign every married woman to a life wholly centered on childbearing, no matter what her talents and aspirations?[38]

The advent of "the pill"—first marketed in the United States in 1960— simply complicated matters. Oral contraceptives raised potential difficulties for the standard Catholic argument against contraception, which turned on the deordination of a natural act by means of artificial barriers or the act's lack of completeness. Neither factor was relevant, strictly speaking, to the pill. In consequence, as John T. Noonan has noted, "the pill became the center and symbol of efforts to modify the Catholic position on birth control."[39] Given various papal statements seeming to condemn the pill, the theologian-modifiers necessarily had to work circuitously. Might the pill not be taken for a time—six to nine months was typically suggested—to regularize a woman's menstrual cycle, so that she might practice rhythm successfully? A sufficient number of moral theologians had endorsed the idea by 1963 that a confessor could feel justified in espousing it.[40] Might the same logic not apply to the years preceding menopause, when the menstrual cycle often became irregular? Father Bernard Haring, a widely known and well-respected theologian, was arguing by 1964 that a premenopausal woman might take the pill for such regularizing purposes for a period of four to six months; "after that they should then try the use of rhythm."[41] Even use of the pill during lactation, initially regarded by nearly all theologians as overtly contraceptive and hence forbidden, had come by 1965 to be widely regarded as licit. Chicago's newly ordained priests were told that women might use the pill for nine months after childbirth, regardless of whether they intended to breastfeed their infants.[42] Developments like these helped to liberate confessors, providing an "out" in certain hard cases, while making the teaching in general even harder to defend.

By the mid-1960s, then, the confessional was contested terrain. Very different advice was suddenly on offer. Some priests still required a firm purpose of amendment when penitents confessed to birth control. Many more simply absolved their contracepting penitents without comment, a practice decried by the Jesuit moralist John Ford as "guilty connivance with the sin of contraception."[43] Some confessors made generous and creative use of the various therapeutic exceptions theologians had come up with for taking the pill. Others did not, either because they disapproved of such venturesome moral theology or simply did not know about it. None of these strategies, however, was necessarily effective with penitents who believed that the teaching was in error. Even if absolution were readily forthcoming, why was it necessary to brand as sinful something the penitent regarded as moral, at least in her circumstances? Then there were those many penitents, too scrupulous—or, as some would have it, too neurotic—to act independently on their convictions, who wanted a confessor's permission to take the pill for overtly contraceptive purposes. A great many priests, even those who had private doubts about the teaching, did not feel able to give such permission, particularly in those many instances where a bishop or superior had expressly forbidden it. It was more prudent and, often enough, the more principled stance to advise the penitent to consult her conscience, as was frequently also done with penitents who contested the teaching.

In the end, many penitents stopped mentioning birth control when they itemized their sins—the logical outcome of a "consult your conscience" strategy. Catholic contraceptive practice, in the meantime, accelerated rapidly. Some 53 percent of Catholic wives in their childbearing years were employing forbidden modes of contraception as of 1965, with the pill the most popular choice. The figure stood at 68 percent by 1970, with even higher numbers among the youngest cohort. It was reasonable to assume by then, as in fact came to pass, that Catholic contraceptive practice would eventually be indistinguishable from that of other Americans.[44] In the circumstances, it was probably a relief to most priests to have penitents decide the matter for themselves. But consider how passive a role this putative solution assigned to the clergy, hitherto accustomed to speak with authority on sexual matters above all else. If the laity, moreover, could make judgments in conscience with regard to birth control, what was to stop them from doing so in other matters? And if they did, what substance would remain to the priest's historic role, most fully realized in confession, as moral authority, guide, and judge?

Confessors first noticed a declining number of penitents in 1966, even as growing numbers were turning to the conscience solution for birth control.[45] Nearly all were surprised, perhaps especially those who believed that invoking conscience made confession a happier experience for all concerned. In retrospect, however, the diminishing numbers—which accelerated dramatically over the ensuing years—are anything but surprising. As the laity began to articulate their grievances over contraception, they were learning to speak—and for public consumption—the language of experience. In the Catholic and even the secular media, in living rooms and parish halls, husbands and wives gave voice with unprecedented frankness to the intimate side of marriage. Long bouts of marital abstinence were devastating to a marriage. ("Everyone is extremely nervous and quarrelsome and the children particularly have been damaged emotionally.")[46] The needs of very young children were inevitably neglected when the babies came too fast. ("The priest does not see a baby's buttocks bleeding from diaper rash; he does not see the baby who has its bottle 'propped.'")[47] The basal temperature system of rhythm, which required a woman to take her rectal temperature every morning before rising, was both "repulsive" and, for busy mothers, wholly impractical. ("It is our view that if the clergy took rectal temperatures that Catholic marrieds would not still be waiting for an answer on contraception.")[48]

The result was to privilege, for growing numbers of Catholics, the lived reality of human relationships as a critical factor in moral deliberation. Was contraception immoral? The answer depended on motives and circumstances—a conclusion that posed grave difficulties for confessors. Even the gentlest, given his celibacy, was at a disadvantage when it came to understanding the relevant particulars of his married penitents' lives, or so growing numbers of laity professed to believe. Nor was the sacrament itself, which typically involved a rapid-fire itemization of sins and a presumption that the priest alone was to judge the penitent's conduct, congenial to the dialogue required by this frankly psychologized approach to morality. When priests in the mid-1960s urged troubled penitents to follow their consciences, they could easily have been heard as conceding their own and even the sacrament's inadequacies. "Confession has become a styled ritual—stand—advance a few paces—enter the box—use only [the] socially determined amount of time for accusing one's self," responded a highly educated Catholic woman to a 1966 survey. "Exploring the conscience, or rather forming it, is a solitary experience—not for the confessional."[49]

Humanae Vitae had the ironic effect of further marginalizing the confessor. The encyclical was issued after several years of uninhibited debate among lay Catholics and unbridled speculation among moral theologians, many of whom believed as early as 1966 that the teaching on contraception was objectively doubtful. It was issued, moreover, after a papal commission, dominated in its final year by cardinals and archbishops, had recommended to the pope that the teaching be revised. "Social changes in matrimony and the family, especially in the role of the woman; lowering of the infant mortality rates; new bodies of knowledge in biology, psychology, sexuality and demography; a changed estimation of the value and meaning of human sexuality and of conjugal relations"—all these things, in the view of the commission's majority, mandated a less rigid and absolute approach to the problem of family limitation.[50] The commission's report, tendered privately to the pope in 1966, was made public in April 1967, when it was published—without papal permission—in the *National Catholic Reporter*. The effect, not surprisingly, was electric. In the words of a sharply observant Detroit priest, writing in 1967: "The pope is quickly being confronted with a de facto solution to birth control. I am quite sure, from conversations with many theologians and parish priests both, that a new consensus is rapidly forming which is contrary to the established teaching of the magisterium."[51]

For the many Catholics who were using contraceptives by 1968, *Humanae Vitae* meant a direct confrontation with church authority. Were Catholics free to reject a definitive statement by the pope in the realm of morality? Could individual conscience be legitimately invoked in such circumstances? For their confessors, it meant much less wiggle room, given that the teaching had been so vigorously reaffirmed. The encyclical was indeed remarkably pastoral in its rhetoric and orientation: confessors were exhorted to be gentle and encouraging even with recidivist penitents, who—assuming a right interior disposition—should not let their contraceptive lapses keep them from receiving the Eucharist. But by the summer of 1968, as nearly every confessor knew, a majority of the laity had already decided that marital contraception was not in most circumstances sinful. They were not about to change their minds or abandon the moral logic that had brought them to this conclusion. The effect of the encyclical in the United States was almost certainly to increase the numbers of Catholics who seldom or never went to confession. As early as 1969, knowledgeable observers were predicting the sacrament's collapse.

Abandoning frequent confession did not mean, for the great majority of Catholics, forgoing frequent communion. After the late 1960s, it was increasingly the norm for nearly everyone at Mass to receive the Eucharist, in stark contrast to the devotional habits of previous generations. Liturgical participation alone was apparently for most regularly practicing Catholics an emotionally satisfying source of forgiveness for sin, or so their behavior suggested. Few evinced much nostalgia for the weekly or monthly confessions that had until recently been integral to their lives of faith. Whatever comfort it might have afforded, the sacrament of penance had typically been experienced as burdensome—a necessary dose of spiritual medicine, but medicine all the same. That is why it took so long for significant numbers of the laity to have become habituated to frequent confession in the first place. An increasingly educated laity in the later 1960s embraced their morally autonomous status with genuine enthusiasm, speaking of themselves—in the period's hyperbolic parlance—as the first truly mature Catholics. Staying away from confession, indeed, became for some an ironic badge of Christian authenticity. They do not seem to have worried that their newfound autonomy would erode their connections to the institutional church or diminish their Catholic identity. "Against the current, if necessary, accepting the risks inherent in responsible choice, morally serious, the theonomous Catholic tastes the joy of the free man," as Michael Novak articulated the ethos in 1967, with explicit reference to individual decision making about contraception.[52]

Many committed adult Catholics in the wake of *Humanae Vitae* continued to attend church regularly; reasonably well educated in the Catholic tradition, theirs continued to be distinctively Catholic moral imaginations. But by the later 1960s, Mass attendance in the United States had begun what proved to be a steady downward plunge, with young Catholics the group most dramatically affected. (Roughly 37 percent of American Catholics today claim to attend Mass weekly, compared to 75 percent in the mid-1950s.)[53] Catholics born since the council seem increasingly ignorant of their tradition and increasingly detached from it. A recent national study "found that U.S. Catholic teenagers are *behind* their Protestant peers—sometimes by as much as 25 percentage points—when measured by many standards of religious belief, practice, experiences, and commitments," in the words of the Jesuit sociologist Thomas Rausch, who saw the results as congruent with his own long experience of Catholic college students.[54] The great majority of young Catholics have had to confront the sexual upheavals of recent decades with very little protection from the culture's ethic of expressive individualism. No wonder so many of them today regard the church as marginal to their moral decision making, as several recently published studies have made distressingly evident.[55]

For priests, the rapid erosion of confession caused more immediate problems. Hearing large numbers of confessions had in some respects been a burden. But hearing confessions affirmed for priests both their status as moral authorities and their intimate connection to the faithful. The rapid diminishment of this role was very bad for morale. With confession in decline, what good was the priest's prodigious learning in moral theology—his preparation to be both judge and doctor of souls? Where did he fit in a world of seemingly omnicompetent secular professionals—the psychiatrists, social workers, and marriage counselors whom more and more Catholics now consulted rather than their clergy? Given the large size of most Catholic parishes, moreover, it was probably true, as a Jesuit claimed in 1965, that for most Catholics "confession is the only personal contact with a priest."[56] In the context of a rapidly escalating priest shortage, there was not much chance of replicating this contact in other venues. "Is confession, as some supposedly knowledgeable theologians predict, on the way out?" asked a young priest from Syracuse in 1968. "If so, where do I fit in as a priest? How am I valuable to people?"[57] Unprecedented numbers were leaving the active priesthood by 1968; some 10 percent of American priests are estimated to have done so between 1966 and 1971.[58] One can hardly imagine more dangerous circumstances in which to be prey to such anxieties.

The collapse of confession obviously points toward a larger problem. After *Humanae Vitae*, an enormous gulf opened up between official church teaching in the realm of sex and the thinking of the faithful. The clergy, to all appearances, have responded to this uncomfortable reality by simply ceasing to talk about it. Birth control provided the template: by early 1969, following an intense flurry of dissent over the encyclical, public silence prevailed in Catholic circles on the topic of contraception. Moral theologians were clearly bored by it and increasingly preoccupied with other issues, including abortion, divorce and remarriage, and—with initially greater tentativeness—homosexuality. The many priests who disagreed with the encyclical were seldom eager to make that disagreement public, out of concern for their relations with ecclesial superiors. (Private counsel was another matter, but the laity after *Humanae Vitae* were less and less likely to consult even sympathetic priests about contraception.)[59] Those bishops and priests who admired the encyclical tended toward public silence, too, reluctant to antagonize a laity whose contraceptive practice more and more resembled the American norm. Even publicly funded birth control programs failed to draw the bishops' collective ire after 1968.[60]

On the fifth anniversary of *Humanae Vitae*, the late theologian Richard McCormick called on the American bishops "to stimulate and support" a communal conversation on the dissent that had greeted the encyclical. Why had that dissent occurred? What meaning did it have for Catholics' collective understanding of the church's teaching authority? Should the bishops choose to maintain their silence, largely unbroken since 1968, the effect—in McCormick's view—would almost certainly be "to seriously compromise the credibility of the teaching office of the Church in the long run."[61] McCormick recognized, as did legions of his fellow priests, that silence on contraception meant refusing to speak honestly about sex in terms that most laity could respect and understand. He knew how unhealthy that silence was in the context of an already demoralized priesthood and a seemingly anarchic sexual revolution.

The public conversation McCormick called for never took place. And the consequences have been precisely those that McCormick predicted. A plurality even of older Catholics today regard the individual as the proper locus of moral decision making when it comes to sex, with somewhat smaller numbers opting for dialogue between church leaders and the faithful. (When it comes to contraception, a substantial majority sees no role at all for church leaders; the individual reigns supreme.) Large numbers of Catholics, in other words, do not regard their church's teaching as binding—or even, necessarily, terribly relevant—when it comes to nonmarital sex, remarriage after divorce, homosexuality, or abortion, which the American bishops have called the most important moral issue facing American Catholics today. What better evidence could there be of a seriously compromised teaching office? We can also see in these numbers why the sacrament of penance continues to be marginal to the lives of a great many laity, particularly since women—historically the more devout sex—have emerged in the polls as more likely than men to champion independent moral deliberation.[62]

The pattern that has prevailed since the late 1960s—silence on sexual subjects generally, punctuated on occasion by what Gerard Sloyan has aptly called "prohibitions without explanation"[63]—stands in poignant contrast to the heated debates of the mid-1960s. (Let me acknowledge parenthetically that the bishops have indeed been vocal on the subject of abortion, which transcends sex; their limited success with even Catholic audiences, however, reflects a larger impasse over sexual morality.) For a brief few years, from 1964 until mid-1968, Catholic married couples spoke with remarkable candor and a surprising theological literacy about their experience of marriage. Their testimony had profound impact on many parish priests, as well as a number of theologians. The late Richard McCormick, for example, had initially been attracted to what later came to be known as the theology of the body, in which the evil of contraception is said to lie in its falsifying the physical language of love.[64] It was the testimony of married couples that ultimately changed his mind. The theology of the body, he told me some years ago, was too abstract—oddly enough, too disembodied—to address the complexities of human sexuality.[65] A genuine personalism, as he wrote in 1989, "commits us to an inductive method in moral deliberation about rightness and wrongness in which human experience and the sciences play an indispensable role."[66]

The silence McCormick rightly deplored is rooted in part in church structures. Once the pope had spoken, dissent became risky. Only those who supported the teaching on contraception—or those, at least, with no public record of dissent—were made bishops during the latter days of Pope Paul's pontificate and that of John Paul II.[67] (The late Kenneth Untener was a notable exception, but it took a trip to Rome by Detroit's Cardinal John Dearden to ensure that Untener's appointment went through.) Nor does the church possess an institutionalized means by which the laity might contribute to the development of teaching on marriage and family life. But this silence is also rooted in the defensiveness—should we call it lack of courage?—that characterizes too much of the church's leadership today. Church authority, our leaders seem to believe, is credible only if one can point to a history of changeless teaching. One must at all costs maintain the fiction, which everyone knows it to be, that the teaching church is never wrong. Such a posture has doubtless reinforced the clericalism that lies at the heart of the sex abuse scandals to which the church has recently been prey, although here, too, dishonesty about sex—which is what silence aids and abets—is also to blame.

There were certainly pastoral reasons in the 1960s to worry about the effects on the faithful of a change in church teaching on birth control. Countless couples had suffered in the teaching's service. A male correspondent to *Jubilee* magazine predicted, not entirely tongue-in-cheek, in 1964 that a change would result in "a March on Rome by millions of men, who[,] having been rejected by their wives, live lives of continence in close proximity to the opposite sex."[68] (Women marchers would presumably have had their own bill of particulars.) Could a church that had erroneously demanded such sacrifices of its people ever again be trusted, especially since the Protestant churches had apparently gotten it right? "If the Church can have erred so egregiously," said the eminent moral theologian John Ford, "then the faithful can no longer believe in her teaching authority."[69] That his argument was rejected by the ecclesiastical members of the papal birth control commission to whom it was addressed does not mean that it lacked substance.

Authority, however, can be undermined in multiple ways. Refusing to engage in honest dialogue, keeping silent when social developments cry out for a wise and nuanced response—such things condemn an institution to irrelevance. Irrelevant institutions, by definition, lack authority. When it comes to sex, I very much fear, the Catholic Church has drifted into irrelevance with near-disastrous consequences. The hopes of the 1960s had to do with more than a change in the teaching on contraception; they centered on the fuller development of what had already emerged as a rich and positive theology of marriage, a theology to which sex was integral but of which it was only a part. At what time in our history have lay Catholics been in greater need of such theological development than the decades since the council? What greater service could the church have performed for those numerous societies, including our own, where marriage is a rapidly eroding institution? Not that innovative theological development with regard to marriage would have solved all problems, most notably those posed by homosexuality and, given demographic realities, premarital sex. Nor would Catholics, in all likelihood, have been spared rising rates of divorce, although such are not beyond the influence of church or synagogue. Still less would Catholics have continued to confess at the rates of the 1950s, for—at least in its preconciliar form—the sacrament has clearly ceased for most Catholics to be an adequate means of spiritual discipline and moral growth. (Would the revised rite of penance have fared better, one wonders, had the postconciliar laity been less alienated?) But the church would surely have earned the respect of a great many Catholics and a voice in our national conversation about the purposes of sex and marriage. Even the young, who clearly hunger for greater stability in marriage than their society appears to support, might have heard that voice and found it worth listening to.

NOTES

1. Joseph Fichter's study of Mater Dolorosa parish in New Orleans in the late 1940s found that 80 percent of parishioners confessed at least once a year, although New Orleans had a cultural heritage of relatively lax Catholic practice, at least by American standards. A National Opinion Research Survey in 1963 found 18 percent of respondents going to confession "practically never" or "not at all." See Joseph H. Fichter, S.J., *Dynamics of a City Church* (Chicago: University of Chicago Press, 1951), 54–55; Andrew M. Greeley, *The American Catholic: A Social Portrait* (New York: Basic Books, 1977), 127.

2. James D. Davidson, *Catholics in Motion: The Church in American Society* (Liguori, MO: Liguori, 2005), 154–155.

3. The definitive account in this regard—at least until the same author publishes his book-length study—is James M. O'Toole, "In the Court of Conscience: American Catholics and Confession, 1900–1975," in *Habits of Devotion: Catholic Religious Practice in Twentieth-Century America*, ed. James M. O'Toole (Ithaca, NY: Cornell University Press, 2004), 131–185. Much of what follows is based on O'Toole's masterful essay, although it is also based on my own research over the past twenty years.

4. Leslie Woodcock Tentler, *Catholics and Contraception: An American History* (Ithaca, NY: Cornell University Press, 2004).

5. My research was carried out in the Archives of the Archdiocese of Detroit; James O'Toole found similar reports in the Archives of the Archdiocese of Milwaukee.

6. Pastors seem typically to have excused themselves from long hours in "the box," except during periods of unusually high demand.

7. Joseph Schuyler, S.J., *Northern Parish: A Sociological and Pastoral Study* (Chicago: Loyola University Press, 1960), 190.

8. Joseph Fichter, S.J., *Priest and People* (New York: Sheed and Ward, 1965), 186.

9. Author interview with Father Kevin O'Brien, April 28, 1999, in Farmington, MI. O'Brien was ordained in 1954.

10. Author interview with Father Ferdinand DeCneudt, October 19, 1998, in Roseville, MI. DeCneudt was born in Belgium; his family emigrated to Detroit in 1920.

11. Quoted in John T. Noonan, *Contraception: A History of Its Treatment by the Catholic Theologians and Canonists*, rev. ed. (Cambridge, MA: Harvard University Press, 1986), 427, 431. Noonan's is a masterful analysis of the encyclical and the circumstances surrounding its genesis.

12. See, for example, Arnaldo Cortesi, "Pope Pius XI, in Encyclical, Condemns Trial Marriage, Divorce, and Birth Control," *New York Times*, January 9, 1931, and especially the editorial "Roma Dixit" in the next day's edition, January 10, 1931. Like a number of other U.S. papers, the *Times* reprinted the full text of *Casti Connubii*.

13. Tentler, *Catholics and Contraception*, 31–32.

14. Ibid., 23–29, 57–60.

15. Ibid., 38–40, 58.

16. Ibid., 32–37.

17. Ibid., 16–19, 27–28, 43–44, 79. The textbook in question was John A. McHugh, O.P., and Charles J. Callan, O.P., *Moral Theology: A Complete Course*, vol. 2 (New York: Joseph F. Wagner, 1930).

18. Tentler, *Catholics and Contraception*, 81–85.

19. Ibid., 86–93. The quoted words, common to many period documents, come from a sermon by the Redemptorist Alfred Menth and a pamphlet by the Jesuit Jones I. Corrigan. Both date from the early 1930s.

20. Ibid., 100–103.

21. Ibid., 122–127.

22. Joseph Reiner, S.J., to Wilfrid Parsons, S.J., March 2, 1933. Georgetown University Library Special Collections, Wilfrid Parsons papers, box 8, folder 12.

23. Tentler, *Catholics and Contraception*, 104–111. Father John A. O'Brien's *Legitimate Birth Control* carried an imprimatur by Fort Wayne's Bishop John Francis Noll.

24. Tentler, *Catholics and Contraception*, 119–121.

25. Ibid, 192–196.

26. Norman B. Ryder and Charles F. Westoff, *Reproduction in the United States: 1965* (Princeton, NJ: Princeton University Press, 1971), 86.

27. George A. Kelly, "Catholics and the Practice of the Faith" (PhD Dissertation, School of Social Science, Catholic University of America, 1946), 58–59, 61–63; Joseph H. Fichter, S.J., *Social Relations in the Urban Parish* (Chicago: University of Chicago Press, 1954), 83, 87–88; Schuyler, *Northern Parish*, 218–220.

28. Author interview with Msgr. William Sherzer, October 18, 1998, in Ann Arbor, MI. Sherzer was ordained in 1945.

29. N.N. to the editor, *Liguorian* (October 1957), 29.

30. *Jubilee* 11 (December 1963) carried articles by Bruce Cooper and Rosemary Radford Ruether. Readers' letters appeared in subsequent issues.

31. William G. Keane to the editor, *Commonweal* 79 (March 20, 1964), 752.

32. Mrs. K. B. Lake to the editor, *Jubilee*, December 11, 1963. Georgetown University Library Special Collections, Ed Rice papers, box 4, folder 55.

33. Letter, signature deleted, to Pat and Parry Crowley, undated but ca. 1965. Archives of the University of Notre Dame, Crowley papers—SPCBPC, box 15, folder 11.

34. Author interview with Msgr. Vincent Howard, October 27, 1998, in Chelsea, MI. Howard was ordained in 1947.

35. J. McCarthy, "The Recidivist," *Priest* 6 (May 1950): 352.

36. Sherzer interview.

37. Michael Novak, ed., *The Experience of Marriage* (New York: Macmillan, 1964), 160. All contributors to the Novak anthology were anonymous.

38. See, for example, Anne Martin, "Time to Grow in Love," in *What Modern Catholics Think of Birth Control*, ed. William Birmingham (New York: Signet, 1964), 198.

39. Noonan, *Contraception*, 472.

40. Tentler, *Catholics and Contraception*, 240–241.

41. Fr. Bernard Haring, C.Ss.R., "Questions and Answers," in *The Priest: Teacher of Morality* (Detroit, MI: Midwestern Institute of Pastoral Theology, 1965), 145.

42. Joseph T. Mangan, "Questions on 'The Pill' and the Practice of Artificial Birth Control," *Chicago Studies* 5 (Summer 1966): 198–199. This article reprints the "norms for confessors" given to newly ordained priests in April 1966.

43. John C. Ford, S.J., "Commentary on 'The Projected "Pastoral Instruction,"'" undated but 1965. Archives of the New England Province of the Society of Jesus, John C. Ford, S.J., papers, box 8 [preliminary cataloguing].

44. Charles F. Westoff and Larry Bumpass, "The Revolution in Birth Control Practices of U.S. Roman Catholics," *Science* 179 (January 5, 1973): 41–42.

45. Tentler, *Catholics and Contraception*, 244–246.

46. "Mother of Six, Arizona" to the editor, *Jubilee* 12 (June 1964): 26.

47. "Mother of Six, East Coast" to the editor, *Jubilee* 12 (June 1964): 23.

48. Written on questionnaire form, undated but ca. 1965. Archives of the University of Notre Dame. Patty Crowley papers (SPCBPC), box 3, folder 2.

49. Sally Cunneen, *Sex: Female, Religion: Catholic* (New York: Holt, Rinehart and Winston, 1968), 62.

50. Quoted in Robert McClory, *Turning Point* (New York: Crossroad, 1995), 113.

51. Msgr. William J. Sherzer to Msgr. Arthur Valada, January 21, 1967. Archives of the Diocese of Lansing, MI, Alexander Zaleski papers, folder: "NCCB Committee on Doctrine: Bishops' Response to Cardinal Ottaviani's Letter, 1967."

52. "Adult Obedience," in *A Time to Build*, ed. Michael Novak (New York: Macmillan, 1967), 158. The article originally appeared in a 1967 issue of *Marriage*.

53. Andrew Greeley attributes the decline, which accelerated sharply after 1968, primarily to *Humanae Vitae*. See Andrew M. Greeley, *The American Catholic: A Social Portrait* (New York: Basic Books, 1977), chapter 7.

54. Thomas P. Rausch, *Being Catholic in a Culture of Choice* (Collegeville, MN: Liturgical, 2006), 5, 17. The study referred to was published in 2005; it utilized a nationwide sample of American youth age 15 to 17. See Christian Smith and Melinda

Lundquist Denton, *Soul Searching: The Religious and Spiritual Lives of American Teenagers* (New York: Oxford University Press, 2005).

55. William V. D'Antonio, James D. Davidson, Dean R. Hoge, and Mary L. Gautier, *American Catholics Today: New Realities of Their Faith and Their Church* (Lanham, MD: Rowman & Littlefield, 2007), 98–101; see also William V. D'Antonio, *American Catholics: Gender, Generation, and Commitment* (Walnut Creek, CA: Altamira Press, 2001), 77–80.

56. Lawrence A. Castagnola, S.J., "Wanted: Confessors with Time," *Pastoral Life* 13 (December 1965): 687.

57. Joseph Champlin, "Sex and Confession," part one, *Pastoral Life* 16 (May 1968): 272.

58. "A Report on the Condition of Priestly Ministry and Celibacy in the United States Made to the Canon Law Society of America," no author or date, but 1971. It was evidently the product of a symposium on mandatory celibacy held at Cathedral College, Douglaston, NY, August 19–22, 1971. Archives of the University of Notre Dame. Association of Chicago Priests papers [CACP], box 2, folder 15.

59. "Catholic Parish Priests and Birth Control: A Comparative Study of Opinion in Colombia, the United States, and the Netherlands," in *Studies in Family Planning* (New York: Population Council, 1971). No author listed, although the various research collaborators are listed in the introduction.

60. Tentler, *Catholics and Contraception*, 257–260.

61. Richard McCormick, S.J., "The Silence since *Humanae Vitae*," *America* 129 (July 21, 1973).

62. D'Antonio et al, *American Catholics Today*, 77.

63. Gerard Sloyan, *Catholic Morality Revisited: Origins and Contemporary Challenges* (Mystic, CT: Twenty-Third, 1990), 100.

64. For an early example of the genre, see Paul M. Quay, S.J., "Contraception and Conjugal Love," *Theological Studies* 22 (March 1961): 18–40.

65. Author interview with Richard McCormick, S.J., November 12, 1998, at the University of Notre Dame.

66. Richard McCormick, "Moral Theology: 1940–1989: An Overview," *Theological Studies* 50 (March 1989): 16.

67. Richard A. McCormick, S.J., "'Humanae Vitae' 25 Years Later," *America* 169 (July 17, 1993): 8; Avery Dulles, S.J., "'Humanae Vitae' and the Crisis of Dissent," *Origins* 22 (April 1993): 775.

68. "Physician, father of six, New Orleans," to the editor, *Jubilee*, January 10, 1964. Typescript of original in Ed Rice papers, Georgetown University Library Special Collections, box 4, folder 55.

69. John C. Ford, S.J., "Statement of Position," May 25, 1966. John C. Ford papers, Archives of the New England Province of the Society of Jesus, box 9 [preliminary cataloguing]. The statement was delivered orally at a meeting of the Pontifical Commission for the Study of Population, Family and Births, popularly known as the "birth control commission."

12

Assessing the Education of Priests and Lay Ministers

Content and Consequences

Katarina Schuth

Introduction

As new generations of priests assume their responsibilities, the approaches they employ in the exercise of ministry become unmistakable signposts to the future direction of the church. Clerical leadership is singular in its power to shape the life of the Christian community, and so in the parish it is the pastor who has the most immediate authority and control. Lay ministers and parishioners undeniably contribute their insights and views, but their influence on parochial life is restricted without the approbation of the pastor. Thus the formation of men in seminaries and schools of theology[1] is a major determinant of whether, as future priests, they will be effective in their leadership roles, collaborative in their approach, and able to bring faith alive in parishes, schools, chaplaincies, and other ministry situations.

Some seminarians who become priests seem to have a natural talent for entering into and enlivening the spirit of the communities to which they are assigned. They make an effort to understand the aspirations and challenges, the needs and gifts of the people they encounter. As evangelizers, they read the signs of the times, taking into account the background and context of the parishes they serve. They become familiar with the experiences of joys and sufferings and the unique ministerial requirements of individuals, families, and groups. As leaders and catalysts, they exercise their authority by drawing all together to form vibrant communities where the members are respected, their minds are enlightened, and their spirits nourished. With this firm foundation and with the support of their communities, parishioners are encouraged to express their faith by extending their religious commitment in service to the broader community.

Priests who are able to generate such enthusiasm and cooperation are often said to be expressing the servant-leader model of priesthood. This form of leadership requires collaboration with laity, especially with lay ministers, and therefore is perceived by critics as blurring the identity of the priest and thus diluting his authority. Priests who are in their forties and older usually describe their ministry in these terms. Younger priests and seminarians are more likely to see themselves as separate and ontologically different from the laity and often are reluctant to embrace this approach to ministry. They are regarded as expressing the cultic model, which is identified with an earlier understanding of priesthood. This model has resurfaced since the 1980s and represents an approach supported by many in the hierarchy. Thus one of the ecclesial dilemmas the church currently faces is the disparagement of the servant-leader model by new generations of priests precisely at a time when the number of priests is declining and meaningful collaboration with the laity is indispensable.

The newly ordained cultic-model priests who have begun serving as pastors in recent years often come to the position with strong ideological preferences that may or may not match those of the community they are called to serve. They are well intentioned and pious and usually can fit in easily and work successfully if the staff and parishioners are like-minded. Frequently, more experienced pastors have difficulty working with these men since they seem to have little interest in the customs of the local parish or the concerns of parishioners. Rather, they understand themselves as bearers of the true interpretation of the doctrines of the faith and sole guardians of proper ministerial practice, especially as it pertains to liturgical expressions. They come ready to impose their own particular spirituality and worship style on the existing community. Since so many bishops are serving as ordinaries far from their home dioceses, the seminaries they choose for their seminarians are often near the bishop's former diocese rather than that of the seminarians. Practices and approaches to ministry in those schools may be quite incompatible with the dioceses where the seminarians will eventually serve as pastors. The newly ordained may not even be aware of the incongruity between their beliefs, practices, and attitudes and those of their parishioners. In these situations, reports circulate of disheartened and dispirited parishioners who too often feel they must flee their home parish because it begins to feel like an alien land to them under the authoritative power of these priests.

But has it not always been the case that the newly ordained came to ministry with similar dispositions and outlooks, whether of more liberal leanings in the 1970s or more conservative leanings since the 1990s? Perhaps, but circumstances have changed. In the past, these young priests usually served long apprenticeships and therefore were formed by seasoned pastors in parishes that were more stable. The pastor had several years to initiate the new priest into ministry and help him understand the requirements of pastoral life. At best, the mentor-pastor taught the apprentice by his example of prudence and patience. In the process, this experience would temper the new priest's idealism and, if necessary, his insensitivity toward parishioners. Absent was the inexperienced priest in charge of the parish who could change the customs and traditions of a long-established parish overnight as he came fresh from the seminary with little understanding of or attachment to the community. The situation is usually different today. In most dioceses, newly ordained priests become pastors within three years or less. Thus theologates carry heightened responsibility for preparing men to be effective pastoral leaders immediately after ordination.

Given the significant role theologates play in orienting future priests to appropriate ministry, this chapter will analyze the status of theologates engaged in this task. It addresses concerns arising from the changing characteristics of those who are assuming pastoral leadership, whose views of church sometimes stand in contrast to the ecclesiological understandings and dispositions of many Catholics today. It begins with an overview of the background and context of church ministry. Then it examines theologate-level education and its implications for the church, taking into account the number and types of theologates and how these institutions have changed, especially over the past two decades. It makes note of the growing differences between diocesan and religious order schools and the introduction of lay students to ministerial education in theologates. Using the same time frame, it considers the faculty, students, and all aspects of formation, including human and spiritual, intellectual and pastoral.

The final focus of the essay is to evaluate how well priests and lay ministers are meeting the challenges of ministry in the church as it exists today. Toward that end, it is important to consider the places of convergence and divergence between those who constitute the Catholic population and those who minister to them. Changes in the characteristics of students, both seminarians and lay, highlight the tensions surfacing in ministry settings as new priests take their places beside pastors with a radically different theology of priesthood and with dissimilar ecclesiologies. The conclusion offers some suggestions to enhance the multiple relationships that are part of ministry today. It recommends some adaptations in the education of future priests and lay ministers so that they can reconcile their understanding of what is involved in being Catholic in the twenty-first century with those of the people they propose to serve. The chapter concludes with suggestions for fruitful engagement on the part of all who constitute the church today. To reduce tensions and polarities and resolve ecclesial dilemmas, several tasks must be undertaken.

Background and Context of Church Ministry in the United States

The narrative is familiar. Since Vatican II, the number of Catholics in the United States has grown rapidly, from 46.9 million in 1967 to 68.1 million in 2009.[2] On average, some 500,000 Catholics were added to parish rosters each year almost without fail.[3] Four major changes affecting church ministry, among many others, have come about as a result of the tremendous growth in the number of Catholics and the parallel decline in the number of priests, sisters, and brothers: church membership is more diverse, attitudes and values among church members are equally diverse and in flux, those who minister represent different vocations than in the past, and the sizes and structures of parishes have shifted. A fundamental question is whether the church will be able to provide ministerial leaders who can meet the needs of contemporary Catholics represented in this portrait of membership.

Evolving Church Membership

In addition to the dramatic increase of 20 million, the composition of the Catholic population has shifted even more radically since the 1970s. Not only the universal church but also local dioceses and many individual parishes are marked by diversity that cuts across social and cultural categories. Racial and ethnic mix, places of origin, educational levels, and rural, urban, or suburban location are among them. These shifts in membership and context have over-whelmed many church leaders who were not fully anticipating the effects of the transformation. The steady stream of immigrants, especially from Latin America and Asia, has changed the face of many United States parishes. Studies indicate that in less than twenty years from now, more than half of Catholics in the United States will be other than European in background; already, 39 percent are Hispanic.

At the same time, the educational level of Catholics has increased to the highest of nearly any religious group. A third shift comes in the form of an outflow from rural to suburban parishes and, to a lesser extent, urban parishes. The movement has left much of rural America depleted of population and suburbs burgeoning with new inhabitants in need of church leaders and structures. The small Catholic parishes that once dotted the landscape are decreasing in number as parishioners age and retire. Fewer farmers own more land, and consequently their numbers and the communities supporting them are shrinking. In a recent interview, a priest in a rural diocese exclaimed, "This is the death of rural America and along with it the diminishment of the rural church." Moreover, regional population movements from North and Midwest to South and West have further unsettled the situation, as personnel, facilities, and other resources are in short supply in parts of the country where the Catholic population is growing. Catholics are on the move.

Changing Attitudes of Catholics

What is more, like their Protestant neighbors, Catholics hold more sharply differing opinions than ever on critical social and moral questions, such as those pertaining to beginning- and end-of-life issues, immigration, and the death penalty. They identify with church authority on these matters to varying degrees, some fully accepting the guiding force of church teachings and others taking decisions into their own hands. Differing liturgical and devotional preferences also divide parishes, especially as newly ordained priests enter ministry with an ecclesiology less influenced by Vatican II. Often these variations are linked to generational differences and sometimes to gender. These layers of complexity mark and sometimes polarize the Catholic population, thus expanding the range of ministerial services priests and others in ministry must provide.

 Attitudinal disparity is especially sharp among generations. Using Vatican II as the marker, the adult Catholic population can be divided into four groups (see table 12.1, left-hand columns), each carrying distinctive traits.[4] Pre–Vatican II members are now older than 65 and comprise 17 percent of the population, down 14 percent from 20 years ago; Vatican II members are between about 45 and 65 and comprise 35 percent of Catholics, down 12 percent from 20 years ago; post–Vatican II members are between about 27 and 44 and comprise 40 percent, up 9 percent from 20 years ago; and millennials are between 18 and 26 and comprise 9 percent of adult Catholics, none of whom were adults 20 years ago and some not yet born. Catholics have shifted from 78 percent adults at the time of Vatican II to about 52 percent now. Those who experienced the aftermath of Vatican II as young children are now 40 percent of the Catholic population, and the millennial generation is 9 percent, which means Catholics are split virtually in half relative to their experience and understanding of Vatican II. Given such divergent experiences of church, the importance of being Catholic

TABLE 12.1. Strength of Catholic Identity by Generation, 2005

	Generational %		Strength of Identity		
	1987	2005	Low %	Medium %	High %
Pre–Vatican II	31	17	22	45	33
Vatican II	47	35	31	44	25
Post–Vatican II	22	40	27	50	24
Millennials	0	9	47	46	7
Total Catholics	100	100	29	46	24

and what it means to be identified as a Catholic vary considerably among the four groups.

The consequences of this split are enormous for parish life because of the conflicting experiences of Catholics on either side of Vatican II, those who were adults in 1965 and those who were children or not yet born at that time. An important element to examine is the strength of Catholic identity of each group (see table 12.1, right-hand columns), as measured by level of agreement with statements such as "Being Catholic is a very important part of who you are," "It is important to you that younger generations of your family grow up as Catholics," and "You can't imagine yourself being anything but Catholic."[5] Older generations are much more highly identified, according to these self-descriptions. The most startling finding is the extremely low 7 percent of the youngest generation who strongly identify themselves as Catholic. Much of this decline in identification with the church is often attributed to the crisis in catechesis over the past four decades.

The dilemmas and divides created by various commitments continue to affect Catholic practice and are vital to understanding what might be the future of the church. Considering the four groups, it is evident that each has enormously different experiences of church and society. Though it is not possible to detail the gaps and incongruities between generations, one key factor deserves mention: the difference in identification with and participation in a secular culture that had moved away from religious ideals. Pre–Vatican II Catholics were largely outside the mainstream and viewed the values of society with skepticism and disapproval. The Vatican II generation moved from holding a negative view of a modern society that seemed hostile to the Catholic faith to a more positive view, seeing the whole world as part of God's creation. Post–Vatican II Catholics gradually blended in and became more comfortable with social structures, while millennial Catholics in some respects seem born into and firmly embedded in the culture. Yet the representation is not so simple. Especially during the last twenty years, the influx of new immigrants has further complicated the picture. Young immigrant generations are infused with values they have carried from another culture rather than fitting neatly into their own age bracket of Americans. On issues of immigration, abortion, war, taxes, the death penalty, health care, the role of women, the conservative resurgence, the role of technology—for many reasons, Catholics hold divergent views, making ministering to them a major challenge. The authority of the church, represented in the person of local pastors, carries considerably less influence than in previous decades when Catholics consider these issues.

Shifting Vocational Status of Church Ministers

At the same time the Catholic population has been growing in size and becoming more diverse in composition, vocations to the priesthood and religious life have spiraled sharply downward. The loss of priests has had the most immediate impact on parish structures and sizes, with a decrease of 18,403 since 1967—from almost 60,000 to 41,489 in 2009. Both diocesan and religious order priests have experienced loss, but religious at a higher rate. In sheer numbers, the decline in women religious is even more drastic with almost 116,000 fewer sisters than the 177,000 of 1967. Furthermore, the average age of the remaining 60,715 is nearly seventy. Those who joined communities in the late 1950s and early 1960s never would have anticipated that in their sixties they would be among the younger members of their congregations. Brothers have fared no better, with about 5,000 remaining compared with 12,500 in 1967. Taken together, the number of priests and vowed religious has declined by 142,000 in forty years and stands now at 107,000. Necessarily, the church depends today on a very different set of people to provide ministry for its large and diverse population.

Steadily declining ordination numbers are indicators of the diminishing situation. In recent years, about half as many men have been ordained as forty years ago; for example, 994 men were ordained in 1965 and 438 in 2006, representing a modern low in number ordained; in 2009, a total of 482 were ordained. The decline has been gradual, with 771 ordained in 1975 and 533 in 1985, equaling a drop of more than 200 ordinations per decade. Since then, the decline has not been as steep, though the figures vary considerably from year to year. By considering three-year averages, the trends can be more accurately identified: from 1990 to 1992, the average number was 708, up from 1985 by almost 200, but the increase was not sustained. From 1993 to 1995, the number went down to 587 and since then has leveled off just short of 500. The decrease naturally contributes to the overall decline in the number of priests, with only one man being ordained for every three who retire or leave the ministry.

The good news for the church is that even though the numbers of priests, sisters, and brothers diminished, deacons and lay ministers have stepped up to serve by the thousands. Following the action of Vatican II, the permanent diaconate was restored in 1970. By 1975, about 900 men in the United States had been ordained to this office. The numbers have risen rapidly in the three decades since then, with 13,348 ordained by 2001 and 16,935 by 2009. They now are serving in almost every diocese in the country. Making up for the loss in numbers of religious sisters and brothers are 167,861 lay teachers in Catholic schools and some 30,000 lay ecclesial ministers in other church service, including directors of religious education, youth and adult ministry, and liturgy, as well as pastoral administrators and business officers in parishes. Generosity comes in the form of a variety of vocational calls. Ministries have expanded to include many new forms as these more than 200,000 laypeople join the ranks of priests and religious working for the church in full-time ministry. Thousands of lay volunteers augment the numbers by providing countless hours of service. These changes require additional educational opportunities at all levels. Along with dioceses, colleges, and universities, theologates have played a major role in preparing people for ministry since the 1980s. The new vocational configuration requires adaptation and flexibility by all those involved in this pioneering effort.

Structural Changes

The new composition of ministerial personnel has resulted in sweeping adjustments in parishes, perhaps most noticeably their size, organization, and structure. Rural parishes often are diminishing in size, and some are reduced to the status of missions. Priests are assigned two, three, four, or more parishes and missions in these situations. By 2005, some 4,500 priests served more than one parish, and 9,109 parishes and missions (44 percent) were clustered in one way or another. The average age of these priests was fifty-six; some 24 percent were older than sixty-five. Parishes are sharing not only priests but also deacons and lay ministers, if the parishes are large enough to employ them. Increasingly, the same phenomenon of multiple parishes served by one priest is showing up in urban areas as well, but the priest shortage is handled in other ways in suburbs and cities. In many cases, urban inner city parishes are closing in favor of a single larger parish, or they are linked in some other way; at the same time, suburban parishes are growing to megachurch proportions. This latter case frequently results in a social situation that is impersonal and isolating for parishioners in their relationships with both parish staff and each other. Besides these rural and urban reconfigurations, regional differences are also significant. The growth of

Catholic numbers in the South and West leaves many dioceses without the infrastructure needed to minister effectively in these locations, while declining numbers in the North and Midwest are left with unused space and buildings.

The context just described involves a literal transformation of the pastoral outlook of the church. The demands for ministry would be enough with the increased number and diversity of the Catholic population, but the simultaneous decrease in numbers of priests and religious deepens the complexity. Taking their places are tens of thousands of lay ecclesial ministers and lay volunteers. The relocation of centers of the Catholic population adds another dimension. This revolution has placed greater demands on priests who remain responsible for most of the local leadership of parishes, but in markedly new circumstances. The need for theologates to respond to these changes is evident. The formation and education of future priests, deacons, and lay ministers calls for adaptation to the conditions of the local churches for which they are being prepared to serve. A significant consequence is the delegation of authority, once so closely held by priests, to deacons and lay ecclesial ministers.

Preparation for Ministry: The Evolving State
of Theologate Programs

The level of awareness of changes in parochial life varies among administrations and faculty members of theologates, as does their response to the conditions of the church today. From year to year, the casual observer may detect little change in theologates. Careful scrutiny, however, reveals notable modifications in these institutions: their numbers, their mission statements, and their ecclesiological self-understandings have changed, and formation programs have been refined and adapted according to church directives. In turn, these adaptations have had a ripple effect on faculty and students—who they are and how their education is structured. Adjustments in the theological program are evident in four areas, known as the four pillars of formation: human, spiritual, intellectual, and pastoral. These changes are found in the approach to each area: to human formation, especially as it relates to celibate chastity; to spiritual formation in the style and variety of religious exercises; to intellectual formation in the academic focus of courses and the way they are taught; and to pastoral formation in the setting and extent of ministerial experiences. Some might call the cumulative effects of the adaptations a sea change; others might see them as representing only a gradual evolution.

In either case, closer examination suggests that the revisions have not moved along a smooth pathway in one direction. Institutions differ greatly from one another, and within a particular school, drastic shifts can come about almost overnight. In some cases, the theological orientation of an institution reflects the demands of new bishops or vocation directors to return to more traditional format and content. In other places and at other times, the schools have brought together clerical and lay students, urging faculty to explore and teach new avenues of collaboration. Then at later times, they have reversed direction and returned to structures that separate students. Whatever the pathway chosen, the characteristics and preferences of students, along with those of bishops, have deeply affected the quality and content of formation programs; in turn, the ministry provided by the graduates, lay and clerical, has been influenced perceptibly by the circumstances and nature of their education. As vividly portrayed in the research presented in *Evolving Visions of Priesthood*,[6] a shifting emphasis in ecclesiology is evident in the growing divergence between the so-called Vatican II priests and John Paul II priests. Another divide emerging from recent program changes is between diocesan and religious order theologates and their students, especially affecting lay students and the role they will play in ministry. Seminarians who become new diocesan priests are much less inclined to see the value of working with lay ministers and therefore less likely to favor collaborative ministry.

Number and Mission of Theologates

In 1967, theologates numbered about 110, most of them small institutions operated by religious orders for their own candidates. About two dozen archdioceses and dioceses owned and operated schools for diocesan students; religious orders ran an equal number of schools for diocesan seminarians and their own candidates. By the mid-1970s, only about seventy theologates were still open. Religious orders had closed nearly forty of their small schools in favor of sending their candidates for priesthood to one of two theological unions. Catholic Theological Union in Chicago and Washington Theological Union, both founded in 1968, soon enrolled the vast majority of religious students who were once distributed among the many small schools. Dominicans, Jesuits, and a few other religious orders maintained theologates for their own men, but within a decade, half of those schools closed. At the same time, almost all of the remaining religious order schools opened their doors to lay students. By the 1980s, more than half of the diocesan theologates had followed suit by enrolling not only seminarians but also lay students in programs designed to prepare women and men for the growing ministerial needs of their dioceses.

The situation by 1987, then, found 54 theologates in operation, 38 of them primarily for diocesan seminarians and 16 primarily for religious order seminarians. By then, half the diocesan seminaries and almost all the religious order schools also enrolled lay students. The landscape had changed considerably in twenty years, and so had the missions of most of these schools. They expanded their enrollments and adapted their programs to accommodate students whose ministerial goals were somewhat different from those studying for priesthood. At the same time, most theologates were focusing their energies on full implementation of the directives coming from the Second Vatican Council and the 1981 (third edition) of the *Program of Priestly Formation (PPF)*.[7] It continued to give considerable attention to the academic and spiritual programs for seminarians but recommended more thorough pastoral formation.

Changes in Theologate Enrollment

Opening enrollment to lay students from the mid-1970s onward had a profound impact on theologate structures and programs (see table 12.2).[8] Several patterns emerged. Within a decade, by 1987–1988, some 2,276 lay students were enrolled in theologates. In the case of several diocesan schools, mostly located on the East Coast, separate parallel programs were established for lay students and were heavily subscribed. A second model, involving other theologates operated for diocesan candidates by both dioceses and religious orders, allowed lay students to enroll in some classes with seminarians. The third model, theologates operated by and for religious orders, enrolled both seminarians and lay students in most of the same classes. In 1987–1988, about two-thirds of lay students were enrolled in theologates operated primarily for diocesan seminarians, and one-third were enrolled in religious order schools. By 2007–2008, the total number of lay students increased only slightly to 2,631, and the proportion enrolled in each type of school remained relatively stable. Even though religious order schools have vigorously recruited lay students, their gains in enrollment have been modest. Diocesan schools have tended to further separate lay students from seminarians in classes and programs.

   Although bishops and religious superiors have made valiant efforts to set in motion plans and projects to recruit more vocations to the priesthood, the dividends have been meager. The record of trends in the number of seminarians and the resulting ordination rates serve as a prime example. Since 1967, when 8,159 seminarians were enrolled in theological schools,[9] 13,401 in college seminaries, and 15,823 in high school seminaries, the decline has been continuous. In 2007, colleges enrolled 1,365 students and high schools only 729. In effect, the traditional feeder system has all but vanished. For theology-level students, the decline was especially sharp through the twenty years from 1967 to 1987, during which time the number fell to 3,896, less than half the

TABLE 12.2. Catholic Ministry Formation Directory Statistical Summary: 2006–2007 Theologate Enrollment

Year	Seminarians		Lay Students	
	#	%	#	%
1967	8,159	–	*	–
1977	4,447	–	**	–
1987	3,896	63.1	2,276	36.9
1997	3,229	58.5	2,292	41.5
2007	3,274	54.9	2,685	45.1

* Lay students were not enrolled in theologates in 1967.
** The record of lay students enrolled in seminaries was incomplete in 1977.

enrollment of its high point of more than 8,000. From 1988 until 2007, the number dropped by only 622; in fact, the 2001 figure was just 300 fewer than in 1987 and was showing a modest recovery. The news of the sexual abuse scandal sent the numbers in another downward spiral, especially among high school and college enrollments, but also among those studying theology. In just four years, the decline overall was 680 seminarians, an 11 percent drop. The past two years have remained more or less steady.

When the decrease is analyzed, it is evident that several phenomena have contributed to the apparently slower rate of decline among theologians in the past twenty years. From a numerical standpoint, those being counted as theology students has changed, and an influx of international seminarians has augmented the numbers. First, the classification of seminarians is different. Beginning in 1980, pretheology was added as a new program to accommodate older men who were entering seminaries in substantial numbers. Often they had earned college degrees some years before and had worked during the intervening years. When they decided to pursue priesthood, it was evident that these men lacked the philosophy required for the study of theology, so special programs were instituted. At the beginning, the number of students in pretheology was relatively small—between 100 and 200—and programs were condensed to one year so these older men could begin theology as soon as possible. Their ranks swelled to about 400 per year for the next ten years and now to more than 600. Meanwhile, the program was expanded to a required two years. The consequence is that 18 percent of those counted as theologians are now in pretheology, and the enrollment is spread over six years instead of four. In actual numbers, seminarians who are ready for ordination have declined even more sharply than it appears.

Besides expanding the length of the program, the other phenomenon greatly affecting the relatively slower decline in numbers studying theology is the substantial increase in foreign-born seminarians. In 2009, about a quarter of all theologians came from countries outside the United States and numbered 825 of 3,357. As recently as twenty years ago, the number was so small as not to be counted, with estimates of about 5 percent foreign-born. The effects are felt in the number of ordinations each year, since only 16 percent of these students return to their countries of origin. Taken together, the 18 percent of older seminarians enrolled in pretheology and the 25 percent foreign-born boost the numbers in theological studies; without them, the decline would be staggering.

Changes in attitudes within groups of church members, and especially among the hierarchical and clerical leadership, have affected the characteristics of those who feel called and the reasons they are choosing priesthood and religious life. Their sense of vocational call and its meaning for them seems to be altered or at least evolving to a more traditional mode. Their cultural backgrounds, attitudes, educations, intellectual abilities, and experience of church all deeply affect the ways they see their exercise of a future ecclesial vocation.

The study of characteristics of seminarians enrolled in theologates has been quite thorough.[10] The most obvious change over three decades, as noted by faculty, is the academic background of seminarians. Fewer have benefited from a first-rate classical education, which included the classics, as well as philosophy and theology. As in the past, many others have reasonably good college degrees and adequate intellectual abilities. The most drastic change comes in the great increase of seminarians who enter theology with insufficient academic backgrounds—in some schools as many as 40 percent. The deficiencies fall into four categories. Some have weak educational backgrounds, lacking reading comprehension and writing skills, and limited ability to think logically and critically. Others with learning disabilities such as dyslexia or attention deficit disorder often have difficulty with writing, suffer from short attention spans, and lack the ability to read advanced material. The third category includes many seminarians from other countries (one-fourth of all those in theology) who lack sufficient knowledge of English and of American cultural practices. The challenge for seminaries, and later for parishes, is to integrate these men first into American culture and then into parish life. Finally, the last group of students includes older candidates, men in their forties, fifties, or beyond, who have been away from academic study for many years or who may find it difficult to reinsert themselves into an academic environment. Faculty often mention the need to adjust their courses to meet the needs of these less well-qualified students.

At least four distinct categories encompass the religious backgrounds of seminarians. Some are deeply rooted in their faith, others recently converted, and a smaller group only minimally connected to the church. The fourth group is comprised of seminarians whose stance toward church and life in general is rigid and unchanging even in the face of new information and situations.[11]

Those deeply rooted in their faith typically grew up in families where they practiced their faith consistently in a local parish and were involved beyond attendance at Sunday Mass. They have a moderately good grasp of the Catholic tradition and a long-standing commitment to their faith. Initially, they approach ministry in a manner similar to what they experienced in the past. Those coming from a more traditional parish or college setting are likely to prefer something comparable, while those coming from more progressive backgrounds are likely to be comfortable with variety and adaptation. Since a high proportion of seminarians, especially those headed for diocesan priesthood, have experienced more traditional parishes, they retain a similar pattern of preferences when ordained.

Those in the second group have experienced one of two types of conversion: some from another Christian denomination (about 6 percent), but more typically the phenomenon is one of reconversion, where, though baptized Catholics at birth, they have been away from the church for a number of years. These men usually have enjoyed only a short-term or sporadic association with a parish and thus lack familiarity with parish life because of the rather sudden shift in their life direction. A large number of seminarians, at least one-third, come to theological studies with this background. In fact, the study of *The First Five Years of the Priesthood*,[12] about three-fourths of the recently ordained respondents reported that they experienced a spiritual awakening, something akin to a conversion, prior to entering the seminary. The concern of most faculty about them is their tendency to be inflexible, overly scrupulous, and fearful. These attitudes can bring about a strict interpretation of what they think is permissible in the practice of the faith, a sense of wanting things to conform exactly to their limited experience. They may find difficulty in adapting their set notions in relation to religious education, liturgical life, and other dimensions of ministry. Through study and field education experiences, seminaries attempt to introduce these students to the breadth of the Catholic experience. Careful mentoring and supervision by faculty and by parish staffs in extended field education experiences is especially important for this group.

A smaller number of seminarians have had minimal connection with the church before ordination. They formally identify themselves as Catholic but many have not practiced their faith consistently and so they have little sense of the fullness of the church's life and teaching. Usually they have not attended Catholic schools and are experiencing formal religious education for the first time in seminary. They tend to fall into one of two groups: first are those caught up by Spirit who enter fully into the formation process and often become convincing models in parishes for people who themselves may have experienced what it is like to be indifferent to their faith; second are those who never quite find their way and are apt to leave the seminary before ordination or, if ordained, fail to engage fully in parish ministry. Helpful to this group is exposure to a wide range of liturgical and other ministerial experiences.

Faculty members estimate that about 10 percent of seminarians have a rigid understanding of their faith. Generally, they came of age after Vatican II concluded and so have no existential memory of the church before 1970. They lived most of their adult lives during the pontificate of Pope John Paul II, a factor that helps explain their unswerving devotion to him and his outlook on the church. While these men have been greatly affected by American cultural forms like their peers, including the media, technology, and communications, unlike their peers, after having been quite immersed in this culture, their response now is to withdraw and condemn the world as they see it. They tend to experience enormous fear—fear of change and fear of the world—and so they regard seminaries as the last bastions of security. Such men want only clear, distinct ideas that are aligned with their view of orthodoxy. They often seek to restore traditional practices, including devotions such as litanies, novenas, benediction, and, more recently, the Tridentine Mass. As priests, these individuals often cause difficulties in parishes and with their fellow priests, even while they are associate pastors. They are not interested in discussion or dialogue since they interpret the world only from their own perspective.

The task of faculty is to encourage adequate transformation in these men with widely varying backgrounds so that they are prepared to serve a church populated by Catholics whose views often contradict or stand outside the experiences of those preparing for priesthood. While apparent changes can be evident before ordination, once these men are ordained, they frequently revert to patterns more typical of their preseminary backgrounds. Pastors who are their first supervisors find this behavior to be the source of tension within the parish.

Faculty Changes in Theologates: Vocational Status

Theologate faculties have responded in diverse ways to new challenges brought about by changes in students and in the ministry, depending on their views of theology, their teaching methods, and their institutional ethos. During the past two decades, the composition of faculty who are teaching in theologates has shifted in terms of vocational status and the types and sources of their most advanced degrees. Most notable is the decrease in the number and proportion of priest faculty and the corresponding increase in lay faculty from 1986–1988 to the present. The number of women religious remained stable between 1986–1988 and 1996–1998, and then declined sharply by 2006–2008 (see table 12.3). The sources of faculty degrees are less likely to be Roman institutions, reflecting the drop in the number of priests, and more likely to be non-Catholic American universities, reflecting the increase in lay faculty (see table 12.4). As a large number of older religious and diocesan priests retire, they are being replaced by a new generation of generally more traditional younger priests in diocesan schools and by more progressive lay faculty in religious order schools. The results of these changes are profound.

To explore more specifically the faculty data on vocational status, the number of priests dropped 35 percent over twenty years. The major change came between 1986–1988 and 1996–1998, during which time 149 fewer men religious were teaching in theologates. When many religious order seminaries closed in the 1970s, these experienced teachers were welcomed into diocesan seminaries to fill the ranks of faculties as diocesan priests and other faculty retired or moved to other ministries. Ten years later, many religious were at retirement age, and the number of priests never recovered to the high level of earlier times. Women religious and lay women and men became part of seminary faculties in significant numbers only during the 1980s. First, a few women religious were hired, and by 1986 they numbered 93; this level held until recently, when the number dropped to 70, a decline of 25 percent. Given the increased average age of women religious, this pattern is not likely to change, though recently a few members of the newer conservative orders are being hired. Another reason for the continuing drop in numbers is the limited roles allowed women in most diocesan theologates since the Vatican-ordered visitations of the early 2000s.[13] The increase in the number of laymen to 172 and of laywomen to 96 represents a 121 percent increase, twice as many laymen and three times as many laywomen as twenty years ago. Most of

TABLE 12.3. Changes in Theologate Faculty: Vocational Status

Faculty	1986–1988		1996–1998		2006–2008		20 year change	
Vocational Status	#	%	#	%	#	%	+ or − #	+ or − %
Diocesan priests	292	32.5	246	33.2	220	28.1	−72	−24.7
Men religious	392	43.7	243	32.8	225	28.7	−167	−42.6
Women religious	93	10.4	95	12.8	70	8.9	−23	−24.7
Laymen	88	9.8	108	14.6	172	22.0	+84	+95.5%
Laywomen	33	3.7	49	6.6	96	12.3	+63	+190.9%
Total	898	100.1	741	100.0	783	100.0	−115	−2.8%

TABLE 12.4. Changes in Theologate Faculty: Sources of Highest Degrees

Institution	1986–1988	1996–1998	2006–2008
	%	%	%
Roman Pontifical degrees	25.7	23.2	19.9
University of Louvain degrees	5.1	2.5	2.6
Other European University degrees*	9.7	6.9	7.5
Catholic University of America degrees	11.6	12.4	11.1
Other American Catholic University degrees **	30.0	33.7	32.7
Non-Catholic American University degrees **	18.0	21.3	26.1

* Includes degrees from one Filipino university in 2006–2008.
** Includes degrees from Canadian institutions and also one each from Argentina and Colombia in 2006–08.

these increases have occurred in theologates operated by religious orders for their own candidates and a large number of lay students.

Faculty Changes in Theologates: Sources of Degrees

The institutions where faculty have earned their highest degrees have changed noticeably in two ways over the period of twenty years from 1986–1988 to 2006–2008: degrees awarded by European institutions dropped by 10.5 percent, from 40.5 to 30.0 percent, with Roman Pontifical degrees accounting for most of the decline, and degrees from non-Catholic American universities rose by 8.1 percent moving from 18.0 percent to 26.1 percent. One of the reasons for the switch is related to fewer priests holding faculty positions. Generally speaking, diocesan priests are more likely to study abroad, especially in Roman universities, and so the drop of 239 priests (20 percent fewer now than in 1986–1988) accounts for much of the difference. At the same time, the number of lay faculty increased by 147 (21 percent more now than in 1986–1988), and many of these faculty earned degrees from American universities, many of them non-Catholic. One particular factor contributed disproportionately to the swing: a significant number of the new lay faculty serve the theologates as teachers of English as a second language (ESL) and Spanish language; almost always their degrees are from non-Catholic universities. Further, religious-order theologates tend to have a more diverse faculty than diocesan schools, especially if they are associated with universities; they employ proportionately more lay faculty with degrees from secular institutions.

The particular institution where faculty have earned degrees is also shifting. Compared with twenty years ago, about half as many present faculty studied at the Pontifical Biblical Institute (down from 38 to 17). In the opposite direction, more current faculty earned degrees at the Pontifical Gregorian

University (up from 53 to 65); the reverse was true for the Pontifical University of St. Thomas Aquinas (down from 39 to 23). Moral theology faculty continued to earn degrees from the Pontifical Lateran University and its associated Pontifical Institute of St. Alphonsus (14 in 1986–1988 and 18 in 2006–2008). In recent years, five diocesan priests who are teaching moral theology earned degrees at the newly established John Paul II Institute in Washington, D.C. The impact of these changes to the theological and ecclesiological environments of theologates is yet to be determined.

Faculty Changes in Theologates: Proportion with Doctoral Degrees

The degree power of today's theologate faculties has increased since 1986–1988, with particularly large gains for women religious and laymen (see table 12.5). Priests also have a higher proportion holding doctorates, as shown later. The percentage of all faculty with doctoral degrees was 67.4 in 1986–1988; ten years later, it was 74.6 percent, and currently it is 75.2 percent, a total increase of 7.8 percent. The proportion would be higher were it not for changes in curriculum, which required adding many ESL faculty, often laywomen who usually hold masters degrees. Men religious have always had the highest proportion of doctorates, now 87.6 percent, an increase of 10 percent since 1986–1988. Gains for laymen were from 67 percent to 83.7 percent, placing them just behind men religious. Women religious made the most significant advance, with 19.1 percent more holding doctorates than twenty years before. Diocesan priests increased to 65 percent with doctorates, up from 59.6 percent in 1986–1988. The statistics on laywomen holding doctorates are somewhat erratic; their overall number is small (54), and recent additions to their ranks have been in ESL instruction, factors that may account for the changes between decades.

TABLE 12.5.   Changes in Theologate Faculty: Earned Doctorates

Earned Doctorates*	1986–1988		1996–1998		2006–2008		% Change 20 Years
	#	%	#	%	#	%	
Diocesan priests	174	59.6	15	63.4	143	65.0	+5.4
Men religious	304	77.6	206	84.8	197	87.6	+10.6
Women religious	50	53.8	63	66.3	51	72.9	+19.1
Laymen	59	67.0	93	86.1	144	83.7	+16.7
Laywomen	18	54.5	35	71.4	54	56.3	+1.8
Total	605	67.4	553	74.6	589	75.2	+7.8

* Doctorates include 31, 22, and 11 Licentiates in Sacred Scripture for respective years.

Changes in Theologate Formation Programs

Periodically, the bishops of the United States draft a new version of their expectations for the education of men for the priesthood in seminaries at all levels from high school through graduate-level theology. Each edition is entitled *Program of Priestly Formation (PPF)*, with the first issued in 1971, then again in 1976, 1981, 1993, and most recently the fifth edition, published in 2006. Adaptations were often prompted by Vatican decrees following consultations with bishops from around the world. The topic of the 1990 World Synod of Bishops was the formation of priests, which strongly reaffirmed celibacy and also focused on the effects of modern culture on vocations to the priesthood. The bishops at the synod discussed the importance of broad-based priestly formation for pastoral service, incorporating four dimensions: human, spiritual, intellectual, and pastoral formation. In 1992, these themes appeared in one of the most widely accepted and influential documents issued by Pope John Paul II, *Pastores Dabo Vobis (I Will Give You Shepherds)*.[14] This apostolic exhortation became the template for future seminary programs and influenced the *Program of Priestly Formation* issued in 1993, but it was not until the 2006 edition that it was fully represented. Seminaries have responded to these directives by adapting their programs, especially as they pertain to human and spiritual formation.[15]

Human and Spiritual Formation

These two areas were treated as one component and, until 2006, described in various editions of the *Program of Priestly Formation* as communal and personal dimensions of spiritual formation. Spiritual formation was always emphasized, though details have continued to evolve over the years. The underlying importance of human development as the basis of all formation came into focus with John Paul II's *PDV* in 1992. Theologate leaders took the recommendation of making this the fourth "pillar" of formation more or less seriously. Many schools developed rather extensive programs, and a few did very little to address the issues raised in *PDV*. In recent years, preparation for priestly ordination has changed most comprehensively in this area.[16] After the sexual abuse scandals broke into public consciousness in 2002 and onward, bishops scrutinized formation programs to ensure that the topic of celibacy was adequately addressed. In the 2006 *PPF*, the human formation component was added as a separate pillar,[17] with sexuality and celibacy a major focus of the text. Deficiencies were identified, and programs were implemented to respond to the concerns.[18] Spiritual formation was again given resolute support, and certain practices were highlighted, including the reception of the sacrament of reconciliation and Eucharistic devotion.

Perhaps as an unintended consequence, theologate faculty have reported changes in components of their human formation dealing with the way topics of celibacy and homosexuality are treated. Regarding celibacy, in the view of some faculty and students, greater—if not exclusive—emphasis is placed on the spiritual dimensions of living a chaste celibate life, with little attention given to the realities and difficulties encountered every day in living as a celibate priest. Regarding homosexuality, since the 2005 Vatican instruction "Concerning the Criteria for the Discernment of Vocations with Regard to Persons with Homosexual Tendencies in View of Their Admission to the Seminary and to Holy Orders," the presumption is that rarely, if ever, are homosexuals admitted to seminaries. The consequence is that frank discussion about how to live as a chaste celibate priest with homosexual tendencies is for the most part eliminated. Observers from inside and outside seminaries are concerned that both shifts will leave a serious lacuna in these aspects of formation. It will take some time before the effects of these changes are evident.

Intellectual and Pastoral Formation

Comparing the number of semester credit hours and the curricular requirements between 1987 and 2007, only a few changes are obvious. The total number of credits has increased by 8.1 from 107.7 to 115.8, the equivalent of about three courses (see table 12.6).[19] Almost all the increase is absorbed by systematic theology and reflects the concern that seminarians enter theological studies with inadequate knowledge of their faith. Further, the course most often added was one dedicated solely to priesthood, entitled theology of priesthood; celibacy, priesthood, and holy orders; or the like. The only reduction was in field education, with two fewer credits on average. The major shift in pastoral studies was toward requiring education in Hispanic studies, including Spanish language, preaching in Spanish, and similar courses. Fewer theologates now require religious education, spiritual direction, and similar pastorally oriented courses.

The number and distribution of courses provides only partial understanding. Several changes in the focus of courses are noticeable from course descriptions. More attention is given to an apologetic approach to studies, and a significant reassertion of the privileged place of the works of St. Thomas Aquinas is evident in diocesan theologates. Descriptions of intellectual formation in some school catalogues highlight priestly identity, priestly

TABLE 12.6. Credit Distribution for the Master of Divinity Degree

Subject Area	1987	1997	2007
Scripture	17.6	17.1	17.5
Systematic theology *	26.6	30.5	33.8
Moral theology	11.2	10.5	11.7
Historical studies	8.6	8.9	9.9
Pastoral studies **	23.9	22.5	23.5
Field education	11.8	10.8	9.8
General electives/other	8.0	11.9	10.2
Total	107.7	112.2	115.8

* Systematic theology encompasses dogmatic, sacramental, liturgical, and spirituality courses.
** Pastoral studies include pastoral theology/skills, homiletics, canon law, and sacramental and liturgical practica.

ministry, and priestly spirituality in contrast to presenting the broader ecclesiological context that includes all the faithful. In moral theology, more emphasis is placed on sexual morality and biomedical ethics dealing with reproductive technology than on the broader social teachings of the church. In effect, through the voluntary visitations in the late 1990s and the required visitations in the 2000s, the bishops have succeeded in altering the curricular direction of many seminaries, as described previously.

As the composition of the Catholic population continues to change, it will be necessary for faculties to examine the outcomes of their program changes to see if graduates are meeting the needs of young people, immigrants, families, and other subgroups who may need special attention. The strengths and weaknesses of the approaches being adopted will need analysis. If the results of the adaptations in the content and methods of the curriculum and other aspects of formation are not carefully considered, the loss of adult Catholics to other faiths will continue at its unacceptably high rate. To make the appropriate adjustments will demand more interaction between theologates and current pastoral leaders and parishioners of all types. The tendency of some theologates is to produce future ministers for Catholics of the past. A broader, more forward-looking view will be indispensable for a much more diverse church.

Remedies and Modifications to Build Up the Life of the Catholic Community

Theologates have undergone many adaptations and adjustments during the past two decades, some of them viewed as encouraging improvements and others as discouraging backtracking. Seminarians and lay students, faculty and formation programs have all changed in response to various influences inside the church and from the larger society. In recent years, research has revealed several concerns that will require ongoing consideration in developing educational programs for future priests and lay ministers. Tensions between older priests and those more recently ordained have grown as their ecclesiologies have become more at odds over appreciation for and understanding of Vatican II theology vis-à-vis that of Pope John Paul II. Tensions also are present between American-born priests and those who have come from other countries, either already ordained or after studying here. Tensions arise, too, between some newly ordained priests and lay ministers when their approaches to ministry are at variance. Usually this situation surfaces when lay ministers are long established in a parish and encounter a new pastor who is eager to make changes according to his own background and preferences. Finally, tensions are present in some parishes when pastors and parishioners have different visions of parish life, a situation that occurs most often when the pastor is new in his position. Understanding the problem is the first task, followed by some modifications that might remedy or at least lessen the concerns.

Interactions between Priests Currently Ministering and the Newly Ordained

In a comprehensive study of priests, *Evolving Visions of the Priesthood: Changes from Vatican II to the Turn of the New Century,* Dean Hoge and Jacqueline Wenger explored issues relating to ecclesiological differences among priests, pointing out the present disjunction between younger and older priests that arises from their unresolved disagreements over approaches to ministry.[20] As older priests described themselves, they used terms like "servants, servant leaders, instruments, facilitators, enablers, pastoral leaders, and liberals." Younger priests were more likely to identify themselves as "traditional, conservative, establishment, 'unapologetically Catholic,' and 'ecclesiologically sound.'"[21] The metaphors illustrate the distance between the two groups and help explain the difficulties they have in relating to each other at presbyteral gatherings and in parochial settings. According to a survey of priests ordained five years or less, disagreements about ecclesiology and ministry are a problem for 42 percent of them.[22]

More disquieting than these contrasting perceptions are the judgments of each group about the other. "Younger priests called the older priests liberals, leftist fringe, secularized, anti-establishment, a 'lost generation,' and priests with a social work model" and "Older priests referred to the young men as inflexible, divisive, liturgically conservative, institutional, hierarchical, and believers in a cultic priesthood."[23] They worry about what research confirms, namely, that younger priests are out of tune with their lay contemporaries, as well as with many older parishioners. While not everyone uses or accepts these negative descriptions, these stereotypes were used again and again by respondents in the Hoge-Wenger study. This persistent, destructive, and unacceptable pattern can prevent parishes and other ministries from thriving. For congregations experiencing the ministry of both types of priests—older pastor and younger associate—or for parishes going through a transition from one type of pastor to another, the changeover is often disruptive and problematic. For lay ministers caught between the two camps, the consequences may be even more distressing.

Clearly, old dichotomies need to be collapsed and new ways of relating explored. Susan Wood, commenting on priests' search for identity,[24] recommends that our ecclesial imaginations need to be stretched to incorporate more of a communion ecclesiology, where relationship rather than essential differences are highlighted. The path to that kind of unity will be long in coming, she says, for it entails constructive theological work that must be filtered to laity and priests alike. Theological faculties, who are themselves now more diverse than ever, need to model for students ways of overcoming problems of relationship. Required is humble acceptance of the fact that several approaches to theological questions and pastoral issues are possible and even desirable. Achieving a balance that respects both experience and new insights, as well as having a keen understanding of the ministerial situations for which students are preparing, takes time and commitment. If priests young and old are to work together more effectively, they must have an awareness of how to achieve rapprochement on the parish and diocesan level. The first step for faculty members may be a willingness to acknowledge their differences on these issues and agree to discuss them with each other. Only then will they be able to speak respectfully to students about the necessity of a unified approach to ministry when they are in similar circumstances of disagreement.

Incorporation of International Priests into American Church Life

Historically, priests have always come from other countries to serve the church in the United States. The recent influx, however, is dissimilar in many ways. In the past, most international priests accompanied immigrants from their own countries to help them settle in a new country. They shared language, customs, and religious traditions that were a source of support and comfort to the new settlers. Through the centuries, Irish priests came in large numbers and ministered throughout the country in whatever dioceses had need. In recent years, the pattern has varied. Most international priests are being recruited by dioceses that are experiencing a great shortage of priests. Generally they are coming from countries with a limited number of Catholic immigrants, such as Nigeria, Colombia, and India. Many also come from Mexico and in the recent past from Vietnam, and they may or may not be serving their own communities. In some cases, those being recruited are already ordained, but a growing number of seminarians—a fourth of all those studying theology—are from other countries.

The impact of the growing diversity in presbyterates is mixed. The service provided by the priests makes it possible for parishes to be staffed and ministry provided in places where it would otherwise be lacking. A 2006 study of international priests in the United States shows that just over half feel they are totally accepted in the diocese and all but 3 percent feel at least partly accepted.[25] Religious order priests fare better, with 75 percent feeling totally accepted and 25 percent partly accepted. Three arguments are made for bringing international priests: to serve immigrant parishes, to fill gaps in the priest shortage, and to help universalize and revitalize American Catholicism.[26] A longer list of problems is identified in the book: language, cultural misunderstandings, different ecclesiologies, funding and finances, and failure of priests from different cultures to mix in the presbyterate. Others see the problems from a broader perspective, including the irrational deployment of world priestly resources, postponement of restructuring parish leadership, and postponement of lay efforts to recruit vocations.[27] Whichever side is taken, for or against international priests, the effects are considerable, given the fact that about 17 percent of U.S. priests have come recently from other countries, and the proportion is growing.

Theologates can work with two groups to improve the present situation: with American seminarians and with those who have come from another country. Since these men will all be ministering together, efforts to build good relationships will help the newcomers feel welcome and grow more familiar with American culture and religion. Theologates need to make a serious effort to help seminarians acculturate through planned programs that familiarize them with all aspects of American culture, especially religious practices, societal customs, and language conventions. Too often an assumption is made that the international student will learn by osmosis, but the learning environment of the seminary is the place to systematize a program for these seminarians. A more difficult situation occurs when a man comes already ordained. Some condensed programs are available to learn the basics of the culture, but too often these are short-circuited in order to place the priest in ministry immediately. This action is to the detriment of the priests, as well as to parish staffs and parishioners who must suffer the consequences of liturgies, especially preaching, that cannot be understood. A comprehensive plan is needed to help the priests who are ill prepared to serve.

Connections between Pastors and Lay Ministers

Within the past twenty to thirty years, laypeople have taken positions in almost every ministry setting.[28] Parishes, chaplaincies, diocesan offices, and schools employ some 30,000 professional lay ministers and 165,000 teachers. Since this form of ministry was new to both experienced pastors and lay ministers when it began, over time they learned together to work collaboratively. By entering into dialogue about their common goals, they fostered good relationships and came to understand the value each brought to the common mission. As one pastor put it, "Unlike those who are being ordained today, we have gradually grown into this way of ministering." In many studies on parish life, pastors in overwhelming numbers indicate that what contributes most to their success as pastors is their relationships with their staffs. For newly ordained pastors, the situation is often more difficult. The theology of priesthood adopted by many of them places them over and above, ontologically separate from, their lay collaborators and runs counter to the conditions of shared ministry. Stories appear regularly in the Catholic press about the tragedies resulting from changes in pastors when structures of collaboration and shared decision making are ignored or reversed.[29] Without an appreciation of the approved role of lay ecclesial ministry and exposure to good examples of collaboration, problems will persist.

Under these circumstances, it cannot be entirely left up to the recently ordained priest to adapt to a new assignment without the assistance of both pastor and lay ministers. Their role as mentor is critical to the success of the relationship. The newly arrived associate deserves a thorough orientation to the parish, including an introduction to the staff and an opportunity for him to introduce himself to them. A historical overview of the parish, information about the way it has evolved and changed through the years, and a report about the current parishioners are essential. Since liturgy is so often contentious, the pastor and staff should give an accounting of the customs and traditions associated with various liturgical celebrations. The pastor might take the lead in explaining the expectations and acceptable parameters for deviating from the established patterns of worship. For several months, the entire staff should meet regularly with the new priest to exchange ideas and answer questions. A mistaken notion prevails about young priests that, rather than lack of experience and exposure to collaboration, all are alike in their reactionary ways, eagerness to return to the past, and unwillingness to learn. To the contrary, when the pastor and staff engage in open discussion, many are willing to learn, grow in understanding, and bring new energy to the parish. The direction toward collaboration or away from it can be determined greatly by the extent of mutual understanding that is created.

Relationships between Pastors and Parishioners

These days, little time is allowed for apprenticeships, as the transition from seminarian to pastor comes swiftly. In a study of priests ordained five to nine years, 45 percent of diocesan priests became pastors within three years of ordination, and of those, 11 percent were named pastors within a year of ordination.[30] That fact stands in marked contrast to the past, when first pastorates came as long as twenty-five years after ordination. By then, the priest had numerous opportunities to witness differing pastoral leadership styles and sometimes to practice his own by gradually being given more responsibilities. The consequences of being assigned as pastor after only a few years ordained are mixed. Since priests are at least five years older on average when they are ordained now than they were twenty-five years ago, many of them have had experience in secular jobs that prepared them for leadership. For those who are more experienced and/or more willing to adapt and learn from staff and parishioners, the adjustment to becoming pastor is usually smooth. In a recent study of priests with multiple parishes, for example, 96 percent said they were very or somewhat satisfied with the relationship with parishioners with whom they work.[31] They are confident and eager to put their skills into practice in a new setting, avoiding the frustrating years of working under a pastor beyond the time of learning anything new.

For those who have not had a background of leadership or do not have natural abilities in that arena, the prospect of serving as a pastor can be daunting. Besides lack of experience, many recently ordained priests bring with them an ecclesiology that is alien to their contemporaries in the parish and to those who are older. Frequently voiced complaints of parishioners indicate that the recently ordained pastor makes too many changes based on his own desires and preferences without reference to the parishioners. If pastors take time to discover the uniqueness of the parish history and character, of its longtime members and new ones, they usually can avoid some of the problems associated with new leadership. It is imperative to understand who is present in the parish and then work to determine how to meet their pastoral needs. Theologate faculty need to make sure their formation programs prepare future leaders humanly, spiritually, intellectually, and pastorally to overcome their own biases and narrow-minded attitudes to embrace new approaches to their ministry.

Conclusion

The Catholic Church in United States is on the move, and with that movement come many dilemmas and concerns about future leadership. Catholics in great numbers have come from all over the world for many years to this place. They have brought with them diverse interpretations of what the church is meant to be in their lives. Their expectations are as wide as their backgrounds and experiences. As movement of people from outside and inside the United States continues, the contexts of parishes have changed. At the same time, fewer priests and sisters and more lay ecclesial ministers work in these megaparishes and multiple parishes. The comfort of old frameworks has evaporated. In this new world, what are the tasks facing those who will be leading the church into the future?

The first task is to be willing to accept the reality of diversity without destroying essential unity. A constructive starting point for church leaders is to become acquainted with the rich history of the church in its manifold settings, showing how local cultures have enriched rather than diminished the church. Implied in this scenario is an approach to theological studies that incorporates recognition of the cultural variations within the church and the particular pastoral requirements that emerge from it. Pastors who serve as authority figures are likely to be much more successful when they recognize the composition of their parishioners and work with them in ways that are compatible with their cultural backgrounds.

The second task arises because of ideological differences that express themselves in liturgical celebrations, spiritual experiences, and theological diversity. Ministerial leaders need to interact as persons, who, in the philosophy of Parker Palmer, have the ability to "think the world together" instead of apart as they face this perplexing scene.[32] To succeed in this complex task requires a thorough understanding of the essence of the Catholic tradition and of the cultural variation found within the tradition. Carefully honed communication skills will help convey the meaning of the faith to persons from a wide range of cultural backgrounds. According to Cardinal Bernardin's Catholic Common Ground Initiative, as expressed in the document "Called to Be Catholic: Church in a Time of Peril," patterns of mutual respect, renewed dialogue, openness, honesty, and civility must be developed to hold together the communities of faith today. When authority is exercised in the manner described, it is much more likely to be accepted.

The third task is to acquire an understanding of the parishes and parishi-oners by practicing the art of social analysis. Such an undertaking requires a talent for asking the right questions of the right people. After appropriate information is collected, a knowledgeable and representative group can come together to consider the findings. Taking into account the resources available, priorities need to be set among many possible ministerial directions. Above all, virtues like humility and patience are important, since personal preferences must be set aside in favor of the common good. Communicating the rationale for choices is a delicate step in the process that takes time if all those involved are to be integrated and included. Sensitive approaches in the use of authority enhance its effectiveness.

The fourth and final task is to become equipped as individuals, both spiritually and intellectually, to not only preach and teach but also heal and sanctify. Intellectual formation is indispensable as leaders attempt to provide deeper understanding of God's saving presence through the sacraments and the church's teaching, but without a caring heart, all the correct doctrine imaginable will fall on deaf ears. Issues related to family life, care of the poor, social justice, and war and peace touch every parish. Suffering abounds as illness, loss of loved ones, stress, and diminishment touch lives. Those who are afflicted—everyone in some way or another—hunger for comfort and compassion, for a listening heart, a kindly word. The goal is to attend to the life stages and unique pastoral needs of a congregation, bringing to them the grace and salvation won by the life, death, and resurrection of Jesus Christ. In whatever ways the dilemmas facing the church today are described, the point is not to dwell excessively on the problems, but to explore how to convey a sense of hope and expectation for improvement to the church, the world, and every individual living in it.

BIBLIOGRAPHY

"Broken Parish." *America* 198 (2008): 24–25.
CARA Report. Washington, DC: Center for Applied Research in the Apostolate, various years.
d'Antonio, William V., James D. Davidson, Dean R. Hoge, and Mary L. Gautier. *American Catholics Today*. Lanham, MD: Rowman & Littlefield, 2007.
DeLambo, David. *Lay Parish Ministers: A Study of Emerging Leadership*. New York: National Pastoral Life Center, 2005.
Filteau, Jerry. "Focus on Celibacy Grew in U.S. Bishops' Priestly Formation Norms." *Catholic News Service* (March 12, 2004).
Foster, Charles, Lisa E. Dahill, Lawrence A. Golemon, and Barbara Wang Tolentino. *Educating Clergy: Teaching Practices and Pastoral Imagination*. San Francisco: Jossey-Bass, 2006.

Hoge, Dean R. *Experiences of Priests Ordained Five to Nine Years*. Washington, DC: National Catholic Educational Association, 2006.

———. *The First Five Years of the Priesthood: A Study of Newly Ordained Catholic Priests*. Collegeville, MN: Liturgical, 2002.

Hoge, Dean R., and Aniedi Okure. *International Priests in America: Challenges and Opportunities*. Collegeville, MN: Liturgical, 2006.

Hoge, Dean R., and Jacqueline E. Wenger. *Evolving Visions of the Priesthood*. Collegeville, MN: Liturgical, 2003.

Holifield, E. Brooks. *God's Ambassadors: A History of the Christian Clergy in America*. Grand Rapids, MI: Wm. B. Eerdmans, 2007.

Klimoski, Victor J., Kevin J. O'Neil, and Katarina Schuth. *Educating Leaders for Ministry: Issues and Responses*. Collegeville, MN: Liturgical, 2005.

Official Catholic Directory. New Providence, NJ: J. P. Kenedy & Sons, multiple years.

Palmer, Parker. *The Courage to Teach: Exploring the Inner Landscape of a Teacher's Life*. San Francisco: Jossey-Bass, 1968.

Pew Forum on Religion & Public Life. *U.S. Religious Landscape Survey*. Washington, DC: Pew Research Center, 2008.

Pope John Paul II. *Pastores Dabo Vobis (I Will Give You Shepherds): Post-Synodal Apostolic Exhortation on the Formation of Priests in the Circumstances of the Present Day*. Rome-Vatican City, March 25, 1992.

Schuth, Katarina. *Seminaries, Theologates, and the Future of Church Ministry: An Analysis of Trends and Transitions*. Collegeville, MN: Liturgical, 1999.

———. *Priestly Ministry in Multiple Parishes*. Collegeville, MN: Liturgical, 2006.

Schwartz, Robert M. *Servant Leaders of the People of God: An Ecclesial Spirituality for American Priests*. New York: Paulist, 1989.

United States Conference of Catholic Bishops. *Program of Priestly Formation*, 5th ed. Washington, DC: United States Conference of Catholic Bishops, 2006.

Witherup, Ronald. "Will the Seminaries Measure Up?" *America* 194 (2006): 9–12.

NOTES

1. Major seminaries and schools of theology are collectively referred to as theologates. This terminology will be used when referring to graduate-level theological education since it is more specific than the term *seminary*, which applies to high school, college, and graduate-level institutions.

2. Figures are reported in the *Official Catholic Directory* (P. J. Kenedy & Sons) in the respective years. The majority of new members were immigrants. See the Pew Forum on Religion & Public Life, *U.S. Religious Landscape Survey* (Washington, DC: Pew Research Center, 2008), 25. It reported that another source of growth was the 2.6 percent of the U.S. adult population that switched their affiliation to Catholic.

3. The number declined for the first time in the modern era from 69.1 million in 2006 to 67.5 million in 2007. By 2009, the number was up slightly to 68.1 million. Whether that sudden and unexpected drop is significant or simply a statistical anomaly is yet to be determined, but in the context of this chapter, it deserves mention. The *U.S. Religious Landscape Survey* finds that the Catholic Church has experienced the greatest net loss by far of any religious group. "Overall, 31.4% of U.S. adults say that they were raised Catholic. Today, however, only 23.9% of adults identify with the Catholic

Church, a net loss of 7.5 percentage points" (p. 23). In other words, these figures show that 76 percent of those raised Catholic are still Catholic; 24 percent are no longer Catholic.

4. Adapted from William V. D'Antonio, James D. Davidson, Dean R. Hoge, and Mary L. Gautier, *American Catholics Today* (Lanham, MD: Rowman & Littlefield, 2007), table from 11, 21; text from 18–19.

5. Ibid., 20.

6. See Dean R. Hoge and Jacqueline E. Wenger, *Evolving Visions of Priesthood: Changes from Vatican II to the Turn of the New Century* (Collegeville, MN: Liturgical, 2003), especially 47–59.

7. The *Program of Priestly Formation*, a publication of the U.S. bishops, establishes guidelines for seminary education at all levels. To date, five editions have been published: 1971, 1976, 1981, 1993, and 2006.

8. Data taken from *CARA Reports* for respective years: Catholic Ministry Formation Directory Statistical Summary.

9. Ibid.

10. Relatively little research has been done on lay students, but CARA studies on *Catholic Ministry Formation Enrollments: Statistical Overview for 2006–2007*, show lay students enrolled in all types of ministry studies include 66 percent women and 34 percent men; 11 percent are under age 30, 47 percent between 30 and 49, and 42 percent 50 and older. White students are 71 percent, Hispanic/Latino 18 percent, Black 4 percent, Asian 4 percent, and other 3 percent. Lay students are more likely to be white, women, and older than seminarians.

11. Adapted from Katarina Schuth, *Seminaries, Theologates, and the Future of Church Ministry: Analysis of Trends and Transitions* (Collegeville, MN: Liturgical, 1999), 79–85.

12. Dean R. Hoge, *The First Five Years of the Priesthood* (Collegeville, MN: Liturgical, 2002), 13.

13. The Apostolic visitation of U.S. seminaries and houses of formation was ordered by the Vatican in 2002 after the sexual abuse scandal became widely publicized. For a report of the outcomes, see Ronald Witherup, S.S., "Will the Seminaries Measure Up?" *America* 194, no. 10 (March 20, 2006): 9–12.

14. *Pastores Dabo Vobis (I Will Give You Shepherds): Post-Synodal Apostolic Exhortation on the Formation of Priests in the Circumstances of the Present Day* was issued March 25, 1992.

15. For a comparative perspective of Catholic seminary education with Protestant and Jewish models, see Charles Foster, Lisa E. Dahill, Lawrence A. Golemon, and Barbara Wang Tolentino, *Educating Clergy: Teaching Practices and Pastoral Imagination* (San Francisco: Jossey-Bass, 2006). Topics include Catholic pedagogies of formation, pedagogical strengths, spirituality, and movement to professionalism in theological education.

16. Jerry Filteau, "Focus on Celibacy Grew in U.S. Bishops' Priestly Formation Norms," Catholic News Service (March 12, 2004).

17. United States Conference of Catholic Bishops, *Program of Priestly Formation*, 5th ed. (Washington, DC: Author, 2006), 29–42.

18. Major additions to the human formation programs in seminaries were made after John Paul II issued *Pastores dabo vobis* in 1992 and again after the 2006 *Program of Priestly Formation*. Some commentators have associated the sexual abuse crisis with what they perceived as the less stringent seminary formation programs of the 1970s. However, the vast majority of priests who abused were educated prior to the end of Vatican II during the time of very restrictive seminary rules and regulations.

19. For diocesan seminarians, the number of credits required is 119.7 and for religious order candidates, the number is 102.9. Generally, those who are studying for religious orders have taken a year of theology before being admitted to theologates, so they take about 17 fewer credits during the last years of their theological studies.

20. Hoge and Wenger, *Evolving Visions of Priesthood*, especially 113–133.

21. Ibid., 113.

22. Dean R. Hoge, *The First Five Years of the Priesthood* (Collegeville, MN: Liturgical, 2002), 171. This study shows that 12 percent of diocesan priests found the disagreements to be a great problem and 30 percent found them to be somewhat of a problem.

23. Hoge and Wenger, *Evolving Visions of Priesthood*, 113–114.

24. Hoge, *The First Five Years of the Priesthood*, 167–173.

25. Dean R. Hoge and Aniedi Okure, *International Priests in America: Challenges and Opportunities* (Collegeville, MN: Liturgical, 2006), 17.

26. Ibid., 36–49.

27. Ibid., 50–68.

28. See David DeLambo, *Lay Parish Ministers: A Study of Emerging Leadership* (New York: National Pastoral Life Center, 2005) for a thorough report of various lay ministers and their roles in parishes.

29. "Broken Parish," *America* 198, no. 4 (February 11, 2008): 24–25, is one such recent article. The numerous online responses to this and similar articles suggest the frequency of the problem.

30. Dean R. Hoge, *Experiences of Priests Ordained Five to Nine Years* (Collegeville, MN: Liturgical, 2006), 58.

31. Katarina Schuth, *Priestly Ministry in Multiple Parishes* (Collegeville, MN: Liturgical, 2006), 195. In this study, 62.1 percent of pastors were very satisfied with their relationship with parishioners and 34 percent were somewhat satisfied.

32. Parker Palmer, *The Courage to Teach: Exploring the Inner Landscape of a Teacher's Life* (San Francisco: Jossey-Bass, 1998), 62.

Epilogue

The Matter of Unity

Francis Oakley

The chapters preceding may be left to speak for themselves. They do so with clarity and a species of reflective force. But while their several authors approach the matter at hand with intellectual, spiritual, and moral sensibilities shaped by an array of differing national, educational, professional, and disciplinary backgrounds, it is a striking fact, nonetheless, that in their chapters several themes or leitmotivs do surface again and again. By way of conclusion, then, it may not be redundant to draw the reader's attention to four of these.

First, none of the contributors betrays any disposition to downplay or minimize the severity of the ecclesial dilemmas that have come to characterize Catholic modernity, perhaps especially so here in North America. The deepening rift concerning the very interpretation of Vatican II, the widening gap between what layfolk expect of their parochial clergy and the attitudes and sacerdotal self-understanding of the upcoming generation of "JP II" priests, the clash between the anxious traditionalist evocation of a seamlessly continuous two-millennia ecclesiastical tradition and the sobering recognition that not all time-hallowed church traditions have proved to reflect the gospel tradition itself or to pass the test of authenticity related to that, the growing insistence with which church historians and commentators have identified the presence across the centuries of marked discontinuities and transpositions in the church's doctrinal teachings, especially but not exclusively in the realm of morality—such phenomena serve to identify the nature and underline the importance of the present discontents. Nor do those phenomena stand alone. Our contributors are also at pains to note the bewildering contrast between, on the one hand, the lack of humility and all-or-nothing mentality informing so much of official church teaching and, on the other, the mounting confusion and contextual pluralism through which the faithful must struggle in the effort to arrive at correct moral judgments. Or yet again, the unhappy counterpoint between the willingness of some of our bishops to intrude on the electoral choices the faithful are called on as citizens to make in the political arena and the sobering fact that between 1967 and 2007 almost a quarter of those Americans who were raised as Catholics have voted with their feet and quietly left the church, while, it should be added, a clear majority of those who remained have not only abandoned the practice of auricular confession but patently declined to "receive" the papal teaching on artificial birth control that Paul VI in 1968 reaffirmed so forcefully in *Humanae vitae.*

Second, it is not only the social scientists or historians but also the full range of contributors to this book who recognize the drawbacks attendant upon the persistent strain in traditional Catholic thinking of what has sometimes been described as a species of ecclesiological monophysitism, the tendency, that is, in thinking about the church, of focusing too exclusively on its divine dimension—eternal, stable, and unchanging—and underestimating the degree of confusion, variability, and sinfulness that goes along with its human embodiment as it forges its way onward amid the rocks and shoals of time.

Third, a closely related point, the contributors as a group are acutely conscious of the church's embedment in that turbulent flow of time, buffeted by the shifting winds and treacherous crosscurrents it inevitably encounters, shaped willy-nilly by the sometimes startling contingencies that go with historicity, subject, accordingly, to change, and change that has not always proved to be gradual or evolutionary. For our ecclesiastical leadership and those among the faithful of traditionalist bent, such manifestations of historical consciousness have given rise over the years to a good deal of anxiety and stimulated, accordingly, much resistance. Charles Taylor speaks, indeed, of "the blind historical panic of much of the hierarchy" during the two centuries following the great cataclysm of the French Revolution. That fear of history was to reverberate down through the nineteenth and twentieth centuries and was given dramatic voice in Pius IX's *Syllabus of Errors,* in the militant defensiveness of Leo XIII, and in the great witch hunt launched by Pius X against the specter of Modernism. It was still alive and well on the very eve of the Second Vatican Council and is not without a residual latter-day resonance in the anxiety of those advocates of a seamless ecclesiological continuity who continue to bridle at any suggestion that the work of the Second Vatican Council may

have involved some moments of significant, essentially noncontinuous institutional change in the life of the church.

In these chapters, the stubborn fact of change is everywhere apparent and,
perhaps more important, identified as having occurred within living memory.
I emphasize that latter fact because anomic events in the life of the church
or changes, however radical, seem somehow to fail to move us or even catch
our attention if they took place in a past that is now distant from us. In such
cases, they appear long since to have been assimilated into what we have come
to regard as the natural order of things. The conciliar deposition of a pope in
the fifteenth century or the resignation of another a century earlier, the fact that
a millennium and more in the history of Christianity had elapsed before
celibacy was more or less successfully imposed on secular clergy and the
requirement of annual confession to a priest imposed on the faithful as a
whole, and again, the fact that it was only in the eleventh and twelfth centuries
that the papacy transformed itself into a sacral monarchy, with the popes
moving to center stage as the most convincing successors to the erstwhile
Roman emperors—such things most of us have either forgotten or have
somehow contrived to ignore.[1] It is a little more difficult, however, not to sit
up and take notice if one is reminded that Vatican I, by its twin definitions of
papal jurisdictional primacy and infallibility, attempted to consign to oblivion a
half-millennial tradition of ecclesiastical constitutionalism that had once made
possible the ending of a scandalous and destructive schism and that, by the
early nineteenth century, had come to dominate the ecclesiological consciousness right across northern Europe. Similarly, though some have been willing to
make the attempt, it is impossible simply to brush out from the history of the
church the dramatic and radical reversal of a hallowed church teaching dating
back to time immemorial effected by *Dignitatis humanae*, Vatican II's *Declaration on Religious Freedom*. For noncanonists, no doubt it is a good deal easier to
miss the marked shift away from the type of legal tradition embedded in the
old *Corpus Juris Canonici* that the promulgation of the new *Code of Canon Law*
effected in 1917. But it is not so easy, perhaps, if one takes due note of the fact
that Canon 1556 of that new code, in stipulating that the pope can be judged by
no one, had excised with the simple stroke of a pen the qualification "unless he
is caught deviating from the faith" that had been enshrined in the earlier body
of canon law. That significant qualification, itself possessed of a millennial
history, had been the focus down through the centuries of a truly enormous
body of canonistic commentary.[2]

Not all church traditions, it seems, endure. As Cardinal Meyer pointed out
at Vatican II, "they can be subject to the limits and failings of the pilgrim
Church, which is a Church of sinners."[3] If some persist, others come to be

viewed as inauthentic and are abandoned. The church's ecclesiological tradition, certainly, turns out to be richer, denser, more complex, and less univocal than once we thought or were encouraged to believe. And the appeal to tradition, as a result, turns out not to be the simple or necessarily decisive matter that once we were inclined to assume, as, of course, Cardinal Guidi, archbishop of Bologna, was destined to discover when, having argued at Vatican I that the pope was not to be taken to speak "by his own will independent of the Church" but "with the counsel of the bishops who show the tradition of their churches," he found himself suddenly hauled on the carpet by an apoplectic Pius IX who, denouncing his views as erroneous, insisted that that was so "because I, I am tradition, I, I am the Church."[4] One is struck, accordingly, and in the fourth place, by the degree to which, in these chapters at least, the anxious preoccupation with certitude, once so deeply rooted in the Catholic temperament, has now been nudged towards the sideline. Instead, the authoritarian willingness to impose all-or-nothing teachings on the faithful tends to be seen as in some measure analogous to King Canute's mythical attempt by royal fiat to prevent the tide from coming in. Conscious as they are of the "contextual pluralism," the "contingency of the conditions" surrounding moral judgment, and the degree to which it is necessarily "perspectival"; sobered by the realization that even traditionally "ahistorical [moral] norms focused on individual behavior" turn out themselves to have history; and deploring ecclesial inflexibility, "intolerance for ambiguity," and "lack of reserve before the enigmatic," our contributors are apt, accordingly, to call for "magisterial humility," to stress the provisional nature of much church teaching, and forthrightly to confess that "our notions of magisterial authority have been tainted by a failure to observe . . . [due] limits."

That being so, and on the assumption that the surfacing of such views is something of a straw in the wind, a sailor's telltale indicating that more stormy weather and turbulent conditions may lie ahead, one is led to return once more to the theme of unity, to wonder about the precise nature of the unity to which the church of the future can reasonably aspire, as well as the nature of the role to be ascribed to the papacy in securing that unity. Not, it already seems clear, given the cracks and fissures that have appeared in the magisterial edifice amid signs that it has overreached and transgressed its effective limits—not the unity-as-identity or uniformity to which a Leo XIII aspired and that his successors have striven in vain to ensure. That sort of unity is not (or is no longer) a possibility for us.[5] But if, instead, a species of unity-across-difference is to prevail, what would that entail for the whole edifice of papal jurisdictional power erected with such tenacity during the second millennium of the church's history and buttressed so obsessively, as well as defended so aggressively, over the course especially of the past two hundred years? That plenitude of jurisdictional or governmental power is hardly susceptible of being folded back into the more contained primacy of honor that was accorded to the bishops of Rome among the several patriarchates of Christian antiquity. Nor is it easy to imagine its being cabined and confined within the coordinating role that in those days the Roman see appears to have played as "a unifying center of communion"[6] in a universal church characteristically conceived as a family of local episcopal churches, participants alike in a sacramentally based community of faith uniting believers with their bishop in given local churches and, beyond that, uniting all the local churches of the Christian world, one with another. That was a world, after all, in which during those early centuries, every bishop was viewed as a successor of the apostle Peter, "joined" with all his fellow bishops, as Cyprian put it, "by the bond of mutual concord and the chain of unity," and with them responsible, in collegial solidarity for the well-being of the entire Christian church. The institutional expression of such bonds of communion was that complex but vital pattern of collaborative episcopal governance and synodal activity that stands out as so marked a feature of the church's earliest centuries. And rather than to any enhanced role for the papal institution, that essentially conciliar mode of governance pointed ahead to its culmination at the level of the universal church in the great succession of ecumenical councils stretching from Nicaea I (315) to Nicaea II (787).

During the course of the eleventh century, however, a papacy conceived now in increasingly high monarchical terms began the inexorable rise to the position of dominance in ecclesiastical governance that it was finally to succeed in vindicating, despite all the ups and downs of the thousand years ensuing. As a result, between us and the more collegial ecclesial realities of the church's earliest centuries, a great gulf has come to yawn. At the Second Vatican Council, it is true, a few rather tentative moves were made in the direction of bridging that gulf. Significance must doubtless be attached to the fact that the framing of the relationship between primacy and episcopacy in terms of the traditional medieval distinction between "power of order" and "power of jurisdiction" (with the *fullness* of jurisdictional or governmental power being ascribed to the papacy) began to lose ground at that council, as also did resort to the very word *jurisdictio* itself. In its voluminous literature, indeed, that crucial word appears only nine times.[7] A similar significance must also attach to the (presumably related) recuperation in the mid-twentieth century of what has come to be identified as the patristic ecclesiology of *communio*, with its recognition of the centrality to the church's early government of episcopal colleagueship and conciliar activity.[8] It was that, one has to assume, that led at Vatican II to the substitution for the more robust "hierarchical subjection" and "true obedience" bluntly alluded to in Vatican I's *Pastor aeternus*, of the novel, more ingratiating, and certainly less hard-edged "hierarchical communion." Unfortunately, that term is itself quite opaque, and it is regrettably the case that in postconciliar practice, the emphasis has persistently been placed on *hierarchical* rather than on *communion*. And that may in turn reflect the fact that in *Lumen gentium* itself, "the ecclesiology of *jurisdictio*, or rather that of Vatican I, and the still older and now rediscovered ecclesiology of *communio* are [simply] placed side by side but remain unconnected." Moreover, as has further been pointed out, that "lack of connection" seems to have had "more serious [consequences] in Church practice than in theology."[9] Herein, or so I am inclined to think, may well lie the most acute, the most sensitive, and the most intractable of the dilemmas characteristic of Catholic modernity. If the problem itself becomes daily more clearly evident, the route to its solution, alas, does not.

NOTES

1. Thus they came to claim some of the attributes of those emperors (that, for example, of being a "living law"), deployed some of their titles ("supreme pontiff," for example, the old pagan priestly title), garbed themselves in imperial costume and used the imperial regalia, were greeted with imperial acclamations, and ruled with imperial grandeur a highly politicized church (itself referred to as a kingdom) via a centralized bureaucracy modeled on that of the old Roman Empire and informed by a legal mentality that was unquestionably Roman. As a result, the way was opened for the great English philosopher Thomas Hobbes to vent the derisive description of the papacy as "no other than the *ghost* of the deceased *Roman empire*—sitting crowned on the grave thereof"; see *Leviathan*, ed. Michael Oakeshott (Oxford: Basil Blackwell, 1946), part 4, chapter 47, p. 457.

2. That qualification is to be found in the *Decretum* of Gratian (mid-12th century), D. 40, cap. 6: "[Papa] a nemine judicandus, *nisi deprehendator a fide devius* (italics ours), in *Corpus Juris Canonici*, ed. A. Friedberg, 2 vols. (Leipzig: B. Tauchnitz, 1879–1881), 1:146. For the modern, truncated version, see *Codex Juris Canonici* (1917), can. 1556. See also the revised Code of 1983, can. 1404, in *Commentary on the Code of Canon Law*, ed. John Beal, James A. Coriden, and Thomas A. Green (New York: Paulist, 2000). For canonistic commentary on D. 40, cap. 6, see Brian Tierney, *Foundations of the Conciliar Theory: The Contribution of the Canonists from Gratian to the Great Schism*, rev. ed. (Leiden, Netherlands: Brill, 1998).

3. See chapter 4 in this book, Francis A. Sullivan, S.J., "Catholic Tradition and Traditions."

4. See Owen Chadwick, *A History of the Popes: 1830–1914* (Oxford: Clarendon, 1998), 210–211. Many have doubted that Pius IX actually uttered those startling words but have done so, it now seems clear, without reason. See Klaus Schatz,

Vaticanum I: 1869–70, 3 vols. (Paderborn, Germany: F. Schöningh, 1993–1994), 3, App. I, 323–333, where the evidence is carefully weighed.

5. Charles Taylor, *A Catholic Modernity?* ed. James L. Heft, S.M. (New York: Oxford University Press, 1999), 14–15.

6. "Einheitszentrum der Communio" is the formula deployed by Stephen Otto Horn, "Das Verhältnis von Primat und Episkopat in ersten Jahrtausend. Ein Geschichtlich-Theologische Synthese," in *Il primato del successore di Pietro* (Vatican City: Libreria Editrice Vaticana, 1998), 193–213 (at 205).

7. See William Henn, "Historical-Theological Synthesis of the Relation between Primacy and Episcopacy during the Second Millennium," in *Il primato del successore di Pietro*, 222–273 (at 207–208). The *power of order* was defined as the sacramental power priests and bishops possessed by virtue of having themselves received the sacrament of holy orders. The *power of jurisdiction*, at least insofar as it pertained to the public sphere (*potestas jurisdictionis in foro exteriori*), was a coercive power pertaining to a public authority, exercised even over the unwilling and directed to the common good of the faithful. For the distinction, its history, and the pertinent literature, see *Dictionnaire de droit canonique*, ed. R. Naz, 7 vols. (Paris: Letouzey et Ané, 1935–1965), 7:98–100, s.v. "Pouvoirs de l'église."

8. For which see, e.g., J. M. R. Tillard, *Church of Churches*, trans. C. De Peaux (Collegeville, MN: Liturgical, 1992); M. M. Garijo-Guembe, *Communion of the Saints*, trans. P. Madigan (Collegeville, MN: Liturgical, 1994); and the issue of *Jurist*, 36, nos. 1–2 (1975), which is devoted in toto to that ecclesiology.

9. Klaus Schatz, *Papal Primacy: From Its Origins to the Present* (Collegeville, MN: Liturgical, 1996), 170. Compare the language used in *Pastor aeternus*, chapter 3, and *Lumen gentium*, chapter 3, §22, in *Decrees of Ecumenical Councils*, 3rd ed. 2 vols., ed. Giuseppe Alberigo and Norman P. Tanner (London and Washington, DC: Sheed and Ward and Georgetown University Press, 1990), 2:814 and 866–867.

Appendix

Remarks on Interpreting the Second
Vatican Council Pope Benedict XVI

Excerpted from the Pope's Address to the
Roman Curia, December 22, 2005

The last event of this year on which I wish to reflect here is the celebration of
the conclusion of the Second Vatican Council forty years ago. This memory
prompts the question: What has been the result of the Council? Was it well
received? What, in the acceptance of the Council, was good and what was
inadequate or mistaken? What still remains to be done? No one can deny that
in vast areas of the Church the implementation of the Council has been somewhat difficult, even without wishing to apply to what occurred in these years the
description that St. Basil, the great Doctor of the Church, made of the Church's
situation after the Council of Nicaea: "The raucous shouting of those who
through disagreement rise up against one another, the incomprehensible chat-
ter, the confused din of uninterrupted clamouring, has now filled almost the
whole of the Church, falsifying through excess or failure the right doctrine of
the faith . . ." (*De Spiritu Sancto*, XXX, 77; PG32, 213 A; SCh 17 ff., p. 524).

We do not want to apply precisely this dramatic description to the situation of the post-conciliar period, yet something from all that occurred is
nevertheless reflected in it. The question arises: Why has the implementation
of the Council, in large parts of the Church, thus far been so difficult?

Well, it all depends on the correct interpretation of the Council or—as we
would say today—on its proper hermeneutics, the correct key to its interpretation and application. The problems in its implementation arose from the
fact that two contrary hermeneutics came face to face and quarreled with each
other. One caused confusion, the other, silently but more and more visibly,
bore and is bearing fruit.

On the one hand, there is an interpretation that I would call "a hermeneutic of discontinuity and rupture"; it has frequently availed itself of the
sympathies of the mass media, and also one trend of modern theology. On the

other, there is the "hermeneutic of reform," of renewal in the continuity of the one subject-Church which the Lord has given to us. She is a subject which increases in time and develops, yet always remaining the same, the one subject of the journeying People of God.

The hermeneutic of discontinuity risks ending in a split between the pre-conciliar and the post-conciliar Church. It asserts that the texts of the Council as such do not yet express the true spirit of the Council. It claims that they are the result of compromises in which, to reach unanimity, it was found necessary to keep and reconfirm many old things that are now pointless. However, the true spirit of the Council is not to be found in these compromises but instead in the impulse toward the new that are contained in the texts.

These innovations alone were supposed to represent the true spirit of the Council, and starting from and in conformity with them, it would be possible to move ahead. Precisely because the texts would only imperfectly reflect the true spirit of the Council and its newness, it would be necessary to go courageously beyond the texts and make room for the newness in which the Council's deepest intention would be expressed, even if it were still vague.

In a word, it would be necessary not to follow the texts of the Council but its spirit. In this way, obviously, a vast margin was left open for the question on how this spirit should subsequently be defined and room was consequently made for every whim.

The nature of the Council as such is therefore basically misunderstood. In this way, it is considered as a sort of constituent assembly that eliminates an old constitution and creates a new one. However, the Constituent Assembly needs a mandator and then confirmation by the mandator, in other words, the people the constitution must serve. The Fathers had no such mandate and no one had ever given them one; nor could anyone have given them one because the essential constitution of the Church comes from the Lord and was given to us so that we might attain eternal life and, starting from this perspective, be able to illuminate life in time and time itself.

Through the Sacrament they have received, Bishops are stewards of the Lord's gift. They are "stewards of the mysteries of God" (1 Cor. 4:1); as such, they must be found to be "faithful" and "wise" (cf. Lk 12:41–48). This requires them to administer the Lord's gift in the right way, so that it is not left concealed in some hiding place but bears fruit, and the Lord may end by saying to the administrator: "Since you were dependable in a small matter I will put you in charge of larger affairs" (cf. Mt. 25:14–30; Lk 19:11–27).

These gospel parables express the dynamic of fidelity required in the Lord's service; and through them it becomes clear that, as in a Council, the dynamic and fidelity must converge.

The hermeneutic of discontinuity is countered by the hermeneutic of reform, as it was presented by Pope John XXIII in his Speech inaugurating the Council on October 11, 1962 and later by Pope Paul VI in his Discourse for the Council's conclusion on December 7, 1965.

Here I shall cite only John XXIII's well-known words, which unequivocally express this hermeneutic when he says that the Council wishes "to transmit the doctrine, pure and integral, without any attenuation or distortion." And he continues: "Our duty is not only to guard this precious treasure, as if we were concerned only with antiquity, but to dedicate ourselves with an earnest will and without fear to that work which our era demands of us. . . ." It is necessary that "adherence to all the teaching of the Church in its entirety and preciseness . . ." be presented in "faithful and perfect conformity to the authentic doctrine, which, however, should be studied and expounded through the methods of research and through the literary forms of modern thought. The substance of the ancient doctrine of the deposit of faith is one thing, and the way in which it is presented is another. . . ," retaining the same meaning and message (*The Documents of Vatican II*, Walter M. Abbott, S.J., p. 715).

It is clear that this commitment to expressing a specific truth in a new way demands new thinking on this truth and a new and vital relationship with it; it is also clear that new words can only develop if they come from an informed understanding of the truth expressed, and on the other hand, that a reflection on faith also requires that this faith be lived. In this regard, the program that Pope John XXIII proposed was extremely demanding, indeed, just as the synthesis of fidelity and dynamic is demanding.

However, wherever this interpretation guided the implementation of the Council, new life developed and new fruit ripened. Forty years after the Council, we can show that the positive is far greater and livelier that it appeared to be in the turbulent years around 1968. Today, we see that although the good seed developed slowly, it is nonetheless growing; and our deep gratitude for the work done by the Council is likewise growing.

In his Discourse closing the Council, Paul VI pointed out a further specific reason why a hermeneutic of discontinuity can seem convincing.

In the great dispute about man which marks the modern epoch, the Council had to focus in particular on the theme of anthropology. It had to question the relationship between the Church and her faith on the one hand, and man and the contemporary world on the other (cf. ibid.). The question becomes even clearer if, instead of the generic term "contemporary world," we opt for another that is more precise: the Council had to determine in a new way the relationship between the Church and the modern era.

This relationship had a somewhat stormy beginning with the Galileo case. It was then totally interrupted when Kant described "religion within pure reason" and when, in the radical phase of the French Revolution, an image of the State and the human being that practically no longer wanted to allow the Church any room was disseminated.

In the 19th century under Pius IX, the clash between the Church's faith and a radical liberalism and the natural sciences, which also claimed to embrace with their knowledge the whole of reality to its limit, stubbornly proposing to make the "hypothesis of God" superfluous, had elicited from the Church a bitter and radical condemnation of this spirit of the modern age. Thus, it seemed that there was no longer any milieu open to a positive and fruitful understanding, and the rejection by those who felt they were representatives of the modern era was also drastic.

In the meantime, however, the modern age had also experienced developments. People came to realize that the American Revolution was offering a model of a modern State that differed from the theoretical model with radical tendencies that had emerged during the second phase of the French Revolution.

The natural sciences were beginning to reflect more and more clearly their own limitations imposed by their own method, which, despite achieving great things, was nevertheless unable to grasp the global nature of reality.

So it was that both parties were gradually beginning to open up to each other. In the period between the two World Wars and especially after the Second World War, Catholic statesmen demonstrated that a modern secular State could exist that was not neutral regarding values but alive, drawing from the great ethical sources opened by Christianity.

Catholic social doctrine, as it gradually developed, became an important model between radical liberalism and the Marxist theory of the State. The natural sciences, which without reservation professed a method of their own to which God was barred access, realized ever more clearly that this method did not include the whole of reality. Hence, they once again opened their doors to God, knowing that reality is greater than the naturalistic method and all that it can encompass.

It might be said that three circles of questions had formed which then, at the time of the Second Vatican Council, were expecting an answer. First of all, the relationship between faith and modern science had to be redefined. Furthermore, this did not only concern the natural sciences but also historical science for, in a certain school, the historical-critical method claimed to have the last word on the interpretation of the Bible and, demanding total exclusivity for its interpretation of Sacred Scripture, was opposed to important points in the interpretation elaborated by the faith of the Church.

Secondly, it was necessary to give a new definition to the relationship between the Church and the modern State that would make room impartially for citizens of various religions and ideologies, merely assuming responsibility for an orderly and tolerant coexistence among them and for the freedom to practice their own religion.

Thirdly, linked more generally to this was the problem of religious tolerance—a question that required a new definition of the relationship between the Christian faith and the world religions. In particular, before the recent crimes of the Nazi regime and, in general, with a retrospective look at a long and difficult history, it was necessary to evaluate and define in a new way the relationship between the Church and the faith of Israel.

These are all subjects of great importance—they were the great themes of the second part of the Council—on which it is impossible to reflect more broadly in this context. It is clear that in all these sectors, which all together form a single problem, some kind of discontinuity might emerge. Indeed, a discontinuity had been revealed but in which, after the various distinctions between concrete historical situations and their requirements had been made, the continuity of principles proved not to have been abandoned. It is easy to miss this fact at a first glance.

It is precisely in this combination of continuity and discontinuity at different levels that the very nature of true reform consists. In this process of innovation in continuity we must learn to understand more practically than before that the Church's decisions on contingent matters—for example, certain practical forms of liberalism or a free inter-pretation of the Bible—should necessarily be contingent themselves, precisely because they refer to a specific reality that is changeable in itself. It was necessary to learn to recognize that in these decisions it is only the principles that express the permanent aspect, since they remain as an undercurrent motivating decisions from within. On the other hand, not so permanent are the practical forms that depend on the historical situation and are therefore subject to change.

Basic decisions, therefore, continue to be well-grounded, whereas the way they are applied to new contexts can change. Thus, for example, if religious freedom were to be considered an expression of human inability to discover the truth and thus become a canonization of relativism, then this social and historical necessity is raised inappropriately to the metaphysical level and thus stripped of its true meaning. Consequently, it cannot be accepted by those who believe that the human person is capable of knowing the truth about God and, on the basis of the inner dignity of the truth, is bound to this knowledge.

It is quite different, on the other hand, to perceive religious freedom as a need that derives from human coexistence, or indeed, as an intrinsic consequence of the truth that cannot be externally imposed but that the person must adopt only through the process of conviction.

The Second Vatican Council, recognizing and making its own an essential principle of the modern State with the Decree on Religious Freedom, has recovered the deepest patrimony of the Church. By doing so she can be conscious of being in full harmony with the teaching of Jesus himself (cf. Mt 22: 21), as well as with the Church of the martyrs of all time. The ancient Church naturally prayed for the emperors and political leaders out of duty (cf. I Tm 2:2); but while she prayed for the emperors, she refused to worship them and thereby clearly rejected the religion of the State.

The martyrs of the early Church died for their faith in that God who was revealed in Jesus Christ, and for this very reason they also died for freedom of conscience and the freedom to profess one's own faith—a profession no State can impose but which, instead, can only be claimed with God's grace in freedom of conscience. A missionary Church known for proclaiming her message to all peoples must necessarily work for the freedom of the faith. She desires to transmit the gift of the truth that exists for one and all.

At the same time, she assures people and their Governments that she does not wish to destroy their identity and culture by doing so, but to give them, on the contrary, a response which, in their innermost depths, they are waiting for—a response with which the multiplicity of cultures is not lost but instead unity between men and women increases and thus also peace between peoples.

The Second Vatican Council, with its new definition of the relationship between the faith of the Church and certain essential elements of modern thought, has reviewed or even corrected certain historical decisions, but in this apparent discontinuity it has actually preserved and deepened her inmost nature and true identity.

The Church, both before and after the Council, was and is the same Church, one, holy, catholic, and apostolic, journeying on through time; she continues "her pilgrimage amid the persecutions of the world and the consolations of God," proclaiming the death of the Lord until he comes (cf. *Lumen Gentium*, n.8).

Those who expected that with this fundamental "yes" to the modern era all tensions would be dispelled and that the "openness towards the world" accordingly achieved would transform everything into pure harmony, had underestimated the inner tensions as well as the contradictions inherent in the modern epoch.

They had underestimated the perilous frailty of human nature which has been a threat to human progress in all periods of history and in every historical constellation. These dangers, with the new possibilities and new power of man over matter and over himself, did not disappear but instead acquired new dimensions: a look at the history of the present day shows this clearly.

In our time, too, the Church remains a "sign that will be opposed" (Lk 2:34)—not without reason did Pope John Paul II, then still a Cardinal, give this title to the theme for the Spiritual Exercises he preached in 1976 to Pope Paul VI and the Roman Curia. The Council could not have intended to abolish the Gospel's opposition to human dangers and errors.

On the contrary, it was certainly the Council's intention to overcome erroneous or superfluous contradictions in order to present to our world the requirement of the Gospel in its full greatness and purity.

The steps the Council took towards the modern era which had rather vaguely been presented as "openness to the world" belong in short to the perennial problem of the relationship between faith and reason that is re-emerging in ever new forms. The situation that the Council had to face can certainly be compared to events of previous epochs.

In his First Letter, St Peter urged Christians always to be ready to give an answer (apo-logia) to anyone who asked them for the logos, the reason for their faith (cf. 3:15).

This meant that biblical faith had to be discussed and come into contact with Greek culture and learn to recognize through interpretation the separating line but also the convergence and the affinity between them in the one reason, given by God.

When, in the 13th century through the Jewish and Arab philosophers, Aristotelian thought came into contact with Medieval Christianity formed in the Platonic tradition and faith and reason risked entering into an irreconcilable contradiction, it was above all St Thomas Aquinas who mediated the new encounter between faith and Aristotelian philosophy, thereby setting faith in a positive relationship with the form of reason prevalent in his time. There is no doubt that the wearing dispute between modern reason and the Christian faith, which had begun negatively with the Galileo case, went through many phases, but with the Second Vatican Council the time came when broad new thinking was required.

Its content was certainly only roughly traced in the conciliar texts, but this determined its essential direction, so that the dialogue between reason and faith, particularly important today, found its bearings on the basis of the Second Vatican Council.

This dialogue now must be developed with great open-mindedness but also with that clear discernment that the world rightly expects of us in this very moment. Thus, today we can look with gratitude at the Second Vatican Council: if we interpret and implement it guided by a right hermeneutic, it can be and can become increasingly powerful for the ever necessary renewal of the Church.

Contributors

John P. Beal is Professor of Canon Law at the Catholic University of America in Washington, D.C. He is the editor, with James Coriden and Thomas Green, of *New Commentary on the Code of Canon Law* (2000).

Lisa Sowle Cahill is J. Donald Monan Professor of Theology at Boston College. She is the author of *Theological Bioethics: Participation, Justice and Change* (2005) and coeditor, with Kenneth Himes, Charles Curran, David Hollenbach, and Thomas Shannon, of *Modern Catholic Social Teaching: Commentaries and Interpretations* (2005).

Mary Gautier, a consultant on this project, is senior research associate at the Center for Applied Research in the Apostolate at Georgetown University in Washington, D.C. She is the coauthor, with William D'Antonio, James D. Davidson, and the late Dean R. Hoge, of *American Catholics Today: New Realities of Their Faith and Their Church* (2007), from which their chapter in the present volume is excerpted.

M. Cathleen Kaveny is John P. Murphy Foundation Professor of Law at the University of Notre Dame Law School. Widely published in law, ethics, and medical ethics, her book in progress is titled *Other People's Wrongdoing: The Problem of Complicity.*

Joseph A. Komonchak held until his recent retirement the John and Gertrude Hubbard Chair in Religious Studies at the Catholic University of America in Washington, D.C. He is the editor, with Mary Collins and Dermot Lane, of *The New Dictionary of Theology* and coeditor, with Giuseppe Alberigo, of the five-volume *History of Vatican II* (1995–2006).

Michael J. Lacey is a retired historian living on Bainbridge Island, Washington. He is Director Emeritus of the American Program at the Woodrow Wilson International Center for Scholars in Washington, D.C., and a Senior Scholar of the Center. His most recent publications are "Moral Autonomy in the Church: Lonergan and the Natural Law," in *Tradition and Pluralism: Essays in Honor of William M. Shea* (2009), edited by Kenneth L. Parker, and "Losing and Finding the Modern Self: Neglected Resources from the Golden Age of American Pragmatism," in *Figures in the Carpet: Finding the Human Person in the American Past* (2007), edited by Wilfred McClay.

Gerard Mannion is a Senior Research Fellow of the Katholieke Universiteit Leuven, Belgium and a Senior Fellow of the Centro per le Scienze Religiose, Fondazione Bruno Kessler, Trento, Italy. He is the author of *Ecclesiology and Postmodernity: Questions for the Church in Our Times* (2007) and coeditor, with Lewis Mudge, of the *Routledge Companion to the Christian Church* (2008).

Francis Oakley is Edward Dorr Griffin Professor of the History of Ideas, Emeritus, President Emeritus of Williams College, and President Emeritus of the American Council of Learned Societies, New York. He is currently Senior Fellow at the Oakley Center for Humanities and Social Sciences, Williams College. His books include *The Conciliarist Tradition: Constitutionalism in the Catholic Church, 1300–1870* (2003) and *Natural Law, Laws of Nature, Natural Rights: Continuity and Discontinuity in the History of Ideas* (2005).

Katarina Schuth is Professor for the Social Scientific Study of Religion, St. Paul Seminary School of Divinity, University of St. Thomas, St. Paul, Minnesota. Her books include *Seminaries, Theologates, and the Future of Church Ministry: An Analysis of Trends and Transitions* (1999) and *Priestly Ministry in Multiple Parishes* (2006).

Francis A. Sullivan, S.J., is Professor of Theology, Boston College. His books include *Creative Fidelity: Weighing and Interpreting Documents of the Magisterium* (2003), *Salvation outside the Church?* (2003), and *From Apostles to Bishops: The Development of the Episcopacy in the Early Church* (2001).

Charles Taylor is Professor Emeritus of Political Science and Philosophy at McGill University in Montreal, Canada. He was awarded the Templeton Prize in 2007. His most recent book is *A Secular Age* (2007).

Leslie Woodcock Tentler is Professor of History at the Catholic University of America in Washington, D.C. She is the author of *Catholics and Contraception: An American History* (2004) and editor of *The Church Confronts Modernity: Catholicism since 1950 in the United States, Ireland, and Quebec* (2007).

Index

Note: Page numbers followed by "*t*" denote tables.